The Legend of a Hunter in a Bygone Era

By: Ric Palmer-Wilson

IMAGE 1: CLARY PALMER-WILSON. BORN IN NAIROBI, KENYA, IN 1907. DIED 1992. HE BECAME A LEGEND IN HIS TIME WHEN HE HUNTED THE WORLD'S RECORD BUFFALO AND A MASSIVE ELEPHANT NAMED THE CROWN PRINCE. IN SPITE OF BEING ASTHMATIC AND ALLERGIC TO OVER 150 SUBSTANCES, HE SURVIVED A LIFE IN THE BUSH. HE BECAME A SOUGHT AFTER HUNTING GUIDE WITH AN EXCELLENT REPUTATION AS A MAN WHO KNEW THE BUSH LIKE HIS HOME.

Copyright. Ric Palmer-Wilson. 2023
All rights reserved. No part of this book may be reproduced
or used in any manner without the prior written permission
of the copyright owner, except for the use of brief
quotations in critical articles and reviews.
ISBN 978 3 00 076007 5

ACKNOWLEDGEMENTS.
Editing manager. DAVE HENDERSON.
Book cover art and design by GREGG DAVIES.
Interior sketches (17) by GREGG DAVIES.
Book design company. WWW.myebook.online.
Proof reading and corrections by LYNN PRESTASH.
Email:lynnprestash1@gmail.com.
Copy editing by CHRISTINE McPHERSON.
Email:christine@googlemail.com.
Formatting, financing, advice and encouragement. KEVIN
PALMER-WILSON.
Information and suggestions. PETER BAILEY.
Financial contributions. CHRIS BRANHAM.
Maps, pictures by RIC PALMER-WILSON.

CONTENT

NOTES ON THE BOOK.

The 17 sketches by Gregg Davies are to illustrate some descriptive scenes. The art has been purposely drawn in a naiive style to represent an old drawing technique used in the 1930's.

When reading this book, please remember that during this period, 1920 to 1973, Tanganyika was a very different country then. Law and order prevailed in the towns and larger villages only but beyond that were huge tracts of uninhabited and unexplored bushland teeming with wildlife. In 1965 there was an estimated elephant population of 1,200,000 animals roaming over the land. Every river was overflowing with crocodiles. Rhinos, buffalos, lions and leopards, were everywhere. Raw, untamed Africa started just beyond the front door and anyone with enough courage and resources, dared to venture into it.

The understaffed and overworked wildlife department was very grateful for any help they could get in keeping control of marauding animals. Hunters were encouraged to buy licences but sometimes were issued with free permits when a situation got out of hand.

Clary, being a professional hunter, helped out many times in game control measures but he never shot an animal for sport or as a trophy, only for food or to earn his living, or if it was injured.

Look at this book as an historic account of one man living an unusual life in East Africa.

Such a life would not be possible today.

Prologue
In the Beginning

Millennia ago, at the dawn of mankind, the great plains of East Africa were rumbling with mighty subterranean turbulence and volcanos were spewing lava three miles skyward to form Africa's highest mountain. The flatlands were sinking into sheer-walled rifts several miles wide and hundreds of miles long, that would later be filled with more than half of Africa's life-supporting freshwater. Evidence of this tremendous upheaval would scar the face of Africa forever.

Amidst this chaos, when every living thing was adapting to this changing world, walked a two-legged, upright being also trying to survive by any means. One day, this creature picked up a bleached bone from a long-dead animal, or perhaps a jagged stone from underfoot, and learned to use this tool to kill other beasts for food. With this move, the human-like biped widened its vegetarian menu to include fresh meat, thereby increasing its chance of survival so greatly that it was now assured. It was on this day that man, the hunter, was born.

Since then, he has used his superior intelligence to advance his hunting skills and improve his crude killing tools. Those early humans who failed to outwit their swift-footed prey died of hunger or became victims of hungry carnivores. Only the fittest and most skilful hunting clans survived to pass on their genes and hunting instincts to the next generations.

Some two-and-a-half million years later, not far from a place where the fossilised bones of these early hunters and their animal prey had been scratched out from the layers of volcanic ash and dust by inquisitive archaeologists, a modern hunter was born. This is the story of Clary Palmer-Wilson, born in East Africa in 1907.

At the age of 14, he started earning his livelihood by becoming a hunter in a harsh, merciless land, where dangers lurked everywhere and mistakes carried severe consequences. As a young man, he was unable to survive by hunting alone, so he joined a gold rush, tried mining, became a car mechanic, went farming, and took on any foolish task that paid enough to keep him going another day. Eventually, he tried settling down to a normal life with a regular job, but his blood ran hot with the call of wild places he longed to be. However, he was living on a fast-changing continent in the waning days of Africa's last wild game paradise, and was too old to change.

IMAGE 2: THOUSANDS OF YEARS AGO MAN BECAME A HUNTER IN ORDER TO SURVIVE. THIS HUNTING INSTINCT IS STILL LYING DORMANT IN US TODAY.

Chapter 1
First Blood

Clary lay dying on a rickety old wooden sisal-rope bed inside the village headman's mud and wattle hut. A thatched-palm roof kept the room dark and cool from the fierce sun beating down from a cloudless African sky. Dark red blood oozed through Clary's khaki shirt, which he had torn into strips to make temporary bandages for his shredded legs. Ink-black blood had already dried into large dark patches on the off-white cotton bed sheet where he had been placed an hour earlier. Just 17 years old and in the prime of life, he was waiting for his end to come in this dingy hut, miles away from civilisation and medical help. There were only a dozen natives to witness the last moments of a young man who had come to save their dwindling goat herd from a spotted devil – a leopard. Instead, he had become a victim himself.

Why had the gun failed to fire, and why had it failed at the most critical moment when it had worked perfectly a few moments before? These questions raced continuously through Clary's muddled mind as he stared at his double-barrelled 400 Jeffery's Express rifle leaning against the wall of the hut. He waited, hoping that his father William would arrive from far-off Tanga in time to save him.

This whole incident had begun a few days previously in Tanga. A leopard had had the natives' goats on its menu for weeks, taking them with impunity wherever and whenever it liked. All attempts by the locals to chase the sly creature away from the area had ended in failure. Only by them being very fleet-footed natives did it not end in tragic failure. Finally, in desperation, a small delegation from the village travelled the long, winding paths that led through the bush from one mango tree-shaded settlement to the next, until they arrived at the seaport town of Tanga. Here was a game department with armed rangers who would come with their guns and shoot this killer of the night… or so they hoped.

However, the whole country was teeming with toothy, tusky, and horned wild animals, munching, crunching, and trampling their way through the territory. The understaffed game department had their hands full just trying to keep the damned buffalo away from the local railway station waiting room. In addition, they were struggling to keep grey, five-ton maize eaters out of the nearby shambas (native plantations) where, in one moonless night, a small herd of these happy pachyderms could munch their way through a whole season's food crop for a village. No, one little leopard chewing on a few goats in a far-off place was of little priority, and the chief game warden refused to contemplate such a mission.

In desperation, knowing that their goat herd was diminishing each day, the dejected delegation let it be known around the tracker and gun bearer circles of Tanga that a devil, disguised as a leopard and smarter than anybody, was feasting on their goats and needed to be dealt with. Clary's curiosity was piqued when he got wind of this rumour, especially the "smarter than anybody" part. More for the love of hunting than the love of saving goats, he accepted the desperate goat herders' challenge.

Just after sunrise the next morning, Clary got up, dressed into his drab olive fatigues and went to the dark cedar wood gun cabinet standing in the corner of the white-washed living room. He retrieved his double-barrelled 400 Jeffery's rifle from the gun rack. Reaching into the bottom shelf, he picked up two banana-yellow packs of Kynoch soft nose cartridges.

"Ten shots should be enough to pierce any devil's armour", he mused, as he removed the fat brass cases and pressed them, one by one, into loops sewn over the chest pockets of his khaki hunting jacket. Just in case one gun jammed, he grabbed the well-used linseed oil-smelling 303 Enfield military rifle with its stepladder sights (adjustable to two thousand yards,) and two boxes containing 40 rounds of 303 ammunition.

"That should be enough firepower to fight off an army of devils", muttered Clary.

The old 303 rifle and its ammo were designed more for killing people than killing animals, but the war had just ended and there was more ammo around for this gun than there were bottles of gin in the whole country. You could even find boxes of ammo lying where they had fallen on a battleground, or washed up on a muddy riverbank from an overturned army truck that had spilled its cargo while trying, unsuccessfully, to cross a swollen brown river.

Clary carried the equipment out of the cool house and across the creaking wooden veranda, where he handed the 303 rifle, ammo packs, and an old army carrying bag to a waiting bearer.

Squinting past the dark green mango trees to the sky beyond, he murmured to no one in particular, "Looks like another beautiful, bloody African day and not a sign of rain."

Turning towards his father, William, who was sipping hot tea in a big, soft armchair on the veranda, Clary said, "I'll be back in a day or two. Make room for a leopard skin rug somewhere."

Clary, hatless as usual, led the way out the garden gate and along the tree-lined sandy street towards the west of town, carrying the big Jeffery's across his shoulder. There they met the waiting goat herders wrapped in their kikois. Clary led the way, while the gun bearer with the 303 and the carrying bag, which cut deeply into his shoulder, brought up the rear. As soon as they passed the last native huts at the edge of town, Clary let the herders take the lead.

They followed the well-worn footpaths that criss-crossed the country, leading from one neat little community to the next, past maize, millet, and cassava fields, some showing signs of recent feasting elephants. The way led through tree-shaded galleries where long creepers dangled down like green serpents ready to strike at all things passing below. They nervously passed patches of dense thickets that snapped and rustled with unseen fauna scampering away from the human disturbance.

They rested once in a Tamarind tree-shaded village, leaning the heavy rifles against the brown trunk while they sat in its shade, drinking the juice from young coconuts. These had been offered to them by an old man who sent one of his sons to a nearby tree to cut down some of the nuts. By late morning, under a burning sun, the party was loudly greeted with smiles and laughter as they reached the tidy group of huts tucked in a grove of huge Baobab trees.

A hastily built boma (enclosure) of cut thorn bushes and upright sticks against one side of the giant trees was evidence of the inhabitants' futile attempt to protect their remaining goats from the marauding leopard. The thatched-roofed huts were surrounded by stubby dry grass glades and scattered patches of thick, yellow, tangled bush where fan-shaped

Doum palms and fawn-coloured termite castles poked through the foliage. This was perfect country for a leopard to hide.

"This very morning", said the old village headman, standing forlornly in his pale-white kanzu and fez cap, "not far from here, this yellow devil tried to catch our goats! He has lost all fear of us so that he now dares to hunt in daylight. He did not kill today because he has become slow and fat on our goats and has eaten all the slow ones. Now only our swiftest ones survive."

Clary nodded in sympathy. He was eager to get going before the sun made all movement torture. Unshouldering his Jeffery's, he broke open the breech, inspected the bores against the sky for obstructions, and then removed two soft-nose cartridges from his breast pocket loops. He slipped them into the open chambers, closing the gun with a loud "clump", then checked that the safety catch was on. Taking a few steps out into the sun, he waved his gun in the air, and spoke to the headman and the throng of ecstatic natives.

"Show me where this spotted devil tried to have his last meal. I am going to put two more spots on him".

The men and children of the community led the way past a wild fig tree and onto the dusty plain that had been grazed bare of all vegetation. Onward they went, towards a patch of greenish-yellow bush on the far side. Before the group reached the denser bush, one man of some authority stopped in a cloud of light grey dust kicked up by the bare feet of the entourage. He ordered the children to stay behind here, reasoning that they were no bigger than goats and could be mistaken for one by the leopard, should it still be on the prowl. Murmurs of agreement rose from the other men, signalling the non-protesting children to seek the shade of a nearby tree and sit down in the dust and thorns to await events.

Half an hour later, the sweating, dust-covered group stopped at the edge of another open plain, sparsely covered with orange grass stubble and dotted with bare, grey-black soil patches. Not more than two hundred yards away, in the middle of this plain, was an island thicket the size of two tennis courts, covered in thick dun-coloured low bushes that sprouted green palm fronds.

"Therein", said a man, pointing to the stand of bush, "is the cause of all our sleepless nights, our fears, our anguishes – the devil, the leopard."

Clary left the men where they stood in a loose bunch in the hot sun. He held his loaded double rifle across his chest, ready for a quick shot, and walked cautiously towards the leopard's suspected lair. Stepping carefully over dry grass tufts to minimise the noise of his approach, he stopped a safe distance from the thicket. Then he started to slowly circle the island, his keen eyes darting from shadow to bush to grass tunnel, looking for that tell-tale movement of a leopard's twitching ear or flicking tail tip.

Yellow, brown, black, and orange-coloured bush could be mistaken for leopard skin. Leaf shadows threw dark spots onto the underbrush, and little puffs of wind moved these shadows leopard-like across the bushes. The only sure giveaway would be the cat's ear twitch or angry flick of the tail tip.

Clary glanced down at his feet, and there in the sand he saw the big pugmarks of a leopard, leading towards the thicket and into a small tunnel of long dry grass stalks. The tracks were a few hours old, so he continued his slow, heart-pounding circle around the green island until he emerged on the other side, in full view of the expectant group of villagers and his gun bearer with the 303.

Sure enough, where the stubbly grass plain was widest, he saw the unmistakable fresh tracks of a sprinting leopard. Beyond them, were the hoof prints of faster sprinting goats trying not to become breakfast that morning. A little farther around the circle were the pugmarks of one dejected leopard entering his hideout after his failed run on the dining room. Two tracks leading in and only one leading out meant with certainty that the leopard was home.

Clary walked back to the men waiting patiently in the fierce sun. They were deliberating the pros and cons of flushing out the animal by setting fire to the tinder-dry island or by throwing Doum palm nuts in to scare it out. This would give Clary a clear shot as it broke cover and ran across the open plain to the next bushy island. In anticipation of either choice, the men had already collected a pile of dry grass and a heap of rock-hard nuts. But by flushing it with either fire or nuts, the animal could bound out anywhere or turn on the natives, scattering them in all directions and making a safe shot impossible to take. Also, a leopard is capable of forty miles an hour sprints, and a bounding, sprinting animal would be difficult to hit, even for a crack shot. Clary knew he was not in that league.

With growing trepidation, he decided to go into the bushy island as silently as possible, hoping the beast would somehow give itself away.

Like a stalking cat himself, the young hunter, his senses on needlepoints, entered the leopard's domain alone. He had one comforting thought. The soft-nosed bullets fired from his 400 Jeffery's would still possess enough power to kill a leopard, even after smashing through fifty feet of tangled bush.

In the tinder-dry scrub with its carpet of crackling dead leaves, branches, and grass stalks, it was impossible for Clary to slink as silently as the cat he was trying so hard to imitate. Deep inside the bush, somewhere ahead or to one side – or even behind him – Clary felt yellow eyes watching his every move. He sensed that head full of long ivory teeth, perfected over millennia for killing, just waiting to snap shut over his neck. And those razor-sharp claws, twenty of them, able to cut flesh right to the bone!

He spent more than one agonising hour in the clammy heat of the bush, crawling, crouching, looking, listening, smelling, and sensing after the elusive quarry. Yet except for fresh spoor and a pungent odour, there was no cat to be found high or low in this island cover.

Certain that no one was at home, Clary stood upright for the first time in over an hour. He mounted a small termite hill in the middle of the island that was bare, except for a few tufts of foot-high dry grass stalks sprouting out the sides. Standing on this vantage point, calmer now but still sweating and covered with dry leaves, he could see the natives sitting in the same spot as before. He hailed them and said that because they had been chatting like a group of old women at the market and he had been noisily blundering through the bush like a lost cow, the leopard must have slunk out somewhere to seek quieter realms. Unbeknownst to him, however, it was still there. Hiding.

Holding the rifle's muzzle with his left hand and balancing the butt on his foot, Clary raised his right hand to shade his eyes against the glare of the early afternoon sun and scanned the far-off patches of bush beyond the plain for any likely leopard layouts.

Then, out of the corner of his eye, he saw it! That unmistakable twitch of a leopard ear that Clary had anticipated for an hour, was now there, not in the bush ahead but rather at his very feet. Over the rifle's muzzle he saw those yellow eyes, the black-tipped ears that twitched again, and the shiny dark nose above sharp ivory teeth bared in a half snarl, all pointing his way.

Still holding the gun by the muzzle, Clary leapt backwards, landing on his back in a patch of dry bush. In one move that took only seconds, he jumped to his feet, then fought his way out of the dry bush, ran through the thicket and out onto the open plain. Readying his gun, he whirled around to fire at the pursuing cat. But no leopard appeared. Silence! Total silence. That's all there was to hear. Nothing came from the hastily abandoned termite hill: no sound, no movement, nothing.

"Iko hapo. It's right there", Clary squeaked in a high-pitched voice, revealing his fright for all to hear.

The baffled black men, all now standing, had heard the confusing commotion. Seeing Clary's wild dash out of the island, his ragged hair standing on end and his khaki clothes decked out with dry brown leaves and broken twigs, like some old Christmas decorations, they wondered if the devil hadn't taken possession of him too.

He retreated farther onto the open plain, still brushing detritus from his hair and clothes while he walked towards the group of natives. On reaching the gun bearer with the 303, Clary exchanged his 400 for the other gun and all its ammunition.

I'll get that big cat out of there now, good and dead", he said to himself, although loud enough for all to hear.

Clary could see his hasty exit path from the island and could just make out, deep inside the bush, the outline of the termite hill where he had seen the leopard. With his gun bearer holding the 400 Jeffery's loaded and ready, and the crowds safely behind, Clary walked close to his exit point. And from a standing position, he proceeded to pepper the area round the leopard's lair with 303 bullets. The gun barked 30 times, shattering the silence of the noonday heat. Hard metal-jacketed bullets thudded into parched earth, flinging chunks of grey sod into the air or ricocheting off in long, whining whistles through the undergrowth and beyond. The acrid smell of burned cordite hung heavily in the air. Finally, the overheating gun barrel, smoking from burned linseed oil, forced him to cease firing.

No growl nor sound of a fleeing cat was heard during the whole exercise, which meant one of two things: either the leopard was dead; or it wasn't. It was not wounded, because had it been injured, it would have growled loudly or charged out. If it was dead, it was dead somewhere in the thicket; and if it was alive, it was alive and very annoyed somewhere in there, too.

This left only one choice. Clary, the brave hunter, the village saviour, had to go in and find out for himself. Exchanging the searing hot 303 for his 400 Jeffery's, he snapped open the breech, checking that both chambers were free of obstructions and that two cartridges were still loaded.

Nervously, he walked towards the island with the safety catch off and his finger on the trigger, ready for an attack.

Using the rifle barrel to part the bushes, he inched forward through the thicket towards the ant-made mound of earth where he had almost stepped on the cat. He pointed the gun at everything he looked at, and searched the bushes all around the termite mound, circling it completely before climbing once again onto its flat top. He surveyed the surrounding strand from this high point.

Dangling branches showed green gashes where they had been struck by the 303 fusillade, and fresh earth chafes on the ground bore testimony to the same cause, but nothing else was noticeable and nothing moved.

Suddenly, he saw it again. That heart-stopping ear twitch of a live leopard!

At his feet, Clary saw that unique visage of one angry cat with flattened ears, fiery eyes, and a snarling mouth all aimed at him. In the blink of an eye from a man in fear, he swung the gun down, pulling both triggers at once. The double "boom-boom" sounded like one, as both barrels barked when the gun levelled with the cat's neck and shoulder. Flying dust and sand indicated a miss. Clary heard a short, guttural growl as the enraged leopard launched itself out and up, hitting Clary full force on the left shoulder. The impact sent him sprawling down the side of the anthill and under a tangle of low-lying branches. Flat on his back, a bit dazed, and still holding the gun, he wriggled partway out of the low bush. The snarling leopard sprang after him.

Tangled branches low over Clary's body blocked the savage cat, keeping it from reaching his neck and face. Still on his back, he pulled the gun free of the bushes, broke open the breech, fumbled out the empty shells, and slammed two fresh cartridges into the chambers. Snapping it shut, he jammed it through the branches until it touched the leopard's neck, and squeezed both triggers hard. To his horror, no "boom-boom" occurred – only infuriated snarling from an enraged cat at being poked in the neck with a metal stick. Maddened, the cat seized the gun barrel in its jaws and bit hard, at the same time clawing in short, quick strokes with its front legs. Razor-sharp claws ripped Clary's trousers and legs into shreds, from his kneecap down to his leather boots.

In excruciating pain and high on adrenalin, he squeezed both gun triggers once more with all his strength, yet the only sound was leopard teeth breaking on gunmetal. The smell of fresh blood drove it on, and the cat lunged closer to Clary's jugular. Holding the animal at bay with the gun barrel, Clary screamed to the men outside, who deliberated momentarily then leaped into action. They lit bunches of dry grass and hurled them into the bushes, setting fire to the dry underbrush. They threw Doum palm nuts in all directions, shouted like madmen, and beat the bushes with long sticks to cause maximum distraction.

The enraged leopard suddenly jumped away, and in a flash, it disappeared. There was no movement, no sound, no sighting. It was just gone, as though it had not ever been there, never to be seen again. However, danger was not over yet.

The fire was rapidly consuming all vegetation and moving with increasing speed and intensity towards Clary, who lay trapped by the low-lying branches. Yelling above the roar of the fire, he attracted the attention of the men. They used their sticks to hack a path through the bushes to where Clary lay, still clutching his rifle. They dragged him free of the bush and lifted him up.

Supporting him under his arms, four brave men, their eyes stinging from the acrid grey smoke, stumbled their way back through the trace until they reached safe ground. When they released their grip on Clary, he collapsed to the ground like a rag doll. Only then did the murmuring crowd notice the terrible injuries inflicted by the leopard. Pink flesh hung in tatters from kneecaps to blood-splattered boots. White bone showed through shredded clothes, and rivers of blood flowed freely from the open wounds, sparkling like liquid rubies in the afternoon sun. Pools of red blood grew and congealed on the pallid sand as Clary lay there in agony.

Horrified that there was an angry leopard roaming about, a sizable bush fire burning out of control, and a badly wounded white man on their hands, the villagers acted quickly. They carried Clary back to the safety of their huts and laid him gently on a bed in the headman's hut. No one had a clean cloth for bandages, so Clary removed his soiled shirt and had the men rip it into bandages to wrap around his bleeding legs.

Clary's gun bearer could do nothing more for him there, so he ran for help. Leaving the two rifles at the hut and wearing only a tucked-up loincloth, he set off at a fast trot to fetch Clary's father William in far-off Tanga.

Chapter 2
The Rescue

"Your son has been attacked by a leopard and is close to death, Bwana Mkubwa." Gasping for breath, the bearer confronted William, who looked up from a half-skinned bird in his home taxidermy studio. Having run through the hot bushland for two-and-a-half hours, this messenger with bad tidings sagged to the concrete studio floor croaking for water.

William had seen the scars of leopard attack victims and had heard tales of the ferocity of these cats when cornered or injured. None of the tales had a happy ending. Some victims died due to blood loss from their gaping wounds. Some died from a single bite to the neck or a bone-crushing snap to the face. However, worst of all was the lingering death that could take weeks when a deep bite or clawed flesh became infected, slowly decaying, and dropping off the bone in a sticky gangrenous mass. The lucky ones who survived such an ordeal would be scarred for life and would vividly remember the nightmare for the rest of their lives.

William, with visions of his only son dying in agony in some remote outpost, prepared for the trek to rescue his son with speed and determination. He was anxious to get there as quickly as possible, wondering whether he would find his boy alive or if he would be bringing back a dead body.

On the sand at the back of the house, he hastily assembled on two long, stout poles, a heavy blanket, sheets, and some sisal rope to make a stretcher. Then he selected six strong men from his workers to be stretcher-bearers. At the same time, he was coaxing precise directions back to the village from the gun bearer who was too exhausted to make the return journey that night.

The man had done well to make the perilous trek at such a fast pace, and he would be well rewarded later. But for now, haste was all-important, as night was approaching and wild animals would be venturing out of their day beds to forage and hunt. And the longer Clary lay with his unattended injuries, the greater the chance of a deadly infection setting in.

"Twende. Let's go", were all the words necessary to set the rescue party on a forced march out of Tanga and into the fading light of the dying day. By the time they arrived at the last outlying houses of the town, night had fallen. The light of the stars above, and a half-moon low in the night sky, were all they had to guide them as they swiftly trod the barely visible footpaths. They lost their way several times in the dark and in the maze of criss-crossing paths, and had to double back to find the right one.

Later, they were guided by the smell of smoke carried on the wind from the bush fire that had been lit during the leopard fight. Finally, they could see the yellow glow of fire above the distant horizon that guided them in the general direction of the village.

The one and only dim kerosene lantern in the village stood on the floor of the headman's hut. It threw a pale light from an open window to guide William out of the darkness and straight to his son's bedside.

At every window and doorway of the headman's hut, black faces with big white eyes stared into the dimly lit room to watch the activity of this big event in their monotonous lives.

Clary was pale, only semi-conscious, and had lost a lot of blood, as evidenced by the red-soaked bedding and sour stench in the room. There was a look of both agony and shame on Clary's pale face as he narrated the incident to his father. Agony from the unattended leg wounds, and shame at being outwitted and outdone by a wild animal.

However, only a look of great relief prevailed on William's face, knowing that he had arrived in time to find his son alive. Badly mauled, yes, but conscious and alive. He peeled off the blood-soaked shirt strips from Clary's legs, revealing an oozing, bloody mass of exposed bone, shredded meat, and trousers. In this warm, humid climate, infection started quickly and spread rapidly, yet the risk of using dirty, local village water to clean the injury was too great. So the wounds were left open to the air.

Although the porters were exhausted from the journey, they could not rest. Now they had to endure a more difficult journey back to Tanga, as William decided to haul his son home right away.

They tied the blanket by its four corners to the wooden poles, and used the sisal rope to make a stretcher. One sheet was thrown over the blanket and the other one covered Clary, mainly to keep the fine dust that would be flung up during the march home from aggravating his wound.

Clary was lifted from the blood-soaked native bed by many willing hands and placed face-up on the uncomfortable jerry-rigged stretcher. Then four strong carriers heaved it onto their shoulders and were ready to go. Clary would have to endure a long, jolting ride back to Tanga, and it was not going to be easy going for the porters either. They had to carry a heavy load on the thorn-strewn paths through the dark bushland crawling with wild game, slithering snakes, and biting insects.

William handed the 400 Jeffery's and 303 to one of his men, then checked that the chambers of his own rifle were loaded and ready to fire. He turned towards the waiting carriers and, without a word, flicked his hand in a "let's go" motion.

By the light of a weak moon, the entourage moved slowly out into the smoky, still night air, and were soon out of sight and sound of the village, save for the faint glow of the bushfire still visible against the night sky behind them.

Several times William was forced to stop the group with an upheld hand, as heavy crashing in the nearby bush announced something large either coming or going. The porters, burdened with their load, could only stand still and note possible escape routes should the something big prove to be aggressive. From time to time, one fatigued porter cried out for a rest, and another took his place without stopping the march.

Once, William had to jump in the air to avoid a crossing snake, and moments later, the rear guard had to make the same manoeuvre as the snake decided to return the same way. In the early hours of the morning, while the moon was still high in the night sky, the exhausted slowly moving party reached the outskirts of Tanga without any nasty incidents, and staggered home.

Clary, barely conscious after the long jolting ride, was carried up the steps of the house and into his bedroom. Together with the stretcher, he was placed on his bed. The bearers, hardly conscious themselves, cut the sisal ropes holding the bloodstained blanket in place, and carried the poles outside. Then they stumbled to the servants' quarters, where they collapsed on any floor space they found and fell asleep.

A short time later, Clary's father, red-eyed and dead tired, walked into the early morning sunlit room. He was trailed by a Kanzu-clad servant carrying an enamel washbasin steaming with boiled water and a white towel folded over one arm. He placed the washbasin on a wooden bedside table, laid the neatly folded towel next to it, then left the room.

"Doctor" William stepped forward, uncorked a dark green bottle, and poured a good measure of tiny purple crystals into the hot water. Little whirls of violet smoke curled up from each grain, which darkened the water into a deep purple liquid.

"Permanganate crystals", answered William, before his son could ask. "It's the best antiseptic there is, and right now we have to stop the infection from setting in. Otherwise you will get gangrene, and the only way then to save your life is to amputate your legs! Both of them! Leopard claws are full of rotten meat from their kills, and washing out the wound with a powerful permanganate solution is your only chance."

Clary nodded, indicating that he too preferred the first option. William bent over his son, untied his leather boots, and slid them off. Then he carefully removed the torn trousers and dirty khaki hunting jacket, which still contained four brass cartridges in the loops, and threw everything into a heap on the floor. Placing the clean towel under Clary's blood-encrusted legs, William dipped a tin teacup into the purple liquid and lifted out a dripping cupful.

"Son, this is going to hurt like hell, like hot coals on naked flesh. But if I am going to save you and your legs, I will have to do it, so hold tight", he said.

With those words, William poured cup after hot cup of liquid over Clary's legs, washing away dried blood, dirt, and yellow body fluid, and staining the towel a sickly blue-black colour. A sound like a lion roaring with its jaws wired shut escaped through Clary's clenched teeth as he struggled to control the tears welling up in his eyes.

In excruciating pain, he screamed, "You're wrong, Dad! It feels like you're pouring molten lead on me!"

William poured the last cupful of disinfectant over the swollen legs and then removed the soaked bedding, throwing the whole lot next to the hunting jacket and torn trousers.

He replaced the sheets with clean ones, then turned to Clary and said, "I will have to wash them a few more times, at least until the wound scabs over and dries out a little. Now that you are used to it, next time it won't hurt so much!"

To reassure his son of that decision, he went on, "If we had taken you to the hospital on the seafront, the doctor would have sprinkled pure sulphur powder onto your open wound. And that, my son, would have been much, much more painful.

"However", he warned, "the most painful part of your recovery is still to come. That therapy comes later."

With those parting words, William picked up the washbasin, bedding, and clothing, and left the room. Closing the door behind him, he left his son alone in the morning sunlit room to rest and reflect on his ordeal and to contemplate his future… assuming he had one.

"My hunting days are over for good, that's it", Clary sobbed to himself.

This was quite a statement coming from a 17-year-old who had just started hunting, and had suffered a severe mauling from a leopard. But he meant it sincerely. He could not understand how he had missed that leopard lying at his feet on the anthill, or why the big gun did not fire at the critical moment when the angry cat was on him. He could not comprehend what had gone so terribly wrong the day before, yet the deep red wounds on his torn legs was certain proof that indeed it had all gone wrong. This incident would change his life from that day on.

A servant entered Clary's room bearing a tray with a plate of game-meat soup and a piece of dark bread – his first meal since breakfast the day before. The servant set the soup plate on the bedside table and pulled it in a little closer for Clary to reach. A look of horror crossed the servant's face as he stared at the ghastly leg wounds, then he hastily made his exit.

Clary raised himself onto one elbow, and greedily began to slurp up the thick, hot soup. When it was finished, he wiped the plate clean with the bread. He had not realised how hungry he was, but he felt better with some nourishment in him and could think more clearly.

When the servant returned to clear away the tray, Clary asked him to bring the 400 Jeffery's, which was leaning against the wall. The servant handed over the gun, picked up the tray, and quickly left the room.

Clary examined the gun carefully, turning it over in his hands. He noted some leopard teeth marks and dried white saliva near the ends of the barrels where the cat had taken the gun into its mouth. Apart from some dust and a smear of

Clary's dried blood on the rosewood stock, no other damage to the gun was visible.

Nevertheless, there was something strange about the two triggers. They looked very wrong now. He then realised that they were bent right back against the rear of the trigger guard. Clary put his thumb on the safety catch and pushed forward. There was a "click" as the safety came off, yet to Clary it sounded more like an explosion as he suddenly realised what had gone wrong the day before. The events fell into place like pieces of a puzzle.

It dawned on him that this gun had an automatic safety catch. Open the breech and the safety is automatically pushed to "safe". Yes, he remembered, when he was on the ground under the bush, he had broken open the gun, extracted the spent shells, put in new ones, then closed the breech and rammed the barrels into the leopard's mouth. He had squeezed so hard on both steel triggers that he had bent them back against the rear guard, rendering the gun useless, even if he had remembered to take off the safety afterwards. Now he broke open the breech, extracted the unfired cartridges, and placed them on his bedside table before closing the gun again. Slipping off the safety catch on the empty gun, he tried to pull the triggers. There was no movement at all. The gun would have to be sent to a good gunsmith to be repaired.

For young Clary, it was the most boring three weeks of his life. Confined to his bed while his legs were cleaned daily and healed slowly, he did nothing except eat, sleep, read, talk, listen, and defecate. That is, until his father walked in one morning and announced that the next painful phase of his recuperation would begin. William explained that the damaged muscles in the legs would heal and settle into a new straight position. This meant Clary would find walking upright difficult and painful, and probably he would walk with a limp for the rest of his life. Unless, that is, he started to walk before the muscles set into their new position.

With this short and simple explanation, William took his son by the arms and lifted him into a sitting position on the bed with his legs dangling over the side, then pulled him into a standing position. With a loud squeal of pain, Clary pulled free and sat down hard on the bed. Blood oozed from cracked black leg scabs that had been torn open when he attempted to stand.

"Son", William said, "I warned you it would be painful. Now this is the price the loser of the battle has to pay. If you don't get up and start walking now, you'll be a cripple for the rest of your life."

"I think I'd rather be a cripple than have to endure that dagger-stabbing pain in my legs again", answered Clary, tears streaming down his face as he stared at his bleeding limbs.

However, he knew his father was right, and he would have to endure the pain and start walking, one slow step at a time. So, several times each day, Clary got out of his bed and took one step, and then another and another. He progressed slowly until he could reach the bedroom door unaided by the African servant who stood in attendance, ready to lend a hand in case of a fall. The servant then helped Clary back to bed, wiped away the blood from any newly opened wounds, and applied a soothing ointment.

Within two weeks, Clary was walking around unaided inside the house, even though he moved slowly and painfully. But after each walk, his legs no longer bled, except when he overexerted himself. Thankfully, the feared gangrene never set in.

A month or so after those first agonising steps on the long road to recovery, Clary was taking daily walks about town or out into the countryside, where he much preferred to go. In the late afternoon on these preferred days, he would gather up the trusty old 303 and a pocketful of ammo, whistle for Satan, the jet-black all-sorts dog, and call out to one of the gardeners to act as a porter.

Then together they would amble down the main road of Tanga, past the imposing German era Kaiserhof hotel, continue under the huge shady mango trees, and stroll between the rows of swaying coconut palms. They passed by the railway station with its ugly, corrugated iron waiting room, which had been erected some years before in a vain attempt to stem the numerous complaints from waiting passengers of harassment by buffaloes. Beyond the railway station, there prevailed game country where Clary never failed to flush out a dainty bushbuck or tender bush pig. Sometimes he accidentally flushed out an irate bull buffalo from which a hasty retreat was called for.

Walking back home in the cool evening, with the salty tang of the sea breeze in the air, Satan trotting at his heels, and a fat kill draped over the porter's shoulders, Clary felt his world was in order. Except that, he could not banish his constant feelings of shame about the leopard incident and how the animal had escaped his bullets.

For days, storm clouds had been gathering into huge, woolly towers far out to sea, signalling the coming of the rainy season. The nightly rumblings of thunder could be heard far out over the ocean. The sound carried into the little room where Clary lay awake contemplating his return to the place of his mauling.

He knew he must return in order to finally lay his mind to rest about what had happened that day. How could he have missed a snarling leopard only inches away from the gun's muzzle? He would have to leave before the rains came to wash away all evidence of the incident. Now seemed to be a good time to go, so he informed his understanding father of his plans.

Chapter 3
Seeking the Truth

The next day, Clary was up before dawn. He breakfasted on tea and chapattis and was out of town before first light. He took his repaired 400 Jeffery's Express rifle with him plus ten cartridges, and was accompanied by a young helper who carried a haversack containing water bottles, some biltong, and a twist of tobacco as a gift for the village headman on whose bed Clary had laid months before. Satan, whining sulkily, was forced to stay safely at home, as leopards, should Clary meet any on the way, were partial to juicy dogs.

Even without a guide, Clary remembered the route through the maze of footpaths, as very little had changed. The thickets along the way were now drier and mostly bare of leaves, affording better visibility through the tangled undergrowth of any potential dangers. They did not stop until they reached the settlement by the old baobab trees where Clary had lain dying months before.

The villagers were pleasantly surprised to see him alive, thinking he had lost so much blood that he would not have survived the journey home. While gratefully receiving the gift of tobacco, the headman told Clary that nobody had been back to the fateful place since the incident, and the leopard had not been seen or heard of again. Their goats were grazing peacefully once more.

Clary, at first, did not recognise the bush island where he had fought the leopard, until he noticed the anthill. The fire had burned the groves of bush into an untidy mass of blackened, tangled branches over a grey and black carpet of charred leaves, yet had left the green broad-leafed palm fronds only singed brown at their edges. The fire had then jumped to another thicket and razed it before petering out.

He pushed his way through the tangle of burned sticks and leaf ash towards the bare anthill, clearly visible in the middle of the scorched island, until he was standing once more on top of his ant-made castle. He let the events of that fateful day come flooding back as though they had happened only yesterday. Looking down at his feet, as he had done on that same afternoon many months before, he could hardly believe his eyes as he stared right into a large vertical hole in the side of the anthill, deep enough and wide enough to hide a full-grown leopard.

IMAGE 3: CLARY LOOKED RIGHT DOWN INTO THE HOLE WHERE THE LEOPARD HAD BEEN HIDING. IT HAD BEEN PROTECTED FROM THE FUSILLADE OF BULLETS BY THE ANTHILL WALLS.

The big cat had been crouching inside this hole, out of sight and shielded from the fusillade of 303 bullets fired all through the grove. It had been protected by earth walls against the blast from the double-barrelled rifle fired at point-blank range. Inches to one side of its hiding place – just where its neck and shoulder would have been had it had been lying on instead of in the anthill – were two bullet holes where the slugs from the 400 had slammed into the dry earth.

Clary stood for a long time looking at the ground near his feet, summing up in his mind the events of that day. And for the first time in more than a month he felt relieved, knowing the full story of what had gone wrong, almost fatally wrong, that afternoon. He had learned a valuable lesson about hunting, specifically leopard hunting, and concluded that he could now continue his hunting career.

As he hurried back to the community to drop off his guides and take the footpath back home, the first large raindrops from the darkening sky began to fall, raising mushroom clouds of dust as each heavy droplet drummed against the parched earth. They perfumed the air with that unique smell of fresh rain on thirsty soil. The rains had finally started.

Chapter 4
First Years of Life

Clary's life started on the night of February 5, 1907, at the cramped, corrugated iron house number 8 of the Imperial Uganda Railways at Nairobi station. He was born by the light of a flickering kerosene lamp to Mr. and Mrs. Palmer Thomas Wilson, the third and only boy of four children. Clary's full name is Clarence William Palmer Thomas Wilson. What a long name for such a small baby.

Clary's father William was born in India, in the old Portuguese enclave of Goa. His father was an officer in the British colonial army responsible for the construction of the railways in India.

William had followed in his father's footsteps and joined the Imperial Indian Railway, and it was during this time, while travelling widely over the magnificent Indian subcontinent teeming with vast herds of free-roaming wildlife, that his passion for hunting took hold. This passion was passed on to and sustained the next three generations of his family.

Despite more than 20 years of railroading and hunting when it was at its finest in India, William looked forward to his impending transfer to the last untamed and unspoiled frontier of East Africa, where the British colonial government was planning to build a railway line from the coastal port of Mombasa into the interior as far as Uganda.

Just before his transfer to East Africa, William met and married a beautiful, dark-haired, half-Indian, half-Portuguese girl – a real princess. She was the daughter of the Portuguese governor of Goa, who was a descendant of the long-ago deposed Portuguese king of the royal house of Braganza. She accompanied William to East Africa, and was Clary's mother.

It was a British custom in those early days to send the children of colonialists to proper British boarding schools. So, at the tender age of six, Clary was shipped off from East Africa to a school in the beautiful state of Kerala in India. There the colonial government maintained an English school system with its stern, disciplined, cane-wielding teachers, windy, cold dormitories, bland school food, and prison-like atmosphere, all for the benefit of the colonialists' children.

Clary and the other poor pupils learned their schoolwork through the force of fear instilled by indifferent, unloving men in black robes with canes, who beat boys and girls with equal force on their tender bottoms for any misdemeanour. Comforting letters from faraway homes took a month to arrive, and during the war years, up to six months, if at all.

Holidays were spent with relatives or friends in India or at holiday camps, which were run like army camps without the classes but with all the other harshness.

Besides the three R's, Clary learned that school teaches you very little about how to look after yourself. He found that the real lessons of life start after you leave the protected and sterile environment of the institution, and that you have to learn young and fast to survive in the world outside

As his headmaster said to him on his last day, "Try to learn from the mistakes of old men, because you will not live long if you make all those mistakes yourself."

In 1919, with six years of schooling behind him, Clary's formal education was over, and the real world would take over as his teacher. As a 12-year-old, together with hundreds of other young men, he was put on board one of the "lollipop specials". These were steam ships specially designated to carry school children from India back home to East Africa and beyond. Like many others, Clary had left home six years before as a scared, shy boy, and was now returning as a confident young man.

Waiting in port for the steamer to arrive, it was extremely difficult for the parents to recognise their offspring after such a long, changing time away from home. So each child was issued a name tag for identification that was hung around their neck like a dog collar. To facilitate the reunion of parent and child at the disembarkation port, the child's name was read aloud by the ship's steward from the name tag. The child then stepped forward out of the waiting room towards the horde of mothers, fathers, aunts, uncles, sisters, cousins, other distant relatives, and odd friends, all dressed in their finest togs and smelling of perfume and aftershave. Each child was greeted by hugs, kisses, squeals of joy and cries of, "Oh my, how you have grown!"

Clary, poor boy, went through the same routine as he was met by his father and beaming mother in Mombasa port.

The First World War had just ended, and German East Africa – a German colony – was confiscated and mandated to Britain to administer. The first move the British made was to change the name to Tanganyika territory.

During German colonial times, a railway had been built from the port of Dar es Salaam, along the coast to Tanga, and then inland to the west as far as Moshi town, which sits at the foot of snow-capped Kilimanjaro.

As the British took over the administration of Tanganyika, William was transferred from Nairobi to Tanga to help run the newly acquired railway system. And it was here that Clary lived after his schooling in India, together with his three sisters, father, and mother.

William knew India well from his early days there, and listened with interest to his son's stories of his six years in his old stomping grounds. He heard that the railway he had helped build to open up and bring prosperity to India was fulfilling its duty admirably, but was saddened to realise how this was a detriment to the huge forests and herds of game that now had to give way in the name of progress. *Although,* he wondered, *progress to where?*

Like father, like son, goes the old adage. So Clary, at 13-and-a-half years old, decided on the advice of his father to join the railways in Tanga. That was a big mistake, Clary realised later.

All young apprentices joining the railways at that time were expected to learn and be familiar with the complete workings of the system, from the very bottom to the very top. So the apprentice was sent for an hour or two each day to a department head who was supposed to show him the workings of his area of expertise, after which the young man was sent off to another department to learn something there. The apprenticeship took about a year to complete. Then he was sent back to the bottom of the ladder and given a junior position as assistant to a supervisor to start his career.

In his first month as an apprentice, Clary learned to make tea for each department head. In his second month, he perfected his brewing technique. In his third month, he was considered a master at the art of tea brewing. By his fourth month, he knew a dozen different ways to brew the golden liquid in accordance with the various whims and tastes of each of his mentors, whom he visited daily in his eager quest for railway knowledge. He was also bored to death and ready to quit, save for his father's urging him to hold out a little longer.

By the end of the fifth month, Clary realised that he was not learning anything useful except tea brewing, and it had been a mistake to think he would be happy and content to be a railwayman.

It was the cry of the wild, and not steam, that coursed through his veins. His heart beat to the African drum, not to the clickety-click of a steam train. He saw more beauty in a mud-plastered warthog than in a smoke-belching, black, steel railway monster. So, without any regrets, he quit his job as super tea maker for all departments.

Chapter 5
The Start of a Hunter

The ancient hunting instinct has been present in every man for thousands of years. It is still present in all carnivores, from the ferocious buffalo-killing lion down to the lowly mosquito-eating gecko. They must hunt successfully in order to survive. Present day man's easy, modern lifestyle of obtaining food from shops does not require a hunter's instinct to survive, so it is suppressed and lies dormant. However, in some men the hunting instinct arises inside them and won't subside until it is satisfied. In Clary's case, his pent-up desire to hunt was like awakening a chained spirit yearning to free itself from the bondage of civilization.

Being a hunter in those early years was not a profession where you could make a good living, but a work of passion. The days when a hunter could barter a grant from a tribal chief to kill one hundred elephants in his area were long gone.

There were no permanent jobs for hunters, so most of them made a living by running a farm on the side.

Guiding rich foreigners on hunting safaris was a rare event before the Second World War. Only after Hollywood made a few successful films glorifying big game hunters in East Africa did wealthy Americans come in their hundreds to hunt with flamboyant professional hunters.

Some lucky hunters found employment to supply game meat to out-of-the-way mining companies or sisal estates. A few months' work could be obtained by acting as armed guard for prospectors or bush clearing operations. Sometimes a hunter would be asked by the game warden to help in dealing with a rogue animal that had been harassing villages.

In such cases, there was no payment, but the hunter would be allowed to keep one tusk from the rogue elephant or skin of a lion or leopard as compensation.

Clary would have to struggle and live by his wits if he was going to survive as a hunter. He was aware of this, but the alternative was to become a game warden who did more paperwork than hunting or to join the rat-race, both of which were out.

"What do you think you are going to do now?" asked Clary's father after he had heard, first-hand, about his son's resignation from the railways.

For this and the subsequent questions he expected to get, Clary had thought carefully about his answers, and he planned to be straightforward and truthful about them.

He began, "I never want to become a prisoner of the city and join a rat-race of men slaving away at boring, dull jobs, living a monotonous life just to save enough money for retirement, as I have seen men do at the railways. I want to get away from towns and crowds of people. I want to be free to live my life on my terms. I want to be in the bush amongst wild animals. I want to run free, I want to be a hunter."

William was astounded to hear such a mature response from him, though he perceived the sincerity and enthusiasm that this answer aroused on his young son's face. Such resolve reminded him of his own tenacity when, at almost the same age, he had been determined to become a train driver.

"Well, that's good if you have made up your mind about what to do with your life, but have you thought about how you are going to go about it?" enquired William, knowing his son would have an appropriate answer.

"Yes, I have", was Clary's quick reply. "I'll go and find Bazil Reele in the bush and team up with him. He invited me to come hunting with him anytime."

Bazil Reele was a tall, wiry, clean-shaven gentleman hunter who loved the bush, the animals, and hunting, more than anything else. He loved the quiet solitude of a camp in the bush as much as he hated towns and civilization. However, to survive as a wandering nomad, he needed money to buy food, ammunition, and dry-throat-lubricating whisky, so he collected horns and skins of various animals on order for William. Although William was still fully employed by the railways as a Westinghouse brake inspector, he also loved hunting. However, he could not get away into the bush long enough to collect the rare, sought-after species of game and birds that he wanted.

He was turning more and more to taxidermy work in his free time, to fulfil a desire to study closely the animals he so loved. He believed that despite the vast number of game herds in East Africa, there might come a day when they all would be gone, with only his mounted specimens remaining as evidence of their existence. He was a perfectionist, producing some excellent specimens of mounted game heads, as well as the difficult-to-mount bird species. This work resulted in a steady stream of customers who bought examples of his handiwork, giving him extra money to pursue his hobby, and provided Bazil with a source of income to continue with his desired lifestyle.

Bazil would shoot the game ordered by William, and when the quota had been filled – or more likely, when the whisky ran dry – would come into town, drop off what he had shot, collect his cash, buy more whisky, food, and ammo, and head out of town as fast as he could.

William sat for a long time in his favourite kapok-stuffed armchair by an open window. His elbows rested on the arms of the chair and his hands were folded under his chin. He was deep in thought while contemplating his own image reflected in his young son, sitting across the silent room from him in an armchair that seemed too big for such a small boy. He realised that his son had made up his mind to become a hunter and it would be futile to attempt to talk him out of it or hold him back. Hopefully Clary would eventually realise that he could not make a decent living that way and would come back to look for a more civilised job.

No words passed between father and son; none were expected, as each knew the other's stand on the matter, and nothing either one said would sway the argument for or against the decision. It was as good as settled.

Wordlessly, William eased himself out of his comfortable armchair and strode across the room to a red cedar wood gun cabinet set against the whitewashed sitting room wall. He pulled open one half-door and removed from the cabinet's dark interior a double-barrelled rifle, turning it over in his hands in admiration. The metallic blue barrels gleamed in the half-light of the room, as did the well-oiled Rosewood stock. This gun had two half-rounded triggers, one behind the other. The front trigger fired the right barrel, and the back trigger the left barrel. Novices usually had to learn the hard way never to put a finger on both triggers when shooting, since the gun's recoil jerked the hand and caused both triggers to be pulled at the same time.

Closing the cabinet door, he walked over to his starry-eyed son who had been watching these proceedings with puzzlement.

"If you're going to be a real hunter, you'll need a real gun, so I'm going to give you my Jeffery's 400 Express rifle. It's big enough to stop anything yet found in Africa, and if you look after it, it will never let you down. Here, my son, it's yours!" said William, thrusting it into the boy's hands.

Clary's "Thanks, Dad" was a grossly inadequate expression of appreciation for such a valuable gift, though his beaming face and ear-to-ear grin said more than any words could have expressed.

He stood next to his armchair, admiring the heavy rifle in his hands, and threw it up to his shoulder, taking aim at an imaginary creature sitting in the dark mango tree just outside the sitting room window. He had carried this rifle before and cleaned it many times for his father after a weekend shoot, although he had never actually fired it. Now it was his very own first rifle.

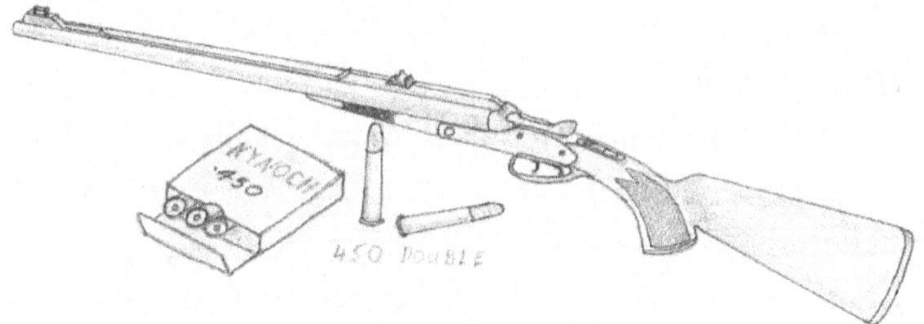

IMAGE 4: CLARY'S SECOND RIFLE.

Clary often shot small game with the military 303 carbine, and bagged game birds for food with the small 22-calibre rifle. He had seen his father shoot an Eland antelope with this big gun, heard the ear-splitting boom, seen the long yellow flame spit from the ends, and noticed the shoulder-jerking recoil on his father's big frame as the Eland went down. But Clary had never fired it, nor any other double-barrelled rifle. He stood the butt of his new possession on the floor and measured himself against it. His shoulders came level with the tops of the barrels. It was, indeed, a very big gun for a 13-year-old boy.

That evening at home, Clary and his father sat on the veranda sharing a cold beer and talking for the first time man to man, not like father to son as they had always done before.

During his youth, William had hunted in India when his dormant hunting spirit craved to be free, so he bestowed this piece of wisdom on his maturing son.

"A true hunter loves all animals, be they big or small, ugly or beautiful, the hunter or the hunted game. He also loves the trees and grassland where they roam, and nature in all its forms. He wants to preserve this for the next generations of wildlife. He will be the last defence against its destruction. When the hunter has gone, the game is not far behind." William paused, then continued, "Your gun is your only defence in nature. Use it wisely."

Clary realised that owning a gun was a status symbol that boosted his standing in life from a boy to a man. He was proud of it, and he let it show.

William knew that in Africa, one had to learn young and fast to assure survival in this hard land, as you could suddenly find yourself alone with no one to turn to for help.

That evening, they agreed that in the morning Clary would take the 400 Express rifle and the 303 carbine and go to look for Bazil Reele's camp. At his father's insistence, two porters would accompany him on the search, in case a mishap happened in the bush. That way, there would be two people to carry a disabled or ill man out. Or, in a serious case, one man could run to the next settlement for help while the other stayed with the downed man to keep hyenas and lions at bay.

After supper with the family, Clary packed a green rucksack with one change of hunting clothes, a towel, a wooden toothbrush with a tin of tooth powder, a bar of soap, and three extra pairs of socks, as these wore out fast while hunting due to the miles of daily foot slogging. He needed no shaving kit because he was too young to show any facial growth, despite now acting like a man. A grey woollen army blanket and a canvas groundsheet, rolled up and strapped below the rucksack, would be his only bedding on this trip.

At the bottom of the bag were the heavy packets of 303 ammo, and in the side pockets were stowed the flat five-shot packs for the 400 Express, whose quick and easy access might save a precarious situation. The amount of ammunition to take was a calculated guess. Taking too much left you lugging the heavy metal cartridges around for weeks on end. Taking too little threatened an early end to the safari, resulting in a shameful return home and the annoyance and disrespect of the safari crews who relied on you. So, you had to take just the right amount and, with experience, you could almost get it right most of the time. Also in the rucksack were a tin plate, tin cup, knife, spoon, gun cleaning kit, gun oil, and a minimum of provisions such as matches, salt, tea leaves, sugar, and some dried game meat to chew on while on the march. One small metal cooking pot that served for all cooking and boiling purposes was strapped to the outside of the rucksack.

The two native porters, dressed in loincloths with their shukas (native blankets) thrown over their shoulders, carried, in addition to the rucksack and one gun, a 20-pound gunny bag balanced on their head. This bag contained posho (native maize meal - their staple diet), tin cups, and some trade goods to exchange for food. Finally, on a waist belt, they had three felt-covered water bottles. The little party would rely on the trade goods to get eggs, vegetables, and fruit at the many friendly native villages they passed through that were scattered throughout the region.

Before dawn broke to the east over the calm blue sea of Tanga harbour, Clary slipped silently out of the house and roused his porters from their beds. Carrying his 400 Express over one shoulder and in his left hand a floppy felt hat that his mother insisted he wear, he was long gone to the west and out of sight and sound of the town before the cook awoke William from his slumber with a steaming cup of morning tea.

For two days, Clary and his doubting porters walked in the sweltering heat from one distant village to the next, enquiring about the whereabouts of the fire-faced Englishman called Bazil. But they received only vague hints that he was ahead somewhere. They stopped once to refill their water bottles from a tepid, gurgling stream, and twice to refill from shallow native wells. At one point, they stopped at a leafy green mango tree festooned with small, yellow mangoes that had not yet been discovered by sweet-toothed elephants. The trio gorged themselves to the limit on the fruit, letting the yellow juice trickle down their cheeks and arms and drip onto the leaf-strewn earth. They stuffed a few more half-ripe mangoes into the top of the maize meal bag for later, and after a well-deserved siesta under the shady tree, they found a pool of stagnant water to wash their sticky hands and faces before continuing on their way.

Before dusk faded into darkness, they looked for a safe campsite for the coming night. They had no lamp so had to collect firewood for light, for cooking their only meal of the day, and to ward off inquisitive animals.

Clary's meal consisted of a cup of sweet black tea, followed by a soupy stew made with dried meat and vegetables given to them by the good, simple people of the last settlement they had passed through. The two porters ate the same stew but included ugali with it. (Cooked maize meal, about the consistency of mashed potatoes. It is the bland, traditional, staple food of the local people.) After dinner, the dirty plates and cooking pot were cleaned with ashes from the fire to prevent them from being stolen by hyenas during the night, who were attracted by the smell of leftover food on the plates.

A patch of ground near the fire was cleared of thorns and twigs to lay out the sleeping mats for the night. The porters placed their blankets on the mats, laid down, and rolled themselves up in the blankets from head to toe like mummies, falling asleep in short order. Clary did the same, except he had the added luxury of a thick canvas groundsheet. He stayed fully clothed, and kept his dirty boots on in case an urgent situation arose during the night. He kept his head outside the blanket and used the rucksack as a pillow.

The 303 stood against a nearby tree, but Clary kept the 400 lying right next to him, loaded, with the muzzle pointing down and ready for quick action. If an unwanted visitor arrived during the night, Clary would shoot into the air first then see who it was. If he needed the second barrel, he would shoot again, but this time not into the air. Nobody stood guard at night, as they were all much too tired and the glowing fire usually warded off wild guests. During the night, someone always awoke, threw another log or two onto the smouldering embers, stoked it a little, and then dozed off back to sleep.

With only a cup of hot sweet tea drunk before dawn, the two men and the boy were on the march before sun-up. From now on, until the evening meal, there would be nothing to sustain them except water, biltong, and the hope of good news.

However, on the warm afternoon of their third day out, the exhausted trio found hope. They entered another tiny, remote village of grass-thatched, round, mud huts, populated by plainly dressed, simple subsistence farmers who scratched a living from their small plots of ripening millet. All eyes were on the little white man with the floppy hat and big gun as he stood tall inside a semi-circle of astonished farmers, listening to one of his porters questioning them about the whereabouts of the mad English hunter.

Clary's heart made a double beat at the word "ndio", meaning "yes"; they had news of him. Two of Bazil's porters had passed through here a few days ago carrying fresh game meat to trade for some cassava and other vegetables that could relieve their camp's daily monotonous dinner of game meat with ugali.

Eager to help, black hands pointed towards the red setting sun, indicating the direction from which Bazil's meat traders had come. The same hands pointed in the opposite direction and skywards when asked about the position of the sun in the morning sky when the traders had passed through. Not more than three hours' walk from here, concluded Clary, as he thanked the men for their help then made his way with his porters to a small band of trees some distance away. There they would make camp and cook their evening meal before the fast-approaching night fell.

The crickets were still in full chirping chorus when Clary was awakened by a yellow half-moon shining into his face from the black, diamond-studded sky. Its eerie light cast strange finger-like shadows over the ground from the overhead branches.

Far to the east, the lowest twinkling stars were beginning to fade, a sure sign that dawn was breaking. As Clary wanted to get a very early start, he woke the sleeping porters with a soft call, then picked up his stained blanket and groundsheet from the hard, packed earth. He shook out the leaves, grass, and sand, then rolled them up ready to be packed. While the porters packed their bedding, Clary opened the breech of the 400 Express, removed both cartridges, and sighted through the empty barrels towards the moon to ascertain that no insects had crawled in during the night. The chambers were clear. He reloaded the breeches, snapped the gun shut, and then looked around the camp to make sure nothing had been left behind. He saw flattened dry grass and a wisp of blue smoke that rose lazily into the cold night air from the sand-doused night fire. These were the only signs that man had ever passed this way.

In the interest of haste, they renounced their usual morning cup of tea, shouldered the rucksack and gunny bag and, gazing up at the stars, picked out a particular group to guide them towards the west on the presumed bearing to Bazil's camp. Leading the way with his heavy rifle acting as a life insurance policy, Clary strode out of the bare campsite and into the bush, the way being lighted by the still bright moon. He was followed closely by his two frightened porters who, despite their heavy loads, still managed to tread lightly on their bare feet, avoiding painful thorns and the stinging scorpions resting on the dark tracks.

They walked silently westwards, their eyes adjusting quickly to the darkness. Pink hues glowed to the east behind, assuring them that dawn was not far off. They avoided dense patches of dark bushes where dangers could not be distinguished from shadows, preferring instead to stay as close to open space as possible. Occasionally they stopped in dead silence for some minutes to listen for sounds that could signal the presence of the dangerous three: elephant, buffalo, and rhino. In the still of the night, noise can be heard three times farther away than in the dampening heat of the day. Human eyes cannot see colours at night or in moonlight, only shades of grey, although they can see movement quite well, and this is what Clary was watching for.

With a silent, motionless lion or leopard, there would be no warning of danger, just a deep, throaty growl a second before it attacked or fled. Suspicious and unidentified noises were given a wide berth just to avoid any possible dangerous encounters.

The dawn finally broke and the sun rose from the mauve-tinged east into a fiery red orb that burst over the horizon like a ball of fire, bathing the harsh land in a new, warm, friendly light.

Clary stopped in a bare patch of ground surrounded by short, dry grass to rest and think about his next move to find Bazil's camp.

In this hot, dry, game-rich countryside, water was the basic need of all creatures, including man. And over the years, this search for water had left distinct animal trails leading to or from the waterholes. Man and animals also sought the cool shade of large, leafy trees during the intense heat of the day, which meant that Bazil had to be camped near water under shady trees. With these clues, Clary started his search for the hidden camp, which he knew was somewhere in those miles of flat, monotonous bush ahead of him.

They rested for only ten minutes then, with a little more energy, continued in the direction in which they had been going, following any prominent game trails, and examining them for human footprints. At any tall trees that afforded a view of the land ahead, Clary stopped and climbed up as far as the thorns permitted, searching for promising bands of trees or greener bushes that could indicate life-giving water.

Before the sun had burned for an hour in the morning sky, Clary spotted a trace of wispy, white smoke curling up through distant trees, which indicated a human presence – perhaps Bazil, or maybe just honey hunters.

Their steps now quickened in time with their heartbeat. They cut straight across the bush towards the smoke, not bothering to keep away from potentially dangerous thickets. Finally, they came within earshot of voices. Clary walked around the last thorn bush and strode, grinning widely, into a relatively comfortable camp situated under the shade of some flat-topped Acacia trees. After three days of hard walking through the wilds of this coastal bushland, Clary had at last arrived at Bazil's camp to begin his hunting career. Little did he know that his career was about to start sooner than he expected.

IMAGE 5: YOUNG CLARY WALKED INTO BAZIL'S CAMP TO START HIS HUNTING CAREER. IT WOULD START SOON THAN HE EXPECTED.

Chapter 6
Thrown into the Deep End

Sitting around a smoky fire watching a kettle of water boil for morning tea were about 25 wide-eyed, open-mouthed, disbelieving natives who stopped in mid-sentence to stare at this boy who had suddenly appeared out of nowhere with nothing except two porters, a gun, and a floppy hat. On one side of the fire pit hung strips of dark meat drying on sisal strings, strung up high between the Acacia tree branches.

On the other side of the fire was a big green canvas sheet stretched over a thick rope. One end of the sheet was pegged into the hard earth, forming an open-ended shelter. Under this shelter were two woollen army blankets strewn over a low, folding camp cot that had recently been vacated. Clary walked past the muttering crowd by the fire and walked over to where Bazil Reele was sitting on a wooden folding camp chair, enjoying the morning sunshine. Next to him was a wooden table with a steaming mug of morning tea on it, from which he sipped from time to time as he stared ahead at nothing in particular.

Being a man of few words and fewer emotions, he waited until his guest introduced himself.

"Hello, Bazil", said Clary.

Bazil Reele's jaw dropped and his eyes widened in astonishment at Clary's appearance. Composing himself, he stammered, "Hello, young Wilson! Do you want a cup of tea?"

"Yes please. I didn't have time to make one myself this morning."

Bazil needn't have asked, because the camp cook had already extracted the tin cup from Clary's rucksack, filled it with boiling hot tea, and was on the way with it, together with a sturdy water can for Clary to sit on. The cook set the tea on the wooden table and the can on the earth, said "Karibu" (welcome), then turned and left the way he had come.

Clary sat down on the upturned can, helped himself to a large spoonful of freshly harvested wild honey from a jar on the table, put it into his black tea, and stirred it slowly lest the overfilled cup spill onto the table.

"What, may I ask, in hell's name are you doing way out here by yourself?" enquired Bazil, as he drained the last drop of tea from his cup and called out to the cook for a refill.

"I left the railways a month ago, because I wasn't learning anything except how to make a perfect cup of tea for each department head", said Clary, as he blew gently over his hot tea before taking a sip.

He then continued, "I have decided to become a hunter like you, and you told me that I could join you on safari at any time. So here I am."

Bazil pondered for a long moment while the cook brought him his fourth cup of tea. Then turning to Clary, he said, "It's lucky for you that you want to be a hunter like me, because I saw that two bull elephants drank from our waterhole last night, and I heard them a while ago feeding near here. I was just about to go and shoot one before breakfast. However, now that you are here, you can do it."

Gulping his tea too fast at the sudden task thrown at him, Clary blurted out, "But I've never shot an elephant!"

"Son", answered Bazil earnestly, "if you start with the biggest game first, the rest will come easy. Are you ready to go?"

"I haven't fired this gun of mine before!" muttered Clary, attempting to delay the chase while he plucked up some courage.

"There is always a first time for everything, and now is a good time", said Bazil nonchalantly, and he walked over to his sleeping place and from a line-up of three guns leaning against a tree, he selected the biggest, meanest gun of the trio. He broke open the breech and from a well-worn ammunition belt studded with fat brass cartridges, he removed two and dropped them into the open mouths of his gun, then snapped it shut. He strapped the ammo belt around his thin waist and reached for his felt hat hanging from a cut branch stub by his tent.

Realising that he could not postpone the inevitable any longer, Clary went to his rucksack and fished out a yellow pack of five 400-calibre solid-nosed cartridges. He put three into his khaki trouser pockets and two into the breech of his 400. Then he shouldered the rifle and looked towards Bazil, half in fear and half in excitement.

Bazil beckoned him on and called out to a tracker to accompany them and show them the way. Led by the loin-clothed tracker, the three made their way silently out of camp towards the place where the elephants had last been heard. Soon they were swallowed up by the dense brown foliage.

The crack of breaking branches ahead alerted the hunters to the elephants' whereabouts. The tracker, his job now done, dropped back. And Clary, with his oversize gun, found himself in the lead. Suddenly, a slate-grey animal came into view about 150 yards away. It towered over the bushes it was feeding on. They saw only one elephant, though they heard noises indicating at least one other giant.

"It's the one you don't see that kills you", Bazil whispered in Clary's ear as they stood still trying to locate other elephants. At every crack of breaking branches, they pointed and held up a finger to indicate a confirmed elephant position. After ten minutes of counting, Clary and Bazil each held up two fingers, confirming that as the tracker had said, there were only two elephants. Glimpses of their dirty, white tusks through the foliage confirmed they were both small bulls carrying tusks of about 40 pounds each, which was just the right size for a porter to carry.

The two bulls ambled forward slowly, stopping often to break off a tender branch and fold it into their mouths before moving on to the next bush.

Bazil whispered to Clary, "You're on your own now. Shoot either one of them."

Clary gripped his gun nervously, moving cautiously and silently from cover to cover. He kept the elephants in sight until he came within 50 yards of the nearest one. He turned to see Bazil still standing in the same place, making "move closer" movements with his hands.

Clary turned back towards his quarry and moved ten yards ahead to a small anthill that gave him a good view of where the elephants were feeding. Being just close enough to aim and shoot, he did not look back at Bazil who he knew would be encouraging him to get even closer. At 40 yards, a massive bull towering at least six feet above the thorn bushes came into view and started to tear off a green branch. Clary had never been this close to a live elephant before and had never realised that they were so big. He put the heavy gun to his shoulder and aimed for the elephant's lower shoulder area, where the vital organs were. He hesitated, then at the last moment decided that two bullets were better than one and jerked both triggers at once. The resulting blast shattered the early morning stillness and sent the broadsided animal crashing onto its side in a plume of pale dust. The double recoil from his rifle sent Clary sprawling onto his back on the hard ground. Dazed but unhurt, he picked himself up, retrieved his gun from under a bush, and looked up to see the wounded elephant staggering to its feet. Fumbling open the breech, Clary extracted the empty shells and dropped in two full ones, then snapped the gun shut. He raised it to his sore shoulder for another shot.

"Boom, Boom!" barked the 400 Express. Again, the shots sent both hunter and hunted sprawling on their backs onto the hard African earth. This time, the elephant stayed where it had fallen and did not move.

Clary, dazed from his fall, was still looking for his lost gun when Bazil came running up. He had been watching the comical proceedings from a safe distance and had kept an eye on the second elephant in case it made trouble, but it had run off at the first round of gunshots. Cautiously and with his gun's safety off, Bazil approached the prone animal from behind. He moved slowly towards its head and poked the open eye with his gun muzzle. It did not blink. It was dead.

Clary had recovered a little from his fall, though he was still covered in dry grass and pale dust. He walked over to the dead elephant where Bazil was admiring the ivory.

"A boy like you would be hard put to withstand the recoil of a single shot from that 400 Express, but you fired both barrels at once, and then you did it again. It's a miracle that you weren't thrown right back into camp!" laughed Bazil.

Clary was too dazed to smile at the joke, and said nothing.

There was a tinge of regret and sadness on Clary's face, feelings which would resurface all his life whenever he shot a beautiful, wild creature. He looked at the enormous bulk of his elephant as he ran his hands over the smooth, curved, ivory tusks. He flapped the huge ear in the shape of Africa, patted the wrinkled grey hide covered in wiry hard hairs, and admired the knitting needle-thick hairs of its tail. Those hairs would soon be woven by a tracker into a wrist bangle - an age-old custom proving that he had killed an elephant.

The two hunters, rifles over their shoulders, walked back in silence through the bush to camp to have breakfast. The birds, who had all fallen silent at the deafening noise of the gunfire, were now singing again as cheerfully as before.

During the hearty breakfast of fried impala steaks on flatbread, washed down with lots of sweet, black tea, Bazil removed his elephant hunting permit from a leather-bound folder to record the date and place of this elephant kill, as required by law.

Clary looked over Bazil's shoulder as he wrote 5 February, 1921. Then he realised it was his birthday today. He had just turned 14 years old.

Chapter 7
Learning the Hard Way

At 4:30 in the pitch-black morning, when most people are in their deepest sleep, Bazil was beginning to stir in his low-slung camp bed under the canvas flysheet. In a few minutes, he was up, had his boots on, and was headed towards the open ground away from camp to relieve himself. He then strode back, passing his empty bed and the sleeping Clary, and moved on towards the faint glow of the smouldering kitchen fire.

He picked up a dry log and poked into the grey ashes until some glowing coals appeared, then began feeding in twigs and small sticks until a healthy, crackling fire was burning in the fire pit. The noisy fire woke the slumbering natives and cast the men and surrounding trees in an orange-yellow glow.

While the cook filled a tin kettle with water and balanced it on three stones straddling the fire, everyone else eased themselves out of their sleeping places and stumbled off in various directions towards bushes to relieve themselves loudly of wind and water.

Bazil grabbed his tin cup, still smelling of whisky from the night before, and filled it with cold water from a bucket. He carefully poured some liquid into the palm of his cupped hand and threw it over his face, rubbing vigorously a few times, repeating this procedure until the cup was empty. This routine was done more to wake himself up and wash the sleep out of his eyes than for hygiene. He dried his hands and face on a dingy towel that had seen whiter days and cleaner hands, and hung it on top of the flysheet pole.

He checked his rifle chambers for obstructions against the kitchen firelight, then walked over to the dining table. Leaning the weapon against a nearby tree, he sat down on his camp chair to await his morning tea to be brought to him and to think about the day's hunt.

Yesterday morning, a porter had been dispatched to the nearest village with news of the dead elephant and an invitation for them to come and help themselves to the meat, as the people of this area loved elephant meat. Soon, half the settlement had grabbed their knives, axes, pangas (machetes), and cooking pots, and were heading out en masse to claim the tons of free meat waiting for them.

The first arrivals – usually young, fit men – were asked to carefully cut out the gleaming white tusks and carry them to camp. By early afternoon there would be 20 or more hungry natives standing near the tusk-less carcass, sharpening knives, pangas, and axes to keen edges and arguing about ownership of choice pieces of the elephant. Ropes for hanging out the fresh meat to dry in the hot sun had already been spun from the bark of surrounding thorn trees, leaving the lily-white trunks out of place, drying and dying in this harsh, red land. Patches of ground had been cleared of thorns and sticks as each family prepared a place to store its share of the meat.

However, not one morsel of elephant meat had been taken. They would never steal another hunter's meat. Never, not even after days of hungry waiting. The meat belonged to the hunter who had killed it, and it belonged to him only.

By the time Bazil and Clary returned from their unsuccessful morning's hunt and ambled over to the bloated elephant carcass, there were a dozen smoky fires burning, ready to grill chunks of fresh meat for immediate consumption.

An older tribesman in a kanzu and a white shirt – a sure sign of authority – approached Clary, not Bazil who was senior, and asked what meat he wanted from the elephant.

"No, I don't want any meat", replied Clary.

Still, not a black man had moved. Then the spokesman asked if he could have the meat.

"Yes, you can", came the expected answer from Clary. Still, not a man moved.

The senior man then turned to his waiting people, waved his hand, and said in his own language, "Take the meat."

Like an army of frenzied ants, a mass of black men swarmed over the elephant, shrieking and laughing, and loudly claiming their desired pieces of meat. Sharp knives, axes, and pangas flailed against the thick, grey hide in complete disregard for the safety of anyone close by. As silver weapons flashed blood-red in the sunlight, there were shouts and curses, pushing and shoving, as many hands vied for the same tender chunks of red meat. Fingers, hands, arms, and legs received cuts, gashes, and stab wounds, and red human blood ran unnoticed beside darker elephant blood.

A fight broke out as two knife-wielding butchers contested the ownership of a chunk of meat. But before their knives came into play on each other, the dispute was settled by a third man who quickly cut the contested meat into two pieces and gave half to each man with the advice that while they were arguing, everyone else's meat pile was growing bigger. Large pieces of elephant hide, with the wet side up, had been laid out on cleared patches of ground and were piled high with meat. The thinner belly hide was cut into long, thin strips to tie up parcels of meat to carry back to the village. Tender neck meat was cut into small chunks, roasted over the open fires, and eaten immediately.

The old folk's food, including the soft heart, liver, and kidneys, would be taken back to the village so that the old and young left behind in the huts would also taste of the feast. Tendons cut from the legs were sliced into long, thin strips and transported back to the village. They would be dried slowly in the shade and rubbed with fat to make excellent bowstrings.

The most prized parts of all were the thick layers of white fat around the heart and in the upper chest cavity. This was carefully cut out and draped like a ragged old blanket over a bush to dry. Lastly, most of the intestines, not the choicest meat, would be removed and cleaned of their green contents. When dried, they would be used as a soup base after all the other meat had been utilized. The elephant carcass was thus reduced to a pile of bones, blood, and body fluids.

A scene that had earlier looked like total chaos and mayhem was replaced by neat piles of fresh meat. Bedlam had been replaced by order and laughter, and happy, singing, contented men.

The smell and sound of freshly roasting elephant meat drifted through the air, mingling with the deep buzzing of bluebottle flies and the sour stench of stomach contents and blood. The surrounding bushes were festooned like Christmas trees almost to the breaking point with strips of dark red meat. Homemade bark ropes, strung between thin trees, sagged to the ground with an overload of drying meat. Grass tufts and anything else that served to keep meat off the ground became drying racks. Upturned elephant hides, now bare of meat, were crawling with ants, flies, and bees sucking at salty liquids. Dung beetles of all sizes were diving into the spilled stomach contents and rolling away round balls of fresh dung in which to lay their eggs.

Some men had already left for the village, hoping to outrun the approaching night and its feline dangers. Meat loads, impaled on long green sticks and carried over bare shoulders, dripped blood in droplets down the backs and legs of the men and onto the ground, leaving an odour trail in their wake that would attract any carnivore for miles around. For those who stayed by the carcass, it would be a sleepless night defending their food against scavengers who were attracted by the smell of fresh meat wafting many miles downwind on the night breeze. All day long, vultures on huge wings circled lazily overhead, assessing the situation below them before gliding down to gather on the larger trees. They were now awaiting their turn at the feast, with their heads hung low between their shoulders in the ghoulish way that only vultures can do.

As the fiery sun relinquished its sky to the twinkling stars, the sound of talking, laughing, contented men, grew louder in their efforts to warn off prowling predators and calm their fears. Tin cans set next to open fires, bubbled away with a bitter brew made from Acacia tree bark and water. Men sipped this brown liquid from time to time while seated on the ground near the fire, cutting off bits of roasted meat and tossing them into their mouths. This sharp brew enabled them to eat meat all night long without feeling full.

The sounds of lowing hyenas and barking jackals echoed throughout the night, intermingled with human voices and an occasional shout as some large animal approached too close to the hanging meat. The sound of a coughing leopard or a roaring lion was not heard. But that did not mean they were not lurking around, only that they had not announced their presence.

At first light the next morning, the remaining villagers packed their meat into portable bundles and trudged home. By late morning, the last villagers had departed, overloaded with their meat and utensils slung over their naked shoulders. They left behind smouldering fires, dried blood, bark-less trees, and meatless bones that would hardly provide a decent snack for the waiting vultures. It took the village inhabitants a few return trips to transport home the hundreds of pounds of semi-dried meat that Bazil had agreed to store temporarily in his camp.

Within a few days of being back at their plantations, the families who had stayed behind would beg for and receive a share of the meat from those who had too much of it. Bland leg meat would be traded for tastier pieces of neck meat. Coveted fat would be traded for a large amount of tough meat, so that in the end, each family ended up with no more and no less than the other. And soon the knife cuts and lacerations would be healed, the arguments forgotten, and life would return to normal.

Some early mornings later, after Bazil had downed his second mug of sweet, steaming tea, Clary joined him with his own mug of tea and seated himself on an upturned water can at the table. Together they decided that in spite of the shortage of firewood, which the villagers had collected and burned during the previous days to smoke their meat and warn away dangers during the night, they could manage with less wood.

The good water in the nearby waterhole was plentiful, so the game would still be here. And leopards and lions may have been attracted by the smell of bloody meat and could be hunted close by. If the wind did not change course and blow the nauseating stench of rotting intestines and blood from the elephant carcass towards camp, there would be no need to move on. So, there they stayed.

Bazil's decisions on where and what to hunt were based on wind, cloud cover, spoor at the waterhole, noises heard during the night, instinct, and, so it sometimes seemed, the strength of his morning tea. All these factors influenced the final decision of where and what to pursue, yet he never kept to a rigid plan. Instead, he changed his mind as often as the situation dictated, and this, Clary learned, was part of what made a good hunter successful.

The routine was the same each day. Up before daybreak, a good, hearty, stamina-building breakfast of fried meat with fresh bread and jam or honey, followed by mugs of hot, sweet tea. Then head out of camp just as the dawn breaks red over the eastern horizon. The early morning is the best time to hunt, as the game is still in the open and just starting to move towards the thickets. During the night, the game move out into the open where they can spot a predator early.

They hunted until midday, then rested under some shady trees, chewing on a piece of hard biltong or flatbread, until the fiercest heat of the day had passed. Then they resumed the hunt until the sun had lost its heat and completed its journey across the sky, ready to fall off the western horizon. This routine was frequently broken at any stage when an animal was shot and the meat, skin, and horns had to be carried back to camp.

Bazil always carried his gun and led the hunt, with Clary following close behind carrying his own gun most of the time. Sometimes, though, after a long, fruitless walk in the scorching sun, Clary, still just a 14-year-old boy, would hand his big double rifle to a bearer to carry. This inevitably drew stern glances of contempt from Bazil.

The rear of the column was brought up by a porter carrying the haversack with water, food, and spare ammunition. A second porter carried the axe, a panga, and a skinning knife. And there was always a relief porter and tracker along. A tracker would carry a gun if required, although it was beneath his dignity to carry anything else, except meat.

During the following weeks in the bush, Bazil and Clary hunted together in silence. Bazil was a man of few words. He believed that man was born a hunter and so the hunting instinct was always inside. It only had to be awakened and put into practice after its long-dormant state in a world that suppressed raw survival in favour of obedient domination to civilization. So, Clary learned bushcraft by watching and making mistakes. Then he learned about hunting by watching, listening, and imitating.

Bazil, however, did spend one evening giving Clary a new bit of wisdom.

"Every hunter will have to undergo three phases of fear during his time in the bush. Not everyone makes it to the third and last stage of fear. Those that do, usually live to have long and successful hunting careers.

"The first stage is pronounced alertness to all movements and sounds, and fear that each strand of bush holds unseen dangers. Every wild animal you see is a threat to your life.

You take no risks, you keep away from thick bush, and you always carry your gun ready to shoot. You play the game as safely as possible.

"After a few years of hunting in this way, you recognise where dangers lie, and you take a few risks that have a successful outcome. Some dangerous situations arise where the only alternative is to shoot your way out or run. You make the right decision and come out unscathed, and your confidence in your skills soars. So, you push your luck and take more risks while hunting dangerous game, and you come out on top every time."

He went on, "Now you enter stage two, the dead-or-alive stage. You take stupid risks while out hunting. You go cool-headed after a wounded buffalo in the thick bush. You hunt late in the evening when the light is poor. Not only that, you work your way unperturbed into a herd of elephants to shoot the big bull in the middle. You have a gun big enough to stop a charging bull elephant dead in its tracks, and your accuracy with it is top-notch. And to prove it to yourself, you have done just that many times. You are now invincible. You have contempt for dangerous game and fear to tread nowhere.

"Then one day, you will be out hunting, and an easy situation will turn deadly.

"Something like this", continued Bazil. "You will be out hunting buffalo with just one tracker carrying a spare rifle. You see a good head on a lone, old buffalo bull. You shoot for the shoulder, but the buffalo moves at the last second and you hit him in the lungs. Still a killing shot, but the buffalo runs off into some light bush. You curse yourself for poor shooting and decide to go after it immediately. At 60 yards you see the injured buffalo at the same time he sees you, and he charges. Overconfident, you wait for a clear shot, and at 45 yards you shoot for the brain. Your bullet hits the big, solid boss of his horn and ricochets into the air. The buffalo shakes his head and continues rushing at you. At 30 yards you fire again and hit him in the right shoulder. He goes down, then gets back up in a second and ploughs on. He is ten yards away now, and you chamber another cartridge and fire too quickly, hitting and knocking off the side of one horn. The buffalo drops, groans, gets up, stands there dazed for a few seconds and then charges you again.

"You panic and try to chamber the last round too hastily, but the gun jams with the cartridge half bent in the magazine. On your left, you see movement and you see a second buffalo that you had no idea was there charging you from less than 15 yards." He paused to let his words sink in.

"Your turning point in life has arrived. If you survive this trial, you enter stage three. The final stage." He hesitated for a few seconds, then continued.

"Now you have respect for all game. You have a healthy fear of dangerous situations. You still take risks, and as a hunter, you must. However, they are calculated risks, and you don't push the situation beyond your limit. Furthermore, you know that the unexpected can occur at any time. That's what makes hunting exciting. Except now you don't go into places where the unexpected could end up in your lap. You walk, stalk, and hunt with a plan on how to get in and get out safely with everybody in your party.

"This incident happened to me", said Bazil, eyeing Clary seriously. "My tracker, carrying my back-up double-barrelled rifle, shot both buffaloes and saved my life."

Clary was entering this first stage of fear. His eyes scanned everywhere, and he suspected all dark, shady areas and bush patches to contain a waiting danger ready to spring, charge, or bite the unwary passer-by. He expected every animal he approached to lower its head and attack with a loud snarl or snort the moment it spotted him. Every patch of grass and overhanging branch hid a poisonous snake that was ready to strike at anyone within range. Every rustle of dry grass, every snapping twig, and every tree waving in the breeze, startled him. Every bird, beetle, or insect movement aroused suspicion. Every hoof and paw print, every sweet, pungent, or acrid smell drifting on the air caused his heartbeat to quicken.

His eyes darted around in search of the perpetrator of the spoor, and with his limited olfactory ability his nostrils sought out the origin of the odour. He could not understand how Bazil could walk, seemingly oblivious to all those signs of potential danger, and not react to any of them.

Nonetheless, Clary decided to keep up his guard, stay alert, and be ready to react at the first sign of danger. Perhaps one day, thanks to his vigilance and quick action, he would save Bazil's life from a springing lion that he had unwittingly blundered into.

"Fresh lion spoor", whispered Clary loudly, as he stopped and pointed to a huge lion spoor on the red sandy soil at his feet.

"Yesterday's", said Bazil in a calm voice, then turned slightly and threw Clary a bored glance, all without looking down or breaking his steady, loping stride through the bush.

"Shhhh!" hissed Clary one midday as he heard the unmistakable crack of a branch close to their path. This time,

Bazil stopped but did not un-shoulder his rifle as he looked towards Clary.

"Crack, crack" came the noise again, however this time from the other side of their track. Clary pointed towards it with a smirk on his face.

"Acacia bean pods bursting in the midday heat. It's their way of spreading their seeds", was the smirk-removing reply from Bazil as he turned back to the path and continued walking.

Another day, during a midday siesta in the shade of a creeper-entangled thorn tree, Bazil lay flat on his back, his head resting on his green haversack and a nondescript floppy hat covering his face. His hands were clasped together over his thin belly. Clary sat under the same tree, leaning back against the trunk with the two rifles resting against a branch next to him. In the light-blue, cloud-scattered sky, he noticed a flock of circling vultures. This could mean a kill in the area, so he decided to bring it to the attention of the snoozing Bazil.

"Vultures", squeaked Clary, breaking the deathly silence of the afternoon calm.

There was a moment of irregular breathing from Bazil as he awoke from his rest, but he did not move. "Huh", he merely grunted.

"Vultures circling over there", repeated Clary, pointing at the big birds in the sky. He noticed that Bazil had not bothered to lift his hat from his face to look.

"At this time of day, they're just catching a rising air current to ascend high without having to flap their wings. Saves them energy", replied Bazil through his hat, then he dozed off again. A short time later, the birds were just tiny black specks high up against the puffy, white clouds, and soon they were out of sight.

After this last embarrassment, Clary vowed to keep quiet, be seen and not heard, and try to learn more by absorbing Bazil's wisdom than by asking stupid questions and making asinine statements.

"How do you know which way the wind will blow today, because I don't feel any wind?" he asked early one morning before leaving camp.

Bazil eased himself out of his chair, walked a little way out of camp, and motioned Clary to come over. Bazil picked up a handful of grey dust and threw it into the air. It fell and drifted in one direction.

"That is the direction of the prevailing wind for today, so we will start off walking into the wind. You can check it by looking at the clouds; which way are they moving? Later in the morning the wind will pick up, so we can use our little bag of ash to check the direction", answered Bazil.

Early one bright, golden morning, as Clary got up and made for the dining table where a hot mug of tea awaited his attention, he heard some voices, louder than the usual morning whispers, coming from the kitchen area. He saw Bazil talking to the cook and his helper. They were running low on food and were completely out of some supplies, such as fresh vegetables and sugar. Bazil was hinting that perhaps they should move camp and pass a plantation where they could obtain fresh vegetables and possibly some fruit.

Bazil walked back slowly towards the dining table, kicking up puffs of dust from the dry ground. On his way, he stopped by the guns leaning against a tree trunk, grabbed the little .22 rifle, checked that the magazine was full of little brass cartridges, then continued ambling towards Clary.

"Would you like a fresh roasted guinea fowl for breakfast?" he asked as he approached the table.

"Yes, I would", Clary blurted out in an unsuspecting squeaky voice.

"Then go and get one!" said Bazil, pointing to the bush as he shoved the 22 into Clary's lap. Then he turned and sat down on his camp chair, examined his empty mug, and shouted over his shoulder at the cook for more tea.

Clary's jaw fell open as he looked from the .22 rifle to Bazil's serious face and then towards the kitchen area, where he hoped to see some sign of a joke being played on him. He quickly realised that it was no joke; rations had run low, and there was nothing to eat for breakfast except, perhaps, maize porridge. Again.

He checked that the little rifle magazine held the full five shots, then shouldered the gun and walked out of camp. Footsteps behind alerted him to the presence of a tracker who had been sent along, no doubt, to help carry back all the freshly shot guinea fowl that Clary was expected to shoot.

Far and wide, not a single bird made a sound or showed itself. After a frustrating hour of walking, stalking, looking, and listening around the empty tract of bush, neither Clary nor the tracker could find a fowl of any sort. So, rather than return empty-handed, Clary shot a dik-dik that was standing motionless less than ten paces from him. The Muslim tracker slit the little animal's throat while it was still kicking, and recited a passage from the Koran as he did so. On the way back to camp with breakfast, Clary missed a francolin on the ground a few paces away and a tiny dove sitting on a thin waving branch, cooing with morning joy.

Although the spiced slivers of fried dik-dik meat, liver, and kidney tasted good even without the usual fresh flatbread, there was an emptiness to the breakfast. The meals were becoming monotonous now without onions and bread, and the tea without condensed milk was not refreshing, however sweet one made it. The staples were finished, and it was time to head back to noxious civilization. Clary sensed Bazil's uneasy mood by the way he stabbed his fork at the pieces of meat on his tin plate.

They were still camped about four days' march from their home base at Tanga. However, the porters would be overburdened with dried meat, sun-bleached skulls, salted skins, and ivory tusks, as well as the usual camp equipment. This meant that they could only manage a few hours of walking between rests in the burning sun. More likely, they could make Tanga in five or six days.

However, the camp was within a day's march of the main railway line running between Tanga and the upcountry terminus of Moshi, situated at the foot of snow-capped Kilimanjaro. With a bit of luck, they could catch the train, for there was one running up-country and one down towards Tanga at least once a week. This might mean spending a few days camped by the railway line waiting for the right train. But even if the wait was long, it would be in a new hunting area and would give the tired porters a chance to rest.

"We'll go for the railway line. Pack your bedding", ordered Bazil. He arose from the breakfast table and walked towards the kitchen area where the porters sat around a smoky fire, murmuring in grumpy tones to each other, and eating their breakfast of thin maize porridge.

There were joyous cries of delight and the sudden burst of activity as busy black men ran in all directions with smiles on their faces – a good indication that the news about the move was well received by all.

Every person knew his station in the camp hierarchy, and each went about his job with respect for the system. No one attempted to usurp another person's rights. The skulls with their sharp horns were bound together, three or four in a bundle, into awkward but manageable loads, which were given to the lowest man in the hierarchy to carry. The next person in rank carried the neatly tied flat bags of salted skins, and the next porter, salt, tusks, food boxes, and camp equipment. The cook carried only the kerosene lamp with its breakable glass and the big axe. His helper carried all the cooking pots and pans and the big kettle, and he sounded like a one-man band as the utensils clinked and clanged against each other in rhythm with his footsteps.

Dried meat, tied into neat long bundles with freshly cut ropes of Acacia bark, were carried by the trackers and skinners. It was considered an honour for a porter to carry a hunter's personal effects, as it meant that he could be close to him and his protection, as well as have some influence on the safari.

Clary and Bazil's bags were handed to the most senior porters to carry, and these men insisted on walking in the privileged position just behind the gun bearers. Proud gun bearers would only carry rifles. However, they also carried a haversack containing ammunition, a gun cleaning kit, and binoculars, as this gear was considered to be part of the gun.

Within an hour, every man stood poised next to his load, ready to go. Those who would carry a load on their head had collected bundles of long yellow dry grass that they had woven into thick rings. These they placed on their heads to act as shock absorbers between the load and their heads.

Bazil, dogged by Clary at his heels, made a last survey of the campsite to assure himself that nothing had been forgotten and that no fire still smouldered that could turn this tinder-dry bush into a raging inferno within minutes. Looking up into the trees as well as down on the ground, Bazil found, stuck in the fork of a tree, a toothbrush made from a short section of a local vine that was not always easy to come by. He held it up in the air for all to see. Smiling broadly, the grateful owner rushed over to retrieve it, stuck it into his curly black hair, and hurried back to his load.

"Haiya, twende, OK, let's go!" roared Bazil, standing on the edge of the campsite where he could observe the men. Loads were heaved onto heads and backs, and slung across shoulders, and then each man moved into his position in line according to his status in camp. The whole column moved off, following Bazil as he led them through the brown bush country towards the railway line in the west.

It would be a two-and-a-half-hour march before the safari made its first rest stop, with the sun shining directly overhead. After a 90 minute pause to let the hottest part of the day drift away, the trek would continue in the same order of rank as it had begun. Every hour after that, a quarter-hour rest would be called so that loosened loads could be tightened, aching backs could be rested, and sore shoulders could be relieved of pain for a while. Sometimes, a deeply embedded thorn in the bare, hard-soled foot of a porter would have to be cut out with a sharp-pointed knife, in which case the rest period would be extended until the successful completion of the operation. The trudging column then continued as before, its progress through the thorn savannah marked by the incessant clanging of the kitchen toto's (young boy) cooking pots.

Suddenly, there it was, the railway line! The sinking sun's rays bounced off the shiny, serpentine steel rails as they disappeared in two unbroken lines into the distance.

Cries of, "tume fika, tume fika", meaning, "we have arrived, we have arrived", emanated from the lead porters as steps quickened in a last burst of energy towards the silent railway line. All signs of fatigue disappeared from the faces and steps of the sweating black men as Bazil led them along the rail line towards a likely looking camping spot for the night.

The small group of thorn Acacia trees near the line would be an acceptable campsite for the few days' wait for a down-country train. Heavy loads were dropped to the ground. There were grunts and sighs of relief as the easy work of clearing the ground of dead branches and thorns to accommodate the sleeping mats began. The two resident dik-diks went bouncing off, uttering high-pitched whistles in protest at the unfair intrusion into their home. Some men went off in search of firewood for the night fires. Others tied the bundles of dried meat, skins, and trophy heads high up in the thorny branches to keep them from thieving hyenas and jackals who were sure to pay a visit after dark.

With less than an hour before darkness engulfed the land, Bazil, carrying the .22 rifle, and Clary, with a military-type 303, went across the railway line in search of fresh meat to satisfy the many hungry mouths in camp. Not long afterwards, they heard a flapping commotion coming from a thicket in front of them. Creeping to within 30 yards of the tall trees, Bazil spotted a flock of electric blue guinea fowl fighting for the best branches to roost on for the night. It was the perfect time to catch them.

A shot rang out from the .22 rifle, and a plump bird flopped to the ground. Another shot, and a second bird bit the dust, and then a third and fourth fell dead before the squawking flock realised the danger and flew off into the dimming light to find a safer roosting place.

On the short walk back to camp, Bazil managed to bag another fat bird from a small flock trotting along a game path still looking for a roosting tree.

Back in camp that evening, Bazil ordered that one whole bird be kept aside for breakfast, and the gizzards, hearts, and livers of the other birds be cooked this evening for his and Clary's dinner. The remainder of the plump birds – a great delicacy to the natives – were distributed to the crew. These birds would be hacked into small pieces and boiled in slightly salty water for several hours until a thick meaty soup remained in the bottom of the cooking pot. A large pot of ugali (maize meal) would be prepared, and everyone except the gun bearers and cook would sit by the steaming food pots and stuff themselves with the nourishing dinner.

To eat, they would take a handful of ugali in one hand, roll it into a mouth-sized ball, poke a deep hollow in the middle, dip the ball into the soup to fill the hollow, and then pop it into their mouths – all the while keeping up a jovial banter. The cook and gun bearers, considered a class above the rest, took their fair share of the food from the communal pot, and ate away from the lowly porters.

Bazil and Clary set their table and chairs out in the open under the star-sprinkled night sky. They dined on freshly grilled guinea fowl gizzards, with tiny hearts and livers and steaming uglai, rounded out with the last of Bazil's Scotch.

After dinner, both hunters moved their chairs closer to the embers of the dying fire and sat in silent contemplation. As though in a trance, they gazed up at the twinkling diamonds over their heads and listened to the mysterious cacophony of creatures in the night. A multitude of fragrances drifted by on a light breeze, enchanting their sense of smell. Wisps of blue smoke from the porters' fires glided like ghosts through the trees, imparting a misty effect to the dark scene. It felt as though magic was in the air.

After a while, Bazil said in a mellow voice, "I just love these moments. Being a hunter out here puts me in touch with my ancestors, my roots; it is where I came from."

Equally entranced by the setting, Clary replied, "You know, right now I have such a contented feeling of being at home in this place. As if I have lived here before. There is something in my head that is telling me this is where I belong, and here I will be happy."

"That, young Wilson, is your intuition trying to get your attention", asserted Bazil. "We Europeans long ago lost contact with our intuition. We follow our logic and ignore the little voice in our head that is trying to guide us. The African tribes living in the bush have not lost this contact and still consult their intuition, their spirits, before making big decisions. Being out in the bush in a quiet, calm environment helps us make contact with this part of our brain." He paused to let his words of wisdom sink in. "I learned long ago to heed the urgings of my instinct, and it has saved me from disaster far too often to be a coincidence. I advise you to do the same whenever you get into an awkward situation."

Clary, however, was too absorbed in his own thoughts to respond.

Next morning, after a delicious breakfast of roasted guinea fowl and the last cups of honey-sweetened tea, Bazil called a young porter over to him. Together they walked towards a reasonably shady tree growing a few paces off the railway tracks. From this thorn tree, Bazil cut a three-foot branch with his knife, stripped off the thorns, and tied a bright red and white dotted handkerchief to one end. He gave strict instructions to the young man to sit in the shade under the tree and, pointing to the north, listen for the train coming from that direction. When he heard that train, he was to shout the news of its arrival for all the camp to hear. Then he must stand by the side of the railway line in this spot. Here Bazil marked a big X on the red earth with his stick. Next, Bazil told the boy to wave the handkerchief stick until the train stopped. When the big steel monster came to a stop, he must tell the engine driver that Mr. Bazil wanted to get on board with his crew and equipment.

Leaving the eager young man with his head cocked to one side, already listening for the train, Bazil walked back. He grabbed the 303 rifle, handed it to one of his trusted gun bearers who knew how to use a gun, and told him that when he heard the young porter yelling that the train was coming, he was to fire three shots into the air. Bazil demonstrated the angle and way in which to shoot, and then made the bearer demonstrate the procedure with a dry shot to be certain that he understood his duties correctly.

Just to be safe, Bazil loaded only three rounds of ammunition into the magazine. He knew that even the calmest types can get carried away in the excitement and shoot off many deadly bullets in all directions, swearing afterwards that they had only fired three shots. Bazil feared that he may not hear the train coming if he was hunting too far from camp. By getting his gun bearer to fire into the air, he was ensuring that he did not miss that all-important train. It was common practice for a hunting party to stop the train in the middle of nowhere to load a crew and cargo. The engine driver could not stop too long, though, as he had a timetable to keep to, even if that imprecise timetable stated: Tanga train station, arrival time: Thursday afternoon.

In the early part of the last century, many Africans in towns calculated time by counting the 12 hours of daylight that starts at 6am and ends at dusk at 6pm. The 12 hours of night start at 6pm and end at dawn the following morning. So, when an African says it is 4 o'clock, he means the day has had four hours of daylight. This would translate to 10am Western time. It is a simple and sensible way to mark time. However, the days of the week and months of the year are the same as the West uses.

In the villages where no one has a time piece, time is indicated by the position of the sun in the sky, such that at 7:00 in the morning, the villager would point to the Eastern horizon and at midday a finger would point directly overhead. Distances are also measured by the sun's movement. Distance to the next village would be shown by the position of the sun when the person would arrive there. There is no time indication during the night; it is just night.

Days are calculated by the last significant event that occurred in the community, such as the death of someone, or when an elephant herd trampled their crops into the ground. Months are counted from one full moon to the next, and years are based on the annual rainy season. It is an effective way of keeping track of time in the bush.

For years, Clary never wore a watch, preferring instead to use the easy African method of timekeeping by the sun's position in the sky, which all his crew understood.

For the crew waiting beside the railway tracks, there was a lot of work to do, and no one was left idle. A good supply of firewood had to be dragged in. Fresh and half-dried skins had to be re-rubbed with cold dry wood ash or salt and laid out in the shade to dry. Uncured meat had to be dried on a wooden rack built over a slow, smoky fire. Personal clothing, torn and ripped by the constant battle with thorn trees, had to be repaired before one dared enter civilization without embarrassment. And good water close by had to be located.

During this waiting time, Bazil and Clary made short shooting forays into the surrounding country, but they were careful not to stray too far from camp lest they not hear the three gun shots signalling the arrival of the train. They found some dark yellow rainwater that had collected in a pan where a few years ago workmen had dug out some earth to use for repairing a broken railway line embankment. The water was muddy from being bathed in by wild animals, yet after settling it, by using the crushed seeds of a Moringa tree as a reagent and then boiling it, the resulting liquid would serve as safe drinking water.

A few hours after midday on the third day, the excited cry of "Na kuja, na kuja" (It's coming, it's coming) burst from the young porter at his post under the thorn tree. Bazil and Clary both happened to be in camp attending to some unfinished roasted pigeons when the cry went out.

Bazil gave the order to pack up the camp and carry everything the hundred yards to the railway line, where the eager young porter was now standing at the big X, holding out his green stick with the dotted handkerchief fluttering in the breeze. He would have to stay in that stance for at least another 20 minutes before the train arrived at his position.

Excited porters dashed around camp, collecting drying meat from the racks and personal belongings from the forks of trees. They doused smoky fires with precious water that would no longer be needed. No one noticed the trusted gun bearer who, in all the excitement, realised that he had forgotten his most important duty. Thinking that he had better carry out his task now, he picked up the 303 rifle, ran into the open, and fired three rounds into the air in quick succession, just as he had been instructed to do.

Panic now broke out amongst the excited safari crew. Screams and shouts of confusion added to the mayhem. Believing that a rhino or lion had assailed the camp, some porters raced for the biggest trees and scampered up into the top branches, oblivious to the long, sharp thorns. Others dropped their loads where they stood and high-tailed it into the bush, leaving a plume of dust in their wake. A few confused souls dove for cover into any convenient bush or hid behind dropped cargo.

The guilty gun bearer saw the panicked men running helter-skelter in all directions and presumed that his shots had spooked a rhino, which was now running through camp. He dropped the rifle and bolted after the others as fast as his flying feet would carry him.

Seeing the confusion that only an irate rhino could have caused, Bazil and Clary raced for their guns, grabbed the biggest ones, loaded and cocked them, and stood side by side, looking about in bewilderment for the cause of the sudden panic. They were met with absolute silence.

Seeing no danger, the bravest men slowly crept out from under thorn bushes and climbed down from trees, then set about pulling thorns from their arms and legs. Calls went out to the long-distance runners that it was now safe to return. Soon the first men warily ventured back to the abandoned campsite. When the perpetrator of this chaos returned and told his side of the story, the whole crew burst into uncontrolled laughter. They returned to their loads and unfinished chores, still laughing and telling their stories above the laughter of the others as they carried their bundles to the railway line.

Their laughter was infectious, and both Bazil and Clary could not maintain their composure for long. Soon they too heartily joined in the hilarity.

Lying abandoned by the railway track was a stick with a red-spotted handkerchief tied to it. The flag-waver was nowhere to be seen, so a new man was chosen to stand by the line and flag down the train. The original young flag carrier was finally found some distance away, sitting on the bare ground, shaking and trembling like a leaf. Like the others, he had heard the three shots, seen the fleeing crew, and felt it was time to abandon his position. He had fled to the other side of the line and into the trees beyond. There he had been confronted by some "fierce animals with big white teeth" – most probably warthogs trotting away from the confusion. He then raced to the left and straight into a herd of "red animals, some with long black horns" – likely docile impalas, springing away from the noise. Running away from these wild encounters like a hunted rabbit, the young porter broke right, straight into the path of a galloping giraffe. Believing death was at hand, he stumbled with his last bit of stamina back to where he'd come from and collapsed by the railway track, where he was found shaking and saying his prayers.

Bazil called the gun bearer who had caused the whole debacle and administered a very severe punishment. He was demoted to porter, and a junior porter at that, though the man was still insisting that he had only done the task he was told to perform.

The puffing of the old steam engine could be heard long before the sound of the clickety-click of the iron wheels rolling over expansion joints in the heated rails was audible. Then the dirty, grey wood smoke cloud came into view, roiling over the tops of the dark green Nyika thorn trees. And finally, the hissing, black, snaking monster, growing louder and louder, could be seen, chugging and wobbling over the line at no more than a man's running speed.

The steel monster came to a hissing stop in a cloud of white steam next to the flag waver. The curious passengers craned their necks and stared out of the open carriage windows, murmuring to each other about why the train had made an unscheduled stop in such a remote, godforsaken place.

IMAGE 6: THE STEEL MONSTER CAME TO A HISSING HALT IN THE MIDDLE OF NOWHERE. THE STARTLED PASSENGERS CRANED THEIR NECKS TO SEE WHAT THE CAUSE COULD BE.

The safari crew loaded the equipment, tusks, horns, hides, and themselves onto the open goods waggons near the end of the train. Gun bearers and cooks preferred to sit on the hard wooden benches in the third class covered wagons. A uniformed, stern train conductor noted all the additional passengers and cargo that had been put aboard his train. He would present Bazil with a bill for the whole cavalcade when they arrived in Tanga.

At the engine driver's invitation, Bazil and Clary hopped up into the cab, where they could get the latest news shouted to them above the loud chuffing, hissing, and clickety-click of the steam engine as it sped at its full speed of 30 miles per hour towards Tanga. As they rolled along, there would certainly be a drop or two of whisky from the Scottish driver's private stock to oil the parched throats and invigorate the hunting tales.

However, there was a delay before the train could start again, as a few porters were still inextricably caught in some wait-a-bit thorns. They had to be freed by hacking off the offending branches with a sharp panga, allowing the men to be extricated. The hooked thorns were removed from bleeding flesh and torn clothes, then the men were quickly ushered on board the train.

Eventually the train departed in a feisty cloud of choking black smoke and with the sound of steel grating on steel as it gathered speed on its way home. The whisky in the cab flowed freely, and the talk was accompanied by much gesticulating and the laughter of tipsy men as the engine swayed from side to side over uneven rails, while the miles rolled lazily by.

As the train lurched to its final screeching stop at Tanga station by the Indian Ocean on that hot and humid evening, Clary, a little tipsy from too much whisky, staggered down the metal steps of the cab and felt elated and happier than he had ever been. He was certain now that he did not want to be

an engine driver or barkeeper or accountant or anything else.
He wanted to be a hunter. His mind was firmly made up.

Chapter 8
Trying to Survive Without Experience

After a few weeks back in Tanga, Clary felt out of place in the hustle and bustle of a big town, and he itched to get back into the bush with Bazil. Orders for mounted game heads at William's Taxidermy shop were few. The expense of shooting, salting, and storing many sets of horns and skins, in the hope that they could be sold later, was costly. So, Clary, knowing that at 14 years old he was too young to accompany Bazil with a paying client on safari, sat idly by and watched enviously as Bazil, and his motley crew of porters, loaded their fresh provisions into the rail cars for another safari into the wilds then disappeared down the tracks in a cloud of smoke.

However, before Bazil departed, he turned to a sad-faced Clary and said, "Get rid of that floppy hat and buy yourself a proper safari hat".

Living at home with his father, mother, and two sisters, Clary was bored with nothing useful to do around the home except play games with his friends. So he appeased his yearning to hunt by occasionally going alone to the edge of town with his black mongrel, Satan, and the old, trustworthy 303 rifle. Together they would wander about the thickets, admiring the colourful wildflowers struggling against competitors to grow and bloom in awkward places. Satan would occasionally rush after some animal he flushed out of its resting bed, but was too slow and never caught anything. Clary would sometimes throw the gun up to his shoulder and dry fire at a fleeing buck, just to keep his shooting reflexes in trim. Both he and Satan were happy just to be outdoors, roaming free wherever their hearts desired and enjoying the beauty of nature without the need to shoot meat for home.

A wise hunter once said, "You can enjoy the pleasure of hunting without killing." A true statement, with which Clary ardently agreed.

Sometimes a local administrator, bored with the usual weekend of drinking at home, then drinking at the club, and then drinking again at a friend's house, felt inclined to try some hunting. Lacking experience in the bush and being scared as well as unsure of himself, he would ask around the club and office if anyone with some bush experience was willing to accompany him. Occasionally, Clary was asked to act as organiser and guide for such outings where only non-dangerous and small game were hunted.

After conducting a few such trips where the inept guest hunter had missed or crippled an animal that required Clary's skilled tracking and stalking to eventually kill it, his reputation as a good hunter, even though so young, spread rapidly. However, Clary refused to take anyone out after dangerous game unless they had first proved their skill by handling a heavy calibre rifle in the bush while hunting plains game.

Visiting cargo ships to the port of Tanga, while offloading and loading cargo, often gave a salty old sea captain a chance to hunt for a few trophies in memory of his visit to East Africa. Clary managed to land a few of these hunts thanks to his spreading reputation as a good hunter, or perhaps due to the low prices he demanded for his services.

One such request almost ended in tragedy, though, owing to Clary's fearless stupidity and lack of respect for wild game, as well as his lack of experience with lions.

A journalist writing stories for an American outdoor magazine had stopped in Tanga for a few days while his ship discharged cargo and took on provisions. While downing a few drinks at the local bar, the writer enquired of the barman if it was possible to go on a short lion hunt for a story he hoped to write. He was told that Clary was in town and could probably arrange such a quick trip. The word was passed on, and eventually Clary and the writer concluded a deal. However, it transpired that the writer was not only short of money and time, but was not a hunter himself and did not actually want to shoot a lion. He wanted to accompany someone on a lion hunt so that he could write about it from first-hand experience.

At that time, there was a pesky lioness that had been killing native cattle regularly at a small settlement only a few hours' walk from Tanga. This lioness was declared vermin by the powers in the game department, and Clary was issued a free permit to shoot it. The following morning Clary headed out to the troubled settlement, with the writer in tow and two porters carrying food supplies and two folding camp chairs.

Arriving about noon in the heat of the day, the group rested briefly in the shade of a tree by the chief's hut. The chief narrated tales of his people's cattle being taken at night by a lioness and how they had tried in vain to stop the beast.

A few miles from the village was a large, dense grove of trees that was suspected to house the lioness's lair. Most of her strikes had taken place close to that grove, and grazing cattle had been spooked when the wind came from that direction.

The village cattle herders led the party to the location, which seemed to fit the requirements of a lion's den. A short distance inside this grove, in a high, sturdy tree, Clary constructed a machan (tree hide) about 12 feet off the ground. It was nothing more than his two high-backed folding safari chairs lashed side by side and secured to stout tree branches by sisal ropes. More poles were tied to the chair legs for footrests, and a single, notched-pole, removable ladder completed the machan. A few green-leafed branches were tied strategically in place to camouflage the hunters while they were in the tree.

Returning now to the village, Clary went to the goat pen and listened to the incessant "bhaa, bhaa" of its occupants. One particular goat that had recently lost its kid bleated incessantly, and it was this goat that Clary requested to use as bait for the lioness. It took two natives to drag the pitiful, bleating, struggling goat by its ears from the pen to a small clearing by the machan, then tie it by its neck with a short rope to a tree trunk 20 yards away.

Two hours before sundown, Clary and the writer sat on a log near the forest and had a snack of tinned corned beef on thick-sliced white bread, quaffed down with a tepid bottle of beer. Then they walked to the hide, climbed up the wobbly ladder, and sat down in the secured camp chairs. Clary was appropriately dressed in a long-sleeved khaki shirt and tough jacket, with long khaki trousers tucked into his brown leather boots.

A porter passed up the 400 Express rifle. Clary loaded it with two solid bullets, then snapped it shut with a reassuring, dull "thunk". He raised the rifle to his shoulder, aimed at the goat, swung it left and right to check that his field of fire was clear, and noted any branches that could block his firing line. He ran his hands over his breast pockets to confirm that his khaki jacket held spare ammunition in the ammo loops. Then he laid the gun across the chair's armrests, muzzle pointing away from the writer, who sat on the left with pencil and small notebook in hand, ready to jot down notes on all the action.

The reporter – a man in his early forties – wore a thin, light green cotton shirt with pallid, heavy cotton pants and sea blue canvas shoes without socks. Thrown across his shoulders, he had a light brown cardigan, "in case it gets cold tonight", he mentioned to Clary in the 35°C heat of the afternoon. It was not proper attire for hunting, although sufficient disguise for tonight.

A porter passed a double-barrelled shotgun to Clary, along with a leather ammo belt, its loops filled with short, thick shot shells. Clary hung the belt over the back of his chair and laid the shotgun within easy reach across two branches at the foot of his chair. Two felt-covered water bottles were also passed up and hung over the backs of the chairs. The two porters removed the jury ladder from the machan, placed it on the ground a short distance away, and slipped away silently towards the village to sleep for the night. They would return the following morning.

At the writer's request, Clary explained that the plan was to wait quietly in the machan until the lioness heard the bleating goat. Hopefully, she would come looking for it, then spring silently and seize the bait by the throat. In the 30 seconds while the lioness was occupied with the dying goat, Clary would have time to raise his rifle and shoot the lioness through the head, neck, or shoulder, depending on her position. Death would be quick and clean.

If the lioness came early and was shot before nightfall, it would be possible, with a little agility, to climb down the tree via the trunk and walk back to the community. If the lioness was shot later in the evening, Clary and his guest would spend the night in the machan. In the morning, the porters would return to put the ladder against the tree so that the hunters could descend. The shotgun, loaded with buckshot, was insurance in case the lioness was not killed by the first shot or was maimed and had to be followed into the thicket the next morning to finish her off. Buckshot was lethal at close range and would stop any lion in its tracks.

"Look, I'm a writer. I have to write something interesting for my magazine readers, so try to add some excitement to this hunt tonight if you can", muttered the writer.

"Shooting a lion in Africa should be interesting enough for your article, but if you want more of a story, I can add some excitement", Clary assured him.

As the harsh daylight faded, and the sky turned orange, then blue, and finally a sombre grey, the setting sun slowly elongated the dark shadows of the trees and brightness descended into darkness all around them.

Day birds slowly fell silent, making way for the night sounds to wake up. Night prowlers and crawlers came out of their day beds, snapping twigs and rustling leaves on the jungle floor in their endless search for food. An occasional puff of wind brushed the treetops and rustled the branches, but no other movement or sound could be seen or heard.

Out there somewhere was a hungry old lioness who could be ogling them right now through yellow eyes and could appear at their machan at any moment. Or she could be miles away from here and never be seen. There was no way to even guess; they could only wait in silence and darkness and let her make the first move.

True to its suspicious nature, the tethered goat continued its ear-piercing bleats right up to dusk, then laid down, tucked its legs neatly under its body, and never made another sound.

Clary and the writer sat silently and motionless on their perch. In the fading light, their sense of sight gave way to the duller senses of hearing and smell. Gentle breezes stirred flimsy branches and wafted through the undergrowth, carrying the many sweet scents of the African land to their noses.

A quarter moon, high in the night sky, ducked in and out of puffy, off-white clouds as shadows on the ground came and went like ghosts in the forest. This shadow dance went on for hour after hour.

They did not hear the faint rustle of a bush and snap of a few twigs, nor did they see a murky shadow moving below when the moon went behind a cloud. Death had come swiftly and silently for the hapless goat. The big cat had rushed in like a puff of wind and snapped the goat's neck so silently that the waiting hunters had not even noticed it. Only heavy breathing alerted Clary to the lioness lying broadside not 20 paces away, holding the lifeless goat in her powerful jaws.

He nudged the writer, and pointed down at the big cat. With a slow, deliberate movement, Clary lifted the rifle to his shoulder and was just about to shoot when he remembered his client's words about adding some excitement. He replaced the gun over his lap, then took the shotgun, eased off the safety, brought it up to his shoulder and whispered softly to the pen and pad man, "Get ready to write". With the express intention of wounding her and turning her into a wild, aggressive beast, Clary aimed for the rear end of the crouching cat, and pulled the trigger. The still night was shattered by the deafening blast, and the yellow flame from the right-hand barrel lit up the eerie scene as a load of buckshot slugs slammed into the back legs of the unsuspecting lioness.

A sound like thunder, so strong that it vibrated the camp chairs on the machan, emanated from the struck cat as she leaped high into the air, twisted around, and crashed off into the night, growling madly. Pungent blue gun smoke drifting over the machan, and a pool of shiny blood from the dead goat visible in the weak moonlight, were the only signs that something had happened here. Silence was so still it could be heard descending heavily over the scene.

For a long half-hour Clary waited, watched, and listened. With subdued breathing, he strained to catch any hint that something was about to happen, and had the shotgun poised and ready for anything.

The writer, ruddy pencil poised above his white notepaper, took in the scene with quick glances left and right towards the dead goat and over to Clary. In a voice far too loud for the silence he said, "What happens now?"

Before his words had left his lips, a deep snarling howl arose below and to the left of them, followed by the sound of sharp claws slashing dry bark along the tree trunk as the lioness lunged upwards towards them. Clary swung the shotgun down and discharged the left barrel in the direction of the noise, then quickly reloaded the empty gun, letting the spent shells fall to the hard earth below. He waited with bated breath, not knowing if he had hit the cat or not.

Except for a few puffs of dust mixed with gunpowder smoke, there was nothing to be seen, and deathly silence reigned. A few minutes later, the next assault came with the same blood-curdling howl. This time it was directly behind them. In their haste to turn in their camp chairs to face the rush, they almost fell out of the wobbly machan, but managed to grab a thick branch and arrest the fall. Clary fired hastily below and somewhere behind him, but the shot only shattered a low-hanging branch and scared the lioness off for the moment. At the same time, the 400 Express slipped off his lap and almost fell to earth, but Cary just managed to grab it. Now panic was beginning to set in.

The only clear shooting area was directly in front and 20 paces left and right of the goat. But this was the only ground the lioness did not use for her many charges that night.

The next attack came silently from somewhere unknown until claws raking the tree trunk gave the cat's position away. She was directly underneath the machan, though invisible to those above. Another wild shot drove her off.

Again and again, she attacked from the left, on the reporter's side, or from the right, on Clary's side. She charged through thick bushes or from the most awkward places behind them. Sometimes she charged, growling and snarling loudly, yet sometimes as quietly as the gloomy shadows that flitted across the jungle floor. At each rush, Clary fired a load of buckshot at the enraged attacker, but none found its mark. The shots only drove her off and steeled her for her next assault. Deep angst gripped the reporter as he squealed loudly at each charge. He panted heavily, fearing for his life, and sweat poured out of every pore of his body. The stench of urine confirmed the desperate terror he felt.

The worst part was the waiting, not knowing if or when the next attack would come, from where it would come, and above all, if this time the lioness would reach into the machan and drag one of them down to certain death.

One fact was certain, somewhere out there was one very angry, very aggressive injured lioness who was determined to kill them, and she wasn't about to give up until she did. This fact kept Clary and the petrified writer fully alert and awake the whole long night. The hunters had now become the hunted!

Once, Clary spotted a shadow off to the right, moving quicker than the other shadows, and he fired both shotgun barrels at it. But the shadow must have seen the flash from the gun and jumped to one side, for it grunted, then disappeared into the other shadows.

When the ammunition belt was almost empty of shot-shells and the ground underneath the machan was littered with spent yellow cartridges, there was still nothing to show for their efforts except torn grey earth and bleeding branches hanging from broken trees.

Clary had lost count of how many assaults he had turned away and how many hours they had been in the tree. He knew that with the quarter moon now below the horizon, there were no more shadows to see. There was only darkness and the occasional sound that tickled the hairs on the nape of his neck to warn him of the lioness's presence.

However, help was on its way from a longed-for quarter, as a faint glow in the east grew brighter and bigger and into a stunningly beautiful red dawn. The trees lost their ghostly dull colours, exchanging them for orange and green hues.

Shadows dissolved into thin air as the welcome sun rose over the land.

Clary and the ashen-faced writer stayed on the machan, not daring to come down just yet. He emptied two more shots into some dark patches of bushes, suspecting it was the cat, but there was no sound or movement. The lioness, a night hunter, would consider her battle lost and flee the area for thicker cover to lick her wounds and perhaps live to fight another day or to die a slow and painful death.

The sun was well up by the time the porters arrived with half the community in tow. No doubt, they had heard all the shooting during the night and wanted to see all the dead lions that surely had been killed. On seeing nothing except a dead, stiff goat, and being told that one very aggressive wounded lioness was still close by, they hurriedly retreated en masse towards the safety of their huts.

The two porters, who had slept peacefully in the village, came to the machan and placed the ladder against the tree trunk. One man climbed halfway up to catch the two guns and an empty ammo belt, and pass them to his companion below. Greatly fatigued from the night's ordeal, Clary managed to climb down the ladder unaided. The writer, however, sat tightly gripping the camp chair, staring emptily straight ahead. His face looked drained and very pale, and he was visibly shaking. He had to be pried forcefully out of his chair and manhandled down the jury-ladder to safety on firm ground. The reporter's notebook and pencil had fallen to the ground, so Clary retrieved it and slapped it a few times against his trouser leg to remove the dust. Dirty white pages with one brown thumbprint and a few dried splashes of sweat were all that was to be seen under the pencilled headline, "A Lion Hunt".

While the porters dismantled the machan and lowered the two sweat-soaked camp chairs to the ground, Clary walked around the battleground to determine the route of the big cat's retreat. He kept the shotgun loaded and ready in case she was lying well camouflaged close by, waiting for the right moment to strike again. The scene was a mess of churned earth, empty shot shells, weeping branches, pug marks, and dried blood, but there was no indication as to which direction she had gone.

In total silence, the three men and a boy retraced their previous day's footsteps back to the settlement. Clary, greatly embarrassed, had to explain to the local chief that he had not killed the marauding lioness despite all the shots the man must have heard. He had only maimed her, and it would be very dangerous for anyone to venture into that tract where they had spent the night.

After taking a long drink from their water bottles, Clary and the dazed reporter made their way along the same well-worn paths towards Tanga, a four-hour trek away. Not a word was spoken on the way back.

Clary felt remorse about wounding the lioness just so that a magazine reporter could write a gripping tale of danger in the African bush. On the other hand, his inexperience in hunting and lack of foresight meant he could not have anticipated the outcome. Now he knew better, or so he believed. His near-death encounter with a leopard was still three years away.

At the whitewashed fortress-like hotel in Tanga, Clary delivered his sweating, exhausted guest to the cut stone steps at the entrance. Without a look back or word of farewell, the reporter made straight for the hotel bar, disappearing behind its double swinging doors and into the cool interior.

Clary turned away, went down the steps and headed home, where he knew he would receive the deserved fury of his father once he told him the story of what had transpired last night.

The scolding from William was more furious than Clary had anticipated.

"You wounded a lioness on purpose just to get your name in a foreign magazine!

"A lion standing on its hind legs can reach ten feet high. Moreover, it can spring at least 15 feet high, right into your lap!

"There will be unsuspecting native herders wandering through there with an injured lioness amongst them!

"You haven't been paid yet, and very likely never will be!"

William's reprimands were severe and without mercy. They echoed throughout the whitewashed living room and outside, for all passers-by to hear.

William dropped the shotgun ammo belt with its few remaining shot shells onto a table.

"Never do such a stupid act again, and never leave a wounded animal to suffer and die an agonising death. One day, you may innocently blunder into a dangerous animal that someone else has maimed and cowardly left to die. I want you to go back right now, track down that lioness, and end her misery", William growled at his cowering son.

Then he turned and walked out of the room, slamming the door hard behind him, leaving Clary to think about the wisdom of his ways in the cool, silent room.

For a long time, Clary sat listening to the silence in the room. Then he rose, picked up the ammunition belt from the table, and proceeded to stuff the empty loops with new bright yellow shot-shells that he had taken from the cedar wood gun cabinet. He had decided that he would rather face the rage of a wounded lioness than the wrath of his father after his afternoon nap, if he found Clary still at home.

The door creaked open, and his mother appeared. Her green eyes showed sympathy for her son, and she felt sorry for him as she had heard the tongue-lashing he had received. She knew her husband was right in his outrage, and she would never interfere with his decisions, even if she believed him to be too harsh in his judgment.

"I have warmed up some food for you, it's on the dining room table. So go and eat before you go out again", she said, then turned and left.

Clary put the last shells into the belt and carried it to the dining room, where he found a white porcelain plate piled high with steaming white rice covered with chunks of meat and sliced vegetables, all swimming in thick brown gravy. He put the belt on the table next to him and then sat down to the huge helping of food – his first meal since the previous day. Two yellow bananas on a separate plate for dessert were too much for him, so he took them to eat later.

He picked up the ammo belt and went back into the sitting room, where he retrieved his 400 Express rifle from the gun cabinet and two five-shot packs of soft-nose bullets. Then he went through the kitchen and out the back door to the servants' house to rouse two porters from their afternoon doze and inform them that the next safari was leaving right now. Everyone in the neighbourhood had heard the scolding Clary had received, and although they did not understand English, the porters suspected that they would be called out again soon. So they had already half prepared to leave, by packing food for themselves.

In an old army haversack, Clary packed water bottles filled with clean drinking water, a few yellow cobs of roasted maize to eat, a thin, hoary cotton blanket to sleep on, his two bananas, and the 400 Express rifle ammo packs. Now the party was ready to go.

Clary led the way with his rifle strapped over his right shoulder, followed by the strong native bearers carrying his meagre provisions and a shotgun. They wended their way down the tree-shaded main street of Tanga, out through the mud and wattle native huts on the outskirts of town, then along the same footpaths they had used before, through the bush until they reached the lion village just as the sun was setting.

It was too late to look for the lioness now, so they would have to spend the night in one of the huts and leave at first light in the morning.

Clary declined the offer of a clean room and a bed in the headman's hut, preferring to sleep outside on a wobbly wooden bed under the front overhang of a hut where a cool breeze would blow all night. He sat on the bed for a while, thinking about how he was going to go about following the crippled lioness tomorrow and not get himself killed. As he had not slept a wink last night and had marched for seven hours today, he was too tired to think straight. So he covered himself with his grey blanket and soon fell into a deep sleep, completely exhausted.

He slept long and well during the night and was awakened by the sun warming his face with its first rays of light and the gentle sounds of the village starting another day. Having slept fully clothed, Clary only had to thump the heels of his boots on the ground to evict any undesirable inhabitants from within, slip them on, lace them up, and he was ready to go.

Breakfast consisted of two squashed brown bananas and a few sips of water. His two bearers had eaten a cold roasted maize cob and drunk a tin cup of warm, freshly drawn goat's milk, offered to them by a herder. They too were ready to start the hunt.

Clary persuaded the eager village helpers to remain in the safety of their huts until he had tracked down and dealt with the injured lioness. Then he set off for the scene of yesterday's events, carrying the 400 Express rifle and followed by his two bearers – one carrying the loaded shotgun, and the other the haversack with spare ammunition.

It was not difficult to find the old machan tree, as there was still the odd hyena lowing in the distance and the first vultures had already started gliding down towards the surrounding trees. Bone splinters, vulture feathers, a piece of rope, and the smell of death were all that remained at the battleground. The previous day, vultures, with their keen eyes, had spotted the dead goat, descended on it, and picked it clean of meat. During the night, hyenas had fought for the remaining bones and skin, and carted off their pieces into the bush to gnaw on at their leisure.

Clary could not see any fresh lioness spoor, which meant she had not returned during the night, although she could still be hiding nearby.

He exchanged the 400 Express rifle for the shotgun, which he loaded with SSG – a larger and deadlier shot at close range than buckshot – then strapped the full ammo belt around his thin waist.

It took at least an hour of searching over the hard sandy ground, through all the hyena spoor, before a keen-eyed tracker found the retreating lioness's spoor, which they confirmed by noting the dried black blood smears on the branches of low bushes.

Following the tracks, the bearer led the way, searching the ground ahead of him to determine the direction that the lioness had taken. Close behind, with the loaded shotgun, walked Clary, scanning the bushes to the left and right, watching for any sign of movement that could signal a lightning attack by the lioness. The second porter brought up the rear, carrying the 400 Express, which was loaded with the safety catch on. His task was to guard the end of the column and warn of a charge from behind.

Two slate-grey doves were almost blown to pieces by Clary when they fluttered out of a thorn tree very close to the hunters who had startled them from their mid-morning rest. An hour passed as the trio, with frayed nerves, stalked silently through the dense bush, which limited visibility around to dangerously close ranges.

Then the lead tracker shouted, "HUKO!" "over there!"

Like greased lightning, Clary swung the gun to his shoulder and aimed to the left, half squeezing the trigger, expecting to see exposed yellow teeth bearing down on him.

But the tracker's black hand was not pointing down to the bush where an assault was expected, but up to some distant treetops where vultures were sitting and a few more were descending from the sky above. Breathing out with relieved tension, Clary ordered the lead porter to abandon the spoor and drop back, while he himself went on cautiously to see what had attracted the vultures. One porter reached over and snapped over a large green branch, which he left dangling and bleeding clear sap to mark their last position on the lioness's spoor, in case they saw nothing of interest at the gathering of vultures and they needed to pick up the trail again.

Approaching the vultures, Clary heard much squawking, hissing, and flapping as they fed. About ten paces from them, the startled birds flapped and crashed away, throwing up clouds of fine dust in their quest to find an open space in which to take flight. When the last bird had gone and the dust settled, Clary was left staring into the hollow eye sockets of a very dead lioness. It was the same lioness that he had wounded two nights ago.

Pale grey intestines protruding from a large, ragged hole in the lioness's side snaked out over the dusty ground. Big blue flies flitted in and out of orifices in the stinking carcass, and Clary had to move upwind to avoid its stench. He flicked the safety catch on and leaned the shotgun against a thorn tree while he examined the carcass more closely. Next to the hole in the stomach, enlarged by the feeding vultures, were a few smaller holes in the leg muscles where the buckshot had entered and severed some tendons attached to the knee joint.

Clary sat there starring at this noble dead creature in the churned-up earth before him. He realised that his first shot into her rear end had hit the knee joint, maiming the lioness and reducing her ability to leap the 12 feet into his lap that night. That was the only reason that he and the reporter were alive now.

One porter was standing five paces away, pointing out something on the ground. He indicated the lioness's tracks, with their tell-tale limp and blood splats, going right past the bush where she now lay. Clary followed the spoor past the bush and on for another 50 yards before it turned and made a large circle right back to where she now lay dead. She had been so weakened by the gunshot wound that she could not go farther. With her last cunning move, she had laid an ambush – an ambush so perfect that there would have been no escape for anyone following her tracks. She would have been completely hidden behind the thick bush, and anyone following her spoor would have walked right past her then, once passed, she would have had clear ground with which to drive home her attack from behind. A run of two or three seconds, even with a sore leg, was all she would have needed. But she had died where she lay waiting for her pursuers.

Clary realised that had he followed her yesterday morning, instead of going back to Tanga, he would very likely have been lying in this very spot, either dead or badly mauled.

He ordered a tracker to cut off the tail and take it back to Tanga as proof to the game warden that the lioness was dead. He was about to have her four paws hacked off so that he could remove her claws, which he could sell in Tanga to jewellers for a few cents each. Ashamed by this thought, he turned away wordlessly and headed back towards the village.

Heavy wings beat the air above and behind him, signalling the vultures' return to their interrupted meal. In less than half an hour, only pieces of skin and the clean bones of the lioness would remain. By tomorrow, after the powerful-jawed hyenas had their turn at the carcass, there would remain only the largest bones and teeth for ants and beetles to chew over. What an ignoble end for such a beautiful creature. Clary vowed then and there that he would never again intentionally cripple an animal.

In Tanga the next day, word was out and all over town that a young hunter with no hunting experience, called Clary, was a danger to anyone who went out with him.

The reporter had sailed out of port on his tramp steamer the morning after his return from the hunt, still in shock and inebriated from too much Scotch the night before. At the hotel bar, he had ranted and raved the whole night to anyone who would listen about a young lunatic called Wilson, who had almost got them both killed by a wounded, raging lioness.

Despite Clary's efforts to explain to all the listeners why he had maimed the lioness in the first place, how he had kept her at bay the entire night, and eventually tracked her down and found her dead a day later, nobody believed him. His good reputation as a reliable hunter was now mud in town. Nobody wanted to go hunting with him, and strangely, there was no space for him on any of his friends' safari trips. However, what hurt Clary the most was that the reporter never wrote the lion story for his magazine in America.

Chapter 9
Learning to Fix Cars and Drive

Depressed at being the pariah in town and shunned by his friends, Clary decided to put away his guns and find something else to do, at least until the lioness incident was forgotten.

At the encouragement of his father, Clary joined Riddoch Motors, the Ford agents in Tanga, as an apprentice mechanic. He accepted the position, with the clearly stated understanding that he would not have to learn tea making for anybody!

In the country, there were many makes and models of cars and trucks that came into the workshop for servicing and repairs. These vehicles were simple machines to work on, though they needed constant attention to keep them running in these rough, muddy, and dusty African conditions. Travelling one hundred miles in a vehicle without a breakdown was an earnest talking point at the local bars in the evenings.

Spare parts were hard to come by, and an urgent order for a part from America or England could take six months to arrive by ship. Therefore, improvising to keep a car going was the norm. Local modifications appeared on almost every car and truck, and when the correct spare part finally arrived from overseas, it did not fit because the original fitting had been so modified that it could not be returned to its previous condition. This necessitated making yet another modified repair to fit the original part to the vehicle.

This was excellent training for Clary. Many times, that knowledge would save him from being marooned in the bush when one of his own clapped-out cars broke down in the middle of nowhere, miles from any help, with no spares, and no hope of another car passing his way any time that year.

Being only 16 years old, Clary was too young to drive and too young to obtain a learner's licence. He was permitted to start the car he was working on in the workshop, but it was strictly forbidden, under threat of instant dismissal, for anyone except authorised garage drivers to take customers' cars on test drives. After a vehicle had been repaired in the workshop, it was test-driven by a company driver. The mechanic who had worked on the vehicle was required to go along on the test drive to determine if the job was satisfactorily done. Thus, Clary got to ride along in the cars that he had worked on, and could ask the driver how to drive a vehicle.

At that time, an old English lady who lived alone in a big house in an upper-class district by the seafront in Tanga, owned a Ford Model A. She had never learned to drive, so she hired a chauffeur for the car. She was a regular customer at Riddoch Motors, and she knew Clary as one of the mechanics who routinely worked on her car.

One Saturday afternoon, she cornered Clary while he was walking along the road past her house. Not knowing that he had no licence, she asked him if he would drive her to the club on the other side of town. Her chauffeur, she said, was off duty that day, but would be on again at 6:30 that evening, and he would come to get her at her club.

In spite of never having driven a car, Clary eagerly agreed. He followed the old lady along the smooth driveway bordered by yellow flower beds to where her black Ford Model A was parked under the awning by the front door.

Clary opened the car door for her to get into the rear seat, then he went around to the other side and climbed into the driver's seat. He realised that he could not depress the gear pedal down all the way and could hardly see over the dashboard. He explained that he needed two seat cushions to drive this car because he had short legs.

At the lady's command, a house servant dressed in light blue robes brought two small patterned sitting room cushions which Clary placed under and behind him, so that he could now reach the gear change pedal and see over the bonnet. He set the control for starting the engine the way he did in the workshop, then jumped out of the car and moved to the front where the big starting handle dangled from the engine compartment. On the third swing, the engine sprang to life with a bang and a cloud of greyish smoke. Clary jumped back into the driver's seat, engaged the forward lever with a grind, and cautiously let out the gear pedal.

The car moved forward and gathered speed slowly as he gingerly manoeuvred it along the driveway. He had never steered a car before, and it proved to be unexpectedly strenuous on his arms. He zigzagged from side to side across the driveway, almost hitting a large coconut tree, but managed to keep the car out of the flowerbeds and make it out of the main gate and onto the road. By now, he had figured out that gentle movements of the big wooden steering wheel were called for, and not violent yanking from side to side.

"Just testing out the steering", he lied to the lady in the back, in case she thought to enquire about the car's wild gyrations from side to side.

He continued along the road to town with a gentler weave. But since he had no idea of the rules of the road, he was confused as to which way to drive around a roundabout. So, he took the shortest way, which was the wrong way, but luckily, there was no other traffic that afternoon.

"Why did you go around the roundabout the wrong way?" demanded the anxious lady.

"It's shorter", said Clary, on the spur of the moment.

By the time they arrived at the outskirts of town, Clary had almost mastered the steering, gear shift, and most importantly, the brakes. He zoomed through town in a cloud of dust at 20 miles per hour, crossing every crossroad without giving way to other traffic, which thankfully was sparse on a Saturday afternoon. He arrived safely at the clubhouse in record time.

"My driver takes a lot longer to get here, but I suppose with your experience you can drive much faster." The elderly lady smiled as the kanzu-clad club doorman opened the car door and assisted her out.

"Park the car in a shady spot where my chauffeur can find it please, and thank you", continued the elderly lady, then she sauntered off in her long green dress and string of white pearls into the cool interior of the clubhouse.

The doorman, still holding the car door, frowned in indignation at Clary as he sat there grinning from ear to ear with the car engine idling and coughing little puffs of blue smoke around them. He could now drive a car.

Sometime during the following week, Clary went into a car showroom on an errand. He took a little booklet that was given to all new car owners to familiarise themselves with the road signs and general rules of the road. He studied it carefully at home in the evenings and was amazed that there were so many rules and regulations for driving a car.

Some days later, the sweet old lady stopped Clary in town and complained that her car would not start, so she'd had to leave it at home and come in with a neighbour. She asked Clary to collect the vehicle and take it to the garage to be repaired. He readily agreed to look at the car the following day, but explained that he would have to get some tools from the workshop first.

The next day, using the excuse that he wanted to repair a friend's car at home, Clary persuaded the foreman to give him a standard toolset wrapped in a green canvas rollup bag. He signed a receipt for the tools, with a notation that if he lost them he would have to pay for them.

The elderly lady's car proved easy to repair. The fuel tank vent had attracted dust and water, which had settled at the bottom of the tank. The dirt had been sucked into the carburettor and had blocked the fuel valve. Clary cleaned out the simple carburettor, although the fuel tank would have to be removed and cleaned at the workshop, and a locally modified fuel filter installed in the fuel line.

He went into the lady's beautifully furnished living room and, with the house servant's permission, took the same two cushions he had previously used to put on the driver's seat. Now that he was alone in the car, Clary could practise moving off slowly and braking gently, which he tried along the driveway before driving out of the wrought iron gate and onto the main road. He diligently obeyed the rules of the road which he had just studied in his little booklet. He stopped at every intersection to give way to other traffic, and carefully noted the road signs and their meanings. Just before he came to the edge of town, he turned off onto a little-used side road to practise turns, stops, and parking. He even managed to drive a few hundred yards in reverse.

Confident that he knew what he was doing, Clary then drove to the workshop and into the yard. He found an empty work bay and skilfully parked in it. He revved the engine and simultaneously switched off the ignition, listening to the engine die. He had seen the workshop drivers do this and was told that it was to ensure that some unburned fuel remained in the engine to help start the vehicle next time.

Jumping down from the car to the amazement of his workmates, Clary met the icy stares of the workshop supervisor and manager. No one said a word, each waiting for the other to explain the situation.

Finally, breaking the ice, Clary said, "The fuel tank needs cleaning and a modified fuel filter".

"You didn't tell me you could drive", the manager exclaimed in surprise.

"I learned to drive a year ago, but you have enough drivers on staff, so I didn't tell you", lied Clary, turning his face away to hide his blush.

"Issue him a permit to test drive the customers' cars", said the workshop manager to his assistant, as he turned and left the floor.

Clary was duly issued a company permit to drive customers' cars, and carried it all the time while driving. When stopped by the police at a road control point and asked for his driver's licence, he would produce his company driver's permit with the excuse that his real licence was in his shirt pocket back at the workshop. To prove it, he would open the top of his grease-stained overalls to reveal no shirt. This trick worked well, but only during working hours on weekdays when he would be testing or delivering customers' cars. He had to remember to sit on his newly obtained seat cushions, which made him look taller and older than his 16 years.

Luck ran out one day when he was ordered by a suspicious policeman to produce his driving licence at the police station within a week, or face prosecution for driving without a licence.

He was in a serious dilemma.

Clary's father, William, had no idea that his son was test-driving customers' cars using a falsely issued licence. Clary knew he would be unsympathetic to his son's pleas for help for a dishonest situation of his own making. Neither could he approach the company management for help, because if they found out about his lies it would mean instant dismissal, and there would be no hope of getting a mechanic's job with any other company in Tanga. There was also a police prosecution hanging over him if he failed to produce a driving licence within the week.

A day before the deadline to produce his driver's licence at the local police station, Clary realised that nobody could help him. Nobody except himself. So, just before lunch break when he would not be missed at Riddoch Motors, Clary put on his thick-soled hunting boots, making him two inches taller, and took his recently issued hunting licence, which was only granted to people 16 years or older. This age limit was not strictly enforced by the game department, who issued these licences. Although 18 was the official minimum age to hold a full driving licence, he hoped that his two-day unshaven face, high-heeled boots, and hunting licence, would fool the police into thinking he was over 18 years old.

Walking into the clean, white-walled police station as calmly as possible, yet visibly nervous and sweating under his clothes, Clary went up to the neatly dressed African police sergeant sitting at a tidy desk, and said he had come to report the loss of his driving licence. The sergeant looked up without expression, pointed down a long open-ended corridor, and said, "See the officer in room 4".

Clary walked down the corridor and stopped at door number four. He knocked lightly and entered when a booming voice from inside bellowed, "Come in".

The white policeman, dressed in an over-starched khaki uniform, was sitting at his wooden desk which was piled high with thick files. He looked friendly, but had an air of authority about him that was unsettling.

Clary sat down on a hard wooden chair and started to tell his tale. He explained how he had been ordered to produce his driving licence at this office and, because he had only been driving company cars with the company drivers' permit, he had not noticed that he had misplaced his civil licence and now wanted to know what to do.

The police officer pushed his chair back with a scrape and walked to a simple wooden cupboard. He opened it to reveal shelves of files stacked neatly on top of each other. Running his fingers across a row of hardbound files, he stopped and extracted one marked, "Motor Vehicle Driving Licences. Europeans". Then, returning to his desk, he opened the file and studied the index of names.

"What did you say your name was?"

"My name is Clarence Wilson, but I am also known as 'Clary' for short."

The police officer studied each name on the index and then, looking up, said", I don't see any Clarence Wilson or Clary Wilson here. What is your father's name?"

"His name is William Wilson."

Again the policeman studied his index trying to find the name, but to no avail.

"Where did you and your father get your driving licences?"

"In Nairobi", Clary half lied, as his father had obtained his licence in Nairobi.

"Ah, that's why I can't find it here", said the policeman with relief, closing the file with a slap. He returned it to its proper place in the cupboard and then looked through another file and pulled out a clean sheet of paper that was marked "Application Form For…". With a black pen, he completed the sentence with "replacement of a lost driving licence".

He handed this to Clary and said, "Fill this form out in ink and then hand it to the Indian at the registry office. Pay him five shillings, and you can collect your duplicate licence next week."

With a great weight off his shoulders, Clary almost bounded with joy out of the police station. At the registry office next to the police station, he filled out the application form. He entered a false date of birth, making him three years older than his true age, and hoping that no one would check it to determine his real age. He paid his five shillings, and a week later collected his driving licence. Using that licence, he drove for the rest of his life without anyone questioning him about how he had obtained it.

As a thank you for his help with her car, the old English lady invited Clary to come to her house for lunch one Sunday.

She asked him to invite four of his friends to come too. When asked what his favourite dish was, he answered truthfully, "Curry and rice". The English lady was known to have an excellent African cook, so Clary was expecting a delicious fish curry, or preferably a succulent chicken curry with accompanying English-style condiments.

On the appointed day, Clary and his four friends were led into the expensively laid-out dining room, and were seated at a table with real English bone china crockery and silver cutlery. Crystal glasses were filled with chilled water, and an immaculately dressed waiter sailed in bearing a huge serving plate piled high with fluffy white rice. The waiter spooned a generous heap of rice onto each of their plates and quietly retreated to the kitchen. A few moments later, he reappeared with a deep silver dish filled with plain, yellow, mild curry powder and proceeded to sprinkle spoonsful of it over the rice. The lady of the house was served a plate of beans and tomatoes on toast.

"I don't see what you boys find so good about curry with rice", she said. "Anyway, tuck in. There's plenty more if you want it."

The boys looked at each other in horror as it dawned on them that this was the old dear's interpretation of "curry and rice". The African cook had been taught English cooking, but obviously neither he nor the old lady had any idea about Indian food, especially curries.

Clary and his four friends had to finish every last grain of rice on their plates, and not only keep a smile on their faces the whole time, but also laughter in their voices as they answered small talk questions from their host. They were able to very politely decline a second helping without offending the sweet, well-intentioned old lady.

Once again, due to this "curry and rice" flop, Clary became a laughing stock and the butt of jokes amongst his friends. He had to keep a very low profile for a long time.

Chapter 10
A Boring and Deadly Life

Clary continued his apprenticeship at Riddoch Motors and learned so much about motor vehicles that he believed he could repair any machine, anywhere on the road, with the minimum of tools. He eventually rose through the ranks to become the workshop foreman three years later.

He tried very hard to keep from making a fool of himself in front of his friends, and was careful whenever he was invited to hunt with them. Despite his interesting job as foreman, with its steady pay and comfortable, secure lifestyle, his love of hunting and wild places never waned. With a monthly wage coming in, he could afford to indulge in his passion on weekends and holidays.

On Friday afternoons, when the end-of-work whistle blew, Clary rushed home, washed, and changed into stiff khaki hunting clothes. He grabbed his well-oiled guns and waxed ammo boxes, loaded less than basic camping gear and inadequate food supplies into backpacks, and with three sturdy porters, was gone before anyone realised that he had even been home. He was never expected back before the fading light of Sunday evening or, occasionally, even later.

On some weekends, he took with him brave local amateurs who had chosen to ignore the slanderous rumours about his hunting ability. Fortunately, most of them were only interested in plains game or guinea fowl shooting, and were too scared to attempt a true safari after anything larger.

Occasionally, the overworked and understaffed game department of Tanga district would solicit help without offering remuneration from anyone willing to assist with the wildlife problems which sometimes overwhelmed them.

On one such occasion, a native villager from the Digo tribe reported that one of his relatives had gone hunting with his bow, searching for bush meat in the coastal thickets nearby. By yesterday evening, he had not returned. The tribesmen suspected that some evil had befallen him and requested an armed escort to join their search party for the lost relative.

The warden knew that those groves of thickets harboured every horned, toothed, clawed, and fanged animal found in the region, and respected the native's request for some life insurance. However, at that time he could not spare a single ranger to help them.

That afternoon a message for Clary, scribbled on the back of a used report form, arrived at the workshop. It was the game warden's request for Clary to accompany the natives in their search party.

Excusing himself from the workshop, he waved the game warden's letter at the manager, saying it was urgent government business. He dashed home to clean up a little, change into hunting khakis, grab his 400 Express rifle, and pack his ammunition. Then Clary headed down the dusty road to the game department offices, where he met the villager.

Here he listened to the Digo's story of woe, then collected his game warden's special permit that stated, "To hunt and kill any such fauna as may be deemed necessary in the pursuit of official duties."

Clary and the villager set off at a fast pace to the search area. On the way, they passed by the Digo village where six scantily clad men, armed with either clubs, spears, pangas, or bows, were already assembled, ready to start the search with or without an armed escort. There was visible scepticism on the natives' faces when they saw this young man with a large gun who had come to protect them against evil things. The messenger told them that no real game ranger was available in Tanga, so they had to accept Clary or nobody. They were, however, grateful for any sort of protection, and together they headed to the search sector.

As they reached the site – an area of tall elephant grass interspersed with patches of heavy brush and high trees – a few vultures flapped away loudly from some tall thorn trees a distance away. Vultures were a good indication that something was dead nearby.

Clary gave orders for the party to stay behind while he went alone into the high grass to see what lay there. With his 400-Express rifle loaded and ready, he plunged headlong into the long grass and was soon swallowed up by it. He parted the long yellow grass stems with his rifle barrel while listening for any sounds of movement ahead. Then suddenly he heard the sound of many flies buzzing. He parted the last grass strands to emerge into a bizarre scene that told its own easy-to-read story from beginning to grisly end.

Lying on a patch of trampled yellow-green grass was the bloated body of a half-naked black man, his swollen and sunburned face staring emptily skywards. Big bluebottle flies buzzed in and out of his open mouth and wide nostrils. A bushbuck, its glossy dark brown coat dulled in death and its head twisted at an awkward angle, lay with its sharp horns embedded deep into the chest of the dead native. Two light-coloured arrows protruded from the animal's shoulder.

These coastal people did not use poisoned arrows for hunting. Instead, they relied on getting close to the animal and accurately placing a shot to pierce the vital organs of their prey. If it ran away, they tracked it to its final resting place.

This lone hunter had stalked and got close to the bushbuck in a dense thicket, then shot an arrow into its lungs. Mortally injured, the buck had run off, leaving a bright red trail in its wake, and then hidden itself in the nearby grass as blood slowly filled its lungs.

The hunter had picked up the spoor very quickly and followed it until he could hear the heavy, coarse breathing of the dying animal. Then he'd followed the sound into this tall grass. He must have seen the bushbuck and shot another arrow into its shoulder from close range. But the hunter had had no time to escape as the crippled animal attacked with the last of its stamina, managing to plunge its long black horns deep into the hunter's chest, rupturing his diaphragm. Both hunter and hunted, inextricably bound, must have struggled and kicked about in vain for several minutes as their lives slowly ebbed away.

Cries of "AH! AH! AH!" surrounded Clary, as the rest of the search party came through the tall grass, open-mouthed and wide-eyed, and looked upon the death scene before them. They were all hunters themselves and understood the dangers a hunter must face. Even so, they were still shocked by the events clearly presented before them. Each, in turn, pointed out small details marking the final moments of their friend, while the others nodded in agreement and shook their heads in disbelief.

Ashen-faced and at a loss for words, Clary moved upwind away from the smell of putrefying flesh. For the first time he felt helpless to do anything. He felt like an intruder in another world.

There was no need for commands from anyone. Each man set about doing a task he knew was necessary, without being asked. Some long green poles were cut and tied to cross poles with bark strips to make a temporary stretcher. The two corpses were pulled apart amid the loud buzzing of disturbed flies. Snow-white maggots fell in masses from gaping black holes and crawled away into the bloodied grass. Discarded like a dirty rag, the rotting bushbuck was angrily thrown to one side, while the hunter – still in rigor mortis – was lifted carefully by trembling hands from the place he had died, and placed gently, lest he be hurt, onto the stretcher.

A native removed one of his own pallid wraparound cloths from his waist and covered the body from head to foot, leaving only the light-grey soles of the feet visible from behind. Four strong, sad men heaved the stretcher onto their bare shoulders and stumbled through the long grass the way they had come, and back towards their village. Clary followed at a decent distance, but could not keep himself from staring at the pale soles of the dead man bobbing up and down on his final journey above the porters' heads.

Back at the Digo settlement, there would follow days of grieving, wailing, drinking, and exaggerated stories of the dead hunter's exploits and bravery. He would be interred somewhere close by, and life in the community would go on as it always had.

Clary stopped briefly at the village perimeter and was about to go in, but as an outsider, it would have been disrespectful to enter without being invited.

This was the first time he had seen a dead man. He was used to seeing dead animals, yet what he had seen left him drained and feeling numb inside. Little did he know that during his life he would see many more dead people, including some of his own children.

He turned away and started walking back home. He was all alone, still many miles from home and very scared, despite the oversized rifle that he carried. Daylight was fading fast, shadows grew longer and darker, and Clary's pace quickened with each unrecognised noise coming from the bushes.

He had never been so relieved to see the comforting lights of Tanga late that night.

Chapter 11
Clever People

Clary smiled and chuckled to himself one afternoon on the way back to work as he passed a big, newly painted building on the main street. It was a bank. Over lunch, he had heard about the latest woes of the newly arrived English manager.

Several weeks ago, a sly South African businessman had approached this bank for a hefty loan to buy two new commercial trucks. He proposed to use these trucks on a lucrative run ferrying bales of sisal fibre from outlaying sisal estates to the port of Tanga. From there, the bales of fibre would be shipped overseas to meet the growing demand for sisal rope and string.

The manager had approved the loan immediately, as there was a shortage of transportation capacity for sisal. However, he approved the loan without consulting his head office in Nairobi, which under bank rules he should have done. So, the manager was now solely responsible for anything that went right, or wrong.

A week or so after the two heavy-duty trucks had been purchased and taken to a shed "somewhere west of Tanga", the South African was back in the bank manager's office with a dilemma.

The cunning businessman from the south told the white manager from the north that the new trucks were expensive to buy and operate, and other trucking companies with old trucks were undercutting his prices, so he could not get much business. Unless the manager stepped in to help him, the loan could not be repaid. If the manager wished to repossess the trucks for non-payment, he could do so, but he would have to first find the trucks which were "somewhere west of Tanga".

After a tête-à-tête, the poor bank manager, more in order to save his own skin than to help a crook, agreed not to advance any more credit to several sisal estates unless they awarded the cargo run to the South African's transport company. In the end, the bank got its loan back, the manager kept his job, and the South African made a lot of money.

Some weeks later, an incident at the bank would be the final straw for this amicable manager. The bank was situated on the ground floor of the building, with wide front doors and a small back service door. Inside the airy bank was a polished mahogany counter for two tellers to serve customers, and next to it, a wooden half-door that led to an open inner office area, neatly laid out with sufficient working desks for the white-shirted Indian bank clerks. At the back of this room was a wood panelled section where the manager sat at his big desk. In a corner next to his desk stood a large steel safe.

At noon each weekday, the main bank doors were locked so that the staff could have a two-hour lunch break. The manager locked his desk drawers and the big safe, then went up an interior flight of stairs to his private quarters above the bank. There, he took his lunch and had an afternoon nap. The rest of the personnel usually stayed at their desks in the bank to eat packed lunches.

One hot afternoon, when all was quiet in the bank and the snoring manager could be heard above the scribbling pens of the young Indian bank clerks, three African men in blue overalls, entered through the back service entrance pushing a two-wheeled baggage trolley. They said they had come to collect the safe, claiming that the bank manager had complained to the local locksmith that the hinges of the safe were squeaking loudly and were in need of oiling. Everyone in the bank knew never to call the manager or make noise during his afternoon rest period, which often lasted until 2:30 or even 3:00, when the bank closed for the day. No one dared wake the manager to confirm the work order, so the clerks let the men in blue take the safe for oiling, which they duly did, promising to bring it back within the hour.

Almost two hours later, the bleary-eyed manager came downstairs after his sleep and stood, key in hand, in front of the empty space usually occupied by the safe. He enquired as to its whereabouts.

He was informed by one brave clerk that three men from the locksmith's shop had collected it to oil the squeaky hinges and had promised to bring it back in an hour, but had not done so, and how unreliable these people were. A quick call by the anxious manager to the locksmith confirmed his worst fear. His safe had been stolen, in broad daylight, from right under his nose… er, bed.

Three houses away, across the main street, people opened their windows to see where the bellowing, ranting, and raving came from, as the incensed manager vented his rage on the cowering clerks. Within hours, the news of the incident had spread all over town. The poor bank staff, who were being thoroughly interrogated, had to endure the wrath of the manager and the ire of the assistant manager, the chief accountant, and the chief of police. Added to that, they were the butt of jokes in town for weeks afterwards.

It was no consolation to the bank manager and his employees when the police found the safe dumped at the side of a small road a few miles out of town. The safe was unopened, although its door had been hammered, chiselled, and scorched with a welding torch. The lock had been drilled to oblivion but remained locked, so the contents of the safe were untouched.

The battered safe was eventually railed to Nairobi, where it was opened, and its contents returned to a new bank manager in Tanga. The old manager had been sent home to England in disgrace. The three men in blue were never found.

The population of Tanga was increasing rapidly, mainly due to a growing sisal industry in the interior, and the fact that Tanga was a railhead with a good harbour that was small but sufficient for handling the export of raw sisal fibres.

This population increase had both a positive and a negative effect on Clary's hunting expeditions.

There were now more Europeans with money who he could take hunting and who had not heard of his tarnished reputation, but now there were also too many amateurs hunting on their own near Tanga. The game areas, which were within easy driving distance of town, had been badly over-hunted and that made it difficult for Clary to find any game to shoot on weekend trips.

One afternoon, while visiting his father at the railway workshop, Clary saw a car that had been modified to run on the railway lines. It was a complicated machine and needed a crane to lift it onto the tracks. Once it was in place, it could be driven along the rails like a car but without the need of a steering wheel.

This gave Clary an idea. He obtained a set of small running wheels from a disused trolley, and in the workshop at Riddoch Motors he made a set of brackets to hold the wheels and bolt the two units onto the front and back of a car's chassis. Thus modified, the car could travel along the railway lines. A driving mechanism for the rear trolley wheels would have been heavy and complicated, but the car could easily be pushed down the tracks by two men walking at a steady pace. Clary had no need of a crane to lift the car on and off the rail lines. He would simply drive the car on or off the tracks at a road crossing.

Clary bought a cheap, worn-out old Ford Model A which required constant attention just to keep it running. As a trained mechanic, he had no trouble coaxing a few more days of work and a few more miles out of this simple car. He modified it to be compatible with his trolley wheels. It was illegal to use the railway lines in this way, so Clary kept this modification secret.

To use his car on the rails, he would drive out of town to a railway crossing, drive onto the tracks, jack up the front end of the car, bolt the rail wheels onto the chassis, and lower it onto the tracks. Then he would do the same with the back end. His car could only travel at the walking speed of his human engines, but that was fast enough for his purpose. On some sections with a down slope, he could let the car roll at 30 miles per hour down the line while his pushers hung onto the back, ready to jump off and act as brakes if the car went too fast. To stop for the night, he had to find level ground, remove the little wheels, and drive off the lines. Then he would reverse the process the next morning to drive back onto the rails. With the train timetable in hand, he could illegally travel long distances, cross rivers and swamps and rough terrain without difficulty, and above all, reach pristine game country near the railway line. His only difficulty was finding a suitable place to drive off the rails whenever a train came along the line. Black smoke billowing above the trees usually gave Clary ample warning of an approaching train, and plenty of time to get off the line and drive out of sight.

IMAGE 7: THE CAR COULD BE PUSHED, MANY MILES ALONG THE LINE, BY HIS MEN. IN THIS WAY CLARY COULD REACH FAR OFF HUNTING AREAS.

He had a close call one day when he miscalculated the train schedule and his car was on the line. The embankment was too steep to drive off, so his men lifted the car and let it roll down the embankment into the bushes and out of sight. Then it took them half a day to cut a path through the bushes to a suitable place to get the car back onto the line.

Another time, Clary noticed just around a bend, a working party rolling along the line with a trolley. He had to stop suddenly and push his car backwards for a mile until he was well clear of them. However, there was no suitable place to get off the line for several miles. He knew it was not unusual for elephants to drag trees over the line, so he found a small tree trunk at the side of the track that he pulled onto the rails to stop the working crew long enough for him to get further away. The trolley crew would have to clear away the debris before continuing. This would give Clary the extra time he needed to proceed along the line to find a suitable place to get off. Despite several close calls, he was never caught with his car on the rails.

At first, only two passenger trains per week were running – one up the line and the other down. However, soon there were also goods trains running both ways at unscheduled times, including at night. This meant that Clary had to curtail his use of the railway lines or modify the attachment for his trolley wheels so that he could remove them very quickly. With his mechanical skills, he was able to make quick, removable trolley wheel brackets that could be attached and removed from the car in a matter of minutes. Now Clary was able to continue using the rail lines for his hunting trips.

His reputation as a successful hunter spread amongst the amateurs of Tanga as his clients boasted about hunting in far-off places teeming with game. Of course, at Clary's request, they refused to explain to inquisitive amateurs how they reached these areas. Clary's income from these weekend hunts sometimes exceeded his mechanic's salary at Riddoch Motors.

However, the good times were not to last. One day, a brown, official-looking envelope arrived bearing William's name. It was an order for him to move to the railway headquarters in Nairobi, Kenya.

Clary and his one remaining sister, Cynthia, still lived at home. His other sister had died a few years earlier from a brain tumour. Although at 18 years old he felt independent enough to live alone in Tanga and make a go of his life, he was also eager to experience life as a rumbustious teenager in a big, bustling city, and to see his birthplace, Nairobi, again. So he eagerly went to Kenya with the rest of his family.

Chapter 12
Life in the City for a Boy

The transition from Tanga to Nairobi was simple. The family's possessions were loaded onto a railway carriage at Tanga, and two days later, they arrived at the main train station in Nairobi. From there, with the help of natives, a donkey cart, and a bellowing stationmaster, their possessions were transported to their new home. It was in a row of cold, grey, rectangular cinder-block houses with shiny corrugated tin roofs and bare concrete floors. These new houses had replaced the old tin huts where Clary had been born.

Clary and his family, who had arrived a few days earlier by train, moved from their temporary quarters at the railway club into this characterless, unpainted house, and set about making it into a comfortable home.

To Clary's delight, there was plenty of game to hunt only a few miles out of town, at a place called the Athi Plains. As well, ducks and geese were abundant in the swamps that surrounded Nairobi. They would prove to be clever and elusive prey to whoever tried stalking them through razor-sharp swamp grass, because they were constantly being shot at by Nairobi's weekend hunters.

Nairobi was never meant to be anything more than a whistle-stop on the Uganda railway. However, it grew into a city that attracted the aristocrats, the rich, the soldiers, the adventurers, the poor, and everybody in between. It became known for its good water, good beer, good life, and goodbyes.

There was a great shortage of European women in Nairobi. All white women were either married or engaged to be married. Fraternising with the many Asian or black women was not done, so the "hunting" of the European ladies by white men was considered an accepted sport, and was practised by many men. Like any dangerous sport, one could easily get killed – in this case, by being shot by a jealous husband. Except this rarely happened, as the jealous husband was probably away chasing some other married woman!

William now found time to engage in his taxidermy hobby, which he worked on in a shed that he erected in his back garden. He also built a simple cinderblock house with a canvas roof right on the Athi Plains, where he could stay on weekends to observe game in its natural habitat. He made sketches of their movements so that he could pose his mounted animals in natural ways. Although he always carried a rifle on these outings, he never shot from the hideout so as not to disturb the game. On many occasions, wildebeest and zebras came to graze within a few yards of the hide, affording excellent opportunities to study his subjects.

Then, one weekend, William noticed that the game kept well away from the cinderblock house. Looking around, he found empty cartridge cases lying about. Someone had used his house to shoot game and had not even bothered to remove the obvious evidence of their insulting intrusion. There were also empty wine and beer bottles thrown about.

The next day, William was back with a group of strong railway workers to remove the whole hide, brick by brick. He gave his helpers the valuable bricks for their own home use. After that, William bought an old army camouflage tent that could easily be carried by a porter. He could set it up anywhere on the plains for his observations, and then remove it at the end of the day. William did not put up the tent in the same place each weekend, so he permitted himself to shoot from it if he wanted some meat for the pot, or to collect a certain animal that he needed to mount for a customer.

William found that duck hunting in and around the Nairobi swamps at the weekends was futile, due to all the other hunters shooting with shotguns at any fowl on the water or flying overhead. However, he was a very good shot. So, after work on weekdays when nobody was in the swamps, he would find a quiet spot on the reed-covered bank, conceal himself under green mosquito netting, and wait. When a duck came into sight, he used his powerful air rifle to shoot it in the head or neck. The shot made hardly any noise, so the other birds were not disturbed, and by leaving the duck in the water it attracted other fowl that came to join in the feeding. This way, William shot as many birds as he wanted. Being a responsible hunter, he only shot enough for his needs, and never in excess of what he could eat at home.

A few duck hunters on the water, in homemade wooden boats fitted with camouflage nets, were more successful at bagging waterfowl than those who were hiding in shelters on land. These boatmen bagged large numbers of ducks and geese far in excess of their needs, and they almost decimated the wildfowl population. After many complaints from hunters who had spent the whole day in the swamps but returned home empty handed, the Game Department imposed a quota on the number of birds that each hunter could shoot per day to put a stop to overshooting. A quota of six birds, ducks, or geese, was set and was honoured by almost all hunters, except the aristocrats living in Nairobi who believed they were above the law and had large amounts of money to pay any puny fines imposed.

In the years before the quotas were imposed, the swamps became a shooting gallery on weekends, where the first hunters to arrive before dawn took up the prime positions in the reeds around the edges. At first light, when the first shot rent the still morning air with a mighty boom, all the waterfowl in the swamps took to the air, flying disorientated in all directions. Then, for the next few minutes, it was a free-for-all as guns opened up on the airborne quarry. Ducks, geese, moorhens, egrets, herons, and other birds of all sorts fell disabled or dead into the water or in the reeds.

After the shooting stopped, the dead birds were collected by native helpers. The edible birds were piled on one heap, and the non-edible ones that had been caught in the crossfire were admired for a few seconds by the shooter, then tossed away into the tall grass like a piece of trash. It then took an hour or two before the first ducks returned to the water from their refuges, and the shooting would start again. This went on all weekend until it became too dark to shoot, and then peace finally reigned over the swamps.

A major reason for the ducks' eventual demise was due to hunters in armed wooden punts. Some of these hunters had the bright idea to put cannons on the front of their boats to shoot ducks. A short cast-iron cannon, with a mouth opening of about four to six inches in diameter, was affixed to the bow of the boat so it could shoot forward and slightly upward. About one half pound of black gunpowder was rammed down the barrel, followed by wadding and then five pounds of lead birdshot.

The camouflaged gunboat was poled very early in the morning through the swamps towards a large flock of ducks. When within shooting range, the hunter loudly hit the side of the boat with a pole, scaring the birds into flight. The cannon's fuse was lit, and an almighty thunderclap ensued, followed by an acrid cloud of white smoke. The boat shook violently from the gun's recoil and was pushed back through the water for quite a distance. By the time the smokescreen had cleared, the waters ahead were littered with dozens of dying or dead ducks, and now it was only a matter of collecting the prize. Many hundreds of water birds were wounded and died later, and many dead birds were not found.

Other hunters got into the act with bigger cannons, and came home with carloads full of ducks and geese that they had the cheek to sell at the market. Something had to be done to stop the wanton slaughter of fowl, and that is when hunting with cannons was banned and a daily quota was set.

IMAGE 8: A CANNON WAS MOUNTED ON THE FRONT AND WHEN FIRED, KILLED HUNDREDS OF DUCKS.

As Nairobi grew from a railhead into a town, the swamps were slowly drained and filled in with rubble to make way for new industries and houses. The waterfowl numbers slowly decreased to such an extent that duck hunting was no longer worthwhile.

In his youth, Clary did not have a chance to improve his shooting skills, as the cost of ammunition precluded wasting it on target practice. Any shooting competition he entered was a disaster, because he usually came in last place. William, being an excellent shot, took first place every time, and won many silver cups. Clary's only consolation was the fact that an old custom dictated that the worst shooter at the event would get a prize of a wooden spoon. This spoon indicated that the shooter was so incompetent with a gun that he was not able to feed his family with meat, so the spoon was to enable him to eat porridge. Clary delighted in placing his many wooden spoons next to William's big silver cups on the mantelpiece at home, saying that at least he won a prize, whereas the other shooters got nothing.

One old hunter jokingly told Clary, "If you can't shoot straight, just use a bigger gun".

In the end, it became an embarrassment to continually occupy last place in the shooting competitions. In order to improve his skills, Clary bought an old air rifle, for which pellets were plentiful and cheap. His first targets were cut marks on tree trunks and empty tin cans hung on branches. As his aim improved, stationary birds, lizards, snakes, and large insects became his victims. Then came flying birds, scampering lizards, and slithering snakes, which made exceptional moving targets for practising quick shots.

Clary's target shooting improved to the point where he was never last in a competition again, although he was still not good enough to win first prize – especially not against his father. At least there were no more embarrassing wooden spoons on the mantelpiece.

One very positive result of his moving target practice was that now he was able to aim and fire at a running animal and routinely hit it fatally. This skill would save his life, as well as the lives of many of his clients, in his later years as a professional hunter.

However, one day his father saw him shooting small birds out of a tree, picking them up, looking at them with admiration, and then discarding them as rubbish.

Five lashes with William's leather belt on Clary's behind left big red welts that made sitting down painful for days.
To drive home his point, William said to his son, "Remember the old hunter's saying, 'Don't kill it to admire it."

That incident left Clary with a long-standing reminder that one should never kill anything without a good reason, and target practice to avoid the awarding of another wooden spoon was not a valid reason.

One time, Clary's shooting skill won him a hard-contested bet. At some shooting contests near Nairobi, a certain Boer would arrive and challenge any man to shoot against him in a 3-shot shootout. The only stipulation was that both of them use the Boer's old smooth-bore muzzle-loading gun. Many very good British riflemen, too proud to let any challenge go uncontested – especially from a Boer – took up the offer, but they always lost the shoot. Even the Boer's countrymen, who were excellent shots with old rifles, lost to this old geezer.

During one shoot-out with a cocky challenger, Clary was standing right behind the Boer as he was shooting and noticed that the man was not aiming at the centre of his target but rather aimed low and just to one side. Nevertheless, his bullet hit the target's bull's eye. Suddenly, it dawned on Clary that the gun was shooting very much to one side and high, and the Boer was compensating for it by aiming low and to the right.

In his youthful stupidity, believing that he knew how to win the contest, he challenged the Boer to a shoot, placing his week's wages as a bet. Clary took the first shot and aimed at the middle of the target, however, his shot hit high and very much to the left. For his second shot, he aimed low and to the right, the equivalent distance off from his first bullet. To the utter amazement of the Boer, he hit the bull's eye. Clary's third shot also hit the bull's eye.

Of course, the Boer hit the bull's eye with all three shots and won the contest, taking Clary's money with him as he hastily left the field. A day later, the Boer came across Clary and his father out in the duck swamps. He gave Clary his money back, because he realised that his secret had been revealed when Clary had figured out how to shoot the gun accurately.

The Boer said that his gun had been bent in an accident when travelling upcountry with his ox-drawn waggon and became stuck in a drift. As he'd stepped down from the driver's seat to guide his ox-span through the mud, his gun slipped off the waggon without being noticed and fell under the ox-cart wheels. His heavy ox-wagon wheels had run over it twice, bending the barrel, and snapping the stock in two places. He'd managed to make a new gunstock from some dead wood he found in a forest, but he could never get the barrel bent back to shoot straight. However, with some practice shots at a target, he had learned where to aim to compensate for the bent barrel. Now he knew exactly how far low and to the right to aim to hit a target at any distance.

A few years ago, he had won a bet by shooting against another competitor when both of them used his bent gun. After winning a few more challenges, he'd realised that he had a sure way to make some money with that gun. So, he'd attended as many shoots as he could, challenging anybody to shoot against him. He always won these challenges and made enough money to buy a new gun. However, since nobody had caught onto his crooked gun trick, he'd decided to continue making money with it until someone realised what was going on. Now that Clary had discovered his secret, he was going to quit and hang up his bent gun for good.

Nairobi was rapidly growing, and it became known as a frontier town. Here, civilization ended and wild, untamed Africa began, not only just outside the city limits, but very often well inside the city as well, where lions, leopards, and hyenas might be encountered. It was also a town where normal people lived and worked at their jobs from eight to five, Monday to Friday, and went home to their families every day to eat and sleep. Then they got up the next morning and performed the same routine over again.

There were three big hotels in Nairobi. Thors Hotel was situated on the main road and frequented by quiet, sedate, older customers. The wild action took place at the other two hotels, namely the Norfolk and the Stanley.

These hotels were about half a mile apart and situated on a straight road on the eastern side of town.

The Norfolk Hotel was designed to look like an English Tudor house with exposed, black-painted wooden beams, panelled walls, and terracotta floor tiles. The main bar was located beside the road front, with a hitching rail for horses along one side. Horses were a common means of transport throughout the Kenya highlands, and were perfect for Friday night outings. Horses did not dent when they hit something, they did not break down, and above all, they could find their own way home when the rider became so inebriated that he did not know his own name, never mind how to find his home.

The secret was that after a heavy drinking spree in town, you'd ride, sit, lie, or hang onto your horse until it stopped walking. Then, you got off, slid off, or fell off, and you were most likely at home. None of this could be done with a motor vehicle.

The Stanley Hotel was a modern-looking brick building with whitewashed walls and carpets throughout its corridors. It had a long bar set back from the main road and a veranda in front. The usual horse-hitching rail was erected along the veranda. Many years later, when big game hunting became popular, the Stanley, and in particular its long bar, became the place where dashing professional hunters gathered to recite their latest hunting exploits to admiring ladies. It was said that more elephants were shot at that long bar than anywhere else in Africa.

This bar became so renowned for hunting stories that many Nairobians from all professions dressed themselves in hunters' attire, complete with ammo loops on their shirts and leather hunting boots. Of course, a hat with a leopard skin band, mostly imitation, was a must. These pseudo-hunters would hang out at the Stanley long bar, trying to impress unattached ladies with quickly conjured-up hunting stories.

Their aim, of course, was to get the ladies into their bed. Some "hunters" had never been out of Nairobi, yet managed to give the impression of having survived numerous attacks by savage beasts in the uncharted wilds.

It was only on Friday evenings, when the weekend started, that all hell broke loose. It was the time to let go, to drink, to get drunk, and to party like there was no tomorrow. For some, it was time to let off steam, to fight, gamble your salary away, visit ladies of the night, and do what you would never admit to doing in a civilised society. If you could hold your liquor, your age and sex did not matter. If you were man enough to do something, nobody stopped you. It was mainly a question of doing what you could afford to do, with the emphasis on "afford". It was said that often half a man's weekly wage was spent on Friday night alone.

Saturday was for cleaning up Friday's mess, assessing damage, counting costs, and recovering from Friday's excesses. Sunday was reserved for going to church to ask for forgiveness for all the wrongs that you could remember committing on Friday night. It was also for apologising to friends and relatives for what you had done, and for what you had said or implied about their wife, children, horse, car, friend, or property. It was a time to rebuild your courage so that you could face your co-workers on Monday morning.

On Friday nights, friends and acquaintances would meet at one of these main hotels for drinks, then head over to the other hotel for more drinks. Those with cars drove over, and those with horses rode over. It was customary that the last person to arrive would pay for the first round of drinks. Naturally, there was a rush so as not to be the last man in. Traffic on Friday nights favoured horses over cars, because shortcuts could be taken with horses along pavements and uncluttered side roads. Eventually, the car drivers ended up footing the bill each time for the first round of drinks.

It was the habit of the first arrivals to order expensive doubles of their favourite tipple, knowing that they did not have to pay for them. It also became a habit that the last man, knowing that he would have to foot a large bill, simply kept driving and went home for the night. This caused a dilemma amongst the drinkers, as it meant that the second last man to arrive was now expected to pay for the drinks. Consequently, the disadvantaged car owners slowly dropped out, leaving the horsey crowd to fight it out amongst themselves.

By late night, there were only a handful of cars driving around, but herds of half-drunk riders galloping back and forth between the two main hotel bars filled the streets. Collisions with lamp posts, pedestrians, and other horses were common; still, no serious injuries seemed to have occurred. In their haste to get from the bar and onto their horses, some riders tried jumping from the raised veranda into their mounts in a Wild West film style. This manoeuvre seldom went as planned, with the rider ending up flat on the ground next to his horse, or hanging onto the reins while being dragged by his startled mount running in the wrong direction. These horse races from one bar to the next usually ended when riders could no longer sit in the saddle or when their money came to an end.

It was not forbidden for Europeans to fraternise with people of another race, meaning Africans and Asians, although it was severely frowned upon by the stiff upper-lipped British administrators. There were also certain by-laws that gave public places the right to refuse entry or service to anyone they did not want. This meant that Europeans, Africans, and Asians established their own bars, restaurants, hotels, and clubs.

Outside the city centre, other ethnic groups, such as Somalis, Arabs, and Sikhs, established their own little communities and celebrated in their own private ways. These rules of entry were strictly adhered to during the working week, but on Friday nights, they were ignored by many Europeans. At first, the men would wine and dine in the best restaurants with the upper class, but later on they could be found in the cheap bars and brothels with a couple of black beauties at their side. As the night got darker, the black girls became whiter, cheap whisky tasted better, and high moral values were left behind.

Clary could not afford to join these crowds with fast horses and excessive income, so he frequented the many smaller bars and establishments that had lower prices. He still managed to enjoy himself, though he longed to have transport of some kind instead of having to walk everywhere. Finally, he bought a huge horse. It was an old Haflinger, a carthorse that had spent years pulling ploughs and carriages on a farm. The farmer had replaced him with a new tractor, so the horse was made redundant and going cheap to anyone who could look after him.

This horse had the knack of going exactly where you pointed him, and he did not give way to anything smaller than himself. He was not fast, and only had three speeds: dead stop, walk, and trot. However, he had tremendous stamina, and never tired during his long night forays. Clary named him Sir Galahad, after a knight in old England who had ridden a similar horse into battle.

At first, Clary was careful about where he rode, keeping to the less crowded side roads to avoid the fast-racing horses. As his confidence increased, he ventured onto the main roads and let Sir Galahad, who towered over all other traffic, run straight lines from one place to the next, never giving way to lesser mortals. Motorcycles, bicycles, and fast long-legged horses all learned to give him a wide berth when they saw him coming.

For a time, he was regarded as a road hazard, and riders would exchange information about "that damn horse's" whereabouts in order to avoid meeting him. Clary's reputation as a reckless rider became so bad that some people threatened to shoot his horse if it barged them out of the way again. He took the threat seriously, knowing it was no idle threat.

Most people living on the outskirts of Nairobi carried a revolver strapped to their waist for protection against the lions, leopards, and hyenas that ranged freely around the edge of town, and sometimes even in the town. On occasion, gunshots were heard coming from a hotel bar. On closer inspection, one might find an out-of-towner, punch drunk, shooting bottles of liquor off the bar room shelf. Perhaps he was proving to his companions that even when intoxicated, he could still shoot straight or win a bet of some kind. Fortunately, revolvers only hold six shots, so when the shooting stopped, the barman, who had taken cover behind his bar, emerged and started counting the smashed bottles. He quickly calculated the damage and handed the shooter an inflated bill for immediate payment. This bill was usually paid promptly before the local police arrived. After payment in cash, the guilty party was permitted to leave, and no names would be remembered should the police eventually arrive to investigate the shooting. The alternative for refusing to pay the bill meant that the unsympathetic police would arrive, arrest the culprit for disturbing the peace, and lock him up in a dingy cell for the whole weekend. He would then be humiliated by having to appear in front of a judge on Monday morning, be fined for the offence, and have his name smeared in the local newspaper. Paying an inflated bill was the preferred option.

One of the main causes of excessive drinking was due to gin and tonic. Gin and tonic, which originated in British India, was a very popular drink in East Africa, in part because it helped prevent malaria. This disease is spread by mosquitoes, and it became a major killer of European settlers, especially in places near lowland rivers, lakes, and wetlands where mosquitoes breed. The indigenous African populations had their own potions and herbal medicines for warding off malaria, but these were frowned upon as primitive by Europeans, so an effective medicine had to be found. Quinine proved to be very effective against malaria in India, so it was imported into East Africa to provide the same protection. In humans, quinine poisons the blood of a person infected with malaria to such an extent that the malaria parasite eggs in the blood die before they can hatch.

Long-term use of quinine makes the eyes very light-sensitive and produces a ringing in the ears. However, compared to contracting malaria and its aftermath, blackwater fever, it was a small price to pay. The recommended dose was two grains by weight of quinine per day to remain malaria-free. Quinine is very bitter, far too bitter to consume pure, and even when it is dissolved in a large quantity of water the bitterness is still present. It became a daily torture for everyone to down their daily dose.

Gin, a bitter drink in itself, dampened quinine's bitterness so that it was not quite so unpleasant to take. The quinine was first dissolved in a glass of water with a good tot or two of gin added, then drunk leisurely. A British pharmacist in India then came up with the perfect solution to the bitter problem. He dissolved half a grain of quinine in a solution of ginger and carbonated water (ginger ale) and added a tot of gin. This made a very pleasant drink with no hint of bitterness. He called his quinine-laced ginger ale "Indian Tonic Water" and the alcoholic drink "gin and tonic". Children were given a dose of quinine in a concoction of ginger, sugar, and carbonated water, called ginger beer.

Now, no one had an excuse for not taking their daily dosage of quinine. So every adult had good reason to drink four gin and tonics per day, and the incidence of malaria amongst the colonials dropped sharply. However, in the highlands of East Africa, there were no mosquitoes, and therefore no malaria, so there was no reason for local residents to drink gin and tonic. However, it was such a popular tipple that there was always a reason for drinking it, sometimes to excess, with the excuse that if a little is good, more must be better. Or, they said, "I will be off to the coast soon, so I am building up my immunity to malaria". Even if the planned trip to the coast was many months away!

With the arrival of more motor vehicles and motorcycles in Nairobi, the traffic congestion got worse and horses were slowly phased out as a means of transport. Pub-crawls still took place, but usually on foot, after finding a scarce parking spot for the car along the congested roads. Police patrols were increased to keep law and order intact. Nairobi's wild frontier status was waning, so Clary sold Sir Galahad to an upcountry farmer and bought himself an old car.

Chapter 13
William and the Tsavo Lions

The railway line through Tsavo in South East Kenya had been completed for several years, despite the long delay caused by a pride of lions that had repeatedly harassed the indentured Indian railway workmen. The man in charge of construction, Colonel Patterson, managed to shoot most of these lions, thus ending their attacks on the railway builders. The lion attacks resulted from the Indian custom of putting their dead out into the bush to be consumed by vultures instead of burying them. However, in East Africa, lions, leopards, and hyenas also joined in the feast, and so acquired a taste for human flesh.

Although the pride of lions that was mainly responsible for bringing construction to a halt had been eliminated, other lions in Tsavo had also acquired a taste for humans and continued sporadically attacking the workers. Therefore, the game department declared all lions along the railway line in Tsavo to be vermin and placed a bounty on them. This meant that they could be shot on sight by anyone, with or without a licence.

At one time William was stationed for three months at Voi Town, just outside the Tsavo area. Voi was a rail stop for water along the line between Mombasa and Nairobi.

One morning, he was called out of his Voi office to make some railway line adjustments with a crew of Indian coolies. Their destination was quite a distance up the line in the Tsavo section.

William always took his trusty old 303 rifle with him so that he could shoot an occasional buck for food to share with his work crew. His team of Indian workmen used metal-framed wooden trollies with small steel wheels for running along the rail tracks. Everything needed for the job, such as picks, shovels, tools, and bolts, were carried on the trolley. They also packed food and water to last for a whole day's work, as well as blankets in case an overnight stay became necessary. These trollies were powered by two men pumping a T-bar up and down to drive a set of back wheels. On straight, downhill stretches of line, the trollies could reach a speed of 30 miles per hour.

William enjoyed this delightful way of sightseeing through dramatic bushland and startled game herds as they sped along on an open platform with a warm wind blowing in their faces.

On this particular day, the repair work had taken longer than expected, which necessitated a return to Voi in the dark. A small kerosene lamp mounted on the front of the trolley to light the way was almost useless for night travel, because animals crossing the tracks could not be spotted in time to avoid a crash. Hitting one of the many elephants or buffalo with the trolley usually provoked a dangerous retaliatory charge by the offended animal.

The memory of the man-eating lions in Tsavo was still fresh in the minds of William's workmen, so they vehemently refused to travel after dark. Therefore, he was forced to pull into one of the many rest huts erected close to the line for just such a purpose. These huts were built with corrugated iron roofs, and sides that were bolted onto steel frames. They had a big sliding door on one side to facilitate access for heavy equipment. There were no windows for ventilation, only a small gap of about three inches all around the bottom edge of the hut to draw in cool air that vented out through a foot-wide gap in the roof. This top gap was covered by a raised iron sheet to keep out rain.

Before it got dark, the coolies lifted the trolley off the line, hastily collected some firewood to cook their food and keep warm in the hut, then locked themselves and William in for the night. The workmen cooked and ate their simple meal of rice and beans, and talked for a time in hushed voices. William ate a tin of corned beef before lying down on his blanket to sleep.

Suddenly, someone noticed heavy breathing coming from outside and realized that lions were sniffing at the ground around the hut! William awoke with a start at the commotion raised by his horrified crew. He grabbed his 303 rifle and ran to the big sliding door, intending to open it a little so he could shoot a lion or possibly two. The Railway paid a reward of two hundred rupees, the equivalent of a month's wages, for anyone killing a lion near the line. William wanted to shoot as many lions as possible to claim the generous reward.

As he was about to open the door, his coolies pulled him away, begging him not to open it. They believed these Tsavo lions were very cunning and would find a way to get inside and kill them. Even under threat of dismissal, they refused to let William near the door. The terrified coolies armed themselves with whatever tools they could get their hands on and stood guarding the big door, expecting a lion to break in at any second. They stoked their cooking fire until it blazed brightly, hoping the lions would go away, but the brutes did not leave.

The lions could be heard prowling and growling lightly very close by, occasionally sniffing under the bottom of the iron walls. One lion jumped onto the roof and was heard padding around above them. Then William saw its two front paws hanging over the gap in the roof ridge. A lion was lying on the roof and looking down on them from above. But luckily the roof gap was too small for it to crawl through.

Estimating where its chest should be, William took his 303 rifle, aimed, and fired a shot up through the thin iron roof. There was a thunderous roar from above, then a heavy thud as the lion hit the ground outside the hut. Deep rumbling and snarling from the remaining lions continued for many long minutes before it finally receded and an eerie quiet descended. William assured his crew that the lions had gone, and he wanted to see if he had killed the one on the roof, but they adamantly refused to let him near the door for the rest of the night. Even early the next morning when it was light outside, they refused to open the door, still fearing that the lions could be waiting in the bushes.

By late morning, a search party arrived to see why William and his crew had not turned up for work. Only at the sound of human voices outside did the coolies allow the door to be opened. They were overjoyed to be alive, describing in detail to the rescue party how they had survived a night of sheer terror as the pride of vicious lions circled their hut. Close to a patch of bush, they found one very dead lioness with a bullet hole through her chest from William's shot. He cut off the lion's tail as proof of the kill, and on returning to Voi, he sent it to Nairobi with the required paperwork, and eagerly awaited his reward of two hundred rupees.

Many weeks later, a check for 192 rupees arrived with a note saying: "One damaged corrugated iron sheet - 5 rupees. Replacement of said sheet - 3 rupees." The Railways had the nerve to charge him for the damaged roof. William never forgave them for that one.

Although the reward money for killing the lion was welcome, he looked for other means to earn extra money or save on expenses.

One way was to hunt small game, mainly to supplement his family's food supply when cash was low. Elephant hunting for ivory, however, could be profitable if you could afford to undertake such a safari and be brave enough to hunt these massive creatures. Even with enough money and courage, there was no assurance of success once you had reached your hunting grounds. Both William and Clary had hunting permits allowing them to buy six elephant licences. This enabled them to double their yearly income from the sale of ivory, provided they could track and shoot big tuskers.

Guiding foreign clients on hunting safaris was another way to supplement one's income. However, professional hunting was still in its infancy, and paying clients were few and far between. There were quite a few people advertising themselves as guides for safaris, but most of these guides were farmers with very little experience in guiding and who just needed an extra income to support their struggling farms.

William did not like the idea of shooting elephants just for the sake of money, so he took up taxidermy in his spare time to supplement his income. There were many Sunday hunters who, having shot a trophy animal, wanted its skin tanned and its head mounted on a plaque to hang on their wall. Books were available on taxidermy, though they were mainly for English game. However, with a little creativity, these methods would also work for African game. The few skilled people who did it professionally could not keep up with the demand for their work, so they willingly shared their African game-mounting methods and knowledge with amateurs such as William, who loved working with his hands.

After a few years of practice, William's reputation as a good taxidermist spread quickly, and a lot of work came his way. This extra income that it generated allowed him to rent a bigger studio in which to work comfortably. He pursued taxidermy and continued with it as a second income earner all his life.

Chapter 14
A Good Reason to Change Your Name

Many a time Clary and William would be walking in Nairobi doing some shopping when suddenly an acquaintance would stop in front of them and, looking very surprised, say, "I heard a rumour that you had been killed by an elephant last week!"

"No, they haven't got me yet", replied Clary to the startled individual.

The acquaintance would then repeat the rumour he had heard about a Wilson who had been killed while elephant hunting. This often happened to them, because Wilson was a common English name in Kenya, so whenever news came through to Nairobi that a Mr. Wilson had been killed while elephant (lion, buffalo, leopard, or other animal) hunting, anyone knowing a Wilson who hunted, suspected it was the one they knew, and they spread the rumour of their demise. Later, when each of the suspected victims turned up alive and well, the missing Wilson was finally identified by the process of elimination.

William was contemplating a legal change of his name just to avoid such embarrassment, but then he realised he was not alone, since this same error happened to all people with common names such as Smith, Baker, or Rogers.

However, an incident happened that gave William a good excuse to alter his name so that he would never again be mistaken for dead.

There was a land surveyor called Robertson living in Nairobi, who was married and had a young son. He also hunted elephants for their ivory to supplement his income, as did quite a few other Europeans living in Kenya. Robertson and a friend decided to make a one-month foot safari to hunt elephants in the north of Kenya, where large tuskers were rumoured to be. The hunters bought three elephant licences each – the maximum allowed in one year – and hoped to fill their quota with some good ivory. Having told their relatives and some close friends of their hunting plan, they set off from Nairobi with their caravan of 35 porters laden with provisions for the month-long trip.

At Baringo, the last police post before the uninhabited wilderness started, it was customary to sign a visitor's book with your name and expected return date. This was necessary in case you did not return, and anyone searching for you knew where to start looking.

The hunting in this northern part of the rift valley, where the daytime temperature often reached 38 degrees Celsius, was hot, tiring, and difficult at the best of times. Nonetheless, the two hunters managed to bag a few good tuskers. After three weeks, when their provisions were running low, they should have headed back home, but by chance, they met up with another hunting party. The second party was also hunting elephants, except they were going farther north to Lake Rudolf (now Lake Turkana), where many big elephants could still be found.

Robertson and his friend were asked to join the second party, and as they still had a few elephants on their licences, they readily agreed. In order to save on costs and provisions, Mr. Robertson sent most of his porters back home with orders to wait for his return, when they would be paid.

The two expeditions, with four hunters, continued their trek north towards Lake Rudolf.

At the same time, unknown to the first party, there was an up-country farmer from Eldoret – a small community 150 miles west of Nairobi – by the name of Robertson, who was in no way related to the first man. The second Mr. Robertson was also hunting elephants in the same area. He had not passed the police station in Baringo to sign in, because he had come to the area via another route.

Sadly, he was killed by an elephant that he had injured and followed into the dense bush. Robertson's porters buried what was left of his body in a shallow grave, then took all his belongings and made their way back home to the farm at Eldoret. They stopped at native plantations along their journey to beg for food and water, and told their hosts that their hunter, named Robertson, had been killed and they were trying to get back home.

This news eventually reached the police post at Baringo. Believing that the man who had been killed was the same Mr. Roberson who had signed in, the police officer in charge transmitted this name by wireless to the police headquarters in Nairobi. Mrs. Robertson in Nairobi was duly informed of the possible death of her husband, although his demise would not be confirmed until Mr. Robertson either failed to return or his death was verified by some other means. So Mrs. Robertson could do nothing except wait and hope for her husband's safe return.

Meanwhile, the four hunters, including Mr. Robertson, worked their way towards Lake Rudolf, shooting meat for the pot and the occasional big elephant. However, by the time they had reached the lake, they had actually shot more elephants than their licences allowed. They were unlikely to meet game rangers this far north, so were not worried about being caught with the extra tusks. The problems would occur when they returned to Nairobi and tried to register and sell their excess ivory. For this reason, they decided to continue north into neighbouring Ethiopia, all the way to the capital, Addis Abeba, where they knew they could safely sell their ivory without problematic queries.

In Addis Abeba, they needed permission from the Ethiopian king's minister to sell ivory, and the minister needed his palm greased in the old African tradition. After some weeks without the promised sales permit being issued, and their ivory stocks slowly depleting from greasing more palms, buying food, and paying for expensive accommodation, the four hunters and their porters escaped with hired asses and their remaining ivory down the mountains of Ethiopia to the port of Asmara on the Red Sea. Here they met Indian and Arab traders who offered them very good prices for their ivory, which turned out to be enough to cover all their expenses, plus give them a handsome profit.

From Asmara, they hoped to catch a ship going along the coast to Mombasa in Kenya, but they had to idle away the time until passage could be found on a trading dhow. When the four hunters finally arrived in Mombasa, it had been almost a year since they left home. From Mombasa, they went by train to Nairobi and back to their waiting families.

Mr. Robertson got the shock of his life when he walked into his house to find his wife had married again, and was pregnant with a baby by her new husband.

During the following court case, Mrs. Roberson explained that on hearing the news from the police of the possible death of her husband, she had waited three months for his return from a one month expedition. When she received no news of his whereabouts or any sign of life from him, she assumed he was the Robertson reported killed by an elephant near Baringo. She had him declared dead and her marriage officially terminated so that she was free to marry again. She knew there was an acute shortage of young, eligible women in Kenya at that time and did not wish to spend the rest of her life alone. In such conditions, any single or widowed woman in Kenya did not have to wait long for her next suitor.

According to the law, she was legally married to her new husband. However, since her first husband was not dead, her marriage could not be ended on the grounds of his death. Neither husband would back down on their legal right to be married to Mrs. Robertson. So followed one legal case after another. This went on for months, and no decision acceptable to both parties was ever reached. The matter was further complicated by the fact that one husband was a Protestant and the other Church of England. The only ones to profit from this were the lawyers, with their outrageous fees.

The final outcome has been lost in time, but it is believed that Mrs. Robertson was so fed up with the constant court cases and stubbornness of her two husbands to come to an agreement that she divorced one, or both, and married again.

William followed this story in the newspapers with great interest, and it was due to this incident with the Robertsons that he decided this was never going to happen to him or his family. He applied for a surname change from Wilson to Palmer-Wilson; Palmer being his grandmother's maiden name. After his name had been altered and registered, he made sure that all his friends and colleagues were aware of his new name so that he would never again be mistaken for dead. To complete the process, he altered all his documents and postal address to reflect his new name. To this day, he and his descendants are the only Palmer-Wilson name-holders in the world.

Chapter 15
Trying to Get a Start in Life

Just as his taxidermy business in Nairobi was doing very well, William had to sell up and move back to Tanga, as he was still employed by the railway and was needed to fill a vacant position there.

So, he and his family took all their belongings to Tanga and set up a home not far from their old house. Their new house, like all government buildings at that time, was just a simple, square, whitewashed structure with a corrugated tin roof and a covering of plaited palm fronds to reduce the heating effects of the tin. William rented a separate workshop/sales office within walking distance of his house and the railway station where he worked. He hired an assistant to look after the shop and keep an eye on the business when he was at the railway station.

He partnered again with his old friend, Bazil Reele, in Tanga. Bazil was still hunting, and as there was a growing demand for mounted game heads, he would go into the bush to collect specimens for William to mount and offer for sale. On weekends, when the opportunity arose, William would hunt on his own to collect various bird specimens, which he loved to mount and display. Clary helped in the taxidermy office and was astonished at the fine class of customers who entered his father's humble little shop to do business.

One day, a French expedition from the natural history museum in Paris passed through Tanga and, on seeing William's work, awarded him a multi-year contract to collect local insects and invertebrates for them. They left specimen boxes with formaldehyde-filled glass tubes and long silver pins with which to preserve and spike the collected specimens. For this, he was paid a good price per specimen box when the consignment arrived in Paris. In the following years, he collected thousands of insects, beetles, lizards, and many other flying or crawling creatures. William's work in this field brought him a steady income for many years afterwards. (Forty years later, a French museum curator from Paris who was visiting East Africa told Clary that they were still sorting and cataloguing his father's specimens.)

During this time, an Austrian prince who was on tour along the East African coast made a stop in Tanga, specifically to acquire several rare bird specimens from William. Somewhere in the royal household of Austria today there is a collection of wild birds from William's shop in Tanga.

Another time, William was asked to accompany one of Teddy Roosevelt's natural history museum expeditions to Mkomazi – a region at the foot of the Pare Mountains in Tanganyika known for its rare duiker and bird species. However, he was too busy filling game-mounting orders for clients, so he sent Clary in his stead. Although Mr. Roosevelt was not present, only his collectors, the expedition was meticulously well organized, which one can imagine if Teddy Roosevelt had anything to do with it. They had a complete railway goods waggon packed full of everything they were likely to need on the expedition.

When Clary asked if anyone had leather bootlaces for him, he was immediately shown a boxful by a member of the team who found them in box seven, drawer D. Everything they might ever need on safari could be found by looking it up in a comprehensively compiled notebook; it was all there and quick to locate. Clary was truly impressed by the meticulous amount of detail someone had assembled so that even the smallest thing one may need in the bush was listed. He made a mental note to copy this same system so as never to be short of even the smallest items on his own safaris.

The expedition lasted only eight days in Mkomazi, where they obtained the rare duiker species and birds they were seeking. After that, they moved to another location where Clary's services were no longer required. Although he was well rewarded for his efforts, it was too short a time and too little money to help him start a hunting business of his own.

Clary was working full time in a local garage but was not happy, for it only gave him weekends in which to pursue his passion for hunting. He could have taken a boring job as a line supervisor with the railway, which would have allowed him to work up and down the line with the prospect of hunting game along the way. Nonetheless, he decided against joining the railway again due to his earlier unhappy experience as a "teaboy". His only real passion was to be a hunter so that he could be out in the bush alone or guiding like-minded clients on hunting safaris.

He knew that start-up costs for new safari equipment were prohibitive for him, and this precluded him from fulfilling his dream of forming his own company. He did occasionally get the chance to join Bazil on a short hunting trip, but only when he could get time off from his regular garage job. So, for the time being, he continued working as a mechanic.

William was now only employed part-time by the railway, but this still gave Clary access to certain railwaymen's privileges that would prove useful in his later hunting career.

In the meantime, he learned taxidermy from his father, something he loved to do, and helped out at the workshop whenever free time allowed. His view was that preparing animal specimens would suffice as a second profession should the worst happen, and he was no longer able to hunt.

As he endeavoured to obtain money to start his own hunting business, Clary heard that one could get a loan from the local bank with a surety for the equivalent value of the loan. But he had nothing of much value, so this was not an option. His only alternative was to take out a life insurance policy in his name, which would be acceptable as a surety against the loan. To get a life insurance policy, he would have to undergo a medical examination to certify his good health, and then pay a monthly fee to the issuing insurance company. After one year, the bank would give him the loan, using his policy as a surety.

Clary could now see his way forward. He was young, fit, and healthy, except for a mild asthma allergy, but had no doubt about sailing through his pending medical examination. His physique was good too, so he was certain nothing could go wrong.

However, when the doctor performed a Bencarts test, which was to determine if he was allergic to any substances such as pollen, dust, bee stings, nuts, etc., out of the 180 allergens commonly occurring in East Africa, Clary proved sensitive to 140 of them! This meant that he failed the health test for the life insurance policy, which shattered his dream of forming his own hunting company.

The day after the test, Clary was given the full report by his doctor, who said in a very solemn voice that if Clary wished to live longer than the next six months, he should immediately pack his bags and take the first steamer out of East Africa back to England, and never, ever set foot in Africa or any tropical country again.

At 18 years of age, Clary was shocked to the core by this revelation. He sat for a long time outside the doctor's office, contemplating his future. Then he trudged dejectedly home in the afternoon heat to relay the bad news to his father and mother and ask for their advice. They told him that they had distant relatives and friends living in England with whom he could stay for a while, and offered to give him letters of introduction should he heed his doctor's advice and move to England. However, the final choice was Clary's.

He had never been to England, but had heard many stories from people who had lived there. It was a green and pleasant land in the summer, very advanced in industry and infrastructure. However, the cities were big and generally crowded, and the inhabitants were not too friendly either. Jobs were difficult to get and not very well paid. It was also cold, windy, and stormy during the winter, and fog was common. Snow lay on the ground for months, and worst of all, there was no free-ranging game to hunt. It seemed that all the game belonged to a few rich landowners who did not want commoners like him hunting the wildlife.

Clary felt that for someone who had been born and raised in such a free and exciting place as East Africa, moving to England would be like entering prison.

With his mind made up, next day Clary went to see his doctor and told him that he would rather live six months in his beloved Africa than a lifetime in that far north, cold, dull, miserable, boring country that had nothing in common with East Africa except the language. He tore up his insurance application form and immediately felt much better. He had made another major decision in his short life, and felt very happy about it. He even outlived his doctor by many decades, who, ironically, retired to England and died there soon afterwards, probably from the cold and boredom.

This same doctor had once examined an old retired Tanga resident who drank heavily with his friends, and whose health was failing. The doctor had ordered him to stop drinking many months earlier, but to no avail. In a last desperate attempt to stop the drinking bouts, the doctor wrote out a banning order forbidding all local bars, hotels, and stores from selling any alcohol to the old man, under threat of prosecution.

At the weekend, the old man visited all his usual drinking places and was steadfastly refused alcohol of any kind. He went to the local stores looking to buy a bottle of alcohol, but was turned away. His friends were also too scared to break the doctor's orders by offering him a drink. With all his drinking possibilities exhausted, the old man returned to the club where he had been renting a room for years. He went to the bar, where the barman offered him an orange juice, which he declined. Turning to the bar guests, he said, "If I can't enjoy another drink, then there is no purpose in life".

With those words, he left the bar, went up to his room, lay down on his bed, and died. The coroner's report stated that the cause of death was natural, simply old age. However, the real reason he died, which everyone knew, was that he had lost his will to live.

At this time, any car – whether new or second-hand – was expensive for the average person to buy, and even more expensive to run. They were also considered by some to be an unreliable means of transportation due to constant breakdowns in remote places. It was a good day if one managed to drive 100 miles without a malfunction.

Clary had the good fortune of being an exceptional mechanic, due to his experience working with cars at Riddoch Motors. He could repair any vehicle in East Africa, often using old parts from other vehicles to get it running and keep it going. However, even one of these old jalopies, if it was capable of being used as a hunting car, was out of Clary's meagre financial reach. Instead, he opted for a motorcycle, which was becoming a very popular vehicle throughout East Africa, because they were in many ways better suited to the very poor roads. However, even a new motorcycle was still far beyond his budget.

Clary came up with the brilliant idea of buying one piece by piece. He started by buying only new parts as money came in, and assembling them at home. It took him almost two years to build his motorcycle, and it cost him double the price of a new BSA 250 cc motorcycle by the time it was ready for its first trial run. However, he did now have a brand-new motorcycle.

Just as he had taught himself to drive a car, Clary would teach himself to ride a motorcycle – something that was not easy to do on roads that were dusty and full of hidden potholes. On his first attempts at riding his new motorcycle, he fell off – as did everyone else, he was told. In spite of falling off too many times to be funny, he persevered, and with dogged determination mastered the art of staying upright in the saddle and making the beast do what he wanted and not go where it wanted to go. It was a new and uncomfortable experience for him to wear a pilot's leather helmet with goggles and a scarf around his face while riding. Nonetheless, it was better than being bombarded at 50 miles per hour on the open road by thousands of flying insects, such as large dung beetles and locusts.

After mastering the two-wheeled brute, Clary was free to travel the whole country wherever he liked, even during the rainy season when most roads become a muddy and impassable morass for motor vehicles. This is where a motorcycle came into its own. With two saddlebags strapped over the back wheel, a rifle holstered across the handlebars and a backpack on the pillion, he became self-sufficient and free to explore far and wide. He could carry food for several days' journey, a tarp to sleep under, spare petrol, and a small tool kit. His biggest problem turned out to be punctures, punctures, and more punctures. He tried in vain to avoid running over the ever-present thorns which were scattered everywhere, even on the main roads. He heard from another motorcycle rider that if he pumped up the tyres much harder than the recommended pressure, the inner tube would seal up around a thorn, stopping air from leaking out. This trick made the ride very hard and tiring on rough roads, but it worked well. The only problem was when the tyre did go flat, there were multiple thorns to remove and many holes in the inner tube to patch.

However, one could not use a motorcycle for hunting, as there was limited space for carrying home any animal that was shot. Still, it was an excellent way to survey potential new hunting grounds in remote and inaccessible localities.

A pillion on the back of his motorcycle also enabled Clary to carry his girlfriends around town and out to remote beaches on the coast, when he was not away scouting new hunting grounds. A favourite spot was an hour's drive outside Tanga, where wild mango trees were bursting with fruit in season and coconuts could be harvested. Whenever Clary needed a cool drink of coconut water, he either shimmied up the tree himself or found a local native who would do it for him. As a last resort, he tried to shoot one out of the tree with his rifle. (This method hardly ever succeeded owing to the strength of the thin, tough coconut fibres holding the nut. There was also the hazard that when trying to shoot the stalk, he would hit the nut, which usually resulted in a shower of coconut water and bits of husks flying all over him.)

Another attraction of this place was its coral reef right near the beach, which was a great place to swim. The reef was swarming with succulent fish and sweet lobsters. He could walk right out onto it and spear fish or catch lobster to grill over an open fire on the beach.

In short, the motorcycle gave him the freedom he longed for to go anywhere he liked and to impress his girlfriends.

Chapter 16
Do Stupid Things

Being young and inexperienced, Clary sometimes made stupid mistakes and foolhardy decisions that could have cost him his life.

One afternoon just before sundown, he took a quiet stroll without his trusty 303, going out of town along one of the many native footpaths that led away into the interior. The evening was cool and pleasant, and he felt at ease walking alone, deep in his own thoughts. As the sun slowly sank behind the trees, he looked back along the path and realised that he may have gone too far to make it home before dark. The footpath was easy to see in the last light, so he hurried back along it, hoping to outrun the darkness. He picked up a long stick so that he could flip out of his path any snakes he saw.

As he rounded a bend in the path, the lights of town were visible in the distance. Suddenly he was distracted by a movement off to one side. He stopped dead in his tracks and stared. It was a lioness crouching in the short grass not ten yards off the path. Man and beast had spotted each other at about the same time and were now sizing each other up. Running away was the worst move Clary could make.

Run? he pondered. *Where to? Back down the path into darkness?* That would be a fatal mistake, as the lioness would instinctively give chase. His only weapon was the flimsy stick in his hands, so that was what he had to use. He raised it with both hands above his head, ready to strike, and walked on. He noticed that the lioness's ears were not laid back and her tail was not twitching violently from side to side, so she was not about to attack. He kept eye contact with the crouching animal and walked on nervously.

As he passed her, he turned his head and kept staring straight into her eyes. She did not move. He had to walk backwards for some distance so as not to break eye contact. He desperately hoped that she was alone and not part of a pride that was lurking near the path along which he was walking backwards. When he lost sight of her, he turned and quickened his pace towards home, still keeping a watchful eye to the rear as well as to both sides in case the rest of her gang were waiting ahead for him. By the time he reached the safety of the first houses in town, his pulse was still racing, and he was trembling and sweating just as he had done during his encounters with the leopard and the lioness at the machan. He swore to himself then and there to never venture out into the bush without a suitable weapon.

At his taxidermy studio, William received a request from a customer for a leopard skin. He did not have any pelts in stock, so he asked Clary if he could go and shoot one, because leopards were everywhere. The scars from Clary's leopard mauling a few years earlier were still very visible, and the incident was burned into his memory. However, he had learned a valuable lesson and would not repeat the mistakes of that encounter. Besides, if he was going to be a successful hunter, he should fear no animal, not even leopards. So, Clary accepted the job.

There were leopards to be found close to town and very often in town, so there was no need to make a camp out in the bush. He could leave home early in the morning, hunt all day, and be back before dark with a leopard pelt – or so he hoped.

Leopards living close to towns were wary of humans and kept well out of sight. They preferred to lie up and sleep in dense groves during the day, but prowled around freely at night. Clary hunted them for days on end through the thickets of Tanga, with not even a fleeting glimpse of these elusive cats. After a few more days of failure and scorn from William, Clary conceded defeat and changed his hunting methods. He packed some bedding and food and walked half a day to a village where he was certain to find leopards. He rented an empty native hut to sleep in and store his rations.

Leopards leave their daytime lairs in the late afternoon and usually start to hunt after it gets dark. They are still actively wandering around in the very early hours of the morning. By getting up before dawn and being in the bush before sunup, Clary hoped to catch a leopard in the open bushland before it found a daytime resting place. If the early morning hunt failed, he still had another chance late in the afternoon until nightfall.

The village where he slept was close to where he hunted the big cats and always within earshot, so he was in no danger of getting lost. At night, while lying awake in bed, Clary could hear the leopards coughing all around his location. During his morning hunts, he saw their fresh pugmarks, smelled their urine territorial insignia, and even heard one dashing off into thicker undergrowth. However, after days of careful hunting alone using all his skills, he was not able to find one to shoot.

Hunting these evasive cats now called for radical measures. He would hunt the wary leopards at night, right on their home ground. At that time, they become brave, losing their fear of humans and their respect for them. So they should be easy prey, theorised the ignorant Clary.

He borrowed a hissing kerosene Tilley lamp from the village chief and found a brave soul to carry it while they walked together through the open glades, hunting leopards late into the night. These pressure kerosene lamps gave off a very bright light, illuminating the ground for a hundred yards all around but made a loud hissing sound when operating. Clary worried this noise might scare off the animals. On the other hand, he hoped it would also arouse their curiosity so that they would come and investigate the source of the noise.

Night after night, Clary and the brave young villager stalked for hours throughout the open glades and grassland with their noisy lamp, scaring away civet cats, bush-babies, duikers, and the odd hyena, but they found no leopard. They did not even get a fleeting glimpse of one. Clary was dejected. He decided there remained only one way left to bag a spotted feline. It was to hunt them in the thickets, in their bedrooms, at night, reasoning that if they were not in the open glades, they must be in the thickets. Now Clary and the brave young fool crept into the leopards' homes with their hissing lamp late at night.

While they were in the middle of a very thick stand of bush, they heard the crashing of heavy animals nearby. Not knowing whether they were charging or running away, Clary had no choice other than to stand his ground and wait, ready to fire. The crashing died down as whatever it was went the other way. It was at that moment, as Clary stood shaking like a leaf, looking into the trusting eyes of his Tilley lamp carrier, that he realised what a stupid fool he had been. A more foolish undertaking could not be imagined than trying to hunt leopards at night in thick bush with a noisy lamp. He realised that he had not learned sufficient respect for leopards even after his mauling a few years ago.

They left the bush as quickly as they could and went back to the village for the rest of the night. Clary was still shaking from fear and his folly when he went to bed that night. The next morning, he paid off his lamp carrier, packed his bedding, gave away the last of his meagre food supplies, and stormed back to Tanga. The leopard hunt was over.

Clary felt so ashamed of his foolishness that he never mentioned the night hunting escapade to anyone, not even his father, for fear of the severe scolding and ridicule that surely would come. (Only in his old age did he tell the full story to his hunting friends) As for the leopard skin, Bazil Reele filled the order on his next safari.

Chapter 17
Umba River Elephants

There were rumours amongst the hunting fraternity that big elephants were regularly seen around the north-western border between Kenya and Tanganyika in the Tsavo area. It was well known that Tsavo, in Kenya, had some massive tuskers. William had seen them when he worked on the railway line running through Tsavo. Since it was a national park, hunting in Tsavo was not permitted. However, mused some hunters, if there were big elephants in that sector, then some would likely stray across the border into Tanganyika where hunting was allowed, as there was no park there.

In order to confirm the rumours, Clary organised a foot safari for himself to this region. He was accompanied by a small band of porters carrying the minimum of food and equipment. The area he intended to explore was along the Umba River, close to the border between the two colonies of Kenya and Tanganyika. The Umba River had water year-round, vast stretches of very dense Acacia thorn trees growing throughout the region, and a few Digo tribal villages scattered far and wide. It was elephant country at its finest.

After a seven-day march from Tanga, Clary arrived at the Umba River and erected a riverside camp under some wild fig trees. While his men were setting up the camp, he walked out with his 303 rifle to an open plain and shot a Kongoni (Hartebeest) for food for his camp staff and himself. That evening, his protein-starved town men gorged themselves on freshly grilled meat until their stomachs ached. They considered it a small price to pay for so much free meat.

Next morning, Clary took a walk close to the camp to look for signs of elephants. Old bull elephants mostly live solitary lives and leave large smooth footprints, because their soles are worn away with age. These old bulls carry the heaviest tusks that every hunter is searching for.

Elephants rely on their keen sense of smell and superior hearing to detect danger, and only use their eyesight to confirm what they have smelt or heard. With their huge ears they can catch very low frequency sounds from a mile away, such as those made by heavy boots pounding dry ground, or thorns sliding over thick cotton hunting clothes. The mighty rumblings of thunder can be heard by elephants from 30 miles away.

In dense bush, elephants have the advantage, as they can hear or smell a hunter long before he can see them. A hunter will know he has been detected when he hears his quarry crashing away through the bush. Therefore, a hunter must approach an elephant silently, with the wind in his favour. Winds usually blow steadily from one direction only in the early mornings and late afternoon. During the rest of the day, they blow haphazardly from different directions as heated earth and cooling bush tumble the turbulent air. A hunter must get close enough to an elephant to see and judge the weight of its ivory before shooting, so it is futile to hunt when the wind is constantly changing.

There were elephant tracks and dung lying about, as well as freshly broken branches, indicating that they had recently been here. Elephants in a herd communicate with each other through deep rumbling noises that they emit through their trunks, and because they must eat vast quantities of vegetation each day to survive, their stomachs are constantly rumbling with the sounds of digestion. They will also squeal or trumpet loudly when another animal gets too close to their food source. All these noises are audible to hunters and give away the elephant's location in the bush.

Later that same morning, Clary heard branches being broken in a thicket a short distance away from him, which made him suspect elephants were close by. His gun bearer's little bag of wood ash shaken in the air confirmed that the wind was in their favour, so they crept in to investigate. Clary could estimate how far away the elephants were by listening to the breaking branches. When he heard the stomach rumblings, he knew he was very close, but the bush was so dense he couldn't see them. He edged closer still until he could hear them chewing leaves. He knew he must be within ten yards of them, but still could not even glimpse an elephant.

The wind suddenly turned towards the elephants, as confirmed by the wood ash bag. Seconds later, the whole herd stampeded away through the thicket. Clary and his gun bearers extricated themselves from the thick bush and walked on through less dense woodland where visibility was better.

A little while later, they heard more elephants and crept into the bush after them, but with the same result as before. The elephants scented the hunters before they could get close. Clary and his bearers walked on to the next elephant herd, but experienced the same problem. There were not only elephants in this patch, but also buffalo and rhinos, who liked to rest deep inside the thickest bushes during the heat of the day. It was very easy and very dangerous to overlook a sleeping rhino in this dense bush.

Running away from danger was never an option in these circumstances, since a hunter must run around the bushes to escape while a charging rhino simply goes straight through them. Trying to climb a thorn tree to get out of danger was also out of the question, for thorns on Acacias can grow up to four inches long and are as hard as nails. Shooting your way out of this precarious situation was the only option. However, once a shot was heard by the big old bull elephants, they knew that hunters were about and tended to migrate far away to safer regions.

By now it was late morning, and the wind was changing constantly, making further hunting futile. So Clary and his team went back to camp where he could enjoy a swim in the cold river and an afternoon rest on his camp cot.

One morning a few days later near camp, Clary came across the large fresh spoor of a lone bull elephant that had been feeding slowly along the riverbank. Judging by the size of the tracks and the smoothness of the pads it was possibly a big tusker, which made it worth following. One drawback to this hunting method is that even a slowly feeding elephant walks faster than the hunter trying to follow it. The only chance the hunter has to catch up to his quarry is when it rests in the shade at midday and stays there until early afternoon. At midday the wind changes directions constantly, so luck plays a big part in finding the elephant before it smells the hunter.

However, this elephant was alone and not part of a herd, so there was a good chance of getting close to him without being detected. Clary and his two trackers followed the spoor along the river until it veered off into the thorn trees. Here they managed to follow it through the lighter thickets, but walked around the heavier bush to avoid scaring any other animals that might be resting there. Each time they picked up the trail again on the other side of the thick bush. They made as little noise as possible, stepping cautiously over dead branches and communicating with each other by sign language. They tested the wind constantly, and stopped often in silence for a few minutes to listen for the noise of their elephant in the bush and any sounds made by other game that they wanted to avoid.

The going was hard and hot, and it was difficult tracking through the patches of bush as it became denser, blocking any cooling breeze from reaching them. Their two water bottles were long finished.

By late afternoon, with no sign that their elephant had rested anywhere or that they were closing in on him, Clary had almost decided to quit the hunt and head home. Then, the faint noise of breaking branches close by encouraged him to have one last look in that direction. Approaching the location of the noise, he heard stomach rumblings long before he was close enough to see his prey. The bush was so thick that he had to edge very close before he could see the elephant's legs and feet through the bottom branches of the thicket.

For a long time, Clary crouched in complete silence. Suddenly he saw a thick tusk poking below the bushes. This elephant had huge tusks and was worth shooting, Clary decided, as his thumping heart pumped adrenaline through his whole body. He knelt down on one knee, slowly lifted his 400-Express rifle, eased off the safety, and waited to get a clear shot through the thick branches. A feeling of regret, of sorrow, a gut feeling of wrongdoing came over him, but he ignored his feelings, concentrating on the thick, gleaming ivory in front of his gunsight.

The big bull turned its head slightly towards Clary, presenting a perfect brain shot. But as he was about to squeeze the trigger, he stopped as he noticed the second tusk was missing. This elephant was a one-tusker, and although it was huge, a one-tusker was not worth shooting, at least from a financial standpoint.

Clary put the safety back on and made as quiet a retreat as possible, so as not to provoke the elephant into a charge. His two trackers stood bewildered a few yards away as they heard the bull retreating quickly through the bush. They couldn't figure out why Clary hadn't fired despite being so close, until he said, "Pembe moja", meaning one tusk. They immediately understood the situation, turned silently and, disillusioned, trudged back to camp.

Three weeks after their arrival, camp supplies were running low. Soon it would be time to trek back to town. To make this trip worthwhile, Clary had to shoot an elephant with tusks that could be sold for more than the cost of the safari. Though time was running out, he was determined not to return home empty-handed.

Now that he knew this tract of bush better and had some experience finding elephants in the thick Acacia scrub, he got braver and became careless as he stalked his prey. He began to take foolish risks when creeping up to the elephants.

One morning, he crawled close to a lone bull in very heavy bush but could not see its ivory to judge if it was worth shooting. He was squatting on his haunches when the bull turned and came towards him, unaware of his presence. It stopped just yards away from him, hidden only by one dense bush. The huge animal was far too close to try to get away. Just steps away. Any second now the bull would get his smell and with one step be on top of him.

Clary saw the white tusks glinting through the thicket with the massive elephant's head towering over him. He had left it far too late and had to make a split-second decision about where to aim. A brain shot up through the lower jaw would probably drop the animal dead on top of him, so the only safe alternative would be a heart shot, with the hope that the heavy bullet's impact would push the enormous elephant backwards.

Aiming up into its chest, Clary fired the first barrel from point-blank range. The animal staggered backwards, turned, and ran back the way it had come. As it turned broadside, Clary fired the second barrel, then reloaded quickly. He and the trackers could hear the bull crashing through the bush for more than two minutes before all became silent. They waited quietly for some time, listening for any sound of movement from the direction the elephant had run.

All was quiet, so they followed the wide trace made by the animal through the bushes which were trampled, broken, and splattered with drops of blood. It was an easy spoor to follow.

A half mile farther on, they found the elephant lying on its side, dead. In spite of the perfect heart shot, the bull had still had enough strength to run that far. Clary could only imagine what would have happened if the elephant had run forward instead of back. He was becoming careless and stupid, and it scared him.

Next time, in such thick bush, I will go for a brain shot before the elephant gets too close or get out sooner, thought Clary.

He was elated, as the tusks were bigger than he had anticipated. They would fetch a good price from the Indian ivory trader in Tanga, and the money would easily cover all safari expenses and provide a small profit.

One tracker cut off the tail and handed it to Clary, following an old tradition to confirm ownership of the elephant should someone else in the area come across it.

It was less than an hour's walk to camp, where a soothing, sweet cup of tea followed by a cooling bath in the river awaited them. They were surprised to see all the camp staff out to greet them on their arrival. The porters said that they had heard the shots and believed that an elephant had been killed.

The ability of the native Digo villagers in the area to deduce when an elephant had been shot was quite useful, as Clary discovered the next day when his fallen animal was surrounded by the villagers. They knew that the hunter did not plan on eating the elephant all by himself, so there would be plenty of meat for them, too.

The tribesmen in this area were partial to elephant meat. In fact, they would eat any meat they could snare or shoot with a bow and arrows. Due to the tsetse flies, a lack of sufficient grazing, and an abundance of predators, it was impossible for them to keep livestock in this district. Their main sources of protein were chickens and guinea pigs, which the people bred in their huts. A German missionary from South America, in his futile attempt to convert the locals to Christianity, also introduced them to guinea pigs as an alternative source of protein. The German was long gone but the guinea pigs stayed.

The next morning, Clary and four camp helpers equipped with knives, pangas, and water bottles, set out towards a flock of circling vultures that indicated the location of their dead elephant.

To their surprise, they found a small post had been set up that morning close to the carcass. Men and women were busy sharpening tools, building fires, constructing meat-drying tables, and preparing for a feast. They had left their village that morning at first light, heading this way until they had spotted the first circling vultures just after sunrise.

Not one sliver of elephant meat had been touched. They would never touch another man's food without asking first. It was their custom, and was respected by all who passed this way.

There was no need for the camp helpers to cut the tusks out. The village men would do it swiftly and skilfully, and even gladly carry them to the camp. After the tusks were delivered, the elephant was theirs – all six tons of it. Nothing but blood, guts, skin, and bones would remain at the end of the day. The meat would likely last this small village five months, before the last hard dry scraps were boiled for hours into a thick soup which would be eaten with maize meal.

With his fine pair of tusks in hand, Clary ordered his men to pack up the camp and prepare to return home. Laughter and jovial banter erupted amongst the crew as they quickly packed the few camp utensils into safari boxes and took down the canvas fly sheets that had served as their sleeping quarters. The precious dried game meat was bundled with bark ropes into portable loads, while the makeshift drying tables and grass windbreaks were torn away and heaped onto a bonfire. The men knew that Clary always left his campsites with barely a trace of human habitation, and inspected them thoroughly before he gave the order to leave. When nothing except footprints, gnawed bones, and dying embers were visible in the empty campsite, he finally ordered, "Load up and move out".

As there was no local guide on this safari, Clary led the way through the uncharted territory using the sun's location for orientation. His elated porters, encumbered with bundles of goods, chanted sonorous tunes that throbbed to the tempo of their footsteps as they walked along the paths home.

Just before the safari stopped to make camp for the night, they ran into another small hunting party led by an old British Army officer. He greeted young Clary in the usual haughty way reserved for junior staff, then sheepishly enquired if he had by any chance come across a large tusker without a tail. Taken aback by this question, Clary said that his big elephant definitely had a very nice long tail, then asked why the officer wanted to know. With great embarrassment, the old gentleman had this story to tell.

"Two weeks ago near the lower Umba River, I shot a fine bull elephant through the brain at 40 yards with my 600-calibre gun. The animal dropped dead immediately on all fours and didn't move a muscle. I went up to it and saw the bullet hole right through the top of the skull, so I knew it was stone dead. I had one of my trackers take a few pictures of myself standing next to the elephant and had the tail cut off." He waved the tail under Clary's nose as proof of his story.

"I went back to my base camp, collected a team of men to chop out the tusks, and sent them off to do the job while I rested in camp. About four hours later, my men returned empty-handed and said that they could not find the dead elephant anywhere. 'What fools do I have as porters?' I thought.

"So the next morning, I marched them to the exact place where the elephant had lain dead, except it was not there. There were only a few drops of dried blood and flattened bushes to mark the spot.

"Very mysterious, isn't it?" said the bigwig.

Then with a serious face he asked Clary if it were possible for the local inhabitants to 'carry away a whole elephant', because that was the only other explanation for his elephant to disappear without a trace. With tremendous effort, Clary barely refrained from hooting with laughter at such a ludicrous suggestion.

While Clary was trying to explain to the red-faced dimwit that an elephant's brain is not at the top of its head but is much lower down just behind the earhole, the riled Army man stormed off and disappeared with his motley crew into the fading light, all the while mumbling that no young whippersnapper could teach him anything about elephants.

A week later, Clary was back in Tanga with his happy porters in tow. After selling the tusks, he was now a little richer than he had been a month before.

Chapter 18
An Old-Fashioned Foot Safari

At this time in the 1930s in Kenya, very few safaris were conducted in the old-fashioned way, which used long lines of porters to carry the necessary equipment and supplies. Instead, the guides employed motor vehicles for hunting, and ungainly trucks to carry the equipment to the camping grounds.

In Tanganyika, there were only a few professional hunters and fewer safaris, so less money was available to buy expensive motor vehicles. Many safaris were still being conducted in the old way by using porters. It was only many years after the Second World War, when cheap ex-military vehicles and equipment were being sold off, that professional hunters in Tanganyika started using motorised transport for safaris.

Tanga, on the coast of Tanganyika, was a small town with only four resident professional hunters, including Clary. So a few old-fashioned foot safaris still started from there. These safaris presented a spectacle for the whole town to behold. In the days before the Second World War, when Clary was a young hunter, he and Bazil started all their safaris from Tanga in the old style, using an army of porters to haul all the equipment.

After making a few trips with Bazil organising the whole kit and caboodle, 24-year-old Clary felt experienced enough to organise and run safari on his own, albeit on a shoestring budget. Clary required months and sometimes over a year to plan and organize his safaris. All correspondence with potential overseas clients was done by airmail, but even then, letters to and from the US could take weeks to arrive. Numerous questions had to be answered concerning everything from the food in camp to snakes in beds and scorpions in shoes, as well as the usual ones concerning game to hunt, guns and ammo to bring, medicines to carry, and the safari's duration, starting date, and total cost.

When all queries were answered and matters agreed upon, the real safari preparations started.

Clary would select a hunting area according to the time of year and game required by his client. The most important factor for a successful safari was the availability of clean water, either from a river, waterhole, or a native well. Local newspaper advertisements requesting the services of porters were unnecessary, since word would leak out amongst the native population about the pending safari. There was always great interest in obtaining a portering job on these expeditions, due to the enviable conditions the successful applicants could expect. There was more fresh game meat every day than anyone could consume. Two ample meals per day were provided, with sweet tea at rest stops during the march. There were pleasant evenings sitting around a crackling fire with other porters, yakking about anything and everything while grilling chunks of meat. Best of all, at the end of the safari, the porters received their cash wages. These wages were more than a regular labourer could earn in the same period in town.

Porters on safaris were protected from exploitation by a government-dictated minimum rate of pay, and a maximum weight that they were permitted to carry. There were also regulations regarding food requirements, sleeping arrangements, and medical needs, as well as a plethora of other rules to protect the crews. However, a good safari headman usually found better ways to solve his crew's problems than relying on the legislation. A constantly complaining porter could be summarily dismissed or was permitted to bring extra items from home, if that solved his problem, but was required to carry them in addition to his normal load.

Hunting safaris were from one to three months in duration. They seldom ran for less time than this, as it was difficult to provide a decent safari that lasted less than six weeks. This was mainly due to the great distances to walk to find a reasonable number of trophy animals. At that time, a total of 27 species of game listed on the game licence could be hunted in Tanganyika, and clients generally liked to shoot at least one of each species if possible.

A two-month safari required about 15 porters to carry all the equipment just for the hunters, such as guns and ammo, drink boxes, a medicine box, bedding, and clothes. Another 30 or 40 porters were needed to transport everything else, such as trade goods, bags of fresh provisions, boxes of tinned goods, camp gear, water containers, and salt for skins. In addition to the porters, each safari needed a cook and kitchen helper, personal servants, headmen, and a local guide or two, swelling the total crew to about 65 people, all of whom needed to be fed daily.

Almost half the porters were required just to carry the minimum three-week supply of "posho" or maize flour, the natives' staple food. To make "Ugali" (cooked maize meal), Posho was stirred into lightly salted boiling water to make a thick bread-like dough called Ugali, that was eaten with a sauce of meat and vegetables or boiled kidney beans. It was a quickly prepared and nourishing meal.

As the food supplies dwindled over the days, the number of porters required was reduced, rendering them surplus, although some of them were still needed to carry the clients' salted game skins and heads. Dried game meat was an added luxury that porters could bring back to their families, which also had to be carried. However, as the safari progressed, any men not needed as porters were sent home early to stretch the food supplies.

A very important item on these safaris were the trade goods. They consisted of rolls of unbleached cotton cloth called americani, sugar, tea, salt, tobacco, and coloured beads. A small number of sheath knives, pangas, axes, and hoes were included, but due to their weight there were only a few of these items. Black gunpowder for native-owned muzzle-loaders was worth its weight in gold, because it was restricted by the government so that a gun owner could only purchase a small amount of gunpowder each year.

A wooden box containing coppers was an essential item to have on any safari. Coppers were local coins of one cent, five cent, ten cent, and one shilling value, that could be used to pay for goods at village "dukas" (shops), if the shop owner did not wish to trade meat for his wares. The local Africans were getting used to transactions in coins, but they did not have pockets in their clothes in which to keep the money. The government, in its wisdom, produced the copper coins with holes through the centres so they could be carried on a string around the neck or hung from a belt.

When the safari dates were finalised and a down-payment was received by his bank, Clary could start placing orders at the local shops for his supplies. He would begin interviewing senior porters for the very important jobs of safari headman and headman's assistants. Once chosen, it was then up to the headman and his assistants to recruit the necessary number of experienced men from the porter community for the job at hand. Clary had his own team of trackers, gun bearers, cooks, and personal servants who accompanied him on all trips.

When his first overseas client, Eberhard, finally arrived at Tanga Aerodrome, he was met by Clary and taken to his hotel in town.

Word spread like wildfire through the porter community that the hunter had finally arrived, and in three days the safari would start. In those three days the client had time to get over his "jetlag" and get used to the intense African heat that he was about to experience.

In the meantime, Clary was busy buying game licences for the client, registering his guns, updating the very important medicine chest with the latest drugs, and doing the million and one other last-minute chores that had been overlooked.

Finally, well before dawn on the first day of the safari, the porters started to arrive – the older men dressed in their clean African-style garments, along with a few more advanced young porters, standing proudly in their European-style khaki shirts and shorts.

All of them assembled in front of the hotel where the very important client was staying. The crowd of onlookers got bigger and bigger as the porters' relatives, friends, acquaintances, and well-wishers turned out to see such a rare event as this. The occasion gave the onlookers an excuse to put on their best clothes and dab on a little cheap perfume.

By this time, everything needed for the safari had been purchased from the various storehouses and shops where it had been ordered months before. Now these supplies were brought to the hotel. Each package had been weighed and numbered according to an itemised list of its contents. This was important, because items had to be strapped together into manageable loads. The maximum weight a porter was permitted to carry was 40 pounds, either on his head or strapped to his back. Some loads that were awkward to carry, such as tent poles, were assigned to taller porters to keep the items above others' heads.

By the time the sun was up, total chaos had spilled over onto the road and side streets around the client's hotel. What traffic arrived had to come to a standstill as porters, family members, friends, and onlookers mingled with each other in great jubilation. Yelling at the top of one's voice was the only way to communicate with each other.

However, by late morning Clary's appointed headman, resplendent in his highly visible fez cap and red jacket which demonstrated his authority, together with his three deputies – also with fez caps, but with lower-ranking green jackets – now showed their true worth by shouting louder, shoving harder, and pulling this chaotic mess into an orderly formation. At last, each man stood ready along the roadside next to his allotted load.

It was not until late morning, when the enthusiastic column was ready to leave, that Clary and his client, Eberhard, finally appeared, imposing in their clean, freshly pressed khaki hunting clothes, polished brown leather boots, and topped off with a wide-brimmed safari hat. They also wore conspicuous green hunting jackets which sported big shiny brass cartridges in their breast pocket loops, and each man carried a gun over his shoulder.

They took their place at the head of the waiting column, telling the headman to order "Loads up". With the usual groans and moans of "too heavy", "too bulky", and "straps too tight", the porters heaved their heavy loads onto their heads and backs with eager help from the well-wishers. When the great loads were up and set, shoulder straps tightened, backpacks strapped on, and the moaning had stopped, the safari was ready to start.

With a shout of, "Haia safari!", and a gesture from Clary, he and his client led the smart column in single file through the main street, heading out of town. Practically the whole town turned out to wave and cheer them off, and shouts of good luck came from sidewalks, shops, and windows, wishing them a safe safari. Even the mangy dogs in the alleyways barked their approval. Uninformed townsfolk looked on in admiration at these brave men heading out into the untamed African bush to do battle with wild and savage beasts.

At this point, Clary and his beaming client felt like royalty on a state visit, cheerfully waving back to the crowds while fully aware that the real dangers in these adventures were diseases and illnesses, not animals. At the end of the column came the relatives, dancing and singing African songs of bravery, of loved ones, and of bygone journeys.

As they left the town behind, Clary purposely refrained from mentioning to his trusting client that this was his first safari on his own.

By the time the column passed the last native huts of Tanga town, the singers and dancers had left, and conversation amongst the porters was reduced to a few words as the weight of their heavy loads began to bite into their heads and shoulders.

This was now a good time for the two hunters to take off their showy jackets and hand these and the heavy rifles to the gun bearers. It was also a good time to call the man carrying the box containing the safari comforts - alcohol - so they could take out a bottle of Scotch plus two glasses, and drop back to the end of the line where they proceeded to toast each other, more than once, to big game bags, good times, and any other reason that deserved another Scotch.

Now the headman took over, leading the march along jungle paths, stopping his men every two hours for a half-hour rest, then marching them on again until the next rest stop. At about four o'clock in the afternoon, he called the final halt, and a temporary camp was organised for the night, close to the nearest settlement.

The safari followed the broad, well-worn native footpaths that led from one village to the next. They tried to time their march so as to arrive at a settlement by 4:00 in the afternoon, because they could barter for food and fresh water there and not break into their own supplies. It also allowed them time to set up their camp before dark, as night in East Africa begins at 6:30pm and by 7pm, it is pitch black.

The chief of the village near where they camped the first night approached Clary and the client. Since they were the only Caucasian men and obviously the expedition leaders, he welcomed them and allowed them to camp by his village. Clary asked the chief for fresh, clean drinking water and any food they could spare for his porters. After the food and water was delivered, the chief invited the hunters to a communal meeting hut where he asked many questions about the purpose of the safari, what game they were after, where they were going, and for how long.

After this conversation, Clary estimated how much the food he had received was worth and gave the equivalent amount in trade goods, such as americani cloth and tobacco, from his stock. Given that handshaking was not an African custom at that time, each party thanked the other with a small head nod and departed in peace.

Everyone was tired after such a long walk on their first day, and the camp fell silent fairly quickly when they had all eaten and the sun had set. Then, around midnight, when silence enveloped the land and sound travelled farthest, the village drummer started beating his hollow wooden log in a series of ascending and descending tones that relayed to all surrounding communities the news and pertinent information about the approaching safari. For the next hour or so, drummers in the far distance could be heard repeating this information to the next villages, who, in turn, passed it on all the way down the line to the last village in the region.

The following day, when the safari reached the second village along their route, they found a campsite had already been cleared of brush and the ground swept clean of thorns. Fresh food and gourds full of water were laid out, together with bundles of firewood, all ready for the expected visitors to use. The whole community turned out to greet them and show that they were welcome. The chief invited the hunters to his house for the usual small talk, and he enquired about their gifts to him. There were no other questions to ask, as the chief had heard the drums during the night and already knew all he needed to know about the safari. With the formalities completed, Clary cut off a few yards of americani cloth and put it with a twist of tobacco, some bags of salt and some sugar – the total worth of which equated to the value of the food he had received. He gave all these items to the chief.

That night, the drums talked only briefly, saying that all was well, and the safari was leaving for the next village tomorrow.

These routines went on each day and night for several days until the safari finally reached the last settlement on their route. From here, they would be on their own, striking out into the uninhabited hunting grounds and starting the real safari. They would now start consuming their own supplies and fetching their own water from whatever source they could find.

Even here, at this last village, the chief knew all there was to know about the safari and had prepared his own men for this day.

A few days before their arrival, the chief had sent out his own scouts to check on the waterholes, elephant movements, general game numbers, and the ground conditions that could influence the success of a hunt. This would include information such as stretches of unburned grass and thick wait-a-bit thorn thickets, since they were unsuitable for hunting. Thorn thickets were often impenetrable, and tall green grass concealed the game too well. Also, if the rains had been heavy that year, the grass would have grown taller and stayed green longer, so it could not be burned off. Unburned dry grass was also a problem because it caught fire very easily and could burn down a camp within minutes, before anyone had time to escape the flames

Ideally, the hunters wanted a dry grass area that had recently burned off. A few days after the grass burned, green shoots would appear, attracting grazing animals in large numbers, which made hunting easier. The thick, green wait-a-bit thorn thickets attracted browsers like the shy kudu and gerenuk, although hunting in this type of thorn is unpleasant, difficult, and sometimes impossible, because the needle-sharp, hook-shaped thorns grab at clothes or dig deep into exposed skin, painfully holding the hunter back.

The chief put a guide at Clary's disposal – a man who knew the territory well enough not to get lost and, most importantly, knew the location of all the waterholes. Also from the village came a man who was skilled at finding elephants and would not run in the face of danger. A third man, perhaps a hunter himself, knew where to hunt the elusive lesser kudu and the gerenuk, for these animals were killed and eaten by the local people themselves. Without hesitation, Clary decided it would be a wise move to take them all on as guides.

One of these guides now led the caravan of porters away from well-worn native footpaths, and across an open grassy plain which was surrounded by dense bush. Finally, they reached a group of tall shady trees where they made the first of many camps.

There was a waterhole close by that was filled with clear water for the camp. This water would need to be boiled and filtered before it was safe to drink, but for all other purposes such as washing and cooking it was acceptable.

In spite of the 50 porters being well skilled at carrying loads, it was another matter entirely for them to erect a camp. It was always frustrating for the headman to organise the first camp set up, since many of the porters had never seen a tent before. Their lack of understanding of the technical side of the equipment, such as tent ropes, poles, and pegs and how they were supposed to function together, was exasperating. However, it was not Clary's job to oversee the camp set up; he just gave directions about where everything was to be placed. It fell to the camp headman and his assistants to see that everything was located in its right place, which usually happened only after much bawling, pushing, and coaching, as well as threats of dismissal, and pointed questions about the porters' intelligence and ancestry.

That the camp finally took on a respectable shape seemed like a miracle, after which the astounded client enquired if chaos was a normal state of affairs.

Clary replied, "Actually, this time it went pretty well."

At each set up after the first one, the crew gained more experience, and as they became better and quicker, they required less supervision. By the fourth or fifth camp set up, the headman had very little to do except walk around authoritatively, giving words of praise, testing the guy ropes for tautness, and making suggestions for improvements for the next time.

Safari camps are just basic quarters from which to conduct a hunt, and they have few luxuries. Clary's camp was no exception. Almost all the equipment had been obtained from army surplus suppliers, although some was specially made for expeditions. All the equipment had to be foldable and transportable, because everything was carried on the backs or heads of humans. At the same time, the camp needed to be as comfortable as possible, since the client was paying for and expecting a certain level of comfort. There is an old professional hunter saying that states, "Only amateurs rough it on safari", which holds true even today.

Clary's camp consisted of two lightweight canvas ridgepole tents, one for the client and one for himself, which he shared with boxes of perishable provisions and all the alcoholic drinks. Each tent was equipped with a thick canvas groundsheet, a folding camp bed with a kapok-filled mattress, two plain sheets, two blankets, and a kapok-filled pillow. There was also a mosquito net that hung by a string over the bed, and at night it was tucked under the mattress to keep flying and crawling insects out of the bed. The pampered client also had a woollen carpet in front of his bed.

In front of the tent, under the awning, was a folding table, an enamel washbasin, a towel rack, and a small shaving mirror, which was attached to the tent pole. The towels and bed linen were washed and changed every week, or more frequently if necessary. An improvised shower enclosure, made from thatched grass over a cane frame, was placed next to each tent, and a canvas bucket with a spout strung up over a tree branch completed the shower. The shower bucket was refilled daily with warm water from the kitchen.

The toilet consisted of a four-legged wooden toilet seat set over a three-foot deep hole in the ground. It was surrounded on three sides by a canvas flysheet for privacy. After each use, a spade full of the excavated earth was thrown in the hole to keep flies and smells away. Toilet paper was always kept in the sleeping tent, never by the toilet, because termites love paper and would devour a packet of it in no time.

Fresh vegetables and fruit for the camp consisted of whatever was available in the markets and whatever could be bartered in villages they passed through. Clary only bought fresh vegetables that would keep well in camp, such as green tomatoes, cabbages, potatoes, and onions. Tinned vegetables and fruit preserves in glass jars, imported from England, made up the rest of the food supplies. Any fresh fruits that could be found at the local markets, such as oranges, mangoes, or bananas, were also purchased. From Tanga, Clary brought a side of cured and smoked bacon that had to be ordered well in advance of the safari. It was considered an essential item for any decent English breakfast, as were smoked pork sausages. These were tied together into long strings and hung in a cool, shady place to keep them from spoiling and out of reach of thieving genet cats.

Eggs were carried in a specially made wooden box containing paper egg trays that would keep eggs safe even if the box was accidentally dropped, which inevitably happened. Flour and dry yeast for baking bread were indispensable items, so supplies had to be sufficient to last until the end of the safari, as they were not available in native communities. Due to the weight and fragility of glass bottles, beer and soft drinks were never carried on safaris, with the exception of whisky, bourbon, and brandy, which were considered essentials. French wine, red and white, was limited to a few bottles of each, and at least one good bottle of champagne and a liqueur were a must.

Meals for the hunters were savoured during the day under a green canvas sheet strung between two poles, and enjoyed at night in the open under the stars. Two folding tables tied together and two camp chairs comprised the primitive dining room furniture. A white tablecloth covered the dining table on which condiments were set out in an orderly manner. Dinner plates, soup bowls, and other tableware were all made of durable enamelled steel, because the dish washers used wood ash mixed with sand to clean grease from the plates. Bone China crockery would not last a week on safari.

Only the whisky glasses were real glass, as to drink whisky from a metal cup would have been criminal. The precious whisky glasses were just rinsed out with clean water by the carefully trained waiter. As it was also sacrilege to drink tea or coffee out of a metal cup, a robust earthenware teapot with matching cups and saucers was always on hand, and these were carried in a special wool-lined wooden box. Eating utensils were made of steel with wooden handles, because silver cutlery tended to go missing very quickly on safari, perhaps due to there being a number of Arab silversmiths at the coast who would buy any silver that was offered to them.

The kitchen area was easily recognisable by a stack of firewood and crudely-made tables strewn with blackened cooking pots. The cook had at his disposal various sized pots, pans, and buckets, as well as a complete set of kitchen implements and a heavy wooden cutting board. The actual cooking was done with a cooking pot set over three large stones, placed in a triangle with hot coals in the middle, as has been done by humans for thousands of years. A table made from sticks, bound together by string bark, big and strong enough to hold full pots of food was one of the first kitchen items to be constructed at a new camp.

Another essential item was a charcoal-fired iron for ironing sheets and clothes after they had been washed and hung out in the air to dry. It was necessary to iron clothes to kill botfly eggs, because botflies laid their eggs in the folds of damp clothing where they would hatch into worms. These worms stayed on the clothes until they found a human host. The worms would burrow into the flesh of their victim and grow big and fat until they were large enough to crawl out and drop off their host, leaving a large suppurating hole in the flesh.

Termites were also a constant plague in Africa, especially on safari, where they ate into any wood that was placed on the ground, particularly wooden food boxes. So, the secret was to place the boxes on freshly cut green logs which the ants avoided until the logs dried out and became munchable. Canvas groundsheets, used for tent floors for the hunters and under sleeping mats for the porters, were a termite delicacy, so the groundsheets were impregnated with repellent paraffin wax before the safari started.

The porters slept in groups on plaited reed sleeping mats placed on the waxed groundsheets. Before going to sleep, the men rolled themselves up from head to toe in a long, thin blanket. A large canvas sheet, hung from above and pegged to the ground on one side, and open on the other side, was their only protection from the elements. In uninhabited country, mosquitoes did not carry malaria, so the porters were not issued nets. Flying insects of all types were repulsed by smoky fires smouldering next to the sleeping shelters. As well, the ground around the sleeping quarters was cleared of vegetation for 30 yards to discourage insects and snakes from entering camp.

The porters formed themselves into groups of eight to ten people to eat, sleep, and work together. One porter cooked the food in a large pot for his group, and they all ate together out of this one pot. Their only utensils were a tin cup for tea and a sharp knife to cut off chunks of roasted meat from a never-ending supply. Those skilled crew members such as trackers, gun bearers, waiters, and the cook, who considered themselves above the average porter, took their share of food from the communal pot and ate separately from a plate.

All camp staff ate two meals a day. Breakfast was hot sweet tea followed by a thin maize porridge. At midday, when the sun made it too hot to cook, they snacked on dry salted meat or a small maize cake. In the cool of the evening, they ate the main meal consisting of ugali, with a side dish of gravy made from vegetables and meat, or boiled beans.

About every three weeks, supplies of kerosene, sugar, salt, and posho ran low, so more had to be procured. The little settlements in the bush grew their own maize, which the women pounded into posho with a large wooden mortar and pestle for their own use. However, they never grew maize in excess of their own needs or had extra kerosene, salt, or sugar to barter, forcing the safari to seek it elsewhere. This usually meant a four or five day return trek by 20 porters to a town where supplies of these items were assured. The porters were led by an assistant headman carrying a leather pouch full of shillings to pay for the purchases. Clary hoped that the assistant headman was honest enough not to abscond with the money, and savvy enough to get what he wanted and not come back empty-handed or get robbed along the way – all of which had happened on previous safaris with Bazil.

There was usually an excess of game meat in camp, so sometimes the porters happily gave up the evening meal of ugali in favour of sitting for half the night gorging themselves on roasted meat. They knew full well that in the morning they would all have stomach aches and be constipated, but that was a small price to pay for so much free meat. For the average porter, it was one of the many perks they received in exchange for tolerating safari hardships and dangers.

Sugar was the only food item that Clary strictly rationed on the safari, because given the chance, the sweet-toothed Africans would put half a cup of sugar into their morning cup of tea or a large handful of sugar into their porridge. Refined white sugar was an expensive imported luxury and much in demand, so Clary reserved its use for the hunters only. Locally produced unrefined brown sugar was cheaper, and a ration of it was issued weekly to each porter. Although wild honey was a good substitute for real sugar on safari, it was seldom available as a trade item from local natives, as they used it all themselves.

Clary and his client usually went out to shoot an animal for food on the first day while the camp was still being set up. This was legal and did not count against the game limit on the hunting licence. His client always missed his first shot, so Clary would take the next shot to ensure that they had meat in camp that night. After the first day, whatever the client shot as a trophy animal kept the camp amply supplied with meat.

Unfortunately, that first client named Eberhard (who preferred Hardy for short) turned out to be such a poor shot that he tested Clary's hunting tactics to the limit. Hardy was a tall, thin, jovial individual who wore thick-rimmed glasses for long distance vision but could read without them. He failed to advise Clary that even with glasses, his distance vision was poor, as Clary was to find out during the trip.

A typical day on safari started when the black night's starry sky was cut into red streaks of dawn along the eastern horizon. The cook, who owned no timepiece, started to stir in his bed. Instinctively, he realised that it was time to get up.

He gently awakened his kitchen helper, stoked the kitchen fire into life, poured some water from a bucket into the blackened kettle, and set it over the fire to make tea for himself and the sleeping hunters. Just when the light began to push the darkness away, the rest of the camp arose from slumber and staggered off towards the perimeter to relieve themselves and get ready for work. By the time it was half-light, the cook had made two cups of sweet tea, which the personal servants delivered with a lighted kerosene lamp to the awakening hunters. Hot water would also be brought to the tents for washing and shaving.

An hour before the sun broke over the land, it was just light enough to see, so the hunters headed for the dining area where breakfast was ready and waiting. The cook made fresh orange juice which was followed by a hearty plate of fried eggs, thick strips of smoky bacon, pork sausages, and baked beans smothered in tomato sauce. Blackened toast made by the kitchen toto over an open fire came with tinned butter and jam or honey, all washed down with mugs of hot tea or coffee.

When it was light enough to see the ground clearly, the hunting party silently left camp, heading on a pre-determined route. The two hunters carried their own rifles. The two gun bearers carried a second gun and spare ammunition, and the two trackers brought the food, the water bottles, and the medical kit. The two local guides from the village who knew the area well led the way, carrying the pangas and skinning knives.

In the early morning, snakes lay very still in open patches of ground awaiting the warming sun, so the guides kept a sharp lookout for them. Stepping on a puff-adder or cobra would have provoked an instant attack that could be fatal. In the early years of European settlement, an antidote was only available at some hospitals, and the vaccine had to be kept cold to preserve its potency. A safari such as this could be a two-week march from the nearest hospital. If someone in the party was bitten by a snake, the only course of action was for the bite area to be cut open and the infected blood sucked out. Then the victim would be carried back to camp on a makeshift stretcher, with a belt or strap bound above the slash. The tourniquet would be loosened at regular intervals to let the blood flow. Once back in camp, the laceration was sprinkled with sulphur powder to prevent infection, then bandaged. The victim would then rest and let the body heal itself. The bite was inspected and dressed daily, then given time to heal, because cleanliness and complete rest were the only options available on safari.

Fortunately, the snakes got cold at night and were lethargic in the early morning, so they reacted slowly, enabling the men to jump out of striking distance. As the sun rose, it became too hot for the snakes, so they sought cool, shady places and were no longer a danger.

Every morning, the hunting party of eight men set out in pursuit of a particular species. However, this plan was seldom followed rigidly, as they pursued any good trophy animal that they spotted along the way. After a successful stalk and shot, assuming Hardy killed the animal and had not just wounded it, there were the usual handshakes and congratulations to the hunter from all those present. A camera was produced, and pictures were taken with the client holding his rifle and standing over the dead animal, as was the custom at that time.

The trophy head was removed from the carcass and, if the client desired, the animal was also skinned. The heart, liver, and kidneys, being a delicacy, were kept aside for the hunters to eat back in camp. Then the rest of the carcass was cut into portable chunks, skewered over long sticks, and given to the men to carry, along with the head and skin. If the animal that had been shot was too big to transport all at once, as much of it as possible was carried to camp while the remainder was guarded by a tracker. A second party of men, large enough to carry the rest of the meat, was dispatched from camp to retrieve the remainder – meat being far too valuable to leave for vultures, hyenas, or jackals to enjoy. After everyone had left the killing ground, the vultures would find only intestines left for them to eat.

Since the trophy and meat had to be brought back to camp immediately after a kill in the morning, the hunt ended there until the afternoon. Back in camp, the hunters ate the sandwiches they had carried with them for lunch, then rested or dozed on their beds until 2:30 in the afternoon, when the heat of the day had subsided somewhat. Afternoon tea was always welcome, even by the coffee-drinking Hardy. Around three o'clock, they went hunting again, but in a different direction from the morning hunt. They tried to be back in camp before 6:00, to have at least half an hour of light in which to have a good hot shower, write up a safari journal, or scan their body for pesky ticks which were abundant in the long grass.

One rule that Clary followed consistently was never to shoot at any large animal within an hour of sunset, because if the creature was only wounded, which happened often with Hardy, there might not be enough time to track it down and kill it before dark. Nobody wanted an injured and often dangerous animal running around in the night close to camp.

After showering and changing into clean clothes, there were drinks with snacks and small talk around the campfire while admiring the sun setting behind the trees.

Just after dark, a big, hearty, hot meal was served by two waiters dressed in white kanzus. The table was laid with a white tablecloth, and a bright, hissing pressure lamp hung on a stand a short distance away to attract flying insects away from the diners' meal

A good safari cook, like the one working for Clary, could prepare an excellent three-course gourmet meal on his three-stone charcoal cooking pit. He would pound a tough old impala steak into fork-cutting tenderness, grill it to perfection over open coals, and serve it smothered with fried onions and tomatoes accompanied by boiled potatoes or rice, with a jus de jour. A good, strong soup with fresh bread was the usual starter, and tinned fruit with tinned cream was the standard dessert.

Certain meals called for a wine, usually red, that had been cooled to a pleasant temperature after being immersed in a basin of cool water. The wine was served in an enamel cup, but tasted just as good as if it were in a glass. Each day had a different meal plan, so there was no monotony in the dining room. Watching the cook in his primitive kitchen make fresh bread in an old baking tin covered with hot coals was an education in itself.

After dinner, freshly brewed coffee was served, and occasionally a tot of liquor rounded out the pleasant meal while the men discussed the strategy and planned the next day's hunt. Then, whilst listening to the many mysterious sounds of the night, it was off to a comfortable bed to sleep and dream under clean white sheets.

Every six to 12 days, the whole camp was moved to a new location, sometimes only a few miles away. If the new venue was not too far from the previous campsite, only half the camp would be moved so that the hunters had half a day to hunt. The rest of the camp was moved the next day.

IMAGE 9: THE CAMPING EQUIPMENT HAD TO BE CARRIED BY PORTERS AND THE CAMPSITE CHANGED EVERY FEW DAYS.

Moving to a distant campsite required a whole day or more, because everything had to be taken in one go. This meant a loss of one hunting day for the client, so Clary tried to make up for any lost time by hunting during the move. Occasionally he went far ahead of his singing column of porters, so his guides would leave visible marks such as cut branches or grass bunches tied into a knot all along the trail for the headman to follow to their new campsite.

On one long move, Clary and Hardy had travelled fast and got far ahead of the porters. The guides had left few markers, causing the headman with the porters to lose the trail. The headman continued along the route he was travelling, hoping to pick up the trail again somewhere ahead. To speed up the search for the trail, the headman reduced the porters' rest periods to 15 minutes at each stop, instead of the usual half hour. The porters became exhausted and stopped singing their usual marching songs. Their singing was important, because it not only boosted their morale but also alerted wild game to the presence of humans.

Suddenly, a scream emerged from someone near the front of the column of weary men. "Faru! Faru!" Rhino! Rhino! The scream was repeated all down the line, as loads were thrown aside, back-packs dropped, and men scattered in all directions, diving under nearby bushes, climbing any tree within reach, or just running anywhere as fast as they could.

A rhino had, indeed, been ambling through the bush, unaware of the silent marching porters, when it happened to cross their path near the front of the column. On hearing the porter's shouts, the animal panicked and stormed towards the first man it saw, then veered off after a few steps and ran into the bush, disappearing in a cloud of dust.

After the rhino had long gone, the porters were still calling out to each other, enquiring if it was safe to return to collect their loads.

Clary and his party heard the men's shouts from afar and assumed someone had been gored by a buffalo or bitten by a snake. They ran back to the column, expecting the worst, only to find 40 porters standing around laughing and joking with each other and reliving the last minutes of their recent incident. No one was injured, except for the multiple thorn scratches and cuts on arms and legs from diving for cover. Apart from a few broken wooden boxes and a broken lamp glass, there was no real damage, except to the pride of some brave men. With a few bashes of a stone, the broken boxes were restored into somewhat original shapes. The lamp glass would later be repaired by gluing it together using Acacia tree gum and baling wire.

After the rhino incident, the men's fatigue disappeared and everyone, still in jovial spirits, picked up their loads and continued along the trail, singing and laughing in true African style. This event would remain a talking point in camp for many days as the story was retold, always followed by much laughter. In those days, black Africans in the bush did not measure dates by a calendar but rather by referring back to the last major incident, in this case, the number of days after the rhino attack. Whenever another big event occurred, it would become the new reference day.

Hardy's shooting ability was poor at best and very frustrating the rest of the time. His three American-made rifles were perfect for the animals he intended to hunt, and were precise enough to shoot accurately at 150 yards, but he kept missing easy shots or merely injuring the animal, necessitating a follow-up that often went on for hours in the hottest part of the day. Most of the time Hardy missed his follow-up shot, too, to the great disappointment of his tired tracking crew who now had to start following the crippled animal again. When the hour was getting late, Clary would leave his client in the care of his exhausted team and hunt the injured animal alone.

One morning, Hardy maimed a bull eland that they had to follow for hours through open bush and tall yellow grass. By the time they finally killed it, it was late afternoon, and they were too far from camp to make it back before dark. Eland meat is very tasty and sought after. Regrettably, they had to leave it all behind. Clary ordered his men to cut off the trophy head and tie it high up in a thorn tree where they could recover it another day, as his porters were too worn out to carry it back to camp that night. Then, with his local guide leading the way, Clary goaded his tired crew back towards camp.

Before they were halfway home, darkness fell, and the men wanted to stop there for the night. However, Clary had been with Bazil on a safari when they were obliged to find their way back to camp in the dark using the stars to guide them. He decided to attempt that feat again rather than spend an uncomfortable night in the bush, feeling cold, hungry, and tired. There was no moon that night, so the stars were out in their full glory from horizon to horizon. The local guide had used the sun for orientation during the day, but at night, he was uncertain how to navigate to camp now.

Before it became completely dark, Clary asked him which way the camp lay. Using that direction to orient himself, Clary picked out an easily recognisable constellation on that heading and, remembering to compensate for the movement of the earth, he started walking towards it with his very sceptical entourage in tow. Two hours later, they were all back in the safety of their comfortable camp. While Clary and Hardy enjoyed a well-deserved drink, they heard their trackers regaling the camp personnel with the tale of Clary's astounding ability to navigate through the bush at night using only the stars. The enthralled audience kept asking which star it was that had the power to lead them home.

Something had to be done about Hardy's poor shooting before the whole camp became disillusioned with him. The trackers and gun bearers had already lost faith in this good-natured hunter, to the point where they made excuses to stay in camp for the day rather than make another long trek after another wounded animal.

The main problem was that Hardy could not see very well at long distances even with his thick-rimmed glasses. They were not strong enough for his poor eyes, so any animal over 100 yards away was just a blur in his view. He had been reluctant at first to admit this to Clary, for fear that the safari would be terminated early. But now that Clary knew about his problem, they had to find a solution.

First, they constructed a tripod from three long sticks so that Hardy had a steady rest for his rifle from which to shoot. Then they built a blind that looked like a bush, using sticks and dry grass tied in place with bark string. This "bush" consisted of two large shields, high enough and wide enough to hide behind, that could easily be carried by two porters. The plan was for the porters to transport the grass-covered shields on their heads while the party searched for game. When the hunters spotted a good trophy animal, the porters would lower the shields to hide behind and walk side by side very slowly towards the unsuspecting prey. Hardy and Clary walked in step behind the porters until they had approached as close as possible, then Hardy could steady his rifle on the tripod and shoot through an opening between the grass covered shields.

The tripod and blind were so successful that Hardy never missed another shot at close range. He used them for the rest of the safari, including on a successful two-hour stalk in open savannah for a big elephant that mingled with a herd of five bulls.

Once, they got so close to a herd of zebras that Hardy's shot went right through the animal he was aiming at and killed a second one standing close behind. Luckily, he had two zebra licences. Another time, a group of inquisitive impala came walking right up to investigate the moving bush. It was the easiest shot Hardy had ever taken on this safari.

Whenever fresh food supplies ran low, Clary consulted with one of his local guides as to which nearby plantations had what to offer, and what in the way of exchange goods would be accepted.

Then a detail of men was selected to journey to all nearby locations to barter for any available food. Game meat, dried or fresh, was the main item of exchange and also the most valuable item to any community, so Clary knew this would be readily accepted. It was always a surprise to see what the detail had been able to exchange for the meat. Cassava, sweet potatoes, spinach, and plenty of corn on the cob were always available. Cabbage, tomatoes, kidney beans, mangoes, bananas, honey, and even eggs were pleasant surprises.

Corn on the cob was a luxury on safari, so the porters held a party when supplies arrived in camp. They roasted cobs on an open fire until the kernels popped like popcorn, and then chomped the cobs clean to the core. Had the headman not limited an estimated week's supply of cobs to two per man, they would have all been eaten on the first night and to hell with the rest of the week.

During the safari, it was the headman's duty to make sure that each porter carried no more than a 40 pound load but also no less than that, so as food supplies were used up, the porters' loads were replaced by dried game meat, heads, and hides. However, after some weeks, the need for so many porters was reduced because overall there was less to carry. So whenever five or more men became surplus, they were sent home to Tanga. They would be given a handwritten note signed by Clary, stating how many days they had worked on safari, including the five days of return travel time. This note could be exchanged for their pay at Clary's bank when they arrived back in Tanga.

Before they left camp, this returning group would be swamped with requests to greet families, relatives, and friends back home with safari news, and they were asked to take gifts of dried meat back to the families of the porters still on safari. Given that hardly any of the men could read or write at that time, all messages were verbal, and these illiterate porters had an uncanny way of remembering, word for word, each and every message and relaying it perfectly to the correct families.

The returning porters would be so overburdened with their own bedding and clothes, in addition to the gifts of dried meat, that their loads far exceeded the regulation 40 pound maximum load by far, but of course, nobody complained about that now. With shouts of good luck and safe journey from those remaining, the group of porters, guided by a local man, would leave camp early in the morning, singing songs of bravery and of loved ones at home as they wended their way back to Tanga and civilization. They would take almost the same route back out as the safari had used coming in, and as was the custom, they would be welcomed and looked after by each village along their way in exchange for a little dried meat. On reaching Tanga five days later, the returnees became the centre of attraction as concerned family members sought news of their husbands, brothers, relatives, or friends. News of the safari itself was also a hot topic, as were conditions in camp, incidents, accidents, and almost anything else that could be asked. Within hours, everyone with any interest in the safari knew everything there was to know.

When the safari was nearly over and the number of porters had dropped from about 50 to less than 30, grumblings of discontent were heard from all quarters for even the smallest of problems. The water tastes muddy, the maize meal is rancid, the vegetables are stale, game meat is getting monotonous – everything in camp was subject to criticism. Fights and arguments amongst the labourers broke out at the slightest provocation. Threats of a walkout were rumoured. The thought of moving again to a new campsite was despised so much by the crew that it required a tactful hand to keep the mutinous men under control. The deteriorating state of morale amongst the disgruntled porters had to be dealt with by the headman.

This was where a good headman and his assistants showed their true worth. It was their duty to see that everybody's problems (and everybody seemed to have a problem) were heard and some sort of solution suggested; even if not an immediate solution, at least a future one. Although the headman could not find solutions for everyone, just listening and sympathising went a long way towards calming nerves and encouraging tranquillity. Clary did not hear about most of the problems, since the headman tried to solve them himself. Sometimes, however, the headman had to present Clary with a particular problem because, although he had a simple solution ready, it required Clary's approval to implement. Such as when game meat was served to the porters too often, it became bland, and complaints mounted. Clary and his client would take a 22-rifle and go out bird shooting for the day. They usually came back with enough juicy guinea-fowl, francolin, bustards, and green pigeons to feed the whole camp for several days, relieving the monotony of game meat. After that, contentment prevailed for a while until the next complaints arose.

Even for the hunters, camp life was becoming mundane and bland, as their own stocks of food gradually ran out. Fried eggs and bacon for breakfast had been replaced by impala steak with baked beans. Maize cakes replaced pancakes and honey on the menu. Porridge boiled in water instead of milk gave even the client reason to complain. Bland tinned vegetables instead of fresh ones accompanied all meals. By this time, the poor cook was forced to compromise on every meal. Still, with the aid of his meat mincer, unripe fruit, and exotic spices, he did a commendable job of procuring tasty meals. However, when the food scouts finally returned with fresh supplies, normality returned to the dining table.

One time, Clary sent a trio of men out with trade goods to buy some goats and chickens from a settlement. They eventually returned with enough bleating and squawking animals to last a whole week. Thereafter, not a single word of complaint was heard from the camp workforce, which sang and feasted almost every night. It seemed that all their problems were forgotten, at least until the last goat had been consumed and the last chicken roasted.

Just when Clary planned another move to a new campsite, there arose so much discontent and disapproval from the ranks that matters were approaching rebellion. The headman's threats of instant dismissal for mutinous porters were actually welcomed by them, as it meant a one-way ticket home, but that would have been a disaster for the safari. Clary and his headman concluded that the only way to get the porters to move camp was to offer them a day of celebration.

To this end, it was decided that Hardy wanted to celebrate his birthday in a few days' time with a big party, but he wanted to do this in a new camp. Now the porters were enthusiastic to make the move, and their mood soon altered from negative to positive.

At that time, the government frowned upon serving porters any type of alcohol while on safari, as drunkenness could get out of hand very quickly. However, alcohol was the last ace the headman had up his sleeve, and he had to play that card now. Clary thoroughly agreed with him.

After the move to the new campsite, Clary and his client went hunting as usual, except they took some extra men to collect wild honey from any hives they found in the bush. Another group of men was sent to a nearby village to trade tobacco for honey. Within a day or two, they had collected enough honey to make several gallons of mead – a mild, sweet alcoholic drink favoured by the upcountry natives.

Three days before the client's birthday celebration, steel buckets, large cooking pots, and water containers were filled with clean water, a good measure of golden wild honey was added, and an overripe mango was put in to start fermentation. The sweet smell of fermenting honey wafted through camp for three days before the brew reached its maximum alcoholic content and sweetness, ready to be imbibed.

Hardy had already shot a tender young eland for grilling whole over hot coals as a special treat for his birthday party, and the clever cook took the opportunity to bake a birthday cake for the astonished client by mixing a tin of fruit salad soaked in brandy with flour, and topping the cake with caramelized honey.

The party was supposed to last a day but ended up being a drinking, singing, dancing, and eating orgy that ran on for two days, then extended another day to let the revellers recover from the after-effects of too much alcohol. Clary and Hardy joined in the drinking and feasting sessions, though in moderation. The only catch was that the client did not really have a birthday that day. It was all a ruse to prevent a rebellion by the porters.

After this memorable party, the porters vowed to follow Clary far and wide wherever he went. His word was their command. This birthday party was the main topic of conversation for the rest of the trip. It was remembered and recounted on many future safaris as well. After this great event, there was no more discontent or grumblings for all the remaining days of the trip. As Clary said, a headman with good solutions is worth his weight in gold.

As the safari was nearing its end, there were still a few animals on Hardy's licence that had not been collected. The local guides told Clary that those final species could easily be hunted on the other side of the Pangani River. However, since it was out of the guides' territory, they could not accompany him there. Instead, they led the safari to a fishing village on the Pangani where Clary could hire several canoes to ferry the party and equipment to the other side.

Clary sited a temporary camp about a mile away from the village, to avoid possible pilfering by the inhabitants, and far from the riverbank because of the mosquitos which likely carried malaria. Also, his porters, now reduced in number to 35 men, had been in the bush for six weeks and were probably so lustful that they would attempt to seduce a local maiden even at the risk of being severely punished if caught by a village guard.

After paying his guides with a generous amount of trade goods, Clary started negotiating with the village headman for the hire of dugout canoes to transport his safari 50 metres across the river. He expected to complete a deal by nightfall and be ready to start crossing in the morning. He could not have been more wrong.

The village headman, dressed in his authoritative pallid kanzu with gold braid and his red fez, and surrounded by his elderly advisers, was a shrewd businessman. He realised that this immature young white man was at his mercy, and so he was going to extract the maximum amount of goods possible from him.

For two straight days, the negotiations went on without coming close to a reasonable agreement. The old headman knew that he had the upper hand and was not about to give it up cheaply. So, on the morning of the third day, when Hardy was prepared to pay extra for the ridiculously high canoe rental fees just so that they could move on, Clary took his headman with a small band of his porters and walked several miles upriver to a small, five-hut, one-canoe village.

To the delight of the canoe's owner, Clary hired the single canoe for two days in exchange for the last of his trade tobacco and americani cloth. Then he sent his men back to the camp with orders to move it to this place and tell the negotiating team in the big village that Clary was away shooting game to feed his men.

Unfortunately, to reach the opposite side of the river, the canoe had first to be poled upstream, hugging the bank for 150 yards, then paddled vigorously across the fast-flowing water to land opposite the tiny village. The canoe was so small that it was only able to carry the weight of two men plus the pole man each time, which was far too time-consuming to be practical. So, Clary, to his own and Hardy's amazement, came up with the brilliant idea of tying some long, dry building poles to the outside of the canoe to increase its buoyancy and stability. Then he removed all his tent ropes and collected as much rope as he dared to remove from the other equipment to make one long line of 120 yards. He stationed six of his strongest men on each river bank, and by attaching the front of the little canoe to the middle of the long rope, the men were able to pull the loaded canoe back and forth across the river until in less than a day everyone and all the equipment was across the river. When the stubborn negotiators from the big village came to Clary to announce that he should come back for negotiations before the price went even higher, he was just pulling over the last of his equipment. The emissaries, however, insisted on at least partial payment for the two days of negotiations, but Clary refused since he was already across the river, which was outside their territory and where they had no influence.

In this final week of the six-week safari, Hardy shot another four animals on his licence, for a total of 23 trophies, 18 of them being separate species. He was a very happy hunter.

Clary reminded Hardy that he did not measure the success of a safari by the number of animals killed or the length of their horns, or even by the weight of the elephant tusks, but rather by the excitement of the hunt and the enduring lifelong memories it generated.

Whereas the safari had started with a big bang in Tanga, it ended eight weeks later with a whimper. Nobody noticed or even acknowledged with as much as a wave the returning horde of scraggly, perspiring men in dirty, tattered clothing, carrying awkward bundles of unknown objects strapped on their bodies or balanced on their heads. It had been a forced march of 15 miles a day for the last five days, and since all the provisions had been used up, they had to rely on the generosity of local farmers for food as they passed through.

The very satisfied client spent a few days in town at his comfortable hotel, drinking cold beers, gorging himself on seafood, and generally recovering from his two-month safari adventure. He spent time sorting through all his safari gear, deciding what to take back to America and what to leave behind for Clary. He caught up on his diaries, and decided which trophies he wanted to keep and which taxidermist to send them to. He determined how much money to tip and to whom, and made all final safari payments before his departure by plane back to his home country.

When the safari was over and his client had departed for home, Clary had numerous boring and unpleasant tasks to complete. After this and every other safari, his equipment had to be cleaned, and either repaired or replaced, for it took quite a beating on safari. Most of the equipment only lasted two years before it was ready for the scrap heap. New carrying boxes had to be made, if the old ones could no longer be nailed back into shape.

Animal skins had to be carefully checked to make sure they were dry and properly salted. If salt ran out before the safari ended, skins were rubbed with wood ash to preserve them, but this meant that now the ash had to be washed out with water, and the skins re-salted and thoroughly dried again. Game skulls had to be cleaned of all meat and the horns checked for dermestid beetles, which live inside the horn and burrow through it from within, eventually ruining the trophy.

Regardless of how vigilant his personal staff had been while on safari, there were always expensive items that had been stolen, such as axes, pangas, and skinning knives, or other items that were damaged or spoiled, like enamelled plates, glass jars or rusty tins of food. If too much equipment had to be replaced and too much had been stolen or broken, Clary would take a loss on the safari, which usually necessitated hunting an elephant to keep him going until the next safari materialised.

With the advent of hunting cars and ex-military trucks to transport the safari equipment, a one-month safari only required a camp staff of about 14 men, instead of the 50 to 60 required for a foot safari. A hunter could overload his truck with all the provisions he would need for a long safari, and the truck never complained. Whenever camp supplies ran low, they could be replenished with a quick drive to the next town, instead of a few days' march by a group of porters to the nearest village. The savings on personnel alone was enough to ensure a profitable safari.

After the Second World War ended and army surplus equipment and vehicles became cheaply available, Clary joined the motorised safari groups and finally started to make money from his chosen profession.

Chapter 19
Germans and Trout

In 1927, when he was 20 years old, Clary married Aline, the daughter of a government official, and attempted to settle down to a sedate married life and raise a family. He was still trying to both hold down a job in Tanga as a mechanic for Riddoch Motors while at the same time hunting whenever a paying client could be found. His love of the bush was always stronger than his love of a regular job with guaranteed pay.

At this time, Riddoch Motors urgently needed a replacement manager for a small garage of theirs in Arusha, in northern Tanganyika. Clary was asked to take this post, as no one else was available. He readily agreed to do so, but only because Arusha was close to some very good hunting territory. Of course, he never told his wife that this was his main motivation for moving.

There were quite a few Germans living in and around Arusha who were running successful businesses. They produced some good German specialities such as schnapps, pumpernickel, sausages, sourdough bread, sauerkraut, jams, and honey, as well as items like soap and toothpaste. Butter, knives, nails, rope, cement, in fact, almost anything one required could be procured from their shops. The local German blacksmith could even forge new car parts from scrap metal by using the old part as a template.

The biggest and most important business in Arusha was the German brewery, which produced excellent German beers. It was the only brewery in East Africa at the time, but it was too small to supply the whole territory with beer. The shortfall was made up by imported beer from England and South Africa.

The reason that the Germans were able to produce such a variety of goods was that any German wishing to live and work in a colony had to attend a colonial training school in Germany and obtain a certificate of competence before being permitted to emigrate. Their teachers were ex-colonialists who had already lived in Africa and knew how to survive off the land. Everything they required had to be made at their new home in Africa, and they were taught how to do it. The new emigrants were told not to expect many goods to be sent out from Germany, because the country was still struggling to pay reparations to the victors of the First World War.

Clary was fascinated by the Germans' technical capability to produce quality metal implements and tools from scraps of metal in primitive foundries. He made many friends in the German community and had his first look at a German-manufactured hunting rifle. He was astounded at the precision workmanship that went into making a Mauser rifle. It was built to last forever, or so it seemed, as the one he was holding in his hands looked brand new yet was already 35 years old. He would have liked to buy one, except that they were very expensive, and the Germans only made light calibres, suitable for small and medium-sized game. Even the Germans who went hunting for large game put their faith in the good old English double-barrelled rifle. Besides his admiration for German ingenuity, Clary acquired a taste for their food, beer, and schnapps, and eventually, years later, managed to buy an excellent Mauser 9.3mm rifle.

Clary stayed for six years as manager of Riddoch Motors in Arusha. Then, with some spare cash in his pocket saved from his monthly salary and the odd hunting trip with a paying guest, he resigned from his job and moved his family to Morogoro – a small town that was just a rest and rail stop on the main road to central Tanganyika. The main reason for his move was to explore new, untouched hunting grounds within easy reach of the town.

With his scant savings, he bought a small garage with which he hoped to make some money, and rented a house for his family.

Fishing in the rivers and streams for indigenous fish near Morogoro was a pastime Clary enjoyed when he only had a few hours of free time from garage duties. As he fished, he noticed that those fast-flowing, clean mountain streams of the Uluguru Mountains would be perfect for rainbow trout to live in.

He arranged with the regional government fisheries department to have a few hundred rainbow trout fingerlings brought in from Kenya to be released into suitable streams. One of the fisheries department's requirements was that the local natives, the Kaguru and Luguru, should be allowed to profit somehow from the fish. This was to ensure that the trout would have value and so be protected by the local Africans. Clary agreed that this was the only way to assure the survival of trout in these waters.

A short time later, baby trout were released into the streams, where they grew and multiplied rapidly in these ideal conditions. A fishing club was established, rules and regulations were spelled out, and keen anglers were asked to become members of the club. In the first few years, only Europeans joined the club, and the fishing was excellent. Africans living in Morogoro had not the slightest interest in joining the club to fly-fish for trout, because that pastime was totally alien to them. To whet their interest, local Luguru and Kaguru businessmen were invited to come and try their hand at trout fishing. All equipment was loaned to them, and the finer points of fly-fishing were demonstrated. A few of those invited found fishing very enjoyable, so they joined the club and became regular members. The European club members were very pleased that they now had some keen African members to assure trout fishing's survival here.

The club further arranged for all the other suitable streams to be stocked with trout so that, a few years later, big fat rainbow trout could be caught in all the streams.

Trout had become so abundant in the streams that there was no catch-limit. The African businessmen who were club members found a good market for these high-priced trout, not only in Morogoro but upcountry as well. So, these men went out almost daily with a group of helpers and caught as many fish as they could. They made a small fortune selling them. When some European club members asked them to stop this practice because fish stocks were now declining, the businessmen refused to forgo this easy, lucrative income. Very soon, more of the Luguru joined the club to partake in the money-making spree, and the streams were soon fished out.

In order to harvest the very last trout, the pools along the streams where the last remaining trout were hiding were dynamited by the African fishermen, killing every last fish in the streams. Trout fishing had lasted just 12 years. There were no more plans to restock the streams, so Clary reverted to hunting in his free time.

A year later, gold was discovered in the Uluguru Mountains, close to Morogoro. Clary still had gold fever in his blood from his Lupa days, so using some of his savings he bought an unworked claim from the government, hoping that this time he would make his fortune. He worked his claim with experienced local African workmen, and for the first time in his life, he made money from one of his hare-brained schemes.

After mining the easy gold down a vertical shaft, he was forced to tunnel horizontally, following a good gold vein. But as luck would have it, one night it rained quite heavily, flooding the mine's tunnel. Work ceased immediately, although expenses did not. The flooding meant he would have to buy an expensive pump to get the water out. Instead, Clary tried to save money in his miserly way by sending his men down the shaft on a ladder to scoop out buckets of water, which were hauled up to the surface by a rope and dumped out. Unfortunately, the rain had soaked the vertical shaft walls so much that they became unstable and collapsed onto four men working below, killing them all. The mine was immediately shut down by the mining commission. Clary lost his operating licence, and he had to pay the dead men's families a hefty compensation for their loss. He continued operating his garage to make ends meet, but his heart was not in his garage work. It never was.

He piled his family and belongings into his old Austin vehicle and drove back to Tanga where, with the help of his father, he found a home to rent.

He kept himself and his family fed and clothed by hunting on his own or by conducting the few long safaris that came his way.

Chapter 20
Dangers Lurk Everywhere

If Clary had calculated his safari costs correctly and been careful with supplies, there would be a small profit left for him to live on for a month or two. However, he only managed to book two or three safaris per year, which was not enough to provide a living, so he had to find other ways to make ends meet. One option was to hunt for big elephants – the large tuskers whose ivory could be sold for a good profit. Clary did not like to do this as he preferred to keep any large tuskers he saw for his future clients. He did not like the idea of having magnificent tusks chopped up to make bangles and trinkets for rich Indians or billiard balls for English gentlemen. He wanted them to be preserved whole and hung on the walls of some rich man's home, which is what his clients did with their tusks.

As time passed and Tanga's population grew, hunting elephants anywhere within a day's walk of the town became a dangerous affair, because too many weekend hunters bought elephant licences, borrowed a small calibre gun from a hunting friend, then went out into the bush with some innocent porters and tried to shoot an elephant. They were not after big tusks, just some ivory to hang on the sitting room wall and brag about. Very often, these amateurs would come upon a sedately feeding herd of elephants, consisting of females with calves, immature bulls, and old matriarchs. All too often, the hunters would fire from too far away at the nearest animal and wound it. As the panicked herd ran off, the hunters kept firing at the wounded animal, but in the ensuing stampede, they usually hit other elephants too. Most of the time, these amateurs would follow the blood spoor of an injured animal until it entered dense bush, then abandon the pursuit due to their apprehension of elephants. These hunters would then look for another elephant herd to harass.

As a result, there were quite a few wounded elephants around Tanga. Many innocent natives, walking through the bush from one village to the next, lost their life when they were suddenly charged by an injured elephant. A game ranger or a professional hunter then had to be sent out to deal with this rogue animal.

One professional hunter from Tanga went out to find a big tusker for himself and ended up being charged by a small bull, which he had to shoot in self-defence. It had a non-fatal, festering bullet wound high on its shoulder. The tusks were small and would hardly cover his licence fee, but he had to take them nonetheless. To make matters worse, on his way back to his car, he was attacked again by another injured elephant, which he also had to shoot. Its tusks were even smaller than the first animal. The hunter only possessed one elephant licence and feared he was in trouble. Fortunately, he was able to persuade the chief game warden back in Tanga that he had only shot the second elephant in self-defence, and could forfeit the tusks without being prosecuted for poaching.

When elephants are constantly harassed, they become very aggressive and will seek out the source of the shot and hunt the hunter down.

Clary lost a friend to elephants because of this.

His friend Edward worked on a sisal farm near Tanga. He was keen on hunting and had been on a few hunts for small game with Clary. Edward wanted to hunt elephants for the extra money their ivory could provide for him. At that time, a hunter was permitted to buy a licence to shoot five elephants per year, and Clary's friend intended to fill his annual quota every year. First, Edward bought an air rifle and spent time at home shooting targets to improve his aim. Then he bought an old 303 Lee-Enfield to shoot at tin cans that he placed on sisal stalks. This was to speed up his reaction time while still shooting accurately. He became a very good shot, able to shoot straight and quickly, even at long distances. Lastly, he bought himself a big enough gun to knock over an elephant at a fair distance, and believed he was ready to go on his first hunt.

Edward knew about the dangers of elephant hunting only from books he had read, but he believed his good marksmanship would keep him safe. He also knew nothing about the particular dangers of hunting elephants near Tanga, so he ignored the warnings of his friends and set out to shoot his first elephant. His body was found many days later by a search party who had been alerted about an elephant attack by a porter who had been with Edward on the hunt.

Edward had been caught by an elephant, thrown high in the air, gored by a thick tusk, and then trampled on by many irate elephants. His remains were covered in safari ants and blue-bottle flies, sucking the last fluids out of his lifeless body. His rifle was close by, crushed into the churned-up earth, its stock broken in three places and the barrel bent. Nearby lay two dead elephants, shot at close range with perfect brain shots. Grass and bushes were ripped up, broken, and flattened by at least two large groups of infuriated elephants. Farther away, they found another dead elephant with large tusks. It had two bullet holes through its head. Using the porter's report and observing the scene, it was fairly easy for the search party to reconstruct the tragic events.

Edward had used good cover to get close to the first elephant, killing it with a brain shot. He then walked up to it and shot the animal again to be certain it was dead. At the sound of the first shot, the other elephants in the herd did not run away as they would normally have done, but instead turned on the hunter. Edward heard them and dodged the first onslaught of the herd by running out of sight and out of the wind, along a line of thickets. Then he hid in the trees. As the herd milled around, testing the air to locate his scent and trying to rouse their dead fellow onto his feet, the hunter ran across an open grassy patch using small bushes as cover, and fled into a grove of big trees. He then sprinted to his right, trying to keep downwind of the milling herd and get as far away from them as he could.

That was when he ran right into a second herd of elephants who had heard the shooting and come looking for the culprit. He shot the first two charging elephants at close range with brain shots, but his gun was now empty. He had failed to put extra cartridges into his trouser pockets, and his tracker had run off with the backpack containing spare ammo after the first elephant attack. The remaining elephants of the furious herd were now on him. He threw his useless gun aside and ran, but it was too late.

Clary was relieved that he was not in the search party, so he did not have to view his friend's mangled body. He was told the story by another professional hunter who had been on the search.

Using Tanga as his base, Clary continued to hunt, though he went far afield, out of harm's way. One time, he took out some local Arab hunters, resplendent in their dishdash garments, muzzar headgear, Yezmeh leather boots, and with their curved jambiya daggers strapped to their waist. They carried beautifully decorated muzzle-loaders with which they shot all their game, big and small. For shooting elephants, they used a heavier charge of gunpowder than they used for an eland. They had an elephant licence and requested young Clary to accompany them with his Jeffery's 400 Express rifle, in case a situation got out of hand.

They camped for the night near a village. Early the next morning, they received word from a villager that he had heard elephants breaking branches close by. It took half an hour to locate the small group of elephants. As Clary was looking over the herd with his binoculars to see if there was a suitable tusker amongst the group, he noticed that the Arabs were holding their guns up, at arm's length, towards the rising sun. Thinking it was a Muslim tradition of offering up prayers for a successful hunt, Clary ignored it. In the herd were only small-tusked animals, so he urged the Arab hunters not to shoot but back away, which they did, very quietly. Later, during a rest period, Clary asked one of the Arab hunters about his ritual of holding a gun up to the sun.

"Ah", said the Arab, "in the early morning, our gunpowder gets wet from the dew, and if it is too wet, the gun will not fire, so we hold it towards the sun to dry it".

Clary was dumbfounded at the revelation but never said a word, although he was laughing inwardly. He told this story to a friend whose grandfather had used muzzle-loaders in his early years of hunting. The man said that his grandfather had almost been killed by an elephant that he was hunting in long grass. The grass had been wet with early morning dew, which dampened the gunpowder in the gun's flash pan. The old man had to cock the hammer and attempted to fire four times at the elephant before the gun went off. After that incident, he made a removable leather cover for the flash pan and hammer.

They did not find any elephants to shoot on that trip, so the Arabs contented themselves with shooting at any other game they saw, as long as it was edible. Whenever they shot an animal, they would run to it, grab its head, and slit the dead animal's throat with a sharp jambiya knife while reciting a ritual Muslim phrase.

During another safari, Clary met two old English gentlemen hunters who were using an ancient 4-bore gun to shoot elephants, and a similar old gun with an 8-bore to shoot everything else. A 4-bore gun shoots a lead ball weighing a quarter of a pound. An 8-bore gun shoots a lead ball weighing an eighth of a pound. These short-range black powder weapons had long ago been replaced by more modern, lighter guns. Nonetheless, these old men insisted on using them and, by the amount of game trophies they had, they were successful. They even had lead ball forms, black powder, and caps to reload their own cases. These guns weighed 16 pounds apiece and required a shooting stick to steady them enough to shoot accurately. Clary did not envy these old hunters with their ancient weapons, though, and he felt pity for the poor gun bearers who had to lug these archaic guns over their shoulders all day long.

One morning in Tanga, Clary received a call from the local game department to help find a lost hunter.

The story goes that two friends had gone out with a car into the bush quite far from Tanga, to hunt small game for meat. They had shot an impala in the leg, but it had managed to run off. Thinking that it could not go very far, one man went after it, telling his friend to stay with the vehicle. The friend in the car heard a shot about 20 minutes later, so he presumed his companion had found and killed the injured impala and was expecting him back at any time.

However, after an hour, his companion had not returned and there were no more shots, so the man in the car became worried. He had hooted the horn many times and even fired a few shots into the air, but there was no reply. As it was getting dark, the young man drove home alone and, early the next morning, went back to the same spot, expecting to find some sign of his friend. There was nothing. He was too scared to try to follow the spoor of his friend into the bush, so he sought help from the game warden.

Clary and another professional hunter called their best trackers and travelled with the young man to the place where the impala had been injured. It was fairly easy for the expert trackers to follow the lost man's footprints in the sandy soil. Less than half an hour later, they came to an area covered by lion spoor. By the number of tracks all over the soft earth, it looked like a large pride had rested there. There was no sign of the missing young man except for his blood-covered rifle and one boot with his foot still in it.

The search party could only speculate as to what happened, although it was quite obvious that the man had been killed and possibly partly eaten by lions. Hyenas had then consumed the rest of his remains during the night, including his blood-soaked clothes. It was likely that this inexperienced hunter had followed the injured impala's blood spoor right into a pride of lions who had just killed it. The young man had probably fired at a lion as it charged him, but missed. Lions will defend their kills from all intruders, including young, inexperienced hunters.

In East Africa, many of the European colonial commissioners would go out on safari for a "spot of hunting", as they called it, just to get away from the office.

Whenever he was hunting alone, Clary sometimes met these commissioners on safari, and custom required that he accept their dinner invitation. Protocol required that if you were invited to dinner by a commissioner, you were expected to attend in formal attire, meaning dinner jacket, black tie, and polished shoes.

Being in the bush on safari did not relieve one of this necessity. Therefore, one of the first items that everyone packed for safari was a formal dress, and woe betide anyone who dared turn up for dinner inappropriately attired. Guests were required to appear at the commissioner's camp at 6:30pm, and dinner was served at 7pm sharp. Clary would carry his suit and polished black shoes in a bag under his arm and wait near the host's camp, keeping out of sight until just before 6:30, then change into his formal attire before entering the commissioner's camp at 6:30 on the dot.

Handshakes and "how do you do's" were followed by drinks of either whisky and soda or gin and tonic, with small talk about this and that around the campfire. At 7:00, an impeccably dressed waiter served dinner on bone China plates, with real glass glasses and white tablecloths. No one ever carried extra camp chairs, so the guests dined by sitting on an upturned steel bucket or a folded blanket placed on a wooden box – one being just as uncomfortable as the other. The meal, cooked by an inexperienced cook, started with game soup broth, followed by the main course of tough, overdone game steak, accompanied by bland tinned vegetables, boiled potatoes with thick gravy, and tasteless tinned fruit for dessert. Strong black coffee afterwards helped to settle the stomach. It was a meal worth forgetting. However, the warm whisky flowed freely, the talk was entertaining, and with a bit of luck, the old boy would offer you a decent cigar to puff on while reminiscing.

At 8:30, you were expected to show concern at the late hour, express your appreciation for the excellent meal and entertaining evening, say goodbye, and leave. Just outside the camp, Clary would change back into proper bush clothes and walk back to his camp. Fortunately, a reciprocal invitation was not expected.

Chapter 21
Do Any Job

On Clary's trips upcountry, he sometimes stopped at a dairy farm to buy cream and homemade butter. It was owned by an old English aristocrat who had been living the high life in England and lost most of his inherited father's fortune on bad investments. He had now come to Tanganyika with hopes of recuperating some of his lost wealth.

On one particular visit, Clary had shot seven plump guinea fowl on the way, so he gave three of them to the dear old gentleman as a present. The man was so pleased to receive the birds that he invited Clary to stay for dinner. Unfortunately, Clary was in a hurry that day to reach Moshi, so he promised that he would stop in for dinner on his return trip.

A month later, Clary dropped in on the aristocrat and his wife to accept the dinner date, and was welcomed with open arms. The two men sat in the elegantly furnished sitting room, drinking gin and tonic and chatting while the lady of the house supervised the cooking of the evening repast. When dinner was ready, a gong sounded, and they moved to the dining room where they were seated at a solid oak dining table adorned with silver candleholders, royal bone China plates, and sterling silver cutlery. The three-course meal was served by a white-gloved servant wearing a black sash tied around his waist and a red fez cap on his head. The first course soup was good, although nothing fancy. However, the main course, which came next, smelt of rotten meat and, as it turned out, was just that. The three guinea fowl that Clary had given the couple a month ago were now served with parsley potatoes and two garden fresh vegetables.

"We made your birds the old traditional English way, you know, aged fowl", said the proud lady, helping herself to a greenish mass of de-boned, stinking guinea fowl.

Aged fowl, Clary learned, meant hanging a cleaned game bird by its neck in a cool place for a month or so until the meat fell off the bone. It was then cooked with dried fruit in a creamy sauce and served hot. It had a sharp gorgonzola cheesy taste to it, and if one ignored the smell, it was pleasantly palatable. The Lord and Lady Aristocrat ate it with delight, even having a second helping, which Clary politely declined. A good claret with the meal helped settle his sensitive stomach.

He never again accepted a dinner invitation from them. When Clary told this story to an acquaintance some weeks later, his friend said, "I gave the old bastard four guinea fowl one time, then waited for three months before I accepted an invitation, and believe it or not, we were served those rotten birds for dinner!"

At the beginning of March, an ad appeared in all the newspapers as a reminder to the public that the rainy season would start on the 26th of March, and only major roads would be passable during the rains. All minor roads would be unusable until June, because the wooden bridges over the rivers would be swept away. The bridges would then be re-built after the rains ended in the first week of June.

In those days, the rainy season was so regular that it could be predicted to start within two days on either side of March 26 and, with few exceptions, it always did. Only the major roads were maintained and had permanent two-way concrete and steel bridges over the rivers. Minor roads became mud slides for vehicles, and the temporary single-lane wooden bridges across streams were washed away by the heavy rain. These temporary bridges were a cost-effective way to keep minor roads passable during the dry season and re-opened as quickly as possible after the rains.

To speed up the reconstruction of temporary bridges, a standard wooden bridge was designed to be adaptable to any river crossing and to be easily built by laymen in a short time. This was accomplished by standardizing the length of each supporting leg and crossbeam, as well as the thickness and length of the wooden road surface planks.

Just before the rains were due to start, Clary heard about a five-ton steel boiler for a sisal estate that had arrived very late by ship and could not be delivered before the rains came. The sisal estate that ordered the boiler was fairly close to Tanga and could be reached by minor roads, with only one bridge to cross. The boiler and truck together weighed over seven tons. However, due to a maximum five-ton rating on the wooden bridges on the minor roads, the boiler would have to be driven far inland to cross this river on a concrete bridge with a 12-ton rating, then travel back down the other side along minor roads to the estate. This route was a long way round and would take at least a week, by which time the rains would have made the minor roads to the estate impassable.

Clary believed he could get the boiler delivered on time, so he persuaded the contractor to give him the job, albeit with the precondition of no delivery, no pay.

He hired two trucks – one to carry the boiler, and the other to carry wooden beams and planks to strengthen the small bridge he intended to cross. Clary omitted to tell the contractor about the second truck's cargo, and instead told him that he planned to transport the boiler on the minor road to the bridge, and with the help of his men, offload the boiler and drag it over using ropes, pulleys, and logs. The truck would drive across empty, and using the pulleys, they would re-load the boiler on the other side, then continue to the estate.

When Clary finally arrived at the 40-foot long, single-lane wooden bridge with the two trucks and his workmen, it was too late in the evening to start offloading the planks and beams and start strengthening the bridge. Rather than wasting the night waiting to strengthen the bridge and unload the boiler in the morning, Clary decided he would risk driving the overweight truck across with the boiler aboard. However, he knew the flimsy bridge would never handle so much weight, so to strengthen the five-ton capacity bridge to take seven tons, he tied long wooden planks on top of the narrow running surface and put some extra cross beams underneath to reinforce it. Then he drove the truck a mile back along the road.

He turned around and, revving the engine, drove towards the bridge as fast as the old girl would go. With the engine screaming at full rpm and belching blue smoke, he smacked the bridge ramp doing 50 miles per hour. He heard the timbers breaking behind him as his momentum carried him forward. He felt the heavy back end of the truck sink down as each crossbeam snapped under the excessive weight, but kept the engine at maximum revs. The sheer momentum of seven tons of steel travelling at 50 miles per hour carried him over the breaking bridge and kept him going for another 200 yards beyond, before he could bring the behemoth to a stop.

Looking back at the bridge, Clary saw that his planks on top were still intact, although the crossbeams underneath were all broken. The upright beams and supports had sunk into the mud a fair bit, but were not broken. He was lucky to have made it across. He had enough spare crossbeams to replace all the broken ones, so an hour later the bridge was repaired, and although it had a noticeable sag in the middle, it was still usable. Clary hurried on that same evening to the sisal estate, delivered the boiler on time, and collected his money.

However, news spreads fast in small communities, and word of Clary's stunt on the bridge eventually reached the ears of the chief engineer in the roads department. The engineer charged Clary with an obscure bridge misuse offence and issued him a summons to appear in court. At his trial, Clary pleaded not guilty to the allegations, and tendered his story of dragging the boiler over the bridge with the help of his men, then driving the empty truck across and reloading it on the other side.

The judge did not believe Clary, but the roads department clerk who was giving evidence did not bring any evidence to prove otherwise. On hearing Clary's blatant lie, the roads engineer was furious and said he would send someone to take pictures of the damaged bridge and bring back broken crossbeams as proof of the illegal deed. The judge postponed the case until the following week so that the clerk could get his evidence. Clary was not off the hook yet.

However, that year the rains came a day early with a thunderous rumble, washing away the bridge and all the evidence. Clary sat at home smiling the whole day as the rain poured down in buckets outside.

Chapter 22
Years of Work for a Lost Eden

Nairobi, the capital of Kenya, was fast becoming the centre for organising and conducting lucrative hunting safaris for wealthy overseas clients. Hollywood film producers found ideal conditions in East Africa to produce box-office hits glorifying big game hunters and hunting. It was good, free advertising for east Africa, and Americans came in their hundreds to experience the hunt of a lifetime. The Kenyan companies received the bulk of the safari business, with Tanganyika and Uganda picking up the remainder. Ironically, many of the Kenya safari companies slipped over to Tanganyika with their unsuspecting clients, to hunt in the more abundant game areas across the border.

More and more people were trying to get into the safari business. Although hunting game was regulated by the government game department, guiding someone on safari was not controlled. Anyone with a hunting licence and enough money to outfit a safari could do it. There were too many inexperienced people attempting to engage in the safari business, often with disastrous results for trusting clients. Many farmers and full-time amateur hunters conducted hunting safaris very successfully. However, there were also clumsy doctors, inept lawyers, unskilled accountants, and other bumbling city dwellers trying to cash in on the business.

After too many lost lives and maulings from wounded game caused by inexperienced amateurs on safaris, as well as complaints of incompetent guides from unsatisfied clients, the government decided to regulate the trade by issuing guide licences to anyone who met certain criteria. At the same time, a group of ex-game wardens, farmers, and experienced hunters formed the East African Professional Hunters Association (EAPHA) in 1934. Its aim was to issue guidelines and codes of conduct to members of the association, as well as any potential candidates seeking a guide licence or intending to become a member.

The association persuaded the government to issue licences only to members of this association who had been vetted by the EAPHA and deemed suitable to hold such a licence. This eliminated all the deficient companies to such an extent that, since then, no overseas client has ever been killed while on safari with an EAPHA member.

When Clary heard about this association and the impending laws concerning safaris, he agreed that it was a long-overdue move and set about applying for membership, as well as applying for the newly required professional hunter's licence.

In 1933, when he was 26 years old, Clary managed to fulfil all the necessary requirements and was issued with a full, unrestricted professional hunter's licence. He was the youngest man to hold such a coveted licence, as well as the youngest member of the hunters' association.

Every professional hunter had a regular hunting ground that he used, and it became an unwritten rule that no other hunter would trespass in this area without the express permission of the "owner". Each locality contained certain species of game in abundance where a client could shoot good trophies. Hunting rights for these areas were always reciprocated with other outfitters, so that each safari came home with a good variety of game which, of course, delighted the clients.

In order to get a better picture of the hunting conditions as well as the amount and species of game in the country, the government wildlife department sent out questionnaires to every person involved in any way with wildlife. It was the first game survey in East Africa, so each recipient was required to complete it as fully as possible.

Clary had made a small region of southern Maasai steppe in Tanganyika his hunting territory. The Maasai and their cattle herds had not arrived this far south due to an abundance of tsetse flies in the area. Also, their herds had been decimated by an outbreak of rinderpest some years previously, and had not recovered. It would be at least another ten years before the first Maasai moved into this region.

This area of southern Maasailand had never been hunted or fully surveyed, as it was protected on one side by the crocodile-infested Ruvu River and on the other side by a vast, uninhabited thorn scrubland. This scrubland was infertile and totally unsuitable for any type of farming. The red stony soil supported nothing except scrubby bush, Acacia thorn trees, and Sansevieria (a sisal-like plant). Other than the Ruvu River, no permanent water occurred in this area except for some waterholes that filled up during the rainy season.

To reach the banks of the Ruvu River near his hunting area, Clary cut a car track off a secondary road that went to a sisal estate, and ran it through the dense bush to the river. Now he could get his old truck to the riverbank where he erected a camp. The river was too deep to drive a vehicle across, so he hired a dugout canoe to cross the dark, lazy, flowing river to explore the other side.

He spent years walking through this completely uninhabited and uncharted territory, cutting rough car tracks through impassable growth, so that one day he could hunt with a car when he could get one across. He later marked these crude roads on an old wartime survey map that was devoid of features for this side of the river. As he progressed slowly inland, he marked waterholes, dry river beds, hills, and open grassy plains that were teeming with a variety of game. Sometimes he spent days exploring an overgrown segment, trying to find an access route through an impenetrable patch. He and his dedicated workforce would sleep rough and eat very little during these hard times. Occasionally they became overwhelmed with the back-breaking work and simply gave up. Then, totally exhausted, they foot-slogged it back to the Ruvu for a few days' rest.

Several years after cutting his many miles of road, Clary was exploring the riverbank upstream from his camp when he observed a small herd of elephants crossing over to the opposite bank. Strangely, only their legs were wet, knee high, when they emerged on the other side. On closer inspection of their fording, he discovered that the river widened at this point and was fairly shallow, with a firm sandy bottom. He thought that if he could get his hunting truck across here, he would be able to reconnoitre the area far beyond walking distance from the river. It was worth a try, so a few days later he drove his Dodge half-ton ex-army truck to the ford with his work crew. He ordered them to cut the low riverbank away on both sides to make a shallow ramp to drive in and out of the river.

It was the dry season, so the water level was lower than usual, only reaching up to the top of the wheels. After removing the fan belt to stop water from splashing onto the spark plugs, he drove down the embankment and steered the growling truck in first gear across the river without any problems. He did, however, bring his entire camp workforce and some heavy ropes, just in case his truck stalled in the middle of the river.

Getting this tough old truck across the river was a major achievement that allowed Clary unlimited exploration opportunities in his territory, and enabled him to travel far into the interior, ranging beyond the blue horizon. With his truck he was able to bring his work crew, bush-cutting tools, simple camp gear, and food for long forays into new places. He could be self-sufficient for weeks before he needed to return to base camp.

His motivated gang of workers proceeded to hack out basic truck trails throughout the region by following well-worn elephant paths that led from one waterhole to the next. It proved easier to cut tracks along these winding paths than to try to hack straight roads through virgin bush. The cut tracks were just wide enough for the Dodge to squeeze through the bush but had no room to spare.

At times, they came across broad, shallow, dry riverbeds, which they could follow for a few miles without having to slash through heavy growth. Whenever they burst out onto an open grassy plain, they could drive across it as far as it stretched, so no bush clearing was necessary, and they made rapid progress.

It took years of backbreaking labour to chop a few miles of rough track through this desolate, hard land. Progress was agonisingly slow at times. Some days they cut a mile or more of track, yet other times they managed much less than a few hundred yards while slaving away from dawn to dusk in the scorching heat.

Then one day, they emerged triumphantly onto a hidden green gem of a place, near a hill that Clary had seen weeks before through his binoculars and had been aiming towards. He and his fatigued crew jumped down from the battered truck and gazed in utter amazement at the scenery. In front of their eyes was a waterhole 200 yards long and five feet deep. It was nestled in a rocky hollow, edged on one side by a short-grass field and on the other side by a grove of leafy green trees. About 60 yards away they saw another waterhole covered with white water lilies, where plump wild ducks and an assortment of water birds frolicked in the clear water or rested on the sandy bank.

They found a third waterhole about 300 yards away. It was 40 yards across and hidden amongst large sandstone boulders. In its crystal-clear water, which was at least ten feet deep, they saw turtles and frogs swimming. The water was clean, cold, and sweet to drink. Clary suspected that all three waterholes must be fed by an underground spring, for he had not noticed any streams flowing into them. Years later, he concluded that they were only filled with rainwater during the rainy season, as he could not find any other source.

Clary marked these three waterholes on his crude survey map but did not name them. Many years later, on new government survey maps, they were called the "Losira Water Holes". The nearby hill that Clary had seen through his binoculars was named "Losira".

There was no sign of human activity here, and Clary believed that he and his men were the first humans to see this gem.

The grazing herds of game around the waterholes confirmed his belief by their lack of fear of humans, as they showed only mild curiosity about these strange new creatures. During their walks in the vicinity of the waterholes, Clary and his crew collected many weathered elephant tusks from long-dead animals, some of the tusks weighing over a hundred pounds each. Other tusks were old and very flaky, so they had no value, and some were too small to be worth collecting. These signs confirmed that Clary and his crew were the first people to set foot here. When they returned home, Clary would hand over the ivory to a game department office in return for a small reward.

Clary and his men made camp under a grove of flat-topped Acacia trees a short distance away from the biggest waterhole. There they sat for a long time, admiring the constant stream of game that came to the waterholes to drink.

Refusing to blight his newfound Eden in any way, Clary drove far away to shoot a large enough animal to satisfy his ravenous crew's hunger for fresh meat. They stayed for ten days, scouting the locality for game and suitable trails to cut access tracks for the Dodge truck. From the top of a nearby steep rocky hill, "Losira Hill", they could just make out a vast open plain to the west. Now they sought a way to reach that plain.

Little did they know they were about to discover another paradise.

Three days later, in the rattling old Dodge, they broke through a heavy band of bush to emerge onto a grassy plain, seven miles long, that was alive with vast herds of game, the likes of which neither Clary nor his crew had ever seen before. As they motored through the enormous herds of wildebeest, zebra, kongoni, impala, and other gazelles, the animals did not run off at the approach of the noisy truck but instead trotted towards it to stare and grunt at this strange creature in their midst.

Lion prides rested under the shade of large trees. Leopards with bulging stomachs lay lazily high up on tree branches. Flocks of ostriches strutted about on their long pink legs through the high grass. Big, sombre elephants, some with large tusks, fed and wandered along the edge of the plain, unconcerned by the presence of people as they drove by in the noisy truck. Tall, majestic giraffes strode from one tree to the next, picking off young tender leaves. Warthog families, tails in the air, hardly bothered to trot out of the truck's way. Flocks of electric blue guinea fowl scratched and pecked at seeds on the ground and were everywhere Clary looked.

Near the edge of the plain, they saw shy bushbuck scuttling away, and a rare lesser kudu standing so still it was hardly noticeable. Buffalo, in herds or small groups, or even old solitary bulls, lay throughout the plain chewing their cud like so many cattle. There were a few waterholes, most of them dry, but some contained dirty brown water where warthogs and buffaloes had wallowed therein, leisurely.

Leading off the plain on one side was a large, well-worn game path that led into the bush. They followed it as far as the truck could go and then continued on foot. Troops of baboons barked at them from all sides as they walked past. This was a sure sign indicating permanent water close by, because baboons need to drink daily. After dodging around the odd rhino and a buffalo or two, they found a small spring emerging from under a granite rock outcrop. The water flowed into a little pool and then for a hundred yards or more over a watercourse, ending in a delta-shaped grassy glade. This pool was most likely filled with rainwater during the rainy season and replenished by small springs during the dry season. These springs, together with the waterholes a few miles away where they had camped, were the main reason for the abundance of game in the area. The grassy plain nourished the herds of plains game, the surrounding thick bush fed the rest of the residents, and all animals had year-round access to water. The area was protected on all sides by miles of impenetrable thorny thickets and, most importantly, it had not been discovered by people, especially the nomadic

Maasai with their destructive herds of disease-carrying, grass-eating cattle.

It was getting late as they wended their way slowly back to camp, feasting their eyes one more time on the immense number of grazing herds of wild African game. They stopped one last time at the place where they had entered the plains that morning. Clary took from his breast pocket the little notebook and pencil which he always carried, and wrote in it, "I have found my paradise on earth." He decided it would be a sin against nature to deface this place by hunting or even firing a peace-shattering shot here. "It must remain a paradise. My paradise", Clary concluded, as he tucked his small notebook away.

He vowed never to hunt here and would keep it secret for himself, or perhaps show it to special clients who would only be allowed to take pictures. Many years later, it would be surveyed and called the "Kitwai Plains".

When Clary and his crew returned to the Ruvu River camp several days later, he updated his map of the area he had discovered, marking on it his newly cut tracks, new waterholes, and his newfound secret game paradise.

However, there was one disturbing fact about this area that Clary did not know. An old German-built car track that ran in a north-south direction, connected some trading posts scattered throughout the bush. It passed close to the west side of his Eden by a few miles. The track was very crude and rough, and had not been maintained since the Germans left, so it was only usable during the dry season.

Clary also did not know that the Tanganyika government had plans to make all parts of the country accessible by motorised vehicle, and one plan called for the widening and grading of this little-used track to make it into a year-round serviceable road. A year after Clary found his paradise, the grading of that road was completed.

A few years after discovering his game Utopia, Clary received the questionnaire concerning game numbers and conditions in his hunting grounds. It was marked, "Confidential and secret, for game department use only". Being naïve and honest, he completed the questionnaire in detail. He included a vivid description of his Utopia, and even attached an accurate sketch map of its location. He was confident that no one would dare hunt in his area without first asking his permission, and believed his hunting grounds were protected from outsiders because he alone knew of the only safe Ruvu River crossing for many miles up or downstream. He had a vision that his Shangri-La could one day become a park for all to see and enjoy.

Clary organised many successful hunting safaris using his Ruvu River camp as a base, and so had no reason to venture anywhere near his Garden of Eden.

About three years after completing the questionnaire, Clary was leading a good-natured American client on safari in the Ruvu River region. The man had shot every animal on his licence that he wanted, and was spending his last few days in the bush shooting game birds. This American client was likeable and easy-going, so Clary believed him trustworthy enough to show him his paradise without allowing him to shoot any animals.

One evening, over cold drinks in camp, Clary described his game Utopia to the client in such glowing terms that the man was willing to waste a hunting day and forego shooting just to be able to see this realm. A Morris box-body, Clary's new hunting car, had been brought over the river to use because it was more comfortable, economical on fuel and faster than the Dodge truck.

Well before dawn, Clary and the client, equipped with only a camera and many rolls of film, set off towards the secret plain. The car bounced and rattled over tracks that only Clary knew. Swirls of red dust thrown up by the tyres blew into the open-sided car, soon covering everything and everybody in a fine red powder. Several hours later they reached the three waterholes at Losira, and had a well-deserved break with hot coffee and biscuits.

There was an acute lack of game by the waterholes. Still, Clary was not concerned, since the Kitwai Plains, the real Eden, were still a few miles away. They travelled on and broke through the last strand of bush onto the Kitwai Plains. Clary could not believe his eyes. The scene was just not possible to comprehend. There were car tracks everywhere. Bleached piles of chalky bones were scattered all along the tracks. Overfed vultures sat assembled in the trees as if expecting another free meal. Clouds of dust in the distance signalled the existence of fleeing game.

He stopped the car in a plume of choking, fine grey dust, and his anger was so great that he trembled with rage at the realisation of what had happened. Big tears of sorrow welled up in his eyes, spilling down his cheeks in long streaks of muddy liquid, falling like raindrops onto his dusty khaki jacket. He let them flow uncontrollably and without shame. His paradise was gone. It had been raped, and had been shot out of existence. It would never return, and it would never recover. Never, never.

Clary's client said nothing but knew that something sickening had taken place here. They motored to the far end of the dry plains, following the many tyre marks running that way. Under a grove of flat-topped Acacia trees, they found a recently abandoned hunting camp. Debris around the camp revealed that it had been used for many years. Empty food tins, scattered papers, torn bags, and discarded burlap sacks all indicated that the supplies came from neighbouring Kenya, and where, almost certainly, the hunter who had caused this desecration was from. Clary collected a few pieces of incriminating evidence, threw them into his car, then stood, engrossed in his own thoughts, staring blankly into space. He decided he was going to find the culprit who did this, come hell or high water.

This scum of a man had not even bothered to hunt the game on foot. He had let his clients shoot from the safety of a car, as evidenced by the numerous tyre tracks criss-crossing over the plains. This was not the work of a hunter, but of a repugnant killer.

The long drive back to Ruvu was conducted in complete silence. Not even an oryx running beside the vehicle elicited a glance from Clary.

Overwhelmed by despondency, he had difficulty concentrating on finishing the last few days of the current safari. His client had paid a small fortune and had taken a lot of time off work for his African safari, so there was no question about cutting it short. The American was very moved by Clary's concern for the welfare of the wild game, even if he hunted and killed a few animals on occasion. The two hunters talked late into the night about anything and everything, which helped Clary to overcome the worst of his depression. By the number of bones that the client had seen scattered over the plains, there was no doubt in his mind that Clary was telling the truth about a game Shangri-La, and it was not a hunter's tale.

As soon as the safari was completed, they hurried to Tanga, where the client caught a plane to Nairobi and then flew back to the United States.

Clary still had to prepare the trophies for shipment, clean his equipment, and complete a huge volume of paperwork before he was able to leave for Kenya to find this damned Satan who had destroyed his paradise at Kitwai.

Weeks later in Kenya, with the aid of his old acquaintances, it was quite easy to find the hunter responsible for desecrating Clary's piece of heaven on earth. After some investigating and a few straight questions to men in authority, the truth finally emerged.

The culprit turned out to be a new, young, professional hunter who could not get established in Kenya, as all the good hunting areas had been taken by old hands. He had to rely on the generosity of other established hunters to let him use their territory.

In those days in East Africa, professional hunters' licences, gun licences, and game licences were accepted in three territories, allowing the licence holder to hunt in all three of them. The only chance this young hunter had of making a name for himself was to look outside of Kenya for a hunting area. Being new and inexperienced, he really did not know which East African country to try and where to start looking.

At the same time, it was an open secret amongst the hunting fraternity that this hunter was having an affair with the wife of a game department officer. She worked as a clerk at the game department and had access to the confidential questionnaires that all hunters had completed. Her hunter-lover persuaded her to "borrow" these questionnaires for him to study one weekend, promising to return them to her by Monday morning. One of these was Clary's questionnaire, with his vivid description of his paradise and its location clearly marked on an ordinance map.

The hunter realised that he would have no chance to cross the Ruvu River, because Clary controlled the only crossing and kept its location secret.

However, it was a simple matter for him to hire a small Cessna plane in Nairobi and survey the site that Clary had so stupidly marked on his map. The newly graded road which connected the small towns had just been completed, and it passed less than 20 miles from the Kitwai Plains shown on Clary's questionnaire. There was a dry riverbed running from the road almost to the plains, and from the air, it looked passable for a hunting car and even a safari truck. It did prove to be passable, allowing the hunter to haul in all his safari equipment via that riverbed.

According to game licences issued to this hunter, he made more than eight successful safaris in the Kitwai Plains during a two-year period, earning himself a reputation as a hunter who conducted successful safaris and shot many excellent trophies with his clients. He was eventually employed by another safari outfitter.

He never admitted to the EAPHA committee that he had done anything wrong by acquiring the hunters' confidential questionnaires from the clerk. He only admitted to hunting on the Kitwai Plains. The information about the borrowed questionnaires only came to light when the husband put an end to his wife's affair, and she admitted giving her lover the questionnaires.

What annoyed and saddened Clary the most was the fact that when the EAPHA board members convened a meeting and were confronted with all the evidence of gross misconduct, they refused to take any action against their errant member, with the feeble excuse that expelling a member might ruin their reputation as an upright institution. Clary left the meeting in disgust. The next day, he handed in his membership resignation with a letter clearly and fully explaining his reason for doing so. He also sent a copy of this letter to the chief game wardens of Kenya and Tanganyika. It was this last act, namely the reports to the game wardens that irked the association so much that Clary was banned for life from the EAPHA.

Clary never applied again, never acknowledged their authority, and kept his professional hunters' licence all his life, in spite of the association's attempts to enforce the rule that all professional hunters be members.

Chapter 23
Hunting for Profit

Clary was as determined as ever to make a success of his hunting career. He had seen the potential of southern Maasailand, so he decided to make this his primary hunting ground. It was only a four-hour drive from his home in Tanga to the Ruvu River in Maasailand, which was a manageable distance.

After he discovered the shallow river crossing over the Ruvu, Clary decided to make his camp on the far bank under a large grove of wild fig trees. From this base camp, he cut rough tracks into the interior to provide access for his hunting safaris.

All along the riverbank lay dead, yellow-barked Acacia trees, known as fever trees. Many years earlier, some ludicrous English colonial medical officer had deduced that people living near these trees often caught malaria, so the trees must be the cause of the malaria fever. In his asinine wisdom, he ordered all yellow-barked Acacia trees to be cut down wherever they occurred. By the time the true malaria culprit was identified (a parasite spread by mosquitoes), large swathes of riverbanks had been denuded of these beautiful trees.

Beginning in 1890, an outbreak of rinderpest raged for decades throughout East Africa and beyond, before it was eventually brought under control by a massive inoculation campaign for cattle and sheep. It was estimated that 90 percent of Maasai cattle died during this outbreak, and 60 percent of the Maasai population died of starvation because their cattle are their sole food source, which is blood, milk and meat.

Most of the other tribes of Africa that relied on cattle for their livelihood were also decimated. Even farming communities that used oxen to pull their ploughs suffered from malnutrition, as they were unable to till the land to grow food.

A second outbreak occurred in East Africa during the First World War. Its cause was traced to infected cattle brought in during the war years to feed the troops. By 1925, it had been brought under control, but still occurred in isolated pockets of cattle that had evaded being inoculated. Later, it was discovered that rinderpest not only infected cattle but also buffalo, eland, warthogs, and other game as well. The infected wildlife caused rinderpest to spread into isolated areas that had previously been pest-free. Due to rinderpest, wildlife populations were decimated throughout Africa. This allowed the thorn bush to retake the open grassland where plains game and cattle had previously grazed. The thornbush environment proved to be ideal breeding grounds for tsetse flies, whose populations now increased and spread out. Tsetse flies carry sleeping sickness – a deadly disease for people and their livestock, which prevents human settlements. All wild game are capable of carrying the sleeping sickness parasite when bitten by a tsetse fly, but are immune to its effects. Tsetse flies are said to be the best game guardians, as they prevent human encroachment in their areas.

Clary always remembered the awful stench of rotting carcasses whenever he journeyed along the roads during these outbreaks. Even while hunting far away from cattle country, a permanent odour of death permeated the air.

Scavengers and predators were immune to rinderpest. Overfed vultures sat lethargically on tree branches, glutted by an overabundance of scavenged meat. Fat-bellied hyenas were so satiated that though they waddled away at any sign of approaching men, they immediately flopped down again a few yards away from the humans. Lions did not have to hunt, but simply sidled up to a weakened prey and brought it down easily with a bite to the sick animal's throat.

There were a few isolated pockets of wildlife that had avoided the ravages of rinderpest, and it was these healthy animals that eventually repopulated the country with game. And it was the proliferation of tsetse flies that kept these areas game rich and cattle-free.

Clary was always looking for an opportunity to go hunting for a few days, preferably with paying guests, although he was willing to take anybody out even for just a day. One of his clients was a local amateur hunter named Gordon who was about to return to England after a five-year contract in Tanganyika. Gordon desperately wanted to shoot a lion. He had shot plenty of small game, whose heads he was taking back as trophies, but he wanted the hide of the King of the Jungle as his ultimate trophy.

They settled on a price, and Clary guaranteed to show him a suitable lion or return his money. It was to be a weekend trip, which meant a basic camp for one or two nights. Lions were plentiful everywhere, but Clary knew a place two-and-a-half hours' drive from Tanga where lions could be hunted in open country, which was safer than hunting them in thick bush.

On their first afternoon at the hunting ground, Clary and Gordon climbed a low rocky hill to survey the surrounding country. Just below the hill, they saw a very sick buffalo, most likely ill with rinderpest. Clary ended its misery with a clean shot through the head, and decided to use it as lion bait. The men knew it would be dangerous for humans to consume any of the contaminated meat, so they prepared the carcass for the wildlife to eat. They cut open the stomach, spilling foul-smelling intestines over the bleak earth to attract lions to the kill. Then they cut a few big thorn branches to cover the dead animal. This would stop hyenas from eating the bait during the night.

"We'll come here early tomorrow morning and hopefully find a lion or two feeding on the carcass. Then you can shoot one", said Clary, as they headed back to base to eat a dinner of cold corned beef on white bread, washed down with a warm beer.

Early the next morning, while it was still dark, they drove to the little rocky hill. They waited in the car until it was light enough to see before climbing up the hill. Even from inside the car, they heard lions snarling and growling near the bait.

"They are at the bait. We are in luck", said Clary to his excited client.

The sun was just peeking over the treetops by the time they had reached the top of the hill. To their amazement, there were 26 lions of all sizes lounging around the dead buffalo just 50 yards below them. Clary immediately spotted a big black-maned lion, the clan chief, amongst the pride. There were three more shoot-able males in the bunch, all with beautiful golden manes.

This was going to be an easy hunt, mused Clary, then noticed that his client was not even looking at the animals. Gordon was in a cold sweat and staring at Clary with wide eyes.

"Take the golden-maned one; it's a beautiful colour", Clary said.

"You must be mad", croaked Gordon, "there are 26 of them down there. We only have two guns. What do we do if they attack us?" With that panicked statement, he crept back down the hill and ran for the safety of the car.

Clary stayed a few minutes longer to enjoy the sight of so many lions up close, knowing he might never see such a scene again. Back at the car, the big-lion-at-any-price hunter only wanted to get away from there as quickly as possible.

Gordon looked grim-faced as he sat in the safety of the car, and he said nothing for a long time while they drove towards camp. On the drive back to Tanga, Clary tried to cheer him up by telling him funny hunting stories, but it was no use.

Then Gordon explained his actions. "I have never been more scared in my life, and back there, I realised that I wanted to get back to England alive and well more than I wanted a lion skin rug for my sitting room."

Clary answered him by saying, "You did not shoot your lion, but you will never forget that moment, looking at 26 lions with nothing but a bit of grass between you and them. It was a very frightening experience, and you will cherish that memory all your life, which is even better than a lion skin rug."

Gordon was content to go home without his rug but alive. And Clary got to keep his fee.

When he had no safaris to lead and got fed up with town life (which was very often), and if his father did not need his help with the taxidermy business, Clary would load his car with camping gear and stay away for weeks at a time to hunt and explore new areas.

One time, when he was in his favourite South Maasailand hunting ground, he had his most frightening and close encounter with an elephant that he would ever experience.

Clary always wore long-sleeved shirts, long khaki trousers, heavy leather boots, and a wide-brimmed hat. An old hunting friend had advised him to dress this way to prevent being scratched by thorns, because those scratches could become infected very quickly. The thick leather boots protected against snakebites, and long-sleeved shirts and a wide-brimmed hat kept the sun off his skin. The old hunter's father had died of skin cancer brought on by overexposure to the sun, so Clary followed his friend's advice closely.

It was late morning when Clary and two trackers came across a large, fresh elephant spoor that indicated it was from a big old bull, so it was worth tracking. They had been following the spoor for half an hour when they heard an elephant feeding in some very thick, tall bushes close by. The fresh spoor was easy to follow in spite of the bush being ten feet tall and very dense. Visibility was reduced to a few feet in the thicket, although Clary could hear the elephant feeding and could judge how far away he was.

He left his trackers outside the dense bush and went on alone. He used his gun to push aside branches as he carefully and silently forced his way forward. He had his thumb on the safety catch and a finger guarding the triggers, ready for a hasty shot. After 20 minutes of spooring at this nerve-wracking, slow pace, Clary concluded that he was not getting closer, although he could hear the elephant clearly only a few feet away. It was feeding as it moved on slowly, not trying to be quiet or stopping to listen for danger. This meant that it had not detected Clary's presence.

He quickened his pace until he felt that the elephant was only inches away from him. At one point, Clary bent down to duck under some low-hanging branches when a hot, steaming elephant turd hit his hat and rolled down to his feet. He stopped dead, his breathing stopped, his heart pounded, and a huge dose of adrenaline coursed through his veins. Slowly, ever so slowly, he put pressure on the trigger and brought the heavy rifle up to his shoulder to shoot. He looked up, expecting to see an elephant's rear end in his face. Instead, he looked right into another fresh elephant turd hanging on thorns above his head. It plopped down to his feet as he touched the branch. The elephant had passed through that spot a few seconds previously, leaving his unmistakable signature stuck on the thorns. The huge creature was still somewhere a few feet ahead.

Clary started breathing again as he stood there shaking from an overdose of adrenaline and fear. Slowly, very slowly, he edged his way out of the thicket and went back to camp to relive his brush with death over a few stiff whiskys.

Chapter 24
Kanga's Story

Old bull elephants try to avoid any place where there is human activity. If they smell the spoor of a man or get wind of him, they will leave that area, travelling for days without resting or eating until they get far enough away to feel secure. They will seek out waterless areas to feed for extended periods of time, and avoid drinking from rivers where there are settlements nearby. They will get their water from chewing the bitter, fibrous Sansevieria leaves or gouging out fleshy pieces of baobab trunks to chew on.

Clary was checking out a dry waterless area for signs of elephants when he came across a large, dense patch of Sansevieria and noticed a wisp of blue smoke emanating from somewhere near the middle. He thought it may indicate a poacher's den. Cautiously, he and his two bearers walked around this patch until they found a well-concealed path leading into the Sansevieria. They followed the path and emerged into a very small clearing, where they saw a primitive grass shelter, some dried game skins, and a blackened earthenware cooking pot standing over a smouldering fire, but no one was there. Although they saw strips of dried meat draped over some branches, there was no sign of serious poaching. It was most likely an Ndorobo honey hunter's camp, they decided, which was quite acceptable, so Clary left again. The Maasai who have no cattle are called Ndorobo, meaning "poor people". They spend their lives roaming the bush, collecting wild honey and fruits to survive and catching small game to eat. They are true nomads of the bush, with no land, homes, or possessions, except what they carry on their backs.

A few days later, Clary realized that the Ndorobo man in the Sansevieria thicket would know if there were any big elephants around, so he went back to the camp to seek his help. Just before he reached the man's refuge, he saw someone running very fast out of the far end of the Sansevieria patch. He shouted for him to stop, but that only made the man run faster as he disappeared into the trees and didn't come back.

Clary and his bearers came back several times to try to talk to the frightened man. However, he ran away each time they approached his hideout. The man was obviously living alone, so he definitely was not a honey hunter, as the Ndorobo never travel alone. But then who was he? Clary would first have to win his trust before the mysterious recluse would come out of the bush and talk to them.

On his next visit, Clary took some tobacco and corn cobs and left them in the clearing by the grass hut. Two days later, when he came back, none of the items had been touched, although there were footprints all around them where someone had walked cautiously by. On the next visit, the tobacco and maize cobs were gone, so Clary left sugar and a blanket. This went on for a few days, although the nomad never showed himself, always running away at their approach. Clary got bored with his efforts and left no more presents, deciding instead to search for elephant signs himself.

After one particularly long day slogging through the bush, Clary and his two bearers returned to camp and saw his other camp staff sitting around a wizened, half-naked man, talking in very broken Swahili. It turned out that this man was the fugitive they had been trying to meet. He had actually walked into camp demanding to know why he had not received any more presents!

The little man's story was most interesting. He had no idea how old he was and didn't know his name. He had been born in a mud hut somewhere far away, where his family were lone subsistence farmers. He was the firstborn child and had to help till their tiny field, fetch water from a waterhole, and lay snares to catch small game and birds in the surrounding bush, as well as look after his younger siblings. When he was still small, his whole family came down with a disease, and they all died one after another, except for him and his father.

When his father had buried his family and recovered from his mourning, he told his son that he would go alone and search for another safer place to live and find a new wife. However, since his father had to walk a long distance very fast, he was to stay there at the farm and wait until his father returned.

The boy stayed at the hut and carried on tilling the ground, fetching water, and catching small game, just as he had done before. He put vegetables and meat into a cooking pot with water and set it over a fire, just as his mother had done. He cooked and ate whatever he could get from their field and whatever he caught in his snares. One night, some elephants came to his tiny farm and ate everything that was growing in his field. He was too scared to try to chase them off in case they attacked him. After that, he had to live off whatever he caught in his snares and any wild berries he found growing close by.

Some months later, when the rains came, his hut leaked badly, and big pieces of the mud walls were washed away by running water. It was no longer a safe place to live, because hyenas could easily enter the hut at night. So, every night, he built a fire in the hut and slept above it on sticks tied to cross beams under the roof.

One night, a pride of lions came to the hut and tried to get in, so he stoked the fire as much as he dared and used a long burning pole to poke at any animal that came close to the holes in the walls. By dawn, the lions had left. He survived the night deathly shaken, but finally decided to run far away from his home as the hut was falling apart and no longer kept out the wild animals and snakes. Also, his father had never returned to collect him and he had no idea what had happened to the man.

The boy took whatever he could carry on his little back and walked away through the bush, sleeping high up in thorn trees at night and scavenging for food during the day. He stayed in one place until he had snared and eaten all the small game he could catch, then moved on to another place. Once, he came to a village and entered it, hoping to live with the people, but due to his wild appearance and his lack of coherent Swahili, they chased him away by throwing stones at him whenever he appeared.

Laughing loudly, the little man told Clary how he lived close to the village for a long time, concealed in his sleeping place high in a tree. He observed the villagers from a safe distance during the day, and at night he stole food from their fields. Sometimes he crept into the village in broad daylight and stole freshly washed pieces of clothing which had been put to dry on the ground in front of a hut. Other times he took chicken eggs and even snared a live chicken, which he grilled over a fire and ate.

Then one day, they almost caught him as he was stealing eggs, and he had to run for his life. They chased him through the bush trying to catch him but gave up when darkness fell. He was far from his sleeping tree, so he climbed the nearest tree and clung to a branch, shivering the night away. The next day, he slipped back unnoticed to retrieve his meagre belongings from his tree, then left the area far behind. After that experience, he vowed never to live close to any community again.

All this had happened many, many rainy seasons ago, he explained. Since then, he had learned to live in the bush on his own and had no fear of any animals. He only feared people.

He knew about tobacco because he had observed men in the fields harvesting leaves, drying and rolling them up, and lighting them to smoke. He coughed intensely the first time he tried tobacco and could not understand why people tortured themselves like this, although now he had got used to smoking and enjoyed a puff now and again. He told Clary that he still stole tobacco leaves at night from nearby villages and rolled his own cigarettes.

He learned how to collect honey from a passing group of Ndorobo honey hunters who took him in and showed him how to follow the honeyguide bird, smoke the bees, take the honey, and never forget to leave a reward for the honey bird. They taught him how to cure animal skins with wood ash and make clothes from them, using Sansevieria twine to stitch them together. From the honey hunters he learned how to form and string a bow with dried animal sinews, and how to make straight, hard, wooden arrows by bending and strengthening them in a fire.

He knew how and where to find water all over the countryside and when and where to find wild fruits. He did not know how to read or write, but he did know how to read signs in the bush that were important to him, and how to leave marks in the bush that any bush wise person could interpret.

The camp staff gave him the name "Kanga", meaning guinea fowl, because he had decorated his animal skin loincloth with guinea fowl feathers. He liked that name and always referred to himself thereafter as Kanga. Clary gave him a panga and a new knife, as Kanga's were worn down to stumps.

From the day he walked into camp, Kanga became one of Clary's most reliable and infallible trackers. To encourage Kanga to stay close-by and work on future safaris, Clary appropriated a fertile piece of land downstream from camp and built a mud hut for the little man, complete with iron cooking pots and a wooden bed. He paid a local tribesman to give Kanga some vegetable seedlings and show him how to grow them. Kanga stayed there contentedly for many years, eventually taking a wife, although he had no children.

On Kanga's first hunt as Clary's guide, he walked so fast that the others could not keep pace with him. He was admonished for walking too fast and not taking precautions to avoid dangerous game. He laughed and said there were no dangerous animals on his route. When asked how he knew, he said it was very clear because during the day, animals rested in the dense patches of bush and there was neither dense bush nor fresh animal odours here.

Late one afternoon, after a very long and hot day in the bush, Clary's party ran out of water and asked Kanga if he knew where to find some nearby. He looked at the ground, shook his head, then walked over to a high thorn tree and climbed it, oblivious to the three-inch thorns on its branches. He descended a few minutes later, pointed with a skinny outstretched hand and said, "This way, not far away is water."

Not far away could mean trekking for a few minutes to several hours. It was futile to ask how long it would take to get to the water, as time was an unknown factor for Kanga. His reasoning was simple; they had no water, but had plenty of time. They eventually stopped in front of an old baobab tree that was regularly used as a resting place by elephants.

Kanga said, "Here is water", and pointed to elephant footmarks high up on the tree trunk, then up to a fork in the tree. The thirsty trackers stared at him, puzzled as to the whereabouts of the promised water.

During the rainy season, water collects inside hollows in baobab trunks where it is protected from evaporation. When the hollow is large enough, water remains all year round. Clary could see where elephants had stood on their hind legs and put their front feet on the tree trunk, so that they could suck out water with their trunks from inside a hollow in the tree. Kanga skilfully clambered up the baobab using uneven bark folds as hand and foot holds. At the top, he grinned down at them and nodded his head.

"Maji mingi", he said. Plenty of water.

Someone threw him a rope with a steel water bottle attached. He lowered the bottle into a hollow in the tree fork and pulled it out full of water. The water was dark and full of larvae and floating debris, but by filtering it through a handkerchief, it became drinkable, although it remained dark, stale, and bitter. Excepting Kanga, they would all have upset stomachs that night, but it was a small price to pay for water in the dry bushland.

One night in camp there was a very heavy downpour which had stopped by early morning. Clary went over to the staff tent that was on high ground to see if any boxes or bags of food had been washed away. Everything was still in place, and even if soaking wet, it would soon dry out when placed in the sun. Kanga preferred to sleep on the bare ground away from the rest of the crew, so Clary walked out of camp a few yards and found him still asleep, wrapped from head to foot in his soaking wet blanket. He was lying in three inches of water. When Clary called out to him, Kanga sat up, looked around in astonishment and said, "What! Did it rain last night?"

Kanga showed no fear whenever they were in a dangerous situation. He was always at Clary's side and never ran away when they were charged by an animal. The only time Kanga did run off was when he went hunting with Clary for the first time. Clary shot at an eland with the .375 rifle. At the sound of the shot, Kanga yelled and ran for his life into the bush as fast as his little legs could carry him. Ten minutes later he came back laughing, shaking his head as he made little clucking sounds. He said he had never heard such a loud bang in his life, except for thunder, when it was raining. He had run away out of sheer terror at such a noise, then ventured back when he realised that no one else had fled. After that incident, he never ran away again from a gun being fired, but refused to act as a gun bearer and carry a gun. He said he was scared that it might go bang and kill him, in spite of Clary's efforts to show him that it could never do so. To make matters worse, a few days later another gun bearer accidentally discharged a gun harmlessly into the air while clambering through a dense bush. It made everyone jump, and this reinforced Kanga's fear of carrying guns.

Clary had to dismiss this same clumsy gun bearer a few weeks later when he ran away with a rifle at a most critical time. It happened this way. Clary was looking through his binoculars at an elephant when they were attacked from one side by a disturbed rhino. He reached around to his gun bearer for the rifle, but the terrified man was already running away with it. Clary ran after him and shouted repeatedly for him to drop the gun. However, on seeing Clary running, the gun bearer ran even faster. He eventually lost his grip on the gun and dropped the weapon. Clary retrieved it from the ground just as the immense rhino thundered past him and disappeared into the thick bush. All the other men dove out of the way when the rhino started its charge, so luckily there were no injuries amongst the party.

The scared gun bearer was found later, hiding in the topmost branches of a thorn tree, refusing to come down. He only relented and climbed down when a tracker stood under the tree and assured him that danger had passed. Clary told him that as a gun bearer he must never run away in the face of danger, but stand by the hunter all the time. A tracker or porter was expected to run when danger threatened, but never a gun bearer. He was immediately demoted to porter and later sent home.

One morning, many years later, when Clary was camped deep inside the southern Maasai steppe on a personal safari to get the last elephant on his licence, he came across a very large elephant spoor. The animal had been to the local waterhole during the night and had gone back into the bush the way it came, leaving clear footprints to follow. By the way its large feet left deep imprints on the ground, it was obviously a huge elephant and very likely carried big tusks, making it well worth following. Clary went back to camp to fetch water bottles and some biltong, then began to give chase with Kanga and another tracker. This was the only fresh elephant spoor they had seen, so it was easy for Kanga to track the heavy footprints over the hard, stony ground.

The animal meandered between the thickets in a leisurely way, feeding as it went. It was not in a hurry to go anywhere. By midday, when the wind turns and twists and comes from all directions, they were concerned that the elephant would catch their scent and run off, so Clary and his men stopped where they were for a rest and a drink of water. Later, when the wind settled in one direction, they continued the hunt. By mid-afternoon they had not caught up to the animal so had to make a decision: break off the hunt now and return to camp in daylight, or continue tracking and spend the night in the bush. They felt there may never be another chance to hunt a large elephant like this one, so decided to continue the hunt.

Late in the afternoon, they heard the elephant breaking branches inside a dense grove close by, but could not find a tall tree to climb to observe it. Cautiously, they walked around to the other side of the grove where they found a big tree that would afford them a good view over the surrounding country. A tracker climbed up and immediately signalled to Clary that he could see the elephant. His pulse racing with excitement, Clary climbed up, and from the top branches he could just make out the ridge of the elephants back above the thicket. Judging the animal against the size of the surrounding trees, he concluded that this was a massive elephant. However, the animal's tusks remained hidden from view in the bushes. The sun was starting to go down, so it was futile to continue the hunt through the thicket with the hope of getting close to the elephant before dark. They would have to find a place to rest for the night, collect some firewood for a fire to ward off curious animals, and continue the hunt tomorrow.

They walked about half a mile away from the elephant and found a small clearing where they could camp. Firewood was plentiful, but they had to keep the fire small, as its smoke might drift towards their quarry and alert it to danger. Elephants associate smoke with the presence of man, and this colossus would surely flee if it smelled their fire.

As darkness fell, they huddled around the flickering flames while chewing on some hard biltong and sipping tepid water. The group slept fitfully on the hard, bare earth by the little fire, its meagre heat radiating little warmth against the chilly night air. Kanga was the only one who slept well, as he was in his element. They were all up before the sun. Breakfast consisted of the last of the water and biltong, then they returned to the grove to seek their prey.

They picked up the elephant's spoor again, not far from where they had last seen it the day before, and continued the chase. The hunting party stopped only twice during the day, once to relieve their hunger by picking a few ripe wild plums, and a second time to collect water from a waterhole a mile off their track which Kanga located by listening to flying sandgrouse going for their morning drink. At midday, they were still a few hours behind the elephant but decided to continue, since the animal was unlikely to move much during the heat of the day, giving the hunters a chance to close the gap. They also realised that this elephant had walked in a half-circle since leaving the waterhole where they had first seen it, putting them within half a day's walk of camp. By early afternoon, they had closed the gap to less than an hour's walk behind the animal, and the spoor became easier to follow on the softer ground.

Just as they were closing in on the elephant, it entered a grove of very dense thorn bushes and spent most of the afternoon feeding noisily there. It would be madness for the men to go into such an impenetrable thicket, so they were forced to wait impatiently outside the grove. However, their quarry showed no intention of leaving its thorny fortress any time soon.

Although they were only half a day's walk from camp, the attraction of such a large elephant nearly within their grasp was too much of a temptation for the hunters to give up now, so they agreed to spend another night sleeping on the trail, hoping for better luck the next day.

They broke off the hunt and found a place to spend the night. Kanga made some string from the bark of a branch and went off to catch something to eat, while the others looked for wild plums and other edible berries. Clary walked to a half-dry waterhole polluted with animal turds, where many colourful butterflies flitted about. Using his hands, he dug a small hollow in the mud near the side of the waterhole and let water seep into it from below. Then he took out of his jacket pocket a small glass jar that contained a piece of Alum wrapped in brown paper. This jar lived permanently in a side pocket of the haversack for just such occasions. He took the piece of Alum and jiggled it in the dirty water. After ten minutes, the mud particles settled to the bottom, and he was able to fill up all four water bottles. It made the water taste tart, but rendered it safe to drink.

Kanga came into their camp beaming with pride, holding a guinea fowl that he had snared with his homemade rope. That night, they dined on freshly grilled guinea fowl and wild plums. Kanga loved the grilled entrails, uncleaned, and finished the whole lot by himself.

On the third day of their hunt, they were pleased to find that the big elephant had not gone very far during the night. The prospect of getting close to it today gave them all a morale boost. Before the sun got too high in the cloudless sky, they came within earshot of the foraging giant. Clary climbed a tree and immediately saw the rump of the big bull a few hundred yards away, browsing slowly through the bush. By the way its back arched low and its wrinkled hide hung loosely over its frame, he knew that this was a very old elephant. The bush thinned out ahead of the animal and the wind was still favourable, so Clary decided to go in after the elephant alone, leaving his men by the tree. He stalked like a silent predator to within 50 yards of the noisily munching creature, but still could not get a glimpse of its tusks. Then it turned sideways and moved into a small opening in the thicket.

Clary's heart fell as he got a good look at the small tusks. It was, indeed, a very old elephant. Its tusks were thick, short, and very stumpy, having been worn down over a lifetime of constant use. They would not even weigh 40 pounds a side, hardly enough ivory to cover safari expenses. It was a heart-wrenching disappointment after such a long and hard hunt. Clary felt inclined to shoot this elephant out of frustration and anger. He put his gun to his shoulder and aimed carefully at the enormous head, but could not gather enough fury to pull the trigger. Instead, he watched as the elephant walked away, unaware of how close it had been to death. Clary walked out to his waiting crew, and told them the bad news. Silent and dispirited, they returned to camp. A day later, they broke camp and trucked back to the Ruvu.

That was Clary's last safari with Kanga. The brave little man eventually grew old and frail. His eyesight failed him. His sense of smell and hearing left him. He could no longer walk or stalk the wild game as he so much loved to do. Kanga did not die; he just faded away until he was no longer there.

Chapter 25
Malaria and Champagne

During this stay on the Ruvu River, Clary contracted a serious case of malaria. He had had this disease many times before without any serious effects. But this time, he had a fever and felt cold all over – a sure sign of malaria. Sometimes he had shivering bouts hour after hour in spite of the hot weather. After taking a few quinine tablets, the fever subsided, the shivering stopped, and he thought he was rid of the disease. However, the fever returned, and the shivering got worse and more frequent.

He took a double dose of quinine, but this merely lengthened the intervals between his shivering bouts. He thought he must have caught malaria before he went after his big elephant, and had overstrained his body during those three strenuous days of hunting. Now he was paying the price for his mistake. Perhaps, he surmised, if he rested in camp for a while, he could recover more quickly. So he took his last quinine tablets and sat in camp, taking it easy, cleaning his guns or fishing from the riverbank for tilapia, which were jumping after flies in the shallows.

However, his condition became worse. His fever rose so high that he had to constantly wash himself with cold water in an effort to cool off. The shivering came more often and was stronger each time. Worst of all, his urine was turning dark red. Clary realised that he not only had full-blown malaria but also blackwater fever, which occurs in the end stage of malaria. Blackwater fever is caused by an excessive amount of red blood cells, which were destroyed by the malaria parasite, flowing through the bloodstream into the kidneys. The kidneys cannot clean the blood quickly enough so it flows out with the urine, causing it to turn black. The final stage comes when the kidneys become totally blocked and can no longer function. The patient eventually dies a slow, lingering death from blood poisoning.

In his weakened condition, it was now too late to try driving to a hospital, as none of his men knew how to drive, and much too late to send a tracker on foot to get medical help. Realising that this could be his last day on earth, Clary wrote an explanatory letter to whoever found his body, informing them that his staff were innocent of any blame for his demise, and that the culprit was blackwater fever. He gave this letter to one of his men, with instructions to hand it to the police or a commissioner if he did not wake up the next morning.

However, Clary knew of one last desperate act that might save his life.

A few years earlier, he had been on safari with a French doctor who hoped to shoot a big elephant. In expectation of success and to celebrate the occasion, the doctor brought a magnum of the best French champagne with him. In the end, he failed to shoot a big tusker. Nevertheless, he left the champagne with Clary, advising him to drink it with whoever shot the next hundred pounder. Being a doctor, the Frenchman also told Clary that if he ever had a kidney problem, he should drink the champagne as it would flush out his system and he would be as good as new.

Clary now took out the oversized champagne bottle, propped himself upright with a soft pillow in his camp bed, and started to drink.

"If I am going to die, I am going to die a very happy man", he said to himself, then added, "a very drunk happy man". He finished the whole bottle that night.

When he awoke the next day in the early afternoon, it was not the face of the devil smiling at him, as he had expected, but rather his grinning cook, bringing him a cup of lukewarm tea.

Clary had one humongous hangover, but nonetheless, he felt on top of the world. He had cured himself of blackwater fever, thanks to a faraway French doctor and excellent French champagne.

Chapter 26
The Lupa Gold Rush

In 1938, gold was discovered in the Lupa river in western Tanganyika. Word of this gold strike and stories of instant wealth obtained by lucky prospectors spread like wildfire throughout the country. It seemed as if everybody was dropping tools and running off to make their fortune in gold.

The news did not escape Clary's attention for long, and he and his cousin Joe, who was in Tanga working at odd jobs, decided to try their luck at gold panning on the Lupa.

The two pooled their money, bought an old Hudson car with a modified wooden pick-up back, and bought spare tyres, inner tubes, tools, petrol cans, oil, tins of food, bags of flour, leather strips, and a roll of baling wire that could be used to repair anything and everything on a car.

The Lupa goldfields were at the other end of the country, a 600-mile journey over rough roads, with sparsely populated areas, a few petrol stations, no places to stay, and very little help if you broke down along the way. Their old car was not only over-loaded with spares but also provisions to last several weeks, as well as picks, shovels, panning plates, and camping equipment, which included beds, mattresses, pillows, blankets, cooking pots, pans, cutlery, crockery, water tanks, stove, and a bag of charcoal. Somewhere in the packed car, they also found a place to stow their clothes, boots, medicine, and bottles of Scotch.

Very early one morning, before anyone saw them in their overloaded, leaning-to-the-left, rattling, squeaking jalopy, they started on their way west towards the Lupa and their hoped-for fortune.

Although the gravel road out of Tanga was smooth and well maintained, they had the first of many, many punctures before noon on the first day, forcing them to make a pit stop for repairs. The next puncture came just before dark on the same day, but instead of repairing it immediately, they pumped it up and raced into the next town before the tyre went flat.

They spent the night in the town, sleeping on the hard earth-packed floor in an empty road worker's hut. The next morning they repaired the flat tyre and put two new tyres and tubes onto the spare rims in anticipation of the next puncture. Before they set off again, the cargo had to be redistributed to reduce the left-leaning list, as this overweight was suspected to be the cause of the previous two punctures.

Amazingly, after the cargo redistribution, the old Hudson ran well for two days without a hitch until a front spring broke while they were speeding over a corrugated section of road, sending them screeching across the road and into the opposite ditch in a cloud of red dust. Fortunately, the main leaf spring broke two-thirds of the way along its length, so it could be temporarily repaired by binding it together with baling wire. It would hold until they reached the next garage, where it could be changed for a spare that they had on board somewhere, deep down underneath everything. The search for the spring would require an hour to unload the car entirely in order to find the part. At the next town, they did just that, eventually finding the spare spring underneath the last item to be unloaded.

After four days of uneventful travelling along smooth main roads, they decided to turn off to take a poorly maintained secondary road that was rougher and hillier but was a shortcut that would reduce the driving distance quite a bit and perhaps the driving time.

Wisely, they drove slowly along this un-kept section of road, as it allowed them to spot and avoid potholes. Driving fast on these corrugated roads shook cars so badly that pieces tended to fall off, unnoticed by the driver. Sometimes, if it was not a critical part that was lost, the car travelled for many miles before the driver realised that something was not right. Then he would stop, get out, look at the void left by the missing part, curse the road, curse the road works, curse Africa, and, having satiated his anger, drive on, making a mental note to stop at the next garage and have the missing part replaced.

Clary, ever the opportunist, kept an eye out for any metal parts lying on the dusty road and stopped to pick them up. Even if they looked broken and unusable, he knew how to repair or alter them to use them again.

The two unshaven, dust-covered travellers celebrated their tenth puncture on the journey by camping under a shady tree by the roadside and getting very drunk. With glass after glass of whisky diluted with warm water, they cursed the roads, the cars, all tyres and their makers, and cursed the heat, the dust, the flies, and their luck.

When rubber gets old, it gets brittle, and when it gets hot, it loses its strength, so when an old and hot tyre is pumped up hard, it will burst. Every spare inner tube of theirs had been repaired so many times that they looked like spotted snakes. Their supply of tube patches and rubber solution to repair the punctures was running out quickly. Some of the tyres were split open along their sides, rendering them all but useless. Clary had learned at Riddoch Motors to fix any car problems by using whatever was available, and now was a good time to try out what he had learned about tyres.

Clary cut part of a tent groundsheet into long, wide strips that he tacked inside the walls and bottom of the best tyres, to strengthen the casing. He then split an inner tube open along the inside and squeezed another inner tube inside the first one, forming a double-walled tube. This double tube was put into the reworked tyre and pumped up hard. It held the air admirably. By doing the same trick with all the tyres on their old iron donkey, they were able to continue their journey at a safe, slow speed, untroubled by more punctures.

However, their vehicle problems were not over yet. Their next major breakdown came just after the halfway mark on the journey. The engine was making a rather unusual noise, and it was getting louder and louder each day until a heavy vibration signalled that something big was about to break. They limped slowly into the next town and shut down at a petrol station. They discovered the knocking sound came from the engine block – a serious problem sector. With some help from the garage owner, Clary took out the engine, laid it on a wooden bench, and opened it up using his own tools. As he suspected, it was an engine main bearing that was worn out and causing the knocking sound, which meant they had a major problem.

Of course, there were no spare bearings for this engine anywhere in town, and none that could be made to fit. Unfortunately, Clary had not bothered to carry spare bearings with him. He was told that the correct bearing could be ordered from the dealer in Kenya and would be here in less than a month.

In a month's time all the gold in the Lupa would be gone, was Clary's answer when the station owner asked whether or not to order the part.

Casting about, Clary noticed that Joe had a very nice, thick leather belt, which he wore with pride every day. It had the same width and thickness as the worn-out engine bearing, so Clary thought it might work as a substitute bearing in an emergency such as this.

With tears in his eyes, Joe watched as Clary cut the middle piece of his beloved belt to fit perfectly into the bearing space. A disbelieving young African mechanic helped Clary assemble the engine and install it back into the Hudson. They were watched by a group of smiling sceptics standing around shaking their heads at this foolish young man who thought he could replace steel with leather.

Their smiles faded into open-mouthed astonishment as Clary started the engine and let it run smoothly for ten minutes. The knock was gone! The engine was repaired! He motioned for Joe to get in the car, waved goodbye, and drove off, leaving the sceptics still shaking their heads and saying, "They won't get far."

But they were wrong, as the leather bearing held all the way to the Lupa and back home.

However, they were fated to be plagued by more car problems before they reached their destination.

At a river crossing, they pulled up under some shady wild fig trees to have a bite to eat, drink from their rations, and perhaps take a little snooze in the shade for an hour.

While lying on the ground close to the Hudson, Joe noticed a thick red wire hanging loose under the engine compartment. On investigation, it turned out to be the positive battery cable with no battery attached to it. On the negative battery cable was a piece of broken battery. Somewhere on the road the battery box had shaken itself loose from its mountings and fallen off, taking most of the battery with it. The old Hudson squeaked and rattled so much when being driven that no one had noticed the noise of the dangling battery as it bounced and scraped along the road until it finally fell off. These old cars could run without a battery as they had a dynamo driven by a fan belt, which produced sufficient electricity to ignite the spark plugs when the engine was running. The dynamo also had enough capacity to supply electric power for the lights and the engine gauges. However, without a battery, the electric starter did not work.

Nevertheless, the engine could be started with a starting handle. This was a "Z"-shaped steel shaft poking out through a hole in the front bumper that was connected to a socket on the engine crankshaft. With a few hefty swings from a strong arm on the handle, the engine would spring to life. The car could also be started by letting it roll down a hill and engaging a gear. The loss of the battery was an inconvenience but did not stop the journey. The last part of their trip was through fairly hilly country, necessitating slow climbs in first gear and resulting in a constantly overheating radiator. Frequent stops were required to let it cool down and be refilled with water. At each river crossing, the water tanks they carried were re-filled.

Somewhere in the middle of nowhere, when they stopped to have a snack and fill the fuel tank from their reserve canisters, they noticed that one canister had sprung a leak and was nearly empty, meaning that they did not have enough petrol to reach the next petrol station. There was nothing they could do except pour in their last canister and drive on as far as it would take them.

By a stroke of good luck, they soon saw a farmhouse a little distance off the road, and drove over to it. They were welcomed by a well-dressed servant into a farmhouse covered with bougainvillea, and invited to partake of cool drinks with the stocky Italian farm owner. He regretted that he had no petrol to spare, having only enough in his car to get him to the next town. He went on to say that many cars had stopped here for food, water, petrol, or to stay overnight on their way to the gold rush.

Clary saw that the farmer had a tractor driving around his fields and enquired about its fuel. The friendly farmer explained that the tractor's engine was started with diesel and, when warm, it was switched over to another tank containing TVO, or tractor vaporising oil, which was a very cheap crude oil, on which the hot engine ran all day.

The Italian had plenty of TVO in drums in his tractor shed, and Clary was welcome to buy some if he could use it. Clary knew that the TVO had to be hot in order for the carburettor to vaporise it for his Hudson engine. He did this by heating the carburettor manifold with burning charcoal on a tin plate which he held under the manifold until it was hot enough to try to start the engine. Strong-arm Joe gave the big steel starting handle a hefty swing. At the first stroke, thick black smoke belched from the exhaust pipe like an old steam train, but the engine kept running and finally settled down to a steady purr. Soon the exhaust pipes below the carburettor kept the TVO hot enough to be vaporised and run the engine.

Clary and Joe filled the car's petrol tank and two spare canisters with TVO. Then, with special thanks to the helpful farmer, they left in their smoking, dirty Hudson, bouncing over the farm road to make a right onto the main road heading west towards the Lupa.

Arriving at the next town with a petrol station, they expected to refuel and be on their way as quickly as possible. Unfortunately, too many cars on their way to the Lupa had passed through here, and the drivers had bought all the fuel. Even the little grocery shops had run out of food. Only the bar where Clary and Joe stopped in for refreshments was still well-stocked with cold beer and hard liquor, and there was a smiling barman behind the long wooden counter to serve them. Having enough TVO in the car to keep them going to the next town, they continued their journey.

Somewhere along the road on their long and boring journey westwards, they decided to stay for the night in the open countryside. They found a hill where they could park the car so that it could be started easily by running it downhill in the morning. During the night, it started raining, and the potential gold-diggers were forced to get up and spend the rest of an uncomfortable night sleeping upright in the car seats. It was still drizzling in the morning, so they could not light the wet firewood to make a cup of tea. However, Clary managed to light some charcoal to heat the carburettor manifold to start the car's engine. With the manifold well and truly hot, they let the car roll down the hill, engaged first gear, and let out the clutch. Much banging and firing emanated from the engine before it caught in a belching cloud of black exhaust smoke, then ran smoothly just as it had done before.

In the next town, they found a dirty place with unappetizing food, but ate there anyway as they were half-starving.

The spark plugs needed constant cleaning because the TVO fouled them very quickly. As Clary was cleaning them with a wire brush, he noticed that the engine oil was low. There was no place here selling oil, but he saw an old, broken-down tractor in a nearby field. The owner of the tractor helped Clary drain some of the tractor's dirty engine oil through a waste cloth to remove most of the soot. Then this half-clean oil was poured into the Hudson's engine. It would do until they reached a proper garage selling clean oil. There was some TVO in the tractor's fuel tank, which Clary also bought.

After 16 days on the road, many breakdowns, and too many punctures to count, the dirty, dusty, unshaven, tired, and hungry pair rolled into the town of Lupa. Finally, they could start looking for their fortune.

Chapter 27
Life on a Gold Field

In Lupa they found organised chaos. Along the wide main road, there was the usual general store, a bank, a post office, a hairdresser, prostitute dens catering to black and white clients, a land and claims office, and at the far end a hotel with an oversize bar. Behind these buildings were wooden shacks, corrugated tin huts, and hundreds of tents, all haphazardly constructed by their owners, making it impossible to walk through in a straight line. Here resided the prospectors, living like dogs and hoping to strike it rich one day.

Clary and Joe pitched their tent in a clearing just outside of town, where they found a place affording some peace and privacy.

Running along one side of the town was a stream from which everyone collected drinking and washing water. This stream was also used for washing the tons of gold-bearing earth through sluices. Since it was the only source of water, it was forbidden for anyone to sluice gold before 9am, giving the townspeople time to collect clean water to use for the day.

To cater to the hygienic needs of the prospectors in the slums, the town council set aside a stretch of ground outside of town where round holes had been dug in the earth at intervals to make "long drop toilets". Small tents for privacy were erected over each hole. After each "visit", a spade full of excavated earth was thrown into the hole to reduce the stench. When a toilet became full with excrement and earth, a new hole was dug three feet away to replace it. As a result, the toilets were moved three feet backwards into new ground every month.

Before they were allowed to start digging for gold, Clary and Joe were required to buy prospectors' licences from the land office and buy a gold claim from the claims office next door. Then they had to hire African labourers who used pickaxes and spades to dig out gold-bearing earth from their claim. The workers then carried the earth to the river in buckets, where Clary and Joe washed it in a pan. Any gold they found went into a clear glass bottle for safekeeping. When the bottle was full it was taken to the claims office where its glistening contents were weighed, assessed, and paid for by cheque.

Most of the gold found at Lupa was flakes of alluvial gold, but sometimes small nuggets were brought into the claims office, and very occasionally a large nugget or clump of gold encased in earth appeared.

When Clary saw the prices at the general store for spades, pickaxes, and buckets, he was happy that he had brought his own all the way from Tanga. Even the prices for tinned food and dry goods were four times higher than at home. He could have sold all his food and equipment and come away with a small fortune. Some prospectors did just that, by giving up their search for gold and selling all their used equipment for more than the price they had paid for it new.

Every morning, women from local communities brought in fresh fruit and vegetables from their gardens, and sometimes beef or goat meat, to sell in Lupa town. However, their prices were so high they were unaffordable for most poor prospectors. Clary found that the prices dropped dramatically at the end of the day so he could bargain them down even further in the evening, although by that time there were only leftover supplies to choose from.

Prospectors came there from all over the world. Some had been at the California gold rush, the Klondike, the Amazon, and many other places that few people had even heard about. They had all made money on gold, but none of them had made enough to permanently retire, so that was why they were there now.

The first week that Clary and Joe were in Lupa, a prospector came into the bar one evening with a round gold-encrusted rock the size of a handball. It was passed around for everyone to drool over and dream about. As the evening wore on, the owner of the gold told and retold the story of how he had found it deep down in his claim. He ordered drinks for everyone to celebrate his find. Then a spontaneous football game started on a cleared space on the bar room floor, using the gold rock as a ball. The game went on well past midnight before the drunks and half-drunks finally staggered back to their hovels.

A few inebriated folks, including the owner of the gold rock, could not even crawl to the doorway to go home, so the bar owner locked the front door and left them asleep on the floor. The next morning, to the dismay of the owners, it was discovered that during the night someone had hacked off a large piece of gold from the rock and made off with it. The culprit was never found.

Clary learned that this wild behaviour was quite common whenever someone hit pay dirt. It was worth being in the bar at these times just for the free drinks and inspiring stories from the lucky fellow.

Late one afternoon when he was in the bar with Joe, two young prospectors arrived and demanded a bathtub be brought in to celebrate their windfall. A bathtub was brought down from one of the upstairs bedrooms and the young prospectors climbed in, muddy boots and all. They ordered the barman to fill the tub with champagne. So, the obliging barman poured bottle after bottle of warm champagne over the two happy men as they sat in the tub, scooping up muddy glasses full of bubbly to slurp or throw over each other or nearby admirers. They announced that they had found some large nuggets on their claim and were expecting to find a lot more. But as life's unpredictable twists and turns prove, they never found any more large nuggets and left a year later, completely broke. Half the money they received for their first nuggets went to the happy barman to pay for champagne and drinks for patrons that memorable night.

An old Klondike prospector named Bill came to Lupa early in the rush. He bought a good claim, found a lot of gold, and built himself a two-room wooden house on high ground above the town, which he outfitted with nice furniture and carpets.

One morning he failed to turn up at his claim to supervise his diggers. This was so unusual that a friend went to the house and found old Bill lying dead in his bed, having died peacefully in his sleep. Word of his death spread rapidly around the community, and a stream of people went to his home to pay their last respects, including Clary and Joe. All of Bill's many bottles of booze were opened and placed on a sitting room table for grievers to help themselves to a drink.

Bill's friends sat there drinking toast after toast to their old friend while a stream of mourners filed through the house.

A griever decided that Bill should have a decent burial in a wooden coffin. Wood was hard to come by, so people were asked to donate any piece of wood that they could spare. Pieces of wood came pouring in from everywhere, and an African carpenter was tasked with turning the pile of donated wood into a strong coffin large enough to accommodate Bill's ample frame.

That afternoon a heavy, rudimentary coffin was delivered to Bill's house and placed on the sitting room floor, while old friends still sat there toasting Bill. One of these friends decided that since the coffin was ready, Bill needed to be buried somewhere very soon. So, a troop of African gold diggers were selected and told to dig a grave at a patch of ground reserved as a burial ground.

Then another half-drunk friend reasoned that before Bill could be officially buried, he needed a death certificate, but as there was no doctor in town to certify Bill's demise, a police constable was asked to write out a certificate of death on police letterhead. The constable duly arrived, looked at Bill on the bed, felt for his pulse and, finding none, declared him dead, then signed his home-made death certificate.

Someone from the group hinted that to bury Bill in the proper manner they would need a priest to preside over the service. However, as no church existed in Lupa, there was no priest or pastor. To solve this dilemma, the bank manager, who was a respected person in the community, was deputised to perform the burial service, which he reluctantly agreed to do.

The next day, almost all the prospectors dressed in their finest had gathered at the burial ground for Bill's funeral. The bank manager was there to say a little eulogy for Bill and send him on his way, but embarrassingly, they had forgotten to bring the coffin. So, four strapping African diggers were told to go to Bill's house and bring it down immediately. In the meantime, a bottle of alcohol was produced and passed around to toast old Bill for the last time.

The coffin eventually arrived, except the Africans had forgotten to bring ropes to lower it into the grave. Another oversight was that nobody had bothered to tell the African diggers how deep to dig the grave, so they had dug until they reached bedrock, which was almost 20 feet down. The stoical bank manager agreed with the impatient crowd's opinion that, because it was Bill's last journey, he would not mind the 20-foot drop. The eulogy was tearfully delivered, and the coffin was dropped into the grave, crashing loudly onto the bedrock below. Everyone in attendance now filed past to say a few final words and toss a handful of earth onto the coffin. Then one by one, all the mourners went home, and the African diggers were left to fill in the deep grave with the remaining earth.

A few of Bill's friends decided to go back to his house to see if there were any belongings of his that should be sent home to his relatives. They went into Bill's bedroom and found him still lying dead on his bed. Someone had forgotten to tell the Africans to put Bill inside his coffin before bringing it down.

With great secrecy and embarrassment, Bill's sobered-up friends had another coffin made, another shallower grave dug next to the first one, and they quietly buried him one dark night, making old Bill the only person in Tanganyika to be buried twice.

After one year at the Lupa, Clary and Joe had exhausted their claim and decided to head home with what little money they had made.

Other than the hardware store owner who made a lot of money on his overpriced goods, there were only three other people who made their fortune at the Lupa goldfields. One was the barman, and the others were two young German prospectors who came very late to the Lupa when all the claims worth working had been dug over a few times. They bought a "dead" claim, which was considered unproductive, and worked it over slowly. Each day they came into the claims office with a few ounces of gold to sell. At the bar, they avoided all questions concerning their method of working the claim. After only four months at the Lupa, they packed up and left with a sizable fortune.

On their farewell night at the bar, they revealed their source of gold. They had worked the dead claim, which was where the public toilets had been situated before they were moved further away. They did not even have to dig out any earth; they simply panned the little leftover mounds of earth dug out for the toilets.

Clary and Joe sold their mining equipment for more than what they had paid for it and sold their claim for almost nothing, which was all it was worth.

On the way home with their Hudson car, they took the longer, smoother road back to Tanga, arriving in record time because the car was much lighter than before. Happily, they experienced very few breakdowns and no punctures.

After deducting all their trip expenses, Clary and Joe shared what money was left and realised that they had the same amount now as when they had left a year before. No loss, no profit, and one dirty, rusty, clapped-out old Hudson car were all they had to show for their venture.

Chapter 28
The War Years in East Africa

In 1939, Clary was in Morogoro running a sawmill when the Second World War erupted in Europe. At first, everyone went about their business as usual, making no distinction between German and British residents. However, the peaceful co-existence in Tanganyika did not last long, as the war in Europe expanded and even peaceful neighbouring countries fell like dominoes under the onslaught of the German Wehrmacht. Former friends now eyed each other suspiciously, and anyone showing sympathy for an enemy nation was branded a traitor.

Finally, the British administrators in East Africa announced over the local radio station that all persons of German or Austrian nationality were to be interned in various centres around the country until the hostilities in Europe had ceased.

Everyone, German and British alike, believed that the war would last only a short time. They thought the politicians of the warring nations would meet and talk to each other, and then a ceasefire would ensue, bringing peace to Europe.

Clary, being British, was drafted into the army reserve in Morogoro, given a few days of military training, handed a rifle and a uniform, and told to follow all orders given to him by a superior officer.

Within days of being drafted, Clary was ordered to take a contingent of African askaris (African soldiers) to a German-owned gold mine in the Uluguru Mountains and arrest all the Germans. He was to take them to a temporary internment hotel in Morogoro.

Despite being only 32 years old, Clary was chosen since he had three advantages over more senior men. Firstly, his defunct mine was in that locality; secondly, he knew the roads well; and thirdly, he personally knew some of the German miners. (He also spoke some German, but now was not the time to boast about it.) However, he was warned that the mine had just taken delivery of a large amount of dynamite a month ago, and that he should be prepared for trouble.

There was a total of 28 Germans at the mine, including wives and children, so four army trucks made up the convoy. Two trucks carried 25 armed askaris, and two trucks would be used to transport the internees back down the mountain.

Clary and his troop left in the early afternoon and made quick progress along the well-used roads leading to the mine. *This would be an easy job*, thought Clary.

As they turned onto the last mile-long stretch of road leading to the mine, his suspicion was aroused, as the road surface looked uneven and disturbed. He feared that perhaps mines or booby traps had been laid on the road. He was not taking any risks on his very first assignment, so he called for his sappers to examine all suspicious road anomalies and embankment cuts for hidden booby-traps. He ordered his askaris to watch for suspicious activities ahead and be prepared for an ambush at any moment.

Progress along the road was now at a snail's pace, even though they did not find explosives or anything unusual. By the time they reached the main gate of the mine, it was already night. They could hear dance music blaring from the clubhouse, and all the lights in the living quarters were on, yet no one was to be seen. Suspecting an ambush, Clary positioned his men in a long line to the left and right of him, and then they crept towards the clubhouse, guns at the ready. Good old German music grew louder as they edged closer to the brightly lit clubhouse.

When they were a few yards from the main entrance, Clary and two askaris rushed the door and threw it open. To their surprise, they found the whole German community, singing, dancing, drinking, laughing, talking, and eating the last of their food with gusto. Clary noticed a long line of suitcases lined up against one wall, and children playing noisily in one corner.

"We have been waiting all afternoon for you! What took you so long?" asked one of Clary's German friends in the crowd, half-drunk from too much schnapps.

"We have our suitcases packed and are ready to go."

The Germans had heard the news on the radio about their impending internment and decided not to offer any resistance, believing that the war would not last long. They insisted that Clary have one last drink with them, and that they be allowed to tidy up the clubhouse before they left, as it was in too much of a mess to leave it as it was.

The German manager gave the keys to the mine houses, storerooms, and vehicles to one of the African staff for safekeeping, with a warning that if anything went missing or lost while they were away, the culprit would be punished when they returned. Still singing and laughing, with an occasional swig from the last of the schnapps bottles, all the German men, women, and children piled into the trucks with their luggage and were driven to Morogoro to be interned.

Being a reserve soldier in Tanganyika was a very dull job. It consisted of endless guard duties at unimportant sites, driving very unimportant people from one building to another, delivering unimportant papers from one place to another, and standing at attention in the burning sun to be inspected by some old man in an ill-fitting uniform.

Clary was never asked to go on patrols into the bush to seek out the enemy or partake in military exercises. He had no proper training to be eligible to fight on the front lines in North Africa, where he yearned to go and see some real action.

He was getting very bored in Morogoro, and longed for a change of environment and job. After his drafting into the Army reserve, he had to sell his little sawmill and rely on his meagre pay to make ends meet. Through his father, he heard that if one was employed in an essential service sector, such as a mechanic, one would be exempt from military duty. So, Clary applied to his old company, Riddoch Motors, for any posting, doing any mechanic job that they had available. He was lucky and got a job managing the company's Moshi garage, which was only an hour's drive from his old workshop in Arusha. Moshi, situated at the foot of imposing Kilimanjaro – the highest mountain in Africa – had a pleasant climate, and was very close to the excellent hunting grounds of the northern Maasai steppe. Most importantly, this job exempted him from military service.

In about 1941, Clary was discharged from the military in Morogoro on the grounds that he was providing an essential service, and moved to Moshi with his wife and three children. He rented a cheap, grass-roofed house to live in, which was close to his place of work.

During the war years, hunting in East Africa was still allowed, although ammunition for sporting rifles was not being imported, so only people who still had ammunition could buy a licence and hunt, as Clary did.

He went out hunting as often as he could in the nearby Maasai steppe and always came home with plenty of meat for himself, as well as extra to barter for scarce goods such as tinned milk, ammunition, and whisky. Eventually he used up all his ammo and realised that no more could be bought, bartered, begged, or stolen from anybody.

In his quest to continue hunting, Clary tried his hand at making gunpowder to re-fill shot shells, so that he could use his shotgun on small game and birds. He thought that it couldn't be that difficult to make gunpowder; after all, it was only charcoal, sulphur, and saltpetre mixed in the right proportions. His German friends had made their own gunpowder in their homes all the time.

His first attempts at creating gunpowder produced big clouds of black smoke but little else. Eventually, he found the right mixture, along with additives such as phosphate, to get a real explosion. He could not get the chemicals to make the firing primers for his shot shells, so he made a steel rod with which to poke out the primers from 303 rifle blanks, which are cartridges without bullets used for firing gun salutes at ceremonies. He even made the lead shot for his shells with lead recovered from old car batteries. He simply heated the lead in a steel pan and poured the molten lead from a four-foot height through a steel mesh into a bucket of cold water. Then he poured the bucket's contents through a coarse sieve, letting the small lead balls fall through onto the ground, where he picked out the size he wanted. The rest of the lead, too big to pass through the sieve, was put back onto the pan to reheat for the next batch.

His efforts enabled him to keep hunting for a few more months, but he soon ran out of old batteries and could not find any more 303 blanks. So, Clary finally admitted defeat and stopped hunting.

He took his three guns out of the gun cupboard, cleaned and oiled them well, removed the wooden stocks, and liberally oiled them with raw linseed oil, then wrapped the steel parts in cotton cloths drenched in engine oil. He took particular care of his recently acquired Jeffery's 450 No. 2 double rifle that he had exchanged for his less powerful 400 express. He wrapped it very well with thick axle grease. Then he stored everything in a felt-lined steel trunk and vowed to leave them there until the war ended.

Desperate to hunt, Clary borrowed an old muzzleloader from an Arab friend, intending to use his own supply of homemade gunpowder, which he thought would work perfectly. Firing caps to ignite the powder charge could be manufactured using match heads wrapped in matchbox striking surface paper. Muzzleloaders have no rifling inside the barrels to keep the projectile on a straight course, so the fired round lead ball travels roughly in a straight line for the first few yards after it leaves the muzzle, then takes on a mind of its own for the rest of the way. Very seldom does the ball travel along the aimed route, so it rarely reaches the intended quarry. After firing off all his homemade gunpowder at various game birds and animals with not even a near miss to his credit, Clary returned the gun to its owner with a thanks but no thanks.

Clary remembered his Uncle Mervin, who had one arm crippled by polio in his youth, yet still loved hunting. He taught himself to rest his 500 Express rifle on his crippled arm and managed to shoot very accurately that way. He still had two rounds of ammunition for his rifle when the war started, so instead of wasting it on shooting meat for home, he shot an elephant for its ivory, which still commanded a good price. The money he received for the tusks enabled him to buy a lot more than just meat for his family. After shooting the first elephant, he still had one bullet left, so he bought another elephant licence and shot one more elephant with his last cartridge.

When he took the tusks into the game department office for registration, Mervin was confronted by the police, who wanted to know where he got all the ammo for his gun. When he told them that he only had two bullets and had shot two elephants, they did not believe him and said he must be mad to go elephant hunting with only one bullet.

Arusha, 40 miles west of Moshi, sat at the foot of an extinct volcano called Mount Meru, which was always covered in mist. The mountainsides were verdant and lush green all year round, thanks to numerous ice-cold clear streams rushing down on all sides. The soil was so fertile that a huge variety of fruit and vegetables could be coaxed to grow throughout the seasons. Most importantly for the European settlers, the climate was cool and pleasant, even in the dry season when the rest of the country was sweltering in almost unbearable heat.

Arusha had such a pleasant climate that the government decided to declare the town a military rest and rehabilitation centre for British soldiers returning from the front lines. This meant that good housing had to be built. Hospitals and recreation areas had to be expanded and suitably equipped. A plentiful supply of food, drinks, and tobacco had to be available for the recovering soldiers and military personnel. Arusha was also designated a restricted access area, complete with machine-gun toting guards patrolling the town and all access roads day and night. Outsiders needed a permit issued by the local army commander to enter Arusha for any reason.

At first, Clary moved around unhindered between his home in Moshi and the excellent shops in Arusha, even without a permit.

When an overzealous British major was put in charge of the town, however, he drastically tightened up security, requiring everyone, including Arusha residents, to carry a permit at all times. Anyone caught without a permit could be arrested and fined, or even jailed. Clary liked shopping in the overstocked military shops in Arusha with their cheap, duty-free prices, and as there were no other good shopping alternatives, he applied for a coveted permit.

He had to fill out the usual forms with supporting documents at the army's headquarters and wait a week for his permit to be issued. However, the new major refused Clary's permit on the grounds that he was stationed in Moshi and had no business in Arusha. Clary did not accept this refusal, so he went to see the major personally. He explained that he needed access to Arusha to collect customers' cars and return them after repairs, as well as collect spare parts from his company's branch office.

The major was still reluctant to issue a permit, but at Clary's insistence and under the threat of involving the Riddoch Motors company manager, the major backed down.

However, just to be spiteful, he issued a restricted permit to "Clarence Wilson", saying that a double-barrelled name like "Palmer-Wilson" was for the aristocracy and not for commoners like Clary.

In addition to the permit, a holder needed to carry additional identification, such as a driver's licence, so that no one could use someone else's permit.

Now Clary was free to move in and out and around the town as he pleased, and his knowledge of Arusha's side roads helped him avoid the inevitable army patrols. However, his restricted permit did not give him access to military areas or permission to shop in army shops. Nevertheless, he ignored these restrictions and went shopping wherever he wanted, buying supplies that were not only cheap, but unavailable anywhere else in the country.

At the army shops, he could buy tax and duty-free whisky for a fraction of the civilian price.

Eventually, the town commandant got wind of Clary's illegal buying activities and tried to put a stop to them by ordering shopkeepers to refuse Clary service, but it was to no avail. Finally, desperate to end the illegal purchases, the commandant issued an arrest warrant for "Clarence Wilson", which was the name on his permit.

Clary only found out by accident that an arrest warrant had been issued for him. He was driving from Arusha back home one afternoon when he was stopped at a roadblock by armed soldiers. They demanded to see his permit, but on that day he had left it at home. A soldier then asked to see some identification, so Clary produced his driver's licence, which read "Clarence Palmer-Wilson". He was promptly arrested and presented to a senior officer at the roadblock, who informed Clary of the arrest warrant issued for him. Clary noticed that the warrant stated "Clarence Wilson" and not his real name of "Clarence Palmer-Wilson", which was on his driver's licence. He informed the senior officer that he was not the person named on the warrant and showed his driver's licence to prove it.

Wilson was a very common name in East Africa, so such mistakes were often made. The officer was sceptical about Clary's explanation, but luckily one of the soldiers was also named Wilson, although no relation. He explained that Palmer-Wilson and Wilson were not the same person. After apologising for the inconvenience, the senior officer released Clary and allowed him to drive home with his large supply of tax and duty-free booze undetected in the trunk of the car.

After that, Clary was careful about where he went, and he managed to avoid army roadblocks. He was still stopped quite a few times by local police, but they did not know about the military arrest warrant, so they were satisfied to see just the permit. Clary avoided arrest thanks to the arrogant town commandant issuing an inaccurate warrant. Much to the humiliation of the commandant, Clary was never brought to book. When the war ended, the arrest warrant was rescinded.

In a case of "just deserts", a very embarrassing incident happened to this pompous town commandant that had everyone talking and laughing at him behind his back.

To make Arusha a good military R and R locale for soldiers and officers alike, there had to be a constant supply of food, drinks, and tobacco. Almost everything could be bought in neighbouring Kenya, except beer and cigarettes, which had to be imported from other countries. Decent beer could only be imported from England or South Africa, but due to the war, weapons and ammunition took priority over beer.

A few months after the war started, beer supplies in Arusha ran out, and soldiers without beer to drink were a cause for serious unrest. No brewery in East Africa existed, except for the German brewery in Arusha, which had been closed and its German brewmaster interned. It proved impossible to find an English brewmaster to come and run the Arusha brewery.

The Arusha commandant had the bright idea of forcing the interned German brewer to come back and restart the brewery. The big, fat German brewmaster was hauled up in front of the commandant and told to immediately reopen the brewery or he would be shot. But as always, the English did not understand the German mentality and pride.

The demand was met with an emphatic, "NEIN!" "NO" in German.

"Then you will be shot for disobeying my orders!"

"That definitely will not get you beer", replied the smug German.

Fortunately for the brewmaster, the commandant realised that beer was an essential commodity to keep the troops happy, and a dead brewer would not solve his problem. So somehow, at any cost, he had to persuade this German to brew beer. After long and heated negotiations between them, the German brewmaster agreed to reopen the factory and run it at full capacity for as long as needed.

In return, the proud German would not be paid, but would be given all the food, booze and cigarettes that he wanted, including German sausages, French cheese and wine, schnapps, dark rye bread, and cigars. His confiscated Arusha house was returned to him, and he had free access to all the restaurants and shops in town, except those within sensitive military areas. He demanded his old Mercedes back, but it had been pressed into military service and was no longer in Arusha. As a compromise, he was allocated an army staff car, with a driver who was permanently at his call. The old brewer still had many British friends in town who preferred his beer to any other, so he was greeted heartily wherever he went. Clary knew him well, and managed to visit him some evenings for snacks and drinks. He even cajoled a bottle or two of good whisky and some schnapps from his friend.

True to his word, the German brewed batch after batch of excellent beer throughout the war years for his "enemies", as he fondly called his customers. The English commandant, however, had the brewery under constant surveillance, as he did not trust the man, suspecting him of being capable of poisoning the whole Arusha garrison with toxic beer. The brewer boasted that he led a marvellous life throughout the war years, with all the comforts and luxuries he desired. Unfortunately for him, his privileged life ended abruptly when the war ended, and he was repatriated to Germany.

Chapter 29
Warthog Pets and Leopards

One day, an African farmer, a Chagga, brought Clary a baby warthog that had been left behind after he had chased a female with piglets off his land. This little one had run the wrong way and got lost in the dense bush where the farmer could hear it squealing for its mother. Lost, lonely, confused, and hungry, the little animal walked up to the farmer's house and laid down next to a sun-warmed wall. Not wanting to kill the baby animal because of his Christian faith, he decided to sell it to a European, for they were known to keep all manner of pets at their houses.

So, Clary bought the little squealing packet and became the owner of a baby warthog. He kept it in a chicken wire enclosure in the back yard, which he equipped with a mud bath and a doghouse. He fed it kitchen scraps, leftover food, and chicken feed. It ate almost anything that was put in front of it. Clary would get into its pen and play with it every day when he got back from work, and he grew very fond of the little creature. He named it "Willy the Warthog".

Soon, Willy grew too big for the back enclosure, and one day simply demolished the chicken wire fence and walked out. Now he was free to run around the yard and, whenever he could, run into the house where he made himself at home on a carpet in the sitting room.

He followed Clary everywhere he went, just like a dog. Whenever Clary went for a walk along the bush paths near the house, Willy followed him faithfully, never showing any interest in the wilderness or in running away. Willy loved to be tickled under his stomach, and when anyone did this, he would lie down in ecstasy and fall asleep right where he was.

After two years of good care and feeding, Willy became a big, ugly, warty, grey animal with long curved tusks that scared the hell out of house visitors. However, there was one big problem with Willy: he would squeal and throw a temper tantrum whenever Clary left the house without him.

The front gate was made of thick steel pipes and kept closed day and night to keep out stray animals. The poor warthog tried in vain to demolish this gate every morning when Clary left to go to work. Willy would spend the whole day by the gate squealing and squeaking like a spoiled child awaiting Clary's return. He became a real problem whenever Clary went away for a weekend, because the house servants were unable to console him.

When Clary was gone, Willy refused to eat anything, even fresh maize cobs, which were normally irresistible to him. Clary was hoping to take two weeks' leave from his job to look at some of the country north of Arusha, but to leave Willy in the care of his servant would be cruel, and to take him on the journey would be out of the question. There was only one solution, and that was to return him to the wild, with force if need be.

So, one weekend, Clary took some camping equipment, a good supply of warthog food, and one delighted warthog, and travelled into the wilderness at least 50 miles from home. He motored to a long, open steppe where he had seen large numbers of warthogs some years ago while on a hunting trip. Since the war was still on, he could not use his own rifles for lack of ammunition. It was acceptable to carry an army 303 rifle for protection against the enemy, but not to use it to shoot game.

Clary set up his tent not far from a waterhole and took Willy there every day for a mud bath, and the warthog showed his gratitude with contented grunts. He also went for long walks along the edge of the plains, with Willy following like an obedient dog. There were groups of wild warthogs all over the place, some coming in at midday to wallow in the nearby waterhole.

One afternoon in camp, while having an afternoon rest on his bed with Willy napping at his side, Clary noticed that Willy heard the wild warthogs romping in the mud. Willy grunted with pleasure a few times, then got up and walked out of the tent.

By the time Clary awoke an hour later, Willy was nowhere to be seen. He was not at the waterhole nor out on the plains. Using this opportunity to escape, Clary unloaded all of Willy's leftover food at the site, packed his tent into the car, and quickly hurried away. He never saw Willy again.

It would have been nice to believe that Willy was finally living with his own kind in his own environment, but on the way out, Clary saw the pug marks of a leopard. Wild warthogs can defend themselves very well against predators, using their sharp tusks, so Clary hoped Willy could do the same. Whatever happened to Willy, he would be living his life in his natural habitat and Clary believed that was the right thing for his warthog.

Clary knew just how vicious and dangerous a cornered warthog could be. Confirmation of this belief occurred one afternoon when a customer came into the workshop to buy four new tyres for his short wheelbase Land Rover. His old ones, which he had brought with him, were cut to shreds along the sides. Clary asked the customer what happened, and the fellow told his story.

"A friend and I went bird shooting with a 22-calibre rifle, just a few miles away from here. We were driving around the scattered brush in our open Land Rover, shooting guinea fowl and francolin. Sometimes a crippled bird would fly up and then fall to the ground a bit farther away. We would leave the car and run after the wounded bird, and most of the time we found it lying dead on the ground.”

The customer paused, then went on, ”Near the end of the day, we chased a maimed bird into a thicket, yet couldn’t find it anywhere. Frustrated, we were walking back to the car when a big warthog came ambling past us about 60 yards away. Louis, my friend, was holding the .22 rifle, so he just aimed at the walking animal and fired, hitting it in the stomach. The wounded animal squealed in agony and took off, running very fast. Louis fired four times at the running pig, hitting it again a few times, however, only in its stomach and back legs. At the last shot, the injured pig spun around and ran in tight circles, still shrieking in pain, trying to gore whatever it was that was biting its back legs.”

He continued with his story. “When it finally stopped running around, it saw us and charged immediately, head down and grunting deeply. We both ran like hell. Louis ran to the nearest tree and swung himself up into the lower branches just in time to avoid being gored by the enraged pig a few feet behind him. He still had the .22 in his hand, but the magazine was empty, so he couldn’t shoot. The enraged pig ran underneath the tree, slashing at the trunk with its tusks. Then it spotted me running towards the car and came after me. I climbed into the open back and stood there, hoping that it could not jump in with me. I had a box of .22 ammunition in the car but no gun. We were helpless.

“That pig could have easily jumped into the back of the car with me, except I think one of the back legs was broken, so it couldn’t jump up. It ran around the car squealing in rage as it tore my tyres to ribbons, all four of them, although, luckily not right through to the inner tubes.” The man’s hands were quivering as he continued to describe the terrifying incident.

"The only weapon I had was a heavy hydraulic jack, which I picked up and threw at the pig, hitting it right on the forehead. This didn't do it any harm at all, only enraged it even more. Now it really attacked the car from all sides and even ran underneath, bending the exhaust pipe and silencer. I got down and lay on the floor in the back so that I was out of sight, and waited. After about 20 minutes of bashing my car to bits, it hobbled off back into the bush. Louis came down from his tree after the pig had long gone."

He paused to calm his nerves and went on, "With four ripped tyres, we couldn't drive fast, as the inner tubes were bulging out and could burst at any time. But we didn't want to walk out and risk meeting that pig again, even if we had a loaded gun now. We only had one spare tyre and nothing to repair the others, so we just limped along the track until we came to the main road. Then we left the car at the roadside and got a lift back to Moshi from a passing motorist.

"We will never underestimate a wounded African animal again, and we will carry a bigger gun", remarked the client.

Clary was relieved to know that this warthog incident had happened far away from where Willy was released.

Clary was also grateful that Willy fared better than a leopard belonging to a friend of his who ran a vegetable farm near Moshi.

This farmer had come across a tiny bundle of fur in a rocky outcrop close to where a poisoned female leopard had been found. The bundle of fur was obviously this leopard's cub and was probably less than a week old, because its eyes were still closed. Its chances of survival were slim.

The farmer's wife mothered it like her own baby until it was a fully-grown animal. It became their house pet and had free run of the whole farm, although it preferred to sleep during the day under a bed in the bedroom. At night it went out into the bush near the farm and hunted rats and small game, and it came home every morning with a full belly.

Clary, as well as other hunters, warned this farmer that leopards are subservient and playful when they are young, but after they grow up, they can suddenly turn into savage killers.

A wise old hunter said, "You can take a leopard out of the jungle, but you can never take the jungle out of a leopard. It will always revert to its nature."

The vegetable farmer was convinced that since he had found it as a tiny baby, it had only known his wife as a mother and had never known the wilderness, so it had no instinct to go back there. To prove how tame and friendly it was, he would pick it up like a big cat, carry it about cradled in his arms, and sit on the couch and cuddle it. Then the inevitable happened.

One weekend, the farmer invited ten of his close friends to celebrate his birthday at the farmhouse. His friends brought their young children with their nannies to look after them. While the party was in full swing in the house, the small children were all on the front lawn having fun playing games, running around, eating cake, and drinking sugary juices. It was almost dark outside, but there were lights strung along the railing of the raised veranda and lanterns on poles around the lawn, bathing it in pale yellow light.

His pet leopard had been sleeping in its usual place under the bed, and now came out and sat on the veranda, watching the children play. The farmer, with glass in hand, was sitting on a chair on the veranda talking to a friend when he noticed his leopard suddenly flatten its ears and slink on its stomach in hunting mode, to the veranda's edge. He saw it leap into the middle of the children, grab something, and leap out again, then run behind a bush in the garden.

The farmer's jaw dropped. His heart raced like a pump gone mad, suspecting that his pet had grabbed a child and was now eating it behind the bush. He rushed into the house and grabbed his shotgun, loaded it, and went after his leopard. He saw it behind a bush, chewing on something. Without warning, his pet snarled viciously at him and lunged forward. The farmer was so startled by this sudden change in temperament that he did not even have time to think about shooting. Fortunately for him, the leopard stopped short, snarled savagely, and bared its long fangs as if to say, "Don't you dare touch my food". The terrified farmer regained his nerve and fired both barrels of his gun from a few yards away, instantly killing his pet.

As it turned out, the leopard had only grabbed a puppy from amongst the children, and not a child. One of the children had brought his new pet, a four-week-old puppy, to show to his friends and the leopard had seen the hapless puppy as food.

The party ended abruptly, and everyone took their children and went home. The next morning, the farmer took his dead pet to the rocky outcrop where he had found it one-and-a-half years earlier and buried it in that same spot.

Clary knew of another leopard incident that happened just outside of town.

He was friendly with a dairy farmer whose wife kept a flock of egg-laying chickens protected behind a 12-foot-high enclosure. They were her pride and joy, because they laid an endless supply of large eggs all year round, which she sold for a good price at a local grocery store.

One night, a civet cat got into the chicken hutch to steal eggs, and it scared the birds half to death. They were so distressed that less than half of them laid any eggs over the next few weeks. It took the frightened birds many weeks to return to full laying capacity. In the meantime, the farmer's wife had the wire fence around the chicken run strengthened to ward off another civet cat attack.

Once more, the civet cat broke into the henhouse and wreaked havoc amongst the poor birds, and again the chickens stopped laying for weeks. This time the wife had a thicker, stronger fence erected outside the chicken run, which she was certain no civet cat could get over.

A few nights later, she heard another commotion coming from the chicken coop. This time she had every intention to kill that damned civet cat. She took her absent husband's loaded .22 rifle and a flashlight, went into the chicken enclosure, locked the gate behind her so that the cat could not escape, and went after it. Just behind the coop, her flashlight beam illuminated the blazing eyes of one very large, angry leopard. It came at lightning speed towards the petrified woman, snarling and growling.

She dropped both the flashlight and the gun and ran for the gate, expecting to feel leopard claws in her back at any second. On reaching the locked gate, she had no time to open it, so she simply "jumped" over the fence and continued running into the house, slamming the door shut behind her, panting like mad and happy to have made it back uninjured. She spent the rest of the night locked in her bedroom.

Her husband was away all night, and when he returned in the morning, she told him in a quivering voice what had happened. She was too scared to go back into the enclosure because the leopard might still be in there. So, she and her husband, armed with a 12-bore shotgun, walked around the outside fence of the chicken run but they could not see a leopard anywhere. Then they went to the gate and tried to open it to get inside. It was still locked from the inside.

Her husband asked how she had got out the previous night with the enclosure door locked. Both were surprised when the wife realised that she had been so terrified that she had somehow "jumped" over the 12-foot fence. To confirm it, they found her fleeing footprints running into the house. The couple managed to open the locked gate and retrieve the rifle intact, but the flashlight showed deep fang marks where it had been bitten a few times. It seemed that the leopard had been temporarily blinded by the light and attacked the flashlight instead of running after the farmer's wife. The cat had then run off without taking a chicken.

Afterwards, the farmer's wife bought some geese and put them in with her chickens. Then, whenever an animal or snake came close to the chicken run, the geese would make such a noise that they woke up the whole farm. The wife also decided that next time if a cat attacked her chickens, she would stay outside the chicken run and shoot it from a safe distance beyond the fence.

Chapter 30
Out With the Old Wife, In With the New

One night, when Clary, his wife, and their three children were at home, it began to rain very heavily, followed by strong winds and lightning. The rain kept falling all night.

During the night Clary heard water rushing through the house, so he got out of bed to investigate. He stepped right into ankle-deep water running through the room and under his bed. He grabbed a flashlight from his bedside table, shone it about, and saw shoes, socks, carpets, and papers floating around the room. Then he waded over to the children's room and saw the same mess, although they were still asleep.

He ran outside the house and saw rainwater rushing down the slope, into the back door, through his house, and out the front door into the garden. The little stream that ran past the house had burst its banks and was now a raging torrent, most of it running through his house. Nothing could be done in the middle of the night, so Clary ordered everyone to stay in their beds while he monitored the water level from his bed.

By morning, the water had subsided to a trickle, but dark mud lay ankle-deep throughout the house. Everything that was on the floor was either waterlogged or had been swept away. Clothes on the lower shelves of the chest of drawers were soaked with dark brown mud stains that would never wash out.

The only dry place was inside the outdoor kitchen, which stood on higher ground next to the servants' quarters. Their clever mongrel guard dog had taken refuge under the cast iron stove in the kitchen, which was dry and warm. The nonpoisonous snake that they kept around the house to keep other snakes away was never seen again.

The most unsettling part of being flooded out was the snakes, rodents, lizards, and insects that came into the house looking for dry ground. They crawled into dry clothes, into shoes, into drawers, up the walls, and took refuge in the rafters, occasionally falling onto the unsuspecting people below.

The person hardest hit by the flood was Clary's wife Aline, who suffered a nervous breakdown. She could no longer take these primitive living conditions with their inherent dangers and moved out as quickly as she could, leaving Clary to look after the children alone. She eventually went to Nairobi in neighbouring Kenya, where she filed for a divorce.

The Second World War came to an end in June, 1945, when Clary was 38 years old. Peace finally reigned over the world. And by good fortune, East Africa had been spared the blood baths and destruction of Europe and North Africa, so there was no rebuilding to do or scores to settle with old enemies. Everyone in the country was now just trying to get back to a normal life.

Clary lived in the same rented house in Moshi, which had been cleaned up after the flood. His children were either at boarding school or a local primary school, so he felt safe leaving the younger ones in the care of a trusted nanny while he travelled to Nairobi to persuade his wife to return to Tanganyika with him.

She not only said "no", but "never!"

She had had enough of this bushman with his hare-brained schemes for making money and his ludicrous way of living. She only wanted to live in a big city where she could feel safe, and said if Clary agreed to live in Nairobi, or any town in England, and get a proper job that paid a monthly salary, she might reconsider her pending divorce from him. She was asking him, in essence, to commit triple suicide, which she knew was out of the question for him.

Clary spent quite some time in Nairobi trying to persuade Aline to change her mind and drop her proposal to live in England, but it was all to no avail. She was never going back to living in a small town. Clary ended up fighting her lawyers and their feeble demand for alimony payments.

Sitting one evening at a popular bar in Nairobi trying to drown his problems, Clary met June – an attractive young green-eyed woman with an adventurous spirit, whom he would eventually marry. She was a natural blonde, with wavy hair falling lightly down to her shoulders. Her white, starched nurse's uniform, with a light blue cardigan, hinted at her profession. She sipped her gin and tonic, ladylike, between stories that she related to Clary.

She was immediately drawn to this pitiful, good-looking hunter with his large-brimmed safari hat and khaki outfit, complete with cartridge loops across each breast. June first thought that he was one of the "woman hunters" who dressed up to look like a hunter and preyed on "any female that could be impressed enough to jump into bed with them".

After a few minutes of small talk, with no mention of daring hunting feats, she realised that he was the first genuine hunter she had met.

She was only 23 and had had an interesting life. She was born in England and started nursing training at the local hospital when she was 16 years old. While there, she fell in love with a young doctor who was nine years her senior.

Then the war broke out.

Her boyfriend, by now her fiancé, was called up to serve as a doctor in the military and was immediately sent to the front lines in Ethiopia, where British soldiers were fighting Italian forces. In order to join him in Africa, June joined the army and took a six-month course to qualify as a battlefield nurse. After completing her course, she asked to be sent to the frontlines in Ethiopia, where her fiancé had been sent.

She had just turned 17 and was too young to be sent abroad, so she lied about her age. By claiming she was 18 she was accepted to go abroad.

She and a contingent of older nurses, together with a battalion of soldiers, were sent by ship to Asmara then by truck to the front lines in Ethiopia.

At last June was stationed with her fiancé in a tented field hospital just a few miles behind the front line, fulfilling her wish that they could be together.

English medical personnel at the field hospitals were required to treat all wounded, regardless of their rank or nationality.

One afternoon, while her fiancé was tending to the shattered leg of an Italian officer, the injured soldier pulled out a hidden knife and fatally stabbed the doctor in the back. He died from internal bleeding within an hour. The sudden death of her fiancé was too much for June to bear, so she was sent to Nairobi to rest and recover from her ordeal.

A beautiful young girl in Nairobi had very little chance of escaping the attentions of colonialists starved for female company. Less than a year after her arrival, she met a rich cattle and fruit farmer, and married him.

Life on a rich man's farm in the fertile highlands of Kenya was pleasant, to say the least. There were servants to clean the house, do the washing and ironing, prepare meals, look after the children, cut the grass, and do the many other household chores. June did nothing in the house except give orders to the servants.

The farmer also ran a very successful butchery in the town of Eldoret. Much money flowed in and out of their lives freely.

One morning when June was strolling through the orchard, she stepped on a young cobra and was bitten just below the knee. Being a nurse, she knew about snake bites and how dangerous they could be if not quickly attended to. She shouted for a servant to come to her aid, then rushed towards the house, but collapsed on reaching the garden gate. Her husband had heard her cry of pain and came running out, catching her as she fell. Under June's supervision, he took off his leather belt and made a tourniquet which he bound just above the knee, then bent down and sucked at the fang marks to draw out as much poison as he could. He rushed her, now unconscious, to the local hospital, where a doctor immediately injected her with a large dose of antivenin.

She stayed there for two weeks and eventually made a full recovery with no after-effects, not even a fear of snakes.

A year after the war ended, the income tax office in Kenya audited the farmer's books, and uncovered a large tax evasion scheme. He was arrested, tried, convicted of tax evasion, and sent to jail. The farm was confiscated and auctioned off to pay the back taxes.

Not wanting to bear the shame of being married to a criminal, June went to Nairobi and stayed with friends while she filed for divorce. She did some nursing to make ends meet and decide on her next move. Her husband was not only in jail but also penniless, and he would most likely be repatriated to England as a pauper after he had completed his sentence.

Now, June was chatting with her husband-to-be at the bar.

Clary returned to Moshi to continue with his job and also have his rented house cleaned, patched up, repainted, and made habitable in preparation for his new lady friend, June.

Now that the war had been over for more than a year, hunting rifles and ammunition were being imported again, which meant Clary could go hunting and start offering safaris to overseas clients. He was excited to be able to walk through the bush again amongst his beloved wild animals and smell the unique African scents.

Somewhere in the back of a storeroom in his house was a steel box containing his hunting rifles, including his reliable double-barrelled 450, dismantled and wrapped in heavy greased cloth. He eagerly went looking for them.

Unknown to him, the car grease in which he had wrapped his gun contained acids which had caused his gun to rust quite badly in places. He should have used a special gun grease to wrap his guns and kicked himself for not knowing this before the damage was done. The gun barrel was covered in rust spots. And in spite of sanding all parts to bare metal and rebluing them, the gun still looked dreadful. However, the metal parts were so thickly built that it was still safe to shoot. Despite its looks, it would serve him well throughout his hunting career. His two other rifles, wrapped in engine oilcloth, had fared no better.

Clary's defaced rifle fared better than an old South African hunter's double rifle that he had oiled with car engine oil and put away in a cupboard for safekeeping until the war ended. When he retrieved it, the insides of the barrels were so rusty that almost all the rifling had been eaten away. When the hunter fired it, he could hear the bullet rattling down the barrel and see it flying off in various directions, though rarely in the direction he had aimed.

It was a useless firearm for hunting dangerous game, where a precise shot was required unless the animal was so close that he could not miss anyway. To overcome the problem, the South African hunter poured cooking oil and table salt down both chambers each evening. By the next morning, the expanded oil/salt mixture had formed a thick coating in the barrel that guaranteed his first two shots were accurate enough to hit whatever he was aiming at, although after that, the gun threw lead in all directions.

This same hunter told Clary of his youth in the veldts of South Africa where he learned to stalk game and shoot accurately.

He said that as a young boy he had gone hunting with his father and learned everything about the bush from him.

When he was 14, his father gave him the old farm rifle, a single-shot Martini-Henry, and one cartridge, telling him to go out and shoot an animal for food. This was the first time that he had been allowed to go hunting on his own, so he was determined to prove himself. Regrettably, he used his only bullet to shoot at a buck that was too far away, and he missed his animal. Dejected at his failure, he walked home, hanging his head in shame.

But worse was to come. When he told his father what had happened, he was taken outside, whipped five hard strokes with a leather sjambok on his behind, told never to miss again, and sent off to bed hungry.

He said from that day on, he never missed another shot. Sometimes he would spend half a day crawling on his stomach through the spiny grass veldt until he got to within certain killing distance of his quarry. At other times, the game moved faster than he could crawl, making it impossible to get close enough to take a shot. Returning home with no animal but with the unfired cartridges was safer and did not rouse his father's anger.

He taught himself to shoot accurately at very long distances by studying the trajectory charts for his bullets. He knew how high to aim above an animal and to compensate for wind, in order to bring down an animal at 400, 500 or even 600 yards. Furthermore, he devised a way to sit on the ground, brace his knees together, and wrap his arms around them to give himself a rock-steady stance from which he could shoot accurately.

He also learned a trick to bring the game within shooting distance. He would fire a shot high over their head so that his quarry heard it go over and hit the ground behind them, which always frightened them so that they ran towards the hunter. Of course, the man's father never knew that his son bought

extra ammunition from other farmers in exchange for meat
so that he could practise shooting to improve his accuracy.

339

Chapter 31
Drink and Drive Up the Hill

After the war, the Tanganyika government had to dispose of all unwanted war materials such as trucks, cars, camping equipment, and tinned rations, as well as all confiscated enemy property, which consisted mainly of houses and farms, but also a few German-owned companies.

The easiest way to get rid of all this was to auction it off for whatever someone was willing to pay for it. The confiscated German properties were advertised in the local newspaper, with a request for interested parties to apply to buy them. They were then sold to the highest bidder. Some German nationals who had been interned in Tanganyika during the war and had not been repatriated were allowed to buy their old property back.

Clary attended some of these army equipment auctions and managed to acquire a complete camping outfit, including plates, cups, saucers, knives, forks, and spoons, for almost nothing. Most of it was unused and still packed in its original boxes. He also bought a Dodge 4x4 truck to transport all his equipment, and a Humber army staff car to travel around in comfort.

He saw an advertisement in the government gazette for a small German coffee farm at a place called Soni in the Usambara Mountains that no one seemed to want. A short walk from the farm was a workshop which was to be sold with the property. Clary made a very low offer for it, and as he was the only bidder, his offer was accepted. Soni seemed to be the perfect place to set up a base and start his hunting business again. The coffee farm and workshop would generate an income when no safaris were underway, and it was only a few hours away by road from his beloved south Maasailand hunting ground. Soni was a small village with one grocery shop, a petrol station, a car workshop, and a lay-by hotel, good for a cup of tea or quick meal. It was only a half hour drive up the mountain to the area headquarters at picturesque Lushoto, which had two good hotels, a well-equipped hospital, government offices, and shops selling a wide variety of goods. Most importantly, Lushoto also had a bank, a post office, and a thriving, colourful marketplace where the local Wasambaa sold a cornucopia of succulent vegetables and fruit.

In 1947, Clary moved to Soni with his new wife-to-be, June, and two children from his first marriage.

June surprised Clary with her good business sense. In spite of knowing nothing about coffee (except how to drink it), she hired some labourers to get the coffee plantation up and running. She organised a proper family homestead in the farmhouse, bought some egg-laying chickens, and made a nice vegetable garden to feed her family and also yielded some extra produce to sell. Clary concentrated on getting his workshop going, although it never did well because he had so few customers.

Once a week or so, Clary and June would drive to Lushoto for supplies and mail, and to catch up on the latest gossip at the Lawns Hotel. Saturday afternoons were reserved for a run to Mombo to collect railed-in spares and heavy goods for the farm. It was also a time to meet old friends who came from the sisal plantations for a weekend of drinking. Anybody travelling north or going south on the main road between Tanga and Arusha would always stop for a drink and a meal in Mombo. Its reputation as a wild weekend watering hole spread quickly.

Clary always took his children with him whenever he went to Lushoto or Mombo, so that they could meet new kids and have a nice outing away from the confines of the farm.

The first time that Clary and June went down to Mombo with the children, Clary started drinking heavily, as was his usual custom, and by 10pm, he was so drunk he could not even stand up. He had to be carried out to his car by the barroom waiters. Unfortunately, June could not drive and refused point-blank to let Clary in his pickled state drive her and the children up the winding, narrow mountain road back to the farm.

A massive argument ensued between them outside in the hotel parking lot, and raged on for a long time, to the delight of the onlookers. Clary insisted that he was perfectly capable of driving safely even if he could not walk. June was shocked that he would even think such a thing. However, no sober person could be found to drive Clary's old army staff car and his family up the mountain, as everyone else was just as drunk. About midnight, with very tired and whining kids hanging around the car, June accepted her fate, got into the car, put the kids in the back, and let herself be driven up the mountain road with its sheer rock wall on one side and a 500-foot drop into the river on the other.

To her amazement and relief, they made it home without incident. Almost every Friday after that, the family made the same trip to Mombo and back and, in spite of his drunken state, there were no objections from June about Clary's driving skills.

So each time, Clary got smashing drunk, had to be carried to his car, tooted his unique horn to call the kids, counted them to make sure they were all in, and then drove carefully and safely home. Once home, he had to be carried by house servants to his bed, where he slept fully clothed, then woke up the next morning with a whopping hangover.

Clary got drunk many, many times in his life, and managed to drive everywhere more carefully when he was drunk than when he was sober. He only had one car accident in his life, and that was when he was driving along a hunting track and another hunter was coming the opposite way. They met head-on, coming around a thick patch of bush. Clary was totally sober at the time.

One drizzly day, while driving home up the mountain from Mombo, Clary noticed a car parked at the roadside. The hood was open, and an old man was leaning over the engine trying to repair something. On the passenger seat was an old lady, resting her head against the side pillar, having a nap. In those days of unreliable vehicles, it was quite normal to see cars stopped at the roadside, so Clary continued on home without stopping.

The next day, a customer came into Clary's workshop to have something fixed on his car. He mentioned that he had just come from Mombo and had passed an old couple broken down at the roadside, with the old man trying to repair something in the engine compartment.

Clary stood staring, mystified at that comment, and said, "But that man was there yesterday when I drove up!"

Both men then stood staring at each other, in utter amazement, as they suddenly realised that something was very wrong. Immediately they informed the local district officer who sent his car with a driver to investigate the situation. They found the old man and his wife dead in their car, still in the same place and position as they had been the day before.

An investigation revealed that the car had, indeed, stopped at the roadside, most likely due to a wet ignition system from a rainstorm that the couple had driven through. The elderly driver had got out and was trying to dry the electrical leads when the car was struck by lightning. Both old people had been killed instantly. This incident reminded Clary how life can be snuffed out in an instant.

Chapter 32
The Mountains and the Greeks

At the foot of the Usambara Mountains was a small town called Mombo. It was a rest stop for travellers on the main road between the port of Tanga and the coffee-growing area around Arusha. It boasted two petrol stations, two garages, three hotels, too many bars to count, and numerous eating places, as well as multiple roadside stands selling freshly harvested fruits and vegetables. There was a small, clear mountain stream running past it that supplied clean water to the town and to a water stop for the railway engines.

Mombo was also the turn-off point for trips up into the Usambara Mountains and to Lushoto and beyond. The cool clean air and fertile loamy soil of the mountains were perfect for growing premium quality tea, excellent Arabica coffee, tropical and sub-tropical fruits, and vegetables of all kinds. The dairy cattle gave creamy milk, and the overfed pigs grew big, fat, and lazy. Virgin forests of African mahogany and giant cedars grew abundantly all over the mountains. The cedar forests were so dense that a flashlight was necessary to find the way through the undergrowth. The strong odour of old cedar wood perfumed the damp air.

One night, Clary rode with an English forester on an old car track through this cedar forest. The forester had a new American-made Phaeton car with wonderfully bright carbide lamps for headlights. As they drove over a pothole in the track, the car's lights extinguished, plunging them into total darkness. A herd of buffalo close by was snorting at them from within the forest.

In spite of the danger, the Englishman was obliged to get out of his car, open the lamp's glass cover and try to relight the carbide gas. He gave Clary a small flashlight and ordered him to shine it about to make sure no animals got too curious or too close while the forester tried to light the headlights with a shaky hand. The matches he had were damp and fizzled when he tried to strike one. Finally, using his last two matchsticks together, he managed to re-light the lamps with a "whoosh". The headlights revealed a herd of curious buffalo ogling them from the sidelines. Fortunately, the beasts let them continue unimpeded as they drove nervously past the herd.

The water ran clear and cold in the mountain streams and provided ideal habitat for rainbow trout, which had been imported from Scotland as fingerlings years before and released into some of the local rivers. Small game roamed all over the uninhabited parts of the mountains, with new sub-species being discovered all the time. The hard-working and friendly African inhabitants, the Wasambaa, lived in unadorned clay-covered huts. They grew a plethora of legumes in their fertile fields, and grazed their cattle on open glades in the forest.

The governor of Tanganyika had built a private lodge in the style of an English country estate in a place called Magamba, situated high in the mountains. He took frequent breaks here in this verdant Nirvana to escape the lowland heat, government problems, and complaining residents.

Even the Catholic diocese built a priests' and nuns' retreat at Magamba. It was a small, castle-like building deep in the lush forest and was quite luxuriously appointed, with a lounge, a library, single bedrooms with attached bathrooms, landscaped gardens, and a complement of staff to cook and clean for the guests. It was built so that local priests and nuns could set aside their duties and enjoy some well-deserved luxury for a few days without having to return to Europe.

The German colonialists were the first Europeans to discover this realm, and they settled here because the lush green forests and open meadows reminded them of home. During the First World War, their properties were confiscated by the British administrators, and they were all repatriated to Germany. When the war ended, many Germans returned, bought back their old properties, and continued with their lives where they had left off before the war.

When the Second World War began, the Germans had their property confiscated again, and they were again repatriated. Once more, when the war ended, many Germans returned to their beloved Lushoto, bought their old farms back and continued farming as before. Sadly, when Tanganyika achieved independence, their property was confiscated for the third time, by the Tanzanian government which did not allow them to buy it back.

The neighbouring territory around Mombo was ideal for growing sisal, a fibre used for spinning rope, string, and twine. Large tracts of bushland were cleared to farm sisal. Heavy tractors needed for clearing bush were shipped by train from the port of Tanga to the railway station at Mombo, and bales of sisal fibres were sent back down the line to Tanga for shipping overseas. Soon Mombo grew into an important waypoint for the sisal industry. It became a meeting place on weekends for sisal estate owners and their senior staff, as well as a drinking place for people coming down from the cold Usambara Mountains, and others coming up from the hot, humid coast.

Greek nationals with large amounts of money invested heavily in new sisal estates and became major owners of vast plantations. The Tanganyika government allocated them as much free land as they asked for, as long as it was cleared and planted with sisal. By the time the sisal boom was in full swing, Mombo had more than tripled in size, with new hotels, eateries, shops, brothels, and low-life bars.

Unfortunately, a few Greek-owned hotels in Mombo became gambling dens where fortunes changed hands overnight, leading to the downfall of many rich Greeks who were known to be serious gamblers. Poker was the preferred game. The town became infamous for how fortunes were made with sisal and lost in one night at the Mombo hotels.

It was said that estate workers had more money than brains, and this adage proved to be true on many weekends.

Clary only bet small amounts and lost most of the time, so he stuck to the cheaper alternative of having a few drinks with acquaintances. He could never afford the minimum entry fees required to join one of the gambling tables, although sometimes he went to observe them in action.

One evening, a young manager had a streak of bad luck and was losing with each hand. After he had lost all his cash, he cashed a cheque at the hotel for more money and continued playing. When that money was lost, he took off his watch and gambled it away. Finally, he put the keys to his new car on the table and lost those too. He pleaded with the winner of his car to give it back because it was all he had left.

The other players said to him, "You know the game, you know the rules". There was no mercy at the gambling table.

That night, he had to get a lift back to his estate with a friend. After that, Clary frequently saw the young manager in Mombo. Quite often he was at the bar, but the man never gambled again.

On one occasion, a sisal estate owner gambled for three straight days in a row, from Friday night to Sunday night. He lost everything he had. All his money, all his savings, his house, his car, and finally his estate were all gone. He went upstairs to an unoccupied bedroom, locked the door, and shot himself.

After this suicide, there were calls from Mombo residents to ban gambling because it was giving the town a bad reputation. These calls fell on deaf ears; the police had better things to do than control weekend revellers having a bit of fun. The gambling continued.

The biggest gambling loss occurred while Clary was there. Two Greek estate owners fought it out over a whole week of gambling. A group of ten Greek men started betting as usual on a Friday evening in one of the upstairs rooms of a Greek-owned hotel. The game went on nonstop all night. Whenever someone had to use the toilet, felt hungry, or even felt like having a nap, he was allowed to leave the table without losing his place. After each hand, a tip was put into a box to cover the cost of any food or drinks, so that no one had to stop and pay for anything while gambling.

By Sunday evening, there were only three players left. Each bet was worth a small fortune. Two of the last players were wealthy estate owners, and the third was an estate manager who was on a lucky streak the whole weekend. At midnight on Sunday, when the gamblers usually stopped playing and made their way home, these three vowed to continue until the end.

They continued playing all night and over the next two days, until one estate owner won back his lost estate. Then he was allowed to quit the game and go home. The last two players – the lowly estate manager and a wealthy hotel and estate owner – played on in the smoke-filled back room until Friday morning. When the game finally ended, the wealthy man had lost everything, including his sisal estate and a hotel back home in Greece. He was left with only the clothes on his back. The winner, the salaried estate manager, was now an extremely wealthy man.

A local Greek storeowner gave the loser a bed in the back of the store for the night, and later, a job helping out in the store. The impoverished gambler worked there for many years, eventually buying the shop from the owner and running the store until he had saved enough money to fly back home to Greece, where he retired.

It was astonishing to see how fortunes were made and lost in Mombo.

Clary remembered a time before the war when he bought a small house in Mombo, as it was close to his hunting area of Maasailand. The ground beyond Clary's house was a tangle of wild bush and stubby trees, with a few outcroppings of black lava rock. He hunted there sometimes with his 22-gauge rifle, hoping to shoot a guinea fowl or some other game bird for food. One time he was sitting quietly on a rock when he saw a fat green pigeon fly past him and land in a little leafy green tree only 40 yards away. He kept his eye on the bird as it landed, picked up his .22 rifle, aimed carefully, and fired. The whole tree exploded in a green burst of colour as about 30 green pigeons fluttered out in every direction. The little tree was almost bare of leaves, for most of the green had been pigeons!

One afternoon, Clary heard the distinctive danger cry of guinea fowl coming from a flock of them somewhere behind his house. Hoping to bag a nice fat bird for dinner, Clary took his little .22 and slipped into the bush to try to shoot one. Following the sound of the birds' cries, he located their position and stalked close enough to see them, but could not get a clear shot through the long grass. Although the birds were now aware of his presence, they did not fly away, but instead continued their warning cries while looking in one direction. Then, something green and moving slowly caught Clary's eye. It was a python crawling between the black lava rocks and bushes, trying to get away from the noisy guinea fowl.

Snakes of any kind were considered vermin in East Africa and were killed by everyone who saw one. Try as he might, Clary could not locate its head to shoot it, this being the only sure way to kill the snake. He stalked closer and climbed onto a flat rock to get a better view. Now he could see parts of a python slithering throughout the tall grass. He thought that this was a small group of pythons fighting each other, so he aimed his gun at what he believed was the largest snake in the bunch and fired. The flock of guinea fowl fluttered up and away at the sound of the shot and soon his dinner disappeared behind the hill.

To his surprise, it appeared that pythons erupted all around him. It seemed as though the whole place was full of writhing twisting snakes. Suddenly he saw a huge snake head rear up over some nearby rocks, and quickly fired at it. The head dropped out of sight and the pythons in the grass slowly stopped wriggling. Ten minutes later, when the wriggling had ceased, Clary grabbed a section of the dead python and pulled. The whole snake moved. He realised that what he had shot was one python, and that there was only one huge python, not a whole group.

Clary had to get some shop workers to help him pull the snake out of its hiding place and back to his house. It was 25 feet long, one of the largest pythons ever recorded in East Africa. Clary skinned it, salted the hide, and later sold it to a crocodile skin merchant in Tanga. That python is probably still walking around as a handbag draped over some rich lady's arm, somewhere in the world.

Chapter 33
A Photo Safari Like No Other

One of Clary's first safaris after the war was not a hunting safari but rather a photographic safari. An American photographer wanted to visit the little-known Ngoro Ngoro crater and Serengeti Park, and asked Clary to arrange a tour. No visitor accommodation was available at these places, so Clary opted to take a complete tented camp and staff with him. It would be a test for his newly acquired Dodge truck and his army camping equipment.

The safari started in Arusha, and it was an easy half-day drive to Mto wa Mbu (Mosquito River), where they made their first camp by a river, under a thick canopy of fig trees. On the first afternoon, while sitting at their camp table under the shady trees and enjoying a cup of tea with sweet biscuits, a troop of baboons decided to sit right above them and stuff themselves full of wild figs. Not only do baboons constantly throw down half-eaten, rotten fruit while eating, they also urinate and defecate at the same time. Jetsam and excreta rained down on cups of tea, on sweet biscuits, and onto the relaxing photographer and guide.

With profane screams, both men hastily vacated the premises for cleaner areas. Clary was so angry that he grabbed his 9.3 Mauser rifle and emptied the magazine into the overhead tree canopy, scattering screeching apes in all directions – although no monkeys fell dead. It took over an hour to clean up the mess, brew fresh tea, procure biscuits, and move the alfresco dining table to a safer, non-fruit-bearing tree.

They stayed three days at Mto wa Mbu, filming the flocks of dancing pink flamingos on Lake Manyara, observing with amusement the tree-climbing lions, and motoring through unperturbed groups of wildlife.

Then they left Mto wa Mbu and crawled up the steep mountain roads to Ngoro Ngoro crater, where they were permitted to camp inside the crater. On the crater floor, they came across an old abandoned German building that the owner had intended to turn into a sausage factory, using game meat. It never went into operation because the butcher could not get his equipment up the steep and slippery slopes of Ngoro Ngoro to his factory. After the war broke out, the butcher had left and the project was abandoned.

At one point in their journey, Clary thought he had lost his client. They were driving along a road on the crater rim when they saw an old bull elephant grazing contentedly nearby. With Clary's permission, the client got out of the car and walked towards the elephant to get a better picture from another angle. On being disturbed by this pesky human, the elephant made a mock charge to chase the intruder away.

The panicky American did not run back to the safety of the car, but instead ran straight down the hillside, through head-high stinging nettles, right into a resting buffalo. The startled buffalo bolted right while the frightened client lunged left, running through more nettles to emerge face-to-face with a group of grazing warthogs. Seeing all those ugly faces covered in warts and with long sabre-like teeth sticking out of their snouts, the horrified man clambered back up the hillside to get away from them. He fought his way through one patch of thorn bush after another and finally emerged onto a grassy field where he collapsed, panting heavily. He was so exhausted that he could not reply even when Clary loudly called his name.

When Clary finally found his client, the fellow's clothes were torn to shreds and covered in blood from his fight with the thorn trees. His face, arms, and hands were bright red and swollen from his battle with the stinging nettles. And he was still shaking like a leaf in a high wind from his ordeal.

Clary took him back to camp where an hour later, in clean clothes and with thorns removed, scratches and lacerations doctored, all stinging nettled body parts covered with soothing camomile lotion, and a good stiff whisky in hand, he told Clary the whole story of his near brush with death.

Clary's sly comment was, "Now you have a little adventure to talk about back home and not only nice pictures to show your friends."

The next stop on their itinerary was the expansive Serengeti Plains, which they had almost all to themselves. The only other people they encountered were the occasional local tourists driving around aimlessly, overwhelmed by the sheer abundance of wildebeest.

The main reason for visiting the Serengeti was that Clary had promised his client that he would get exceptional lion pictures here. Lions were difficult to spot on the brownish kopjes where they liked to lie during the day and where they had a commanding view of their meandering food sources below. Even when stretched out on the short brown grass of the plains, their light fawn pelt blended in so well that they were nearly invisible.

To help the safari guides find lions for their clients, who all wanted superb photos, the park warden allowed visiting hunters like Clary to shoot an animal outside the park and bring it in to use as bait to attract lions. Having shot his bait, the hunter would bring it into the park, cut open the belly, drag it behind his vehicle to a suitable spot for filming, then tie it in place with a strong rope. Lions would smell the bait or come across the drag spoor and follow it to the carcass. Early the next morning, the client would be driven to the bait and have an unparalleled opportunity to obtain spectacular photographs of lions at their kill.

Unfortunately, the lions soon associated the sound of a truck with free food and began to follow the vehicles whenever one drove along the roads. It was no longer necessary to drag the bait through the park, because lions came running after any truck that drove by.

This practice of allowing a hunter to shoot an animal outside the park and drag it inside the park as lion bait had to be stopped after a road maintenance truck, with 20 workmen on board, drove into the park to carry out some necessary roadwork and was attacked by lions. As the story goes, a large pride of lions saw the truck and ran after it, expecting to get a free meal. The terrified workmen who were standing in the open back and being thrown around by the rough road screamed to the driver in the cab that they were being chased by a pride of lions and pleaded with him to speed up as fast as he could go.

However, their old truck could not outrun any lion, even on a good road, and certainly not on that rough, uneven park road. The lions easily caught up with the speeding truck, expecting a nice juicy wildebeest to be in tow behind. When they found no food, one agile lioness jumped into the back of the speeding truck, scattering screaming men in all directions. The panic-stricken men leaped from the truck and fled towards a group of nearby fever trees. They climbed up the vertical trunks into the topmost branches and stayed there the rest of the day. The terrified driver, with a lion still in the back of his truck, never even slowed down. Instead, he sped on to the park headquarters where the disappointed lioness jumped out.

After the driver's shattered nerves had settled down, he told his story to the aghast warden, though he still shook with fright and stuttered badly. A few hours later, when the park warden came in a truck with an armed escort to rescue the workers in the fever trees, the lions had long gone. However, the workers in the trees could not get down. They had no idea how they had got up there in the first place, and try as they could, they simply could not find a way to descend safely. It was only with the help of a strong rope, carried up to the stranded men by an agile scout and tied to stable branches, that they managed to rappel down safely. After that, lion baiting was forbidden, and all trucks passing through the park were given an armed escort until the lions stopped following them.

When Clary and his client were there, the migration of one-and-a-half million wildebeest through the Serengeti was in full swing, and what a marvellous sight it was to behold. There were overfed lions lounging next to every kopje and overstuffed leopards hanging out in every grove of thorn trees. Clary's American client was overwhelmed by the sheer wealth of game here. He took a huge number of excellent pictures, including outstanding photos of lions and leopards. These photographs were so good that a series of them were published in a national magazine back home in the United

States, which helped put the Serengeti Park on a list of world wonders. After the trip, the client was so pleased that he gave Clary an exceptionally large tip.

Chapter 34
World's Largest Buffalo

The client was a Mexican businessman who was interested in hunting as many animals as he was permitted on his licence. He would fly from Mexico City into Nairobi, Kenya, as almost all airlines flying over East Africa stopped there for fuel and services. He would then hire a small Cessna to take him to Arusha, where Clary was to meet him to start the safari.

On his first visit to Mto wa Mbu, the mosquito river, Clary had been amazed at the spectacular scenery and diversity of game, so he started the Mexican's hunting trip there. He pitched his camp under the same trees as he had done a few years ago when the local monkeys had defecated on his afternoon tea and biscuits. This time, he instructed his staff to chase away all animal intruders from the trees around camp.

This stretch of the rift valley was rich in game, mainly because of the abundant water that flowed down from the Ngoro Ngoro escarpment into the alkaline Lake Manyara, and the lush vegetation that grew in the fertile soil around the lake. It was a pleasant safari due to the abundance and variety of animals seen every day. Here they were able to drive through mile-wide, long, open plains teeming with zebra, wildebeest, kongoni, ostrich, giraffe, buffalo, and zebra. In fact, they counted 12 different game species in one afternoon while resting by the Dodge when they parked under a shady flat-topped Acacia tree. There were a few small forests scattered around the plain where elephants fed and rested in the shade during the heat of the day.

For the second time, Clary saw lions resting in trees in one of the forests. Elsewhere, adult lions cannot climb vertical tree trunks, yet here these fully grown lions managed to do it easily. They probably climbed into these trees to catch a cool breeze blowing in off the lake and to get away from the swarms of biting flies near the ground, concluded Clary.

By the third last day of the 30-day safari, the happy client had shot all the game on his licence and was just enjoying the last few days of the safari by driving around, admiring the herds of game, and taking a few pictures. That morning, close to Lake Manyara, Clary was looking through his binoculars at a herd of about 100 slowly grazing buffaloes, when he spotted one animal that towered over the rest. He watched it for a while until it raised its head.

IMAGE 13: THE WORLD RECORD BUFFALO.

Then his eyes popped out and he called out, "Look at the horns on that buffalo! It must be a world record."

Not waiting for a reply from his startled client, Clary grabbed his 450 double rifle from the truck and ran towards the milling herd. The big buffalo was easy to see, towering above the rest of the group. It grazed in the middle of the herd, making it impossible for Clary to take a decent shot. The buffaloes seemed unconcerned by Clary's presence about 100 yards away, as they grazed contentedly in an open glade amongst a few scattered trees. They were moving slowly towards a patch of tall grass, and if they reached it, following them would be futile, because they would disappear inside it.

A buffalo of this size was a chance of a lifetime, and not to be missed. So, against all his hunting ethics, Clary raised his rifle and steadied it against a tree trunk. He aimed at the only part of the huge buffalo that he could see, which was its back, rising a foot higher than all the others. He fired a well-placed shot to the pelvic region, and the buffalo went down. He ran to within 30 yards of the disabled animal as the rest of the herd thundered past.

Just then, his client, who had been observing the drama, ran up with his camera to take some pictures. Clary was so embarrassed at his own selfishness in shooting so hastily without first consulting his client that he grabbed the camera from the client and told him to take the rifle and shoot a few shots over the top of the running herd while he filmed the scene to get some action pictures. The client did as ordered.

When the buffalo herd had disappeared into the long grass and the fine dust had dissipated, the big buffalo was on its front feet, trying to get up and charge them, in spite of its broken back. Clary gave the struggling animal a mortal shot through the heart.

The men walked over to inspect the dead animal and were staggered by the five-foot width of its horns. When the Mexican saw how much bigger these horns were in comparison to his own trophy, he wanted to have them.

Clary was reluctant to forego such a unique prize, claiming that as he had shot it, it belonged to him – even if it was an unethical act on his part. The determined Mexican agreed that Clary had shot the animal and it was legitimately his, but was adamant in his desire to have the trophy, claiming that it would occupy an honourable place above his living room fireplace at home in Mexico.

Clary could not match that place of honour, yet was still unwilling to let his prize go. After a heated discussion, a large financial incentive was promised, and an exchange was agreed upon. The client would get this huge buffalo, and Clary would take the Mexican's smaller one.

However, he later said to the client, "I don't want any dead animal heads on my walls. I live with live ones every day, so you can keep your first buffalo head, too."

One small unforeseen problem with the exchange of trophies occurred when a game warden came into camp to check on the hunters' licences. He had been watching the hunt through a pair of binoculars from the escarpment and had seen Clary shoot the impressive buffalo. However, as no laws had been broken and all licences were in order, the warden agreed to keep quiet and not file a report about Clary shooting it and not the Mexican client who was now claiming it.

Back in camp, the horns were measured with a steel tape. They were a quarter inch over 64 inches at their widest point, which is just over five feet. It was the new world record for buffalo, beating the old record by six inches. At that time in

East Africa, newspapers and the general public could not care less about what was going on in the hunting scene, so there were only a few lines about this record event in the local papers.

The record still stands today, except that this animal was neither male nor female; it was an hermaphrodite, so it was not accepted in some hunting circles, because only male animals can qualify for records. (This record has recently been beaten by another buffalo found dead in Manyara Park, which is a few hundred yards away from where Clary shot his animal. Today, buffalo horns use another method of measurement to determine its trophy size.)

Chapter 35
Crocodile Hunter

There were hardly any hunting safaris coming to East Africa after the war, so Clary had to find another source of income to tide him over during this slack period. One advantage of the war was that no hunting occurred during that time, so wild game had been left in peace to breed undisturbed, and their numbers soon swelled.

The crocodiles increased so much that they became a menace to villages situated near the rivers. There were so many crocodile attacks throughout the country that the government declared them vermin animals. This allowed anyone with a licence to hunt them in unlimited numbers.

Clary left the farm in Soni and made a quick camping trip to his old hunting ground on the Ruvu River to assess the crocodile situation for himself. He hired a dugout canoe from a village downstream and had the men pole him upriver towards his camp. He observed thousands of the reptiles all along the riverbanks. On some sandy banks, there were so many crocs that they were lying on top of each other for lack of space. As the canoe approached, they slid slowly and quietly back into the river, showing very little fear of humans.

Clary noticed that in such a small river the number of crocodiles far exceeded the amount of fish needed to feed them. When fish stocks in a river were depleted, the crocs relied more on land animals that came to the river, including people. The fishermen complained that they hardly caught any fish in their traps and were forced to paddle a long distance from their village to find decent fishing grounds. More and more, they had to rely on what little game they could snare in the bush for food. Almost every week, a crocodile attack occurred on this river, in spite of all the precautions the people took.

A few days after Clary arrived, a man came into his camp and told him that one of their young men had gone to check his fish traps and had not returned. They feared that he had been taken by a crocodile. A search party sent out to look for the man had found only his empty canoe trapped against a fallen tree far downriver. Clary promised to help them catch the killer crocodile.

Early the next morning, villagers led him to the riverbank where the missing man usually laid his fish traps. There were large croc footprints all over the grassy bank where the fish traps were visible in the shallow water. Clary suspected that the young man had anchored his canoe a few feet out into the river and then tried to set his traps in the shallow water between the canoe and the bank. The canoe had probably been drifting in and out from the bank with the river current, and it was at that moment when the canoe had drifted out that the croc had a chance to slip underneath it, grab the man, and drag him underwater. It seemed as though the young man had also managed to grab the side of the canoe and pull it from its anchorage as he was being dragged into the water. No one had heard his inevitable screams for help because their huts were too far away.

Knowing that crocs are cold-blooded and that they like to warm themselves by lying in the sun on the riverbank, Clary walked up and down looking for likely places for the beasts to sun themselves. He built a hideout where he could see several likely sunning spots on the opposite bank. He went back to his camp and waited until the afternoon when the crocodiles liked to catch the last rays of sun before the cold night.

Later that day, he picked up his Mauser 9.3mm with five solid cartridges and walked back to his hiding place on the riverbank. He noticed quite a few crocs sunning themselves on the opposite side, but none that looked big enough to tackle a grown man. At one point, a large crocodile came gliding downriver, scattering all the other crocs from their sunny spots.

This could be the killer croc, as it is certainly big enough, thought Clary. Eventually, the huge crocodile emerged from the river and slithered up the bank to a grassy spot, where it lay broadside. Clary waited until the animal settled in and closed its eyelids, then moved very slowly into a good shooting position. A loud crack from his Mauser sent every crocodile within hearing plunging into the safety of the dark river. The big croc on the opposite bank never moved a muscle. Its brain cover, just behind the eye, was shot clear away.

On hearing the shot, some villagers came poling over the river in two canoes, as Clary had ordered. The dead croc was turned onto its back and its belly split open. The mangled arm of a young man, complete with an armband, flopped out. More human body parts emerged as the croc's stomach contents spilled onto the green grass. No human head was found to identify the body, but the armband was proof enough that it belonged to the missing man. His remains were carried back to the village to be mourned and buried close to his hut. The dead croc was unceremoniously dumped back into the river, where it would be devoured by its cannibalistic brethren.

Returning home to his farm in Soni, Clary learned that as an incentive for hunters, the government was issuing unlimited licences to shoot crocs, and crocodile skin buyers were paying one shilling per foot of belly skins. There was even a bounty on baby crocs of one shilling per animal, and ten cents for each egg handed into the game department office. Here, opined Clary, was a way to be in his beloved bush to hunt and earn some extra money to keep him and his family going a little longer.

Leaving his children on the farm in the care of a nanny, Clary took June on a crocodile hunting safari to his Ruvu River camp. He had obtained a permit to shoot an unlimited number of crocodiles along the Ruvu. This was going to be a money-making trip which would solve his financial problems, at least for a while.

Opposite his riverside camp was a grassy bank strewn with resting crocs. Clary's first shot with his Mauser 9.3 blew the brains out of one animal but sent every other croc within 500 yards splashing back into the safety of the river. It took more than an hour before another brave creature crawled gingerly out onto the grassy bank to lie next to its dead kin. This one was also shot. Another hour later, a croc stuck its head out of the water but was too timid to crawl out onto the bank, so it submerged and disappeared.

Clary went over to the opposite bank with his skinner, cut out the belly skins of both crocs, and pushed the carcasses into the river where they floated downstream on the lazy current. He walked upstream, keeping an eye out for crocs laying on the opposite bank, and managed to shoot two more big animals before the sun got too low in the sky to give enough heat to entice them out.

On his first day of hunting, he had only four croc skins to show for his efforts. The problem was that the loud report from his Mauser rifle sent all the crocs within hearing range diving for cover into the river, where they stayed for at least an hour before venturing out onto the banks again.

The next morning, Clary came up with a new strategy for hunting them. He would leave camp in the morning and walk upriver along one side for an hour, shooting animals on the opposite bank, then cross over and walk back downriver to camp, collecting the skins of the dead ones as he went. Then, in the afternoon, he would walk downriver from camp for an hour, shooting his quarry on the opposite bank, returning along that bank to collect his skins. This method proved successful for a short time, as it gave the crocs time to get over their fear and climb out onto the banks again. However, after a few days of shooting, most of the big crocodiles moved out of this part of the river to safer stretches, and only young small crocs which were not worth shooting remained on the banks.

Next day, Clary drove far downriver in his old Dodge truck until he came to a section with sunny resting places on the opposite bank. He walked upriver for an hour, shooting as he went, then crossed over and collected his skins on the way back to the truck. In the afternoon, he walked downriver on one side and back on the opposite side, gathering the skins as he returned. Every evening, he hurried back to camp where the croc skins had to be well salted; otherwise, they would spoil very quickly in this humid, hot climate.

After three weeks of continuous harassment, the crocs became very wary of any human they saw, and slipped silently away before Clary had a chance to shoot. Crocodiles only like to lie in the sun when it is hot, which means they do not come onto the riverbanks before 9:00 in the morning nor after 4:00 in the afternoon. On a cloudy day, they may only come out around midday, if at all. It was getting harder to find crocs worth shooting on the Ruvu, so Clary decided to take a few days off to rest and allow his salted skins to dry completely before he returned home with his bounty.

Each day that Clary had hunted, June tagged along as his faithful gun bearer, carrying the cumbersome 450 double rifle in case they unexpectedly ran into a cantankerous old buffalo or, even worse, a sleeping rhino, both of which frequented this shady riverine forest.

There was still much fish in the river opposite their camp, so on a lazy afternoon, Clary and June set up a table and camp chairs in the shade on a three-foot high riverbank and threw in a fishing line to see what they could catch. Clary sipped his whisky and soda while June nipped a gin and tonic. Colourful birds flitted overhead, chasing insects from tree to tree, while Sykes' monkeys and baboons chatted to each other on the opposite bank. The lazy green river gurgled past them.

"This is what living in the Garden of Eden must be like", said June, leaning back in her chair with her eyes closed.

A loud screech, followed by the sound of splashing water and barking monkeys, shattered this peaceful idyll. June jumped to her feet and grabbed the rifle from the table, looking for the culprit who had caused the upheaval. But Clary had seen it all unfold before his eyes and did not bother to get up. He had been watching a monkey playing on a branch hanging five feet over the river. A crocodile that had also been watching these antics from afar drifted downstream towards the branch with just its eyes visible above water. At an opportune moment, the clever croc lashed its tail up out of the water and, with a mighty flick, knocked the unsuspecting monkey off its branch. The hapless creature fell into the river, where the crocodile quickly pulled it under the water. The drama was over in a few seconds.

"In every paradise, there is a little corner of hell", sighed Clary.

He told June that he was very impressed with her quick reaction to the incident. In fact, he had been impressed with her conduct during the whole trip, for she had not complained or moaned about anything. She had not grumbled or griped about the unpleasant heat, nor the pesky flies buzzing around her head all day long, nor even about the biting mosquitoes in camp at night. She was brave and adventurous and endured all the hardships of the bush without complaint. Clary concluded that he had finally found the perfect wife for his way of life.

One afternoon, Clary took June out onto the open plains next to camp and showed her how to handle and shoot a gun. He started by letting her shoot the tiny .22 calibre rifle until she was able to hit an empty tin can at 50 yards every time she fired. Then he let her graduate to the more powerful 9.3, but had to restrict her to three shots due to the cost of ammo for this gun. Finally, he let her fire one shot with the 450 double. The recoil sent her reeling backwards.

"Bloody hell, this thing kicks harder than a drunken horse", she uttered loudly, then added, "That's the first and last time I'm shooting that damn thing".

She eventually became a very good shot with all the rifles that Clary owned. Over the years, June hunted every animal on her licence, including eight elephants, although for these huge animals she used a .375 Winchester, as its recoil was manageable for her.

When they left their camp on the Ruvu the next day, the old Dodge was piled high with salted croc skins. The overloaded truck swayed and groaned as it wobbled over the red dirt bush roads until finally reaching the good, smooth main road to Tanga. There it could speed up to 45 miles per hour, a good clip for such an old machine.

Their driver drove directly to the agent who bought crocodile skins in Tanga. It was almost closing time as the smelly truck came through the main gate of the buyer's yard, followed by Clary and June in the old army staff car. The well-dressed Indian clerk was all smiles as he eyed the huge pile of skins on the truck. They would be worth a fortune to him after they had been cured into saleable leather.

He ordered all his escaping employees back to work, warning them under threat of a pay-cut that no one could leave until all the skins were off-loaded, counted, and put into brine vats. It took the complaining tannery workers more than an hour to off-load, roll-out, measure, inspect and dump each skin into the vats of brine.

Clary beamed from ear to ear as he sat in the clerk's office listening to the buyer add up the payment, totalling first quality skins, so many shillings; second grade, so many shillings;, and third grade, still more shillings. He said to Clary and June, while writing out their payment cheque, that this was the single biggest consignment he had ever taken in his life. Clary promised him many more skins in the near future.

The money he was paid would be enough to keep him and the farm going well for at least five months, perhaps longer if they were frugal.

While celebrating his new wealth in a posh bar in Tanga, Clary got talking to a hunter from Kenya who told him about the newest small calibre high-powered rifles from America. They used a new type of gunpowder that was much more powerful than the cordite used in the English ammunition. These new American rifles fired small bullets at very high speeds, allowing accurate shooting at several hundred yards' distance. In addition, they could be fitted with powerful telescopic sights to increase the gun's accuracy.

Clary was fascinated by his account of these new guns, so the next morning he paid a visit to an English firearms dealer in Tanga whom he had known from his early days. The dealer knew about these American rifles, but he distrusted them, preferring superior English weapons of which he had a large stock. However, he gave Clary some good advice about suitable rifles for crocodile hunting.

The gun shop owner reluctantly agreed to import a special American rifle for Clary plus a large amount of ammo, but only because he and his father had previously been good customers of his. Luck was on Clary's side, as he learned the next day from the gun shop owner that some of these new rifles had already been ordered from America by a Nairobi gun shop and were on their way to East Africa by air. One gun had now been reserved for Clary.

While waiting for his special rifle to arrive, Clary decided to give "his" crocodiles a rest by not shooting them and not using his Ruvu camp for any safaris for a while. Then a short hunting safari unexpectedly came his way through an agent in the United States while he was idling his time away at the farm in Soni.

Chapter 36
The Hornet and a Big Friendly Croc

When Clary returned from the short safari, he received news that his new rifle had arrived. It was waiting for him in the gun shop in Tanga. At the shop, Clary was very pleased to see his new rifle was well-made, light, and felt just right in his hands. It was a Winchester .22 Hornet. The brass cartridges were only two inches long, with tiny copper-coloured bullets, about a quarter the size of his Mauser 9.3 bullets. The cartridges looked tiny, and the bullets looked minute, but he was assured that although small, these bullets were made of a new hard metal that didn't deform easily and could penetrate deeper due to higher velocities.

The rifle came with one of the newest four-power adjustable telescopic sights and a thick leather carrying case. Clary bought the shop's entire supply of cartridges for the gun, all 500 rounds of them, and was expecting to use at least that many on his next crocodile hunt.

As soon as he arrived home at his farm in Soni, Clary set up a shooting range in between the coffee trees to try out his new toy. After firing quite a few rounds from varying distances, and adjusting the telescopic sight to be spot on at 200 yards, he left it at that setting. When he saw the tiny bullet punch right through a thick board, he realised that this really was a perfect weapon for croc hunting.

It took almost two weeks to dry, pack, and ship out his Mexican client's trophies, and he took special care with the record buffalo head. Then he was free to head back to his Ruvu river camp and start hunting crocodiles again.

Clary was not the only one who had heard about the bounty on crocodiles, and it seemed every amateur hunter in Tanganyika was out hunting them. When Clary and June came back to their Ruvu camp, some local natives hoping to find work told them that other hunters had already been here shooting crocs. They had shot at many but killed only a few animals, and those were small ones.

There was nothing Clary could do about it, because officially this area was free for anybody with a licence to hunt any animal they wanted. It was only a gentlemen's agreement between professional hunters that they did not trespass on one another's territory. Amateur hunters did not respect this agreement.

On the first day along the river with his new rifle, Clary was very upset that he did not get a chance to try it on a crocodile. Even the next day was a disappointment. There were still quite a few crocs about, but they tended to be watchful and stay in the river, only poking their eyes and noses out for a short time. Whenever Clary saw one resting on a bank, it kept its eyes open all the time and dashed into the river at the slightest hint of danger.

Clary and June had to drive very far upriver to find a place where crocs were not so shy and would remain lying in the sun with their eyes closed. Clary's first shot at a sleeping croc with his new Winchester rifle was more than he expected from such a small bullet. It penetrated the croc's skull and went right through the head, exiting the other side. Most rewarding of all was that the cracking sound when this cartridge was fired did not carry far, so only nearby animals dived into the river for safety.

Clary's previous strategy of driving his Dodge far upstream then hunting on foot along one side of the river, and collecting the skins from dead animals on the way back, worked well. In the afternoon, he hunted downstream. The hunts went very well, mainly because his Winchester Hornet was much quieter than his Mauser 9.3, and it did not scare off the crocs the way the older gun did. Sometimes his quarry was lying at the wrong angle to afford a brain shot, so he tried a neck shot and, to his astonishment, it proved to be just as deadly as a brain shot.

In spite of the four-power telescopic sight, Clary sometimes missed a brain shot, or the bullet hit too low or high to be fatal. A neck shot, however, afforded a bigger, easier target and was just as deadly.

One day he almost got bitten by a croc. He had seen the tail of a fairly large animal on a grassy patch on his side of the river. Not being able to get close enough to shoot, he climbed a convenient tree to where he could just make out the croc's head and body through the grass. It was facing away, so Clary went for a brain shot, aiming at the space right between its eyes. The little hornet bullet hit the skull with a resounding smack, but did not kill the croc; it only stunned it. The animal writhed back and forth, edging closer to the river to escape.

Clary clambered down the tree like an agile chimp and ran towards the thrashing animal which was just about to enter the water. He grabbed its tail and pulled it away from the edge. But the crocodile was fast recovering from its shock. It swung its big head around and snapped at Clary, just missing his face by inches. He dropped the tail, staggered, and fell backwards. June came running up with the Mauser 9.3 and put a bullet through the animal's neck before it could turn on Clary or return to the river. On examining the croc's skull, Clary realised that the shooting angle was too shallow to enable the little bullet to penetrate, so it had simply bounced off the thick, hard skull. He kissed June, giving her a well-deserved thank you for saving his life.

Another day while croc hunting, Clary heard a buffalo moaning in pain. On taking a closer look, he saw on the opposite bank a medium-sized croc, half out of the river, had caught a fully grown female buffalo by its snout and was trying to drag it into the water. The riverbank was muddy and slippery, and the buffalo slid around in the mud as it attempted to pull free. It was a stalemate.

Clary could have easily killed the croc, but it would have fallen into the river and sank out of sight. So, he and his party of skinners sat down to watch the fight and bet on who would win. It took the crocodile half an hour to tire the buffalo enough to pull its mouth and nose slowly underwater and drown it. Once the buffalo was dead and in the water, all the other waiting crocs joined in the feast, tearing off chunks of bloody meat and gulping them down. No crocs came out onto the riverbank, however, so Clary didn't shoot. But watching the buffalo drama compensated for the lack of poor hunting.

After a month of successful hunting along the river, the crocs were getting thinned out quite a bit. During his last week of hunting, Clary only managed to shoot a few crocs each day, and they were mostly small ones which fetched a lowly third grade price.

He stopped hunting, left his camp intact under the watchful eye of a reliable villager, and hurried to Tanga, his truck piled higher with skins than it had ever been before.

Clary could imagine the big grin on the Indian clerk's face when he unloaded this batch of skins in his yard.

By now, however, there was a glut of crocodile skins on the market, and prices had dropped dramatically. Despite delivering many more first grade skins than he had brought in the first time, Clary earned less than half of what he had received previously. The Indian clerk apologised profusely for such low prices and showed Clary his overflowing storehouse, piled to the roof with crocodile skins.

"It seems that everybody in East Africa with a gun is hunting crocodiles and bringing them to me", he said morosely.

Clary and June did not celebrate a windfall this time, but instead drove all night to get home as quickly as possible. They decided that even if the price was low, there was still a lot of money to be made with crocodile skins, and they wanted to go hunting again as soon as possible.

Clary heard rumours that a large number of big crocodiles still swam in Lake Tanganyika – a deep, 200-mile long lake on the western edge of the country. He was curious to know if that was true, so packed a few basic camping supplies and drove there to see for himself.

It transpired that the rumours were true. There were many crocs in the lake, and some very big monsters had been photographed sunning themselves on its banks. However, there were three drawbacks to hunting at this lake. Firstly, the lake was over 200 miles long, with stretches of forest coming right down to the lakeshore, leaving few places for sandbanks to form where crocs could come out to sun themselves. Secondly, wherever a long sandy beach did exist, it was occupied by a fishing village, which deterred crocodiles from using it. Thirdly, there was still so much fish in the lake that crocs did not bother any fishermen or attack people swimming, so they had not been declared vermin. This meant Clary had to buy a licence to shoot crocs here.

Nonetheless, Clary wanted to verify the rumours of how big these crocs were, so he sought to find some of these behemoths. Upon arriving at Lake Tanganyika, he was advised by the local Wafipa tribe to go to a community far up the lake, where he was guaranteed to see a monster croc up close.

When he came to the suggested place, he found a typical Waholoholo village – the local tribe – with round, beehive, grass-roofed huts nestled amongst shady trees and scattered fields of maize. A number of dugout canoes were pulled up on the sandy shore, with drying fishing nets draped over them. Masses of shiny silver minnows were drying in the burning sun on palm thatch mats laid on the beach.

It was customary to pay respects to the Waholoholo headman before going about any business in the village, so Clary paid him a visit. When Clary enquired about crocs, the headman who was decked out in his spotless kanzu with gold braiding around the neck and arms, intoned, "Yes, there are plenty of crocodiles in the waters here, including a particularly large one that can be enticed onto our sandbank if it is offered a meal of fresh meat. But you must buy a few scrawny chickens or an old, tough goat as a sacrifice to entice this reptile out."

He leaned back in his carved wooden chair and advised Clary to buy an old goat that they just happened to have tethered by a hut, because this was the preferred sacrificial animal.

Clary suspected that it was the more expensive option, and that the old animal was probably on its last legs. Of course, the asking price was too high, but after a bit of haggling, the final price came down to the equivalent of four chickens, which was considered the minimum number for a sacrifice.

So Clary paid the agreed price, while a reluctant old goat was dragged onto the sandy beach, its throat ceremoniously slit with a sharp knife, and its limbs hacked off and scattered over the sand. Its blood mixed with sand was carried to the lakeshore and thrown into the water, while a dozen men in loin-cloths assembled on the beach and began to softly recite a mysterious verse. The whole community of men, women, and children stopped what they were doing and gathered in random groups higher up on the beach, while the dozen men started chanting a song that got louder and louder to the accompaniment of beating tom-tom drums.

For a long time, nothing stirred in the water. Almost an hour later, when the singers and drummers were getting hoarse and sweating profusely, a cry went up from the waiting crowd as they pointed excitedly to a small black dot far out in the lake. The dot got closer and closer and grew in size as it neared the shore.

First, a massive crocodile head emerged above the water and eyed the crowd for a few minutes. The singers and drummers found new vigour and amplified their voices almost to shouts as the excitement rose amongst the expectantly waiting crowd. Finally, the big brute slowly came out of the water and strode deliberately up the bank to his sacrificial goat. He sauntered over the blood-soaked beach on his huge feet, grabbing one piece of goat after another and, without chewing, swallowed each piece in a hefty gulp.

Clary estimated the crocodile was about 35-feet long from snout to tail tip, and almost five feet at its widest point, and that it weighed a ton, if not more. It was by far the biggest crocodile he had ever seen. The biggest croc he had shot in the Ruvu River was a 23-foot monster, but this one was much bigger.

The mighty animal, having finished its "snack", laid on his ample belly and rested for 20 minutes on the bloody sand, seemingly oblivious to the cacophonous humanity only yards away. The singers and drummers continued their chorus unabated, although in subdued tones and hoarse voices.

When the croc realised that dinner was over and no second helping was forthcoming, it turned slowly towards the lake and sauntered to the water's edge. Before the croc had gone more than a few feet, Clary's heart sank into his boots as he saw laughing little children run after the ambling animal and climb onto its back, riding it right into the water and far out into the lake until it dived underwater and was gone.

The children splashed their way back to shore, still laughing with delight. Then the singers and drummers stopped their chants and everyone returned to their daily routine.

Clary's biggest regret was that he had not brought a camera to record this memorable event. He had brought his rifle with plenty of ammunition, but his camera was lying somewhere at home. The headman told Clary that they had been calling this crocodile out for food ever since he was a small boy. They believed that this croc was a lake god, and by feeding it sometimes, it would protect the village fishermen from being attacked by the other crocs. It must have worked, since nobody had ever been taken by a croc along this part of the shore.

Some ten years later, Clary heard that one day the croc had failed to appear and was never seen again, in spite of the villagers singing and drumming all day long and slaughtering a big fat cow as an offering to their beloved crocodile. Based on the headman's tales of his youth with this croc, it was probably 70 years old and had simply died of old age.

Chapter 37
A Farm in the Mountains and Baby Crocs

The Soni farm was too small to produce enough coffee and vegetables to make it a viable business. The little workshop was more of a hobby than an income producer, so Clary had to find a better way to make money.

He eventually found a rubber plantation for sale at a cheap price in Korogwe, a small town on the Tanga to Arusha road. He knew nothing about growing rubber trees or harvesting the latex, but bought the plantation anyway, hoping to learn about it in the course of his work there. The trees had been imported from Asia by the German colonial government as an experiment to see if they would grow in this part of Africa. They grew very well and produced good quality latex, so Clary was hopeful that the plantation would provide a good income. In less than a year Clary realised that it had been a big mistake to buy the property, and he discovered why this plantation had been sold so cheaply.

Synthetic rubber for car tyres had just been invented in the United States, and it proved to be more suitable for tyres than natural rubber and less expensive to produce. Natural rubber prices were dropping to such low levels that it was unprofitable to run the plantation. Fortunately, Clary was able to sell it to an Indian farmer for almost as much as he had paid for it. The new owner intended to replant it with kapok trees whose fluffy wool commanded a reasonable price as a filling for life jackets, mattresses, and upholstery.

Clary then heard about a small confiscated German farm still for sale at Malindi, high up in the Usambara Mountains.

His offer on the farm was accepted by the government, and once again he moved to a new home.

This farm was four times bigger than his Soni farm and boasted a large plum orchard, as well as apple, pear, orange, and lemon trees. It had a small cedar forest and a large stand of wattle trees whose dried bark was used for making shoe polish and tanning leather. There was also one fertile patch of land along a stream, which was good for growing vegetables, but the rest of the farm was wild scrubland suitable only for grazing cattle.

The biggest attraction of this farm was a solidly built, two-storey German farmhouse with plastered walls, inside and out. The outer walls were two feet thick and made of compacted earth which was reinforced with wattle. The farmhouse was a long building with a sitting room in the middle, two large bedrooms on one side, and a kitchen and dining room at the other end. A bathroom and a long drop toilet were separately situated at the back of the main house. It had no electricity, no running water, and no telephone. Above the sitting room and bedrooms was a large office, and a storeroom with two small windows overlooking a fruit orchard. There were two big storage barns behind the main house in which safari equipment could be stored.

The farmhouse and compound sat on a flat ridge overlooking the Mlalo Basin, 3000 feet below. June had the business brains, and she soon made plans to use all the farm's resources and exploit its full potential, which left Clary time to concentrate on building up his hunting safari business.

One morning in town, Clary read in a regional newspaper that the game department believed there were still too many crocs in the rivers, despite the high number of them that had already been killed. The department determined that their numbers must be reduced even further. Hunters and native fishermen were encouraged to catch baby crocodiles (hatchlings) for which a bounty of one shilling per head would be paid. Crocodile eggs fetched a payment of ten cents per egg. A single crocodile nest could contain 20 to 30 eggs, so it was possible to earn some decent money by finding the nests.

These bounties on hatchlings and eggs had been in place since crocs were placed on the vermin list, but had largely been ignored in favour of the more lucrative skin trade. To take advantage of this baby croc and egg offer, Clary and June made another trip to their Ruvu river camp to hunt big crocs and perhaps collect some eggs and hatchlings as well. On their first morning at the Ruvu, they walked upriver along one side, as they had done so successfully before. Crocodiles of all sizes dashed out of the tall grass on all sides and made for the safety of the river before Clary could even get his gun up to shoot. There were many sandy banks which showed evidence of constant use by the crocs, but not one animal was caught out in the open.

That first morning, the hunters returned to camp empty-handed. The afternoon was the same. Many miles both upriver and downriver, the crocodiles were equally wary of humans, diving for deep water at the slightest hint of danger. *There must be a way to outsmart these beasts*, thought Clary, and decided to work out new ways to hunt them, as there were still plenty of crocs in this river. The problem was that none of them stayed in one spot long enough for Clary to take a shot.

Clary's first new tactic was to walk parallel to the riverbank, keeping far inland where he wouldn't be noticed. Then he would creep very quietly towards the river, hoping to catch a crocodile out in the open. This worked with two small crocs dozing on open banks, but most of the others were resting in the long grass where they could not be seen. His second attempt at outsmarting these clever brutes was to walk very quietly to the riverbank and climb a high tree from which he could see any crocs resting in the long grass on the opposite bank. This method worked for a few big animals, but many more crocodiles made it into the river after being warned of Clary's approach by barking baboons.

In some places, there were simply no big trees to climb to get a view over the grass, or just no trees at all. At one of these open, treeless places, Clary built a hide of bunched grass close to the riverbank, hoping that some crocs would come to sun themselves. Only one animal came the whole morning, and it was too small to be worth shooting. He spent an entire day making hideouts on all of the sandy banks and cutting paths through the bushes to each one, so that he could enter a blind quietly and without being seen.

The next day, he went from one hideout to the next, shooting any good-sized animals that were lying in the open. Except for a few pesky baboons raising the alarm at Clary's approach, he managed to bag quite a few crocs. By the third day of hunting with the blinds, the crocs learned to avoid all places with a hideout on the opposite bank. Clary came into camp frustrated and empty-handed.

There was one last trick to try, and that was to shoot a large animal such as a waterbuck as bait, then tie it to a stake a few yards from the riverbank. Clary would hide on the opposite bank with a clear view of the carcass, and shoot any crocs eating it. On his first morning with the bait, only two brave crocs came out of the river to consume the meat while more of their cohorts swam nearby awaiting the all-clear. Clary only shot two small crocs feeding on the bait that day, one in the morning and one in the afternoon.

During the night, many crocs came out of the water and devoured the entire waterbuck. Whatever they left, including half a length of bloody rope, was eaten before dawn by hyenas. When Clary arrived the next morning, expecting to see a croc or two, he found nothing except trampled bare ground and one disappointed vulture.

Shooting game at night with a spotlight was prohibited by law but excluded vermin animals such as crocodiles, so this was the next method he tried. This time, Clary shot an old warthog, pulled it to a new place on the river, and threw its stomach into the water to attract customers. He left one of his trackers to watch over the pig in order to keep vultures and hyenas away until nightfall. When it was dark, the tracker paddled his canoe to where Clary was hiding on the opposite side.

It was impossible to see any movement where the warthog was staked out, but by listening to the racket of breaking bones, Clary could guess when a croc was feeding. He waited until the feeding crocs were fully engrossed in their meal before switching on his powerful flashlight. A blaze of eyes reflected in the beam that illuminated a group of startled and confused crocodiles. Clary peered at the nearest croc through the telescopic sight of his .22 Hornet, but he could not make out the scope's crosshairs. He had not bothered to check how his night vision would function with a scope and a powerful flashlight, thinking it would be just like daylight shooting. Now he could only guess where the crosshairs were indicating, so he fired anyway but hit nothing. All the crocs splashed loudly into the river and disappeared. Sound carries very much farther at night than during the day, so not only was the shot heard in camp several miles away, but it also awoke every nearby troop of sleeping baboons into a barking frenzy who warned all crocodiles within miles that danger lurked.

"To hell with you bloody crocs!" shouted Clary, as he turned and made a beeline for his truck to drive home. Crocodile hunting was over. With all his options played out, he had been defeated by these ancient reptiles.

Crocodiles had been living on earth for millions of years before primates appeared. They survived so long because of their intelligence and ability to avoid or overcome danger whenever it appears. This is exactly what they were now doing wherever they had been intensely hunted in Tanganyika. They adapted their habits such as sunbathing in long grass instead of on sandbanks, or if they did come out onto an open sandbank, they kept their eyes open rather than sleeping, and ran for cover at the slightest hint of danger. These strategies proved successful for them, as the number of skins being delivered to buyers had dropped dramatically, despite reported crocodile incidents being down by only a half.

However, crocodile hunting was not entirely over. There were still baby crocs that could be easily caught with a spotlight at night on the grassy shore. Clary had to be wary of bigger crocs lurking nearby, because they also prey on crocodile hatchlings. Night after night, Clary and June went out in the canoe, spotlighting crocs. Many shiny eyes were caught in the beams. Some were frogs, others snakes, but most were crocodile eyes, big and small. However, it proved impossible to paddle close enough to catch one of the small ones by grabbing it behind the head, because it always ducked underwater just at the last moment.

A stroke of good fortune came their way one morning when Clary and June were walking along the riverbank. They heard a muffled squeaking sound coming from a mound of earth and leaves about 20 yards from the riverbank. They watched the mound eagerly as newly hatched crocodiles emerged, all covered in dirt and egg white. The hatchlings instinctively ran towards the river where their mother was waiting in the water to protect them.

Clary had his 450 double in his hands and was watching the river in case the mother crocodile came out to retrieve her young. He instructed June to grab the babies as they came out of the nest and put them into a sack he had brought to collect eggs.

June let out a lot of "Ouch, ouch, you little bugger!" cries as babies scampered past Clary and made it safely into the river.

"Grab them behind the neck, you silly woman!" yelled Clary, as more hatchlings scampered past him.

June had been trying to catch them by the tail, so they turned around and gave her a good nip on her fingers with needle-sharp little teeth. In the end, June got five into the sack, the rest escaping into the river where their mother was waiting to greet them.

Finding crocodile nests proved even more frustrating than trying to shoot the adults. After a fruitless week of searching for nests, Clary and June packed up and went home with their five baby crocodiles and the skins from the harvested ones. Surprisingly, the crocodile skin price had gone up quite a bit due to a shortage of hides being brought in. Clary was pleased with the price he got for his skins, as it meant another few weeks of financial freedom.

At first, Clary had assumed he would collect crocodile eggs for the bounty of ten cents each, but baby crocs were one shilling each. So, suddenly he had the bright idea of gathering the eggs, take them home, incubate them, and collect the shillings for new-born crocs instead of the eggs.

At the farm, before he left to hunt for the crocs, he had prepared a large tank of mud brick walls with dry leaves scattered over the sandy bottom so that he could hatch the eggs. He also built a high-walled tank containing shallow water, rocks, and water-weeds in which to keep the crocs after they had hatched, so that they felt at home before he murdered them. Back at the farm, the baby crocodiles were put into their riverine heaven, fed on scraps of meat, and left to grow so that eventually they became one of Clary's varied pets that he boasted about.

Some months later, when both Clary and June were away on another egg-hunting safari, an army medical team came to the farm. They had orders to spray insecticide on all standing water to kill the mosquito larvae, in an effort to combat the spread of malaria. The army team was equipped with mobile spraying tanks containing DDT. They sprayed all standing water, including the tank with baby crocodiles, unaware that animals were living in those tanks. A day later, one of the farmhands found all five babies floating belly-up in their Garden of Eden. They were all dead.

When Clary returned to the farm, empty-handed, several weeks later, he was livid when he heard that the army had poisoned his crocodiles. He wrote a stinging letter to the army commander, demanding not monetary compensation but rather five baby crocodiles, "namely crocodylus niloticus", to replace the poisoned ones. To add impetus to his demand, he sent a copy of his letter to the district commissioner and the chief game warden. Except for an official letter of regret for their actions from the army, along with a promise of adequate compensation, Clary received no other correspondence and he laid the incident to rest.

However, a few months later, when Clary was at his Ruvu River camp, a troop of weary army soldiers came to seek his advice on an urgent matter. A dishevelled young army sergeant who was at his wit's end, asked where and how he could catch some baby crocodiles on the Ruvu River, or anywhere else in the country for that matter. He explained that his troops had been searching for weeks up and down all the rivers in this area and had not been able to catch a single crocodile. The soldiers were totally fed up with this mosquito-infested, hot and humid hell, and just wanted to get back to civilization.

Upon enquiring why the British Army in East Africa required crocodiles, Clary was told that an army medical team had accidentally poisoned a farmer's crocodile farm. The irate farmer had refused monetary compensation and demanded five baby crocodiles to replace them. Realising that these poor men had been tasked with catching replacement crocs for him, Clary decided not to reveal that he was the irate farmer in question. Instead, he told the young sergeant that this was the wrong time of year for crocs to lay eggs, and that he should try again in the rainy season.

However, said Clary, trying not to grin, if the army offered this farmer decent remuneration rather than the paltry five shillings that had originally been suggested for the dead crocs, then the farmer would most likely accept it.

Much relieved, the sergeant and his ragged troops left camp with a new spring in their step. Weeks later, an official letter from the army arrived in the mail, containing a letter of profuse apology and a cheque for an amount far higher than the 20 shillings Clary had expected to receive.

Chapter 38
The Crown Prince

The Crown Prince of Germany was known throughout Europe as a keen hunter. This was also well known by the German community in East Africa, who had been allowed to return after the First World War. No one expected another war to erupt, so when the Germans returned, life for them resumed where it had left off, with everyone going about their business as usual.

During this period, a German amateur hunter from Arusha who was in the bush hunting small game, came across an elephant with very large tusks. He did not shoot it because he did not have an elephant licence. On his return to Arusha, he boasted about the existence of this huge tusker to his hunting friends. A German nobleman in this community ardently proposed that this elephant be reserved for the German Crown Prince to hunt. He suggested that since the Prince was a relative of the English royal family, he should be given the privilege of shooting this elephant as a gesture of goodwill between Germany and England.

The British administration in Tanganyika, on being told about this goodwill gesture, agreed to have the elephant "marked" as the property of the Prince of Germany, and given protected status in the territory. With this status, no one was allowed to hunt or harm that animal other than the Crown Prince of Germany.

Other hunters who sighted this elephant in various parts of the territory confirmed that it was indeed an elephant with oversized tusks, and they reported its whereabouts to the game department who kept track of its movements.

A formal invitation from the Tanganyika government to the Crown Prince to visit the country and shoot this tusker, was delivered to the German consulate. However, the Prince was unable to come to East Africa to collect his trophy before the Second World War broke out.

During the war years, hunting was severely curtailed due to a lack of suitable ammunition for sporting rifles, so the big elephant was free to wander unmolested throughout his realm, out of sight and out of mind of the people who wanted to kill him. After the Second World War ended, game hunting resumed and the protected status of this huge elephant was lifted, making it available to hunt for anybody with the appropriate licence.

Many hunters, both professional and amateur, hunted this elephant for years without success. Some lucky ones came close enough to take a pot shot at it, but either their gun calibre was too small or the bush was too dense to allow a bullet to penetrate deep enough to make a kill. Being constantly harassed by hunters made the elephant ever more elusive and cunning. Eventually, it disappeared and was not seen for years. However, hunters knew it was still around somewhere, because they occasionally came across its unmistakable footprints.

The elephant had a vast territory of several thousand square miles in which it roamed unseen, according to a variable timetable based on seasons and rains that only the massive creature itself knew.

Clary also tried to hunt this elephant when the rains favoured a certain area in which it had been sighted years before. He came across its fresh spoor one morning and followed it, though he had to give up after a few hours of tracking because the bush it had entered was so dense it was impenetrable for any man. The next morning he picked up the fresh tracks again near a waterhole and gave chase.

The elephant was feeding slowly, moving from tree to tree, breaking off succulent branches to eat. It favoured walking into the wind all the time, so that it could smell dangers ahead but not behind. As Clary followed its unmistakable spoor, he knew he was getting close to it by noticing the freshly broken branches. Suddenly its tracks indicated that for some unknown reason the elephant had stopped eating and made a beeline for a dense grove of bush, as though it was late for an appointment. Clary realised that the wary animal had become aware that it was being hunted so had fled the area. He had to abandon the chase.

On the third day, Clary walked all over the previous day's ground looking for fresh spoor, even climbing trees and hills to scout the surrounding bush for any sign of the animal, but he found nothing. The elephant had probably picked up Clary's scent because of the unsteady wind yesterday and had now left the territory.

Two weeks later, Clary returned to the same spot but only saw two-week-old elephant spoor. So for this year, the hunt for the Crown Prince was over.

Clary spoke to some honey hunters he met a few months later, who told him that they had seen a huge elephant in the bush, far away from waterholes or other sources of water. Clary thought that it was probably just passing through that area, but the honey hunters insisted that it had been there for a long time. Clary did not believe them, because elephants must drink at least once every three or four days, but he decided to check it out for himself.

He took a fly camp and two trackers with him and bashed as far into the dense bush as he could get with his truck, then hiked the remainder of the way to a place called Ndedo, right into the middle of South Maasailand, where he made his crude camp.

To his surprise, he found an old set of large familiar elephant footprints and chewed branches, indicating that the big tusker had remained in this area for a long while, just as the honey hunters had said. The problem was that there were no waterholes or rivers within a three-day elephant march, so where had his elephant found water?

Clary and his knowledgeable guides searched for days for hidden water sources of some kind that the elephant could have used, but found nothing. There were no waterholes or hidden springs, nor were there any large baobab trees with secret pools of water in them. In fact, there were no baobabs at all, nor any other trees large enough to store water. It was indeed a mystery.

Perhaps the elephant had brought some water with him, Clary joked later, sitting in camp waiting for the kettle to boil so that he could have a deserved cup of tea. The blackened kettle sat on three stones over a smouldering fire, burning old elephant dung and dry balls of Sansevieria leaf fibre which the elephant had chewed and spat out. Occasionally someone would throw another dried ball of chewed fibre into the fire to coax out more heat.

"Of course! That's it!" Clary suddenly blurted out to the startled trackers. "This elephant is getting all his water from Sansevieria leaves!"

Picking up a ball of Sansevieria fibres, he remembered how he had followed a group of bull elephants through waterless country many years ago, and how he had come across balls of chewed Sansevieria leaves.

Clary plucked one long green leaf from a Sansevieria plant. He bashed it with a stone, then twisted it over his cup to see how much liquid it contained. About an eighth of a cup of very bitter green juice dribbled out of the leaf. No doubt when chewed by an elephant, even more juice could be extracted from the leaf. The mystery was solved. The evidence lay all around him for everyone to see, except no one had noticed it. This clever elephant was getting its liquid nourishment from Sansevieria.

Every year around the same time, Clary went out after this big tusker, checking each of its favourite haunts in turn, hoping to finally catch up with it. In three years of searching for it, he only once got a far-off glimpse of its arched back as it moved quickly through heavy thorn bushes.

In those three years, Clary formed a picture of the character of this pachyderm. It was a clever and cunning animal. It knew that it was being hunted, and took intelligent precautions not to be caught. It continued walking into the wind or across the wind, and raised its trunk now and then to catch the scent of whatever was ahead. It stopped frequently to listen for the sound of pursuers. It kept to the thickest patches of brush during the day, and only ventured into open territory after dark to graze on sweet grass or drink water. It never drank from the same waterhole twice in a week, preferring to travel many miles for its next drink. It kept away from elephant herds and remained alone in a locality long after all the other animals had gone away. It stayed in waterless regions for long periods, quenching its thirst with Sansevieria leaves. Whenever it picked up the scent of humans in the air or came across their tracks, it would leave the area completely and not return until the following year.

Interestingly, it was not scared of honey hunters, perhaps due to the fact that they had been plying their trade peacefully alongside elephants for hundreds of years. It did not have a set routine; its movements were unpredictable. Some years it did not visit its old haunts, even when the rains were good and the grass plentiful. Nobody knew where it went in those years. From his past encounters with the elephant, Clary worked out that it ranged throughout the Maasai steppe – an uninhabited wilderness of several thousand square miles – for about four months of the year. Yet for eight months every year, it disappeared into some unknown territory that hunters could only speculate about where it could be.

Very large elephants, some with huge tusks, were often seen in neighbouring Kenya, in Tsavo Park. Whether this crown prince of elephants was amongst them, no one could say for certain. Looking at a survey map of Tanganyika, Clary saw that the country contained vast stretches of roadless, uninhabited bushland where game could range freely without interference from humans. The crown prince could zigzag anywhere he liked for years in this territory without being noticed amongst the vast number of other elephants in the area.

Just after the Great War, there was no scarcity of elephants in Tanganyika, as an estimated one million two hundred thousand of them roamed the country. Game rangers were shooting 3000 elephants per year just to protect poor native farmers from crop-raiding elephants. Sadly, it was not only the pachyderms that suffered at the hand of man, for it was the typical, uneducated reaction of the colonial administrators to use a gun to solve any problem. Whenever a complaint came into headquarters involving wildlife, the answer was always to kill it. It seemed to be the only method they knew, whether it worked or not.

IMAGE 15: 1965. 3000 ELEPHANT TUSKS STORED IN A WAREHOUSE IN DAR ES SALAAM READY TO BE AUCTIONED.

Clary estimated that the crown prince had already been a big-tusked elephant in the 1930s, which was 20 years before, so now it must be nearing its last years of life. If it died a natural death somewhere in the vast savannahs of East Africa, its huge body would probably never be found, as it would be consumed by scavengers and maggots until only sun-bleached bones and the great ivory tusks remained. They too would slowly disintegrate into white calcium powder and leach back into the earth, as tusks have been doing for thousands of years. However, Clary was determined to get those tusks for himself, and so were a lot of other hunters in the territory.

A new man, by the name of Salimu, had just started work as a gun bearer on Clary's latest expedition to find the big tusker. He was intelligent and clever; in fact, Clary thought him too clever to be a simple gun bearer. He was dressed unusually well, wearing a brown short-sleeved shirt, long khaki trousers, and brown lace-up shoes, whereas the other gun bearers were barefooted and wore a shuka or kanzu. Salimu's job on this trip was to stay close and carry the heavy 450 Express rifle. Clary was wary of him and kept an eye on his movements.

One hot afternoon while out hunting, the party took a rest under a shady tree. Clary lay down in its shade, placing his double-barrel rifle against the trunk, within easy reach should the need to use it arise. The party rested for an hour under the shady trees and were awoken by the noise of a group of chattering monkeys.

Just then, a large animal, possibly a rhino, lumbered away from them through the bush. Clary picked up his rifle and instinctively opened the breech to check that he had the correct cartridges and that the chambers were clear. He noticed one barrel was obstructed with some debris about halfway down. Thinking that a piece of bark might have fallen in while it was resting against the tree, he tried blowing down the barrel, but the obstruction did not move. So, he cut a long stick and tried poking it out. Still the blockage stayed in place. However, when he rammed the stick hard through the barrel several times, he managed to dislodge a wad of sticks and charcoal onto the ground.

Someone is trying to kill me, was Clary's first incredulous thought. If he had fired with a blocked barrel, his gun would have exploded in his face, with fatal results.

He did not mention the gun blockage to any of his men, but simply led his group back to camp. On arrival, he confronted Salimu with the facts, accusing him of deadly sabotage. Of course, the gun bearer vehemently denied it, although he could not explain how the chamber became blocked while the gun was in his care. He was summarily dismissed.

Much later, it emerged that Salimu was, in fact, a spy for another hunter who was hoping to find the whereabouts of the crown prince by noting where Clary hunted for it.

Clary remembered how in his early twenties he had almost died from being poisoned by a new man on his team. The man had secretly put pieces of dried hyena liver, which are very toxic, into Clary's evening meal. When he started feeling nauseated and had terrible stomach pains, and the new man suddenly ran away from camp, Clary knew he had eaten poison. He sent two gun bearers to the next village for help, and they returned with a gourd containing pungent leaves and a vile smelling liquid concocted by an old Burungi woman. His gun bearer said he must pour the liquid into a cup with sugar and drink it. The concoction tasted like kerosene mixed with castor oil. Clary surmised that if the poison did not kill him, this potion certainly would.

Within minutes of taking the antidote, his mouth and throat felt numb, and he had to empty his bowels. He spent the whole night behind his tent trying to poop his guts out. The next morning, he was utterly exhausted and could hardly stand from his ordeal. For the next three days he felt so weak that he could not walk more than a few yards between rests. Everything he ate or drank passed through his intestines like water out of a tap. However, he had survived thanks to an old Burungi medicine woman who knew what ancient remedy to use. It was highly unlikely that a Western doctor in a hospital would have known what treatment to provide. Since that day, Clary had been very careful with any new men he recruited.

Ironically, the blocked rifle barrel had been caused by a ground hornet trying to build a nest inside it. Clary discovered this sometime later, when he saw a ground hornet flying into his gun's muzzle with bits of charcoal in its mandible. When he opened the breech, a bit of charcoal fell out. It was just a coincidence that the blocked barrel and the spy incident had happened at the same time.

In his fourth year hunting the crown prince, Clary was told by some other hunters that they believed the elephant had died a natural death, because it had not been seen for a long time. Another hunter claimed that it had been spotted crossing into Kenya and was now living in Tsavo Park, a protected area. Yet another man claimed that a group of ivory poachers from Somalia had killed it and smuggled the tusks out of the country. Any of these rumours could have been true, for no one could prove otherwise. But Clary refused to give up until he had irrefutable evidence that the elephant really was in Tsavo or dead.

The rains were short this fourth year, only partially filling the widely spaced waterholes on which the game relied for water. This scarcity of water would force the wild animals to congregate along the permanent rivers that in turn would make hunting easier, since the game would not be so widely scattered about the bush. There were still browsers far away in the bush that did not need to drink to survive, such as greater kudu, gerenuk, oryx, and Grant's gazelle. They could meet all their liquid needs from the plentiful supply of green leaves they ate, and they would have no competition from the grazing animals.

Clary had been camping with a short crew in the northern part of Maasailand, hunting greater and lesser kudu to fill a taxidermist's order for replacement of head mounts that had been spoiled by red fungus – a mould that destroys unsalted damp skins. One of the larger waterholes near camp still held grey, muddy water that could be settled and filtered to use as washing water. However, drinking and cooking water for the camp was used sparingly and came from a steel drum that they carried on the truck.

One morning, while checking spoor around a waterhole to see what game was still in the sector, Clary's heart skipped a beat as he spotted a large elephant's footprints in the mud. On careful scrutiny, he realised it was the crown prince's unique spoor; no doubt about it. The elephant's footprint indicated that it had drunk at the waterhole about three o'clock that morning. That was only four hours ago, giving the elephant a very short head start.

Without returning to camp to resupply with water and biltong for a possible long hunt, he and his two trackers immediately started tracking at a fast pace. At this rate, there was a good chance of catching up with the elephant at midday when it usually rested in a thicket in the hottest part of the day. After an hour of fast, hard tracking, Clary realised that the animal was not stopping to feed or slowing its pace. It was heading out of the area as fast as it could go. Perhaps it had come across Clary's trail somewhere and was leaving that territory.

Discouraged by this realisation, he headed back to camp to think things over. *There could be a chance*, he thought, *a slim chance, that his quarry was making for a region to the south of their camp, about one hundred miles away.* He had seen its tracks there some years before, so he made up his mind to go for this slim chance. The camp was thrown haphazardly onto the Dodge truck, and they sped away, heading for a place only Clary knew about.

It took them ten hours of nonstop driving over rough secondary roads and washed-out hunting tracks before they reached their intended campsite well after midnight. They were so dog-tired that no one bothered to put up a tent or even a bed for the night, each man opting to sleep right where he fell, Clary included.

The next morning, before the new camp was set up, Clary sent one of the local Ndorobo honey hunters to inspect a nearby waterhole for usable water and signs of any elephants. The man returned with the good news that the waterhole still contained some dark, soupy water, although no elephants had been to it recently. There had been only a few warthogs taking a mud bath. Fresh meat for the camp had run out, but Clary did not dare shoot at any animal here, not even with his silent .22, for fear of scaring off the crown prince if it was close by. Little dik-dik, guinea fowl, and spurfowl were perfectly safe as they sauntered around camp with not a care in the world. It was corned beef hash for everyone until further notice.

During the third night in camp, Clary was awoken at about 4am by the twittering of an angry plover – a bird that liked to nest close to water and attempted to chase away any animals that came too close to its nest. *It could be the crown prince,* thought Clary! When it was light enough to see, Clary sent the Ndorobo man to check on the waterhole. Ten minutes later, he came running back, visibly excited. In a squeaky voice, he confirmed that there were fresh footprints of a very large elephant at the waterhole. He was sure it was the crown prince. The three-man hunting party was on the spoor within minutes of hearing the good news.

The big tracks of this heavy elephant were easy to follow on the light, pallid earth as the creature ate and moved slowly amongst the green thorn trees. Hour after hour, they tracked the elephant in the burning heat, as the merciless sun beat down on them from a cloudless sky. They were constantly plagued around their eyes and mouths by tiny, stingless sweat bees sucking their body fluids as the men trudged through the windless thickets. They were constantly alert for other game that might be spooked by their presence and give them away.

Every so often they made five-minute stops to listen for the tell-tale sounds of an elephant or other big game. Whenever they passed a tall tree, someone climbed up to scour the bush ahead for signs of the elephant. At midday, they stumbled into a tangle of impenetrable wait-a-bit and white thorn Acacia trees, where passage was impossible, and visibility was limited to a few feet. The only way through this patch was to backtrack to lighter sections and make a detour to regain the spoor on the other side. The wind was now shifting around and blowing in all directions, which was risky for them, but hopefully it would not blow towards the elephant.

The big elephant was following its usual habit of laying up at midday for a rest in the thickest, most impenetrable thorn patch around. Clary realised that it was hopeless to try to catch up to it in this impassable refuge. The only alternative was to wait until their quarry started to move again after the fiercest heat of the day had subsided. They would have to stay close enough to hear it when it started moving, and hope they were downwind of it.

Sweating profusely and thirsty beyond words, they rested amongst the long, sharp thorns of a skinny, shadeless tree, drank the last drops of water, and put up with the plague of sweat bees buzzing around their faces. They knew this was the inevitable price to pay for hunting here.

Then the little Ndorobo tracker heard it first. He touched Clary's arm very gently, then put a finger to his own ear, which meant, "I hear something." Everyone was awake by now and listening intently. Then it came again – faint yet unmistakable, the rumbling of an elephant's stomach. No one said a word. They only put their fingers to their ears and then pointed in the same direction. An elephant could be faintly heard moving through the bushes not too far away.

A wordless discussion ensued between the men as to what the best course of action was. Clary settled it by deciding that he was going into the thicket alone. The rest were to stay here and only come forward if a shot was fired or if he called them. They only had one rifle, the 450 Express which Clary had, so the others would be unprotected if a dangerous situation arose. They knew from experience to run for cover if they were charged.

Clary removed his heavy leather boots and slipped on his moccasins, which would silence his footfalls like those of an Ndorobo tracker who went about barefoot and moved silently all the time. He removed his hat, wiped his sweating brow with the back of his sleeve, and handed the hat to his tracker. He checked the wind one last time by shaking the bag of ash at head height. It was steady and in his favour, so Clary started the final stalk. It would make too much noise to check the chambers of his rifle now and cursed himself for not doing it sooner.

Walking both upright and silently through this bush was impossible, because thorns and branches scratching against his heavy khaki clothes made a grating noise loud enough to wake the dead. Even crouching low to stoop under the brush was difficult and tiring, so Clary got down on his haunches and waddled along like an oversized goose to get under the low branches. He got onto his hands and knees whenever the lowest branches blocked his way, dragging his loaded gun by the muzzle behind him. The faint click of a gun's safety catch being thumbed off was loud enough to warn an animal with the acute hearing of an elephant, but it was too dangerous to crawl through this thick bush with the safety off and risk snagging a stick in the trigger. He reluctantly left it on, and would have to risk the elephant hearing him thumb it off at the last second. Clary hoped he would be in a position to shoot before he had to push the safety off.

At an estimated 50 yards from the feeding elephant, he could see nothing of the animal through the dense bush. At 40 yards, he had a glimpse through a thicket of some big feet shuffling about, yet still could not see the body above them. At 30 yards, he caught the unmistakable earthy whiff of elephant, which confirmed that the wind was still in his favour. He got down and lay flat on his stomach to get a better view below the bushes and saw the tips of two giant tusks almost touching the ground. Now he had no doubt in his mind that this was the crown prince with its long, heavy, magnificent tusks.

IMAGE 16: THE CROWN PRINCE OF ELEPHANTS.

It was time for the final act. Holding his gun in front of him, Clary elbowed his way under the dense trees on his stomach, oblivious to the thorns sticking into his flesh, until he was six paces behind the animal. He stood up carefully, easing himself between the branches with his gun ready to fire, then took two paces to the left for a better view.

Just then, the elephant heard him and lifted its massive head, turning slightly left, and looked over the thick bush at him. They made eye contact at the same moment. Clary aimed and slid the safety catch off. Then he fired. The colossal crown prince collapsed to the earth and finally met his demise that afternoon in South Maasailand where he had roamed for the last 70 or more years of his life.

Clary waited where he was until his racing heartbeat slowed and his nerves calmed down. Then he pushed his way through the thicket and went up to his elephant as it lay on the hard, grey earth. He touched its open eye to ascertain that it was dead, then caressed its beautiful long curving tusks, and stroked its rough hide. He cut off its hairless tail, to prove his ownership of the elephant, as was traditional. Just as he did many times when no one was watching, Clary said a silent prayer of thanks to the elephant gods for letting him take this animal's life. Then he called out to his trackers to come and bring his hat, while he sat upon the elephant's bloated stomach, pulling thorns out of his hands and knees while waiting for his men to appear.

Cries of "Ah, Ah, Ah", announced the trackers' arrival and their incredulity at seeing such a gigantic creature. Neither tracker had ever seen an elephant with tusks as long as these. They believed that this elephant had evaded hunters and survived for so long because it had been protected all these years by an elephant god, but now it was its time to die, so Clary had been permitted to take it. These true men of the bush always had a simple explanation for all of life's events.

When it was time to leave, the two happy trackers led the way back to camp, talking loudly to each other about their previous hunts and the hardships they had endured. It was difficult to find a direct way through the thorn patches, so they made a long detour to skirt the densest parts. These detours delayed them so much that darkness fell while they were still in the thick bush. Clary took the lead and guided the group towards camp by following the stars overhead. They arrived very late, dead beat, thirsty, and hungry, to find a silent, sleeping camp. The camp staff had thought the hunting party would spend the night sleeping rough in the bush, so they had all gone to bed. Dinner that night was, for the last time, corned beef with ugali.

Clary decided the following day would be a day of rest to remove embedded thorns and pick off blood-sucking ticks, as well as sharpen axes, pangas, and knives for the task of removing the ivory. The two small, trusting dik-diks lost their lives to a.22 rifle to feed a camp full of men hungry for fresh meat.

Next day, they loaded all the tools and equipment onto the Dodge truck, as well as food and the last of their drinking water, then bashed an almost straight path through the dense bush towards the dead elephant. They used a huge flock of circling vultures as a guide, but had to leave the truck a few hundred yards from the carcass, because even that steel monster could not batter its way through more than a few yards of tangled growth before its engine stalled and died.

When they arrived at the dead elephant, Clary examined the carcass closely. He saw that it had at least two old bullet wounds that had healed over. They had probably been made by an Arab ivory poacher using a muzzleloader at too far a distance with too little powder to inflict a deadly injury. Or maybe the injuries had come from one of the many unlucky professional hunters who had been searching for this elephant for years and had managed to fire at it from far off.

Clary noticed that only half a tooth was left in its jaw, and even that tooth was worn down to a stump. It meant that this old boy was on his last set of teeth. Elephants go through six sets of teeth during their life, and once this elephant's last tooth fell out, he would no longer be able to chew food and would die a slow, agonising death by starvation. Clary guessed that this ancient elephant had probably had less than a year to live before its last tooth fell out and it starved to death.

It hurt him to see seven tons of elephant meat left for the dining pleasure of local carnivores and scavengers. However, as there were no villages within a hundred miles to collect the meat, he had no choice except to leave it. Perhaps the carcass would keep the local lions and leopards supplied with enough food for many weeks so that they would not have to hunt for other prey.

After Clary taught his tracker how to take a straight and level picture of him with the mighty elephant, he let them remove the tusks. It took four strong men swinging heavy axes four hours to hack out the two tusks, and same four men to carry one tusk back to the truck. They made six return trips to the carcass to bring the ivory and some meat to the truck. With the Dodge now loaded with ivory, meat, and happy people, Clary pushed his way back to camp along the same path they had just made. He stopped in camp just long enough to pack up all the equipment and load it onto the truck. Then he started the long, dusty drive home.

On the way, the Ndorobo trackers, together with a large quantity of elephant meat, were dropped off at a group of huts. The meat would be grilled that night over an open fire and feasted on by all the villagers, while they listened to tales of the great elephant hunt. The rest of the safari motored on, stopping only once for petrol in Mombo, then continuing to the farm. They arrived tired, hungry, thirsty, dusty, and stinking of sweat, just as dawn broke over the sleeping farmhouse.

A few days later, Clary and June travelled to Tanga with the tusks to register them at the game department office, as required by law. Each tusk was assigned a unique number, which was stamped with a steel dye above the lip mark. This procedure was a feeble attempt by the game department to control poaching, by making it difficult to trade in unmarked tusks. Unfortunately, the dyes used for stamping ivory were also used for other purposes so were available for purchase at any hardware store, thus allowing poachers to stamp their illegal tusks themselves. The unique number was registered in a game department ivory archive book, and a copy of this registration number was given to Clary as proof of legal ownership of the tusks.

At the Indian ivory trader's warehouse, each tusk was weighed separately; the longer one weighed in at 167 pounds, while the slightly shorter one was 163 pounds – a total of 330 pounds. They were the biggest tusks registered in Tanga in the last 20 years, which made Clary a bit of a hero for a day and the talk of the town. The ivory trader paid a premium for such big tusks, giving Clary a cheque for the equivalent of a bank manager's annual salary.

It was regrettable that these magnificent tusks would be exported to India, where they would be cut up to make billiard balls, bangles, statuettes, piano keys, or a thousand other items for which the well-heeled would pay a high price. Looking at his ledger book, the trader moved his finger down the columns of ivory purchases to show Clary that although his tusks were the heaviest ones purchased in the last 20 years, there were at least 60 other tusks that he had bought that weighed over 100 pounds, with one even being 150 pounds. All these tusks had been exported, and received the same ignoble fate of being cut up for trinkets.

Over the next 12 years, Clary would guide his hunting clients on safaris in his South Maasailand realm. On these safaris, a total of 16 elephants with tusks weighing more than 100 pounds each were shot. It was a great relief for Clary to know that the tusks of his clients' elephants would end up in trophy rooms where they would be admired and preserved intact for posterity.

Over his entire hunting career, Clary would shoot almost 100 elephants, most of them would be back-up shots for clients with poor marksmanship. The rest of the elephants were to pay off debts, or just to cover his everyday living expenses. He had a farm to run and six children to feed, clothe, and send to school, and ivory always fetched a good price to pay these expenses. An elephant with big tusks paid for the annual school fees, all clothes, and shoes for his three school-aged children, and there would be some money left over to meet farm expenses for half a year.

Whenever the truck broke down or the car needed major repairs, an elephant had to sacrifice its life to pay for these contingencies. Christmas was a very expensive time because all the workers on the farm expected a present, and so did all the children. A big elephant solved all Christmas problems. At that time, it was the normal way people with hunting licences supplemented their income or solved financial difficulties.

Clary detested those hunters who killed large numbers of elephants in order to become rich, and those who went out every year to shoot five elephants because they could, even though they did not need the money from the ivory. During his lifetime, Clary heard about some men who had boasted about slaughtering hundreds of elephants then bought farms or businesses with their proceeds. They had no regrets about their actions, and in fact, were proud that they had used a natural resource to build a thriving business. Clary was thankful that he never had to meet such a person.

Chapter 39
A Christmas to Remember

One year at Christmas time, Clary asked the next-door farmer who was driving into Tanga for supplies if he could get a lift into town and back home again. The neighbour, being a good friend, agreed. It was a very unpleasant six-hour ride for Clary in the hard-sprung, rattling old farm truck driven by a reckless driver, but it saved him the expense of going with his own car. After arriving in Tanga, he arranged a pick-up time and place with the driver for the next afternoon, for the unpleasant journey back to the farm.

The following afternoon, which was Christmas Eve, Clary was loaded down with boxes crammed full of Christmas presents for everyone, including a few bottles of whisky, gin, and brandy for June and himself, as well as some urgently needed spare parts for the farm.

He waited at the agreed-upon hotel for the driver, but when he had not turned up by late afternoon, Clary feared that the man may have had an accident. So he left his purchases in the care of the hotel reception, and went looking for the truck and driver.

He found out from another truck driver that the farm driver was using the truck to earn his own Christmas presents by doing some extra work transporting goods out of town. He had left Tanga the previous day for an unknown destination, and was not expected back any time soon.

The next day was Christmas Day, so Clary was desperate to get his presents home in time to celebrate with his family. All of the hotels were fully booked with Christmas guests, so there was no way he could stay in Tanga even if he had wanted to. Hiring a car was not possible in those days, so Clary emptied his bank account of all his cash and went looking for a second-hand car to buy. All the car dealerships had closed shop days ago for the Christmas season, and so had all the second-hand car dealers. However, he went to see an Indian friend who was a Muslim and didn't celebrate Christmas, although the Muslim community respected the Christmas tradition by also closing their shops. Clary asked for his friend's help to buy a used car.

Fortunately, his Muslim friend knew a Hindu car dealer a block away, and Clary was able to buy a very cheap, worn-out old Austin after haggling a while over the high price. By the time Clary had bought his car, registered it, filled it with petrol, and loaded his presents and spare parts, it was almost dark, and all offices were closed so he could not get his car insured. However, Clary decided to take the risk and travel without insurance.

Just as he left Tanga, it started to rain heavily. To his dismay, he discovered that the single windshield wiper did not work, and the car leaked, not only through the roof edges but also into the footwell through the rusted floor panels. As there was almost no traffic on the road, he was able to drive carefully and slowly until the rain finally stopped and he could see through the windshield again. When Clary reached the Pangani River ferry, he found that it was deserted and all the boatmen had gone home, even though they were supposed to be on duty until midnight because this ferry was on the main road to Tanga.

To make matters worse, the ferry was tied up on the opposite riverbank. To bring the ferry over to his side of the river, Clary stripped off all his clothes except his underwear, walked a long way upriver, dove into the ice-cold, crocodile-infested river and swam in the dark across and reached the other side before the current swept him past the ferry landing. He made it, but only just, and was shivering from the cold when he clambered onto the muddy bank.

Two startled natives waiting at the ferry landing with their overloaded bicycles could not believe their eyes when a half-naked European crawled out of the dark water, dressed only in a pair of pale underwear. After recovering from their shock, the two men were more than eager to help Clary run the ferry across the river. They pointed out, however, that the ferry's engine room was locked and barred, so there was no way to get the ferry across using the engine.

The ferry was a primitive contraption made of two half-round steel pontoons, held eight feet apart by crossbeams, with a 20-foot deck made of heavy wooden planks. It had an on/off ramp at both ends and an engine compartment in one pontoon. It was capable of carrying two cars or one truck at a time. Its operation was even simpler. A steel rope was suspended across the river and anchored to each side of the riverbank. The ferry was attached to the steel rope by two cables and pulleys, one in front and one in the back. The one diesel engine pushed the ferry across, while the two pulleys rolled along the steel cable, guiding the vessel through the water.

After some thought, Clary concluded that by slackening the rear cable, the ferry would sit at an angle, facing upriver, allowing the current to push the ferry across without an engine. He gingerly unrolled the ferry's rear cable to make it longer, and the ferry began to move slowly across the river. He slackened the cable a bit more and the ferry moved faster through the water. It worked just as he had expected, so the three of them, with Clary still shivering in his underwear, floated across to the other bank at a good speed.

The two laughing, happy, cyclists, having arrived safely on the other side, said, "Asante sana, bwana", which means "Thank you very much, mister", and pedalled off without lights into the gloomy night.

Clary got dressed, then manoeuvred his little car onto the ferry and used the same method in reverse to get to the other side of the river. All alone now, he struggled to keep the rear cable from slipping off its pinion, and almost stopped in mid-stream. But finally he made it across. He tied up the ferry just as he had found it, and drove away.

IMAGE 17: CLARY FERRIED HIS CAR ACROSS THE RIVER ON HIS OWN.

It was just before midnight when he encountered his next obstacle. A loaded truck had slipped off the concrete fording over a shallow stream and was blocking the road. Because he expected no traffic at this time of night, the driver was asleep in his cab, waiting for help to arrive the next morning. Clary could not get past the stranded truck. However, a sleepy turn boy in the back told him to drive upstream a few hundred yards where another vehicle had crossed this evening through the very shallow water above the ford.

Clary weaved his way along the bank until he came to the tracks that showed where the other vehicle had crossed. The water looked shallow enough to drive across even with his small tyres, so he drove in very slowly. Halfway across, he suddenly came to a deeper stretch of water. The little Austin's front end was suddenly submerged, and the engine faltered, spluttered, and died midstream. The turn boy had forgotten to mention that it was a small truck that had crossed here, not a car. When Clary tried the starter, the engine turned over but did not fire, because the radiator fan had thrown water over the spark plugs and distributor, short-circuiting the electrical system.

Somehow Clary would have to get the car out of the stream so that he could dry out the wiring and try to restart. There was not a soul around to help push the car out, except perhaps the sleeping driver and turn boy. They would not be too enthusiastic to jump into the cold water to help a stranded motorist when he could wait a few hours until morning when help would come.

Then he remembered one of his old tricks in such situations. He removed the spark plugs and fan belt, put the car in second gear and pressed the starter button, holding it for 30 seconds. The car rolled forward a few feet, which was just far enough to get the engine out of the deep water. He then dried the whole electrical system with his handkerchief, replaced the dry spark plugs, and pressed the start button. The engine turned over laboriously but did not fire.

He tried again and managed to get one plug to fire, and kept the engine going for a minute before it died. He waited for a few more minutes, hoping that the warmed engine would dry out more. On the next attempt, all cylinders fired nicely, and the car lurched out of the river and onto the bank. He drove back to the road, where he reinstalled the fan belt and continued his journey.

The rest of the trip early that Christmas morning went smoothly until a few miles from home, where he got a flat tyre. It was very cold and misty in the mountains, and the road was slippery from recent rains. Clary did not have the strength left to change the tyre, so he simply pumped it up with a foot pump until it was hard, and drove on quickly before all the air could leak out.

It had rained heavily at the farm, making the driveway up the hill to the house very slippery. However, by rushing the steep driveway at a good speed, he just made it to the top before the little car sank into deep mud and stopped 35 yards from the farmhouse door. It was now 4:30 on Christmas morning. He had made it! It was a Christmas that Clary would never forget.

Chapter 40
On the Nile River

Six months later, a British company was looking for an experienced "bushman" to help with a survey of the Nile River at Jinja, in Uganda, where a large hydro-electric dam called Owen Falls, was planned. The pay was very good, but the contract duration was limited to a maximum of three months, because severe malaria was rampant along that part of the Nile. Whoever took the job was not allowed to take the newly developed antimalarial drugs while there, and would inevitably contract the disease despite other precautions such as mosquito nets on tents, head-to-toe clothing, and the use of insect repellent.

Once the three-month contract was over, the bushman had to leave the area and would be treated with the new, very powerful malaria drug, and be cured. He would never be allowed back into the area in order to prevent mosquitoes from building up resistance to the super drug.

Clary applied for the job and was immediately engaged to take the next available three-month slot. He had to drive to Arusha on his own, where a company car picked him up and took him on to the camp at Jinja.

The surveyors' camp where he would be based seemed quite luxurious for such an out-of-the-way place. It prided itself on having large sleeping tents and comfortable beds. There was a shower and toilet tent behind every main tent. A big mess tent with a lounge attached boasted a good bar that served cold beer and drinks every evening. The campsite was located under a strand of fever and sausage trees about a mile from the Nile river survey site.

There were fewer mosquitoes at this site than near the river, and there was less chance of having problems with the herds of elephants and hippos that moved along the river every night. One day, a technician and his team who had no experience in the wilds of Africa decided to pitch their tents close to the river near the dam site, instead of by the surveyors' campsite. They were armed with one heavy rifle for protection, and so they were not concerned about wild animals near their camp.

After dark, hippos came out of the river and moved onto the grassland to graze. At the same time, other animals such as elephants, buffalo, and plains game, came out of the distant bush and moved down to drink at the river. There was a large amount of animal traffic along the riverbank in the evening, as outgoing hippos grunted and moved out of the path of incoming trumpeting elephants. Buffaloes, caught in-between, bellowed in protest about being pushed around by the others. The plains game had to find their way to the water by squeezing between all the big players while avoiding being trampled or gored by them.

That first evening, the inexperienced technicians in their flimsy tents by the river became alarmed, for they were now caught in the middle of this traffic jam. They decided to scare off the trespassers by firing a few shots into the air. A gunshot during the day will scare the hell out of wild animals and cause them to run in panic, but at night, when the noise carries four times farther, it causes greater panic. So, to say that all hell broke loose when the shots were fired would be an understatement

Trumpeting elephant herds broke off mid-drink and ran helter-skelter back to the safety of the thick bush from which they had just emerged. Startled buffaloes did the same, making a beeline for the safety of the bush, regardless of what was in their way, be it cars, tents, elephants, hippos, or trees. Hippos, those two-ton tanks of fat and bone, chose the shortest distance to the river from where they were amicably grazing, and nothing would stop them.

In the middle of this chaos stood four stupid, terrified technicians, who made matters worse by firing a few more shots into the air, hoping to chase the stampeding herds away from their camp. Not knowing where the shots were coming from, the terror-stricken animals ran wildly in every direction, screeching, trumpeting, grunting, and snorting as they went. Pounding hooves and stamping feet from hundreds of fleeing animals shook the ground like an earthquake.

Clary and his crew heard the shots and the commotion but could do nothing about the situation except listen to the mayhem and wait. Fortunately, only a few buffalo and some lost elephants passed close to their camp and did no harm. Clary, who was the hunter and the only armed guard in the main camp, ordered everyone to take cover behind big trees or in one of the trucks until the commotion had stopped. An hour later, the night became as silent as a graveyard.

The next morning, Clary went to the river with a truck and crew, expecting to find flattened human bodies all over the place. Instead, he saw that the technicians had made one sensible decision, and that was to climb into the biggest, thickest tree they could find. Clary found all four of them still clinging to thorny branches high up in a fever tree, where they had spent the night. They could not find a way to descend the tree trunk safely, despite the fact that they had clambered up it in the dark last night. When a truck was parked underneath the tree, they were able to step onto its high cab and get down.

Their camp and equipment had taken the brunt of the stampede, and it was strewn like rubbish all over the grassy plains behind them. Their brand-new Land Rover was lying on its side, dented and badly bashed about by fleeing wildlife. When it was pulled upright onto its wheels, it started immediately and could be driven into the next town for repairs. Except for a few items of clothing, nothing else was salvageable from the camp. That same afternoon, the four anxious technicians asked to be returned to civilization and never be sent out into darkest Africa again.

Clary's main job was protecting the camp workforce from wild game. He also accompanied the surveyors and helped with their work on the river.

One of his most dangerous jobs was measuring the water depth across the top of the 55-foot high Owen Falls.

Clary did this with two African helpers in a little wooden boat, powered by a 1½ horsepower Seagull single-cylinder outboard motor. This was done with a lead fish attached to a knotted measuring string. Clary let the lead fish sink to the riverbed, then read its depth in the river by counting the knots in his string. One brave native noted the soundings taken in his book as Clary shouted them to him above the din of the engine, while the other brave man manoeuvred the boat through fast-flowing water along the top of the falls, avoiding unseen rocks lurking just below the surface. The boatman never hit any rocks, which could have sheared off the outboard motor's propeller, nor did the little Seagull engine miss a beat. Either event would have sent them plunging over the falls to certain death and to become crocodile food below.

During his tenure on the dam project, Clary only had weekends off. He did not drive into the town of Jinja for endless drinking binges and debauchery like the rest of the surveyors. Instead, he went hunting close to camp, where there was plenty of game. The Europeans in camp did not care for game meat, probably because the camp cook had never been shown how to cook it, whereas the native workmen loved it and were thankful for any game meat they could get. Clary's gifts of meat to them made him a lot of friends amongst the natives, who would willingly do as he requested without question.

On one of his hunts through the reed beds, he saw what looked like a grey rat that was the size of a house cat but had a long hairless tail. Although he only had a large calibre rifle suitable for buffalo with him, Clary shot the rat, believing it to be a new sub-species of rodent. Returning to camp with his prize, he held it up in front of his native crew and asked them if they had ever seen such a big rat.

One man jumped up, said "yes", took the rodent, and was about to start cutting it up when Clary rushed in and snatched it back, saying that it was not for eating. The men laughed when he said that, thinking he was making a joke. When the natives realised that Clary was serious, a local man explained that it was a cane rat. They were very common in swampy areas of Uganda, and were considered a delicacy by the local people because the rats only ate grass and water plants, which made their flesh tender and very tasty.

None of the Europeans working at the site had ever seen a cane rat and became quite concerned when they learned that the grassy plains around camp were the rats' favourite haunt. Waving his buffalo gun in the air, Clary jokingly assured them that he would protect the camp against any rats that came close.

At the end of his three-month contract, his African staff were truly saddened by his departure, for he had treated them well, and his absence meant no more game meat for them.

Clary signed a non-return contract and was returned home with a hefty pay packet equivalent to six months' salary. A blood test showed that he had not contracted malaria during his three-month tenure, so he did not need the strong antimalarial drug. In spite of that, Clary was not allowed to return to this area for at least ten years, and by that time the dam would have been built and no more hunters' contracts would be awarded.

Chapter 41
Roving Over the Land

June had done a good job of running the farm while Clary was away, and in fact had run it better without his intervention. Clary wanted to use some of his hard-earned salary to explore the far reaches of Tanganyika and felt confident that June could continue running the farm without him. He said he wanted to find new hunting areas with different game species so that he could offer his clients a larger variety of game. Secretly, though, he just wanted to be in the bush, for that was where he felt at home.

New roads were constantly being built to connect towns with remote villages and to facilitate easy access to all parts of the country. He intended to make use of them.

For his upcoming trip of two months or more, Clary bought a very good, used, jungle green Land Rover. It was the first of many green Land Rovers in his hunting career.

The East African administrators had ordered thousands of these sturdy vehicles from England, all in jungle green, to be distributed to all government departments as a standard car for the country. There were plenty of them available to buy new or used, and many experienced mechanics to service them. This four-wheel drive car was very reliable, tough, and easy to repair, and spare parts for it were available everywhere, making it the perfect car for travelling around the remotest parts of Africa. Clary was pleased with his choice.

He was planning to camp wherever possible in order to save on hotel accommodation and food. He took along two rifles: a German Mauser 9.3mm for big game, and a .22 long rifle to shoot small game and birds for the pot.

On the day of departure, his car was so chock-full with camping equipment, spare petrol, tools, guns, and food boxes, that there was barely space for his African helper to squeeze into the front seat next to Clary. Since they were late getting away from the farm, they only made it to the foot of the Usambara Mountains, where they spent an uncomfortable first night sleeping on a canvas sheet by the roadside. The first leg of their trip took them towards the southern region of Tanganyika that Clary wanted to see, because it was completely unknown to him and undocumented as a hunting area.

A few years before, a new road had been built linking Tanga with the territorial capital, Dar es Salaam. The new road would knock three hours off the driving time between the two major towns compared to the longer, older route. However, there was a problem for motorists travelling on some sections of the new road that passed through hilly and heavily wooded country. The local Zigua youths in those sections amused themselves by stoning passing cars from the safety of the thick forests along the road. The stone-throwers always chose a spot with a high embankment and a thick stand of trees to run into and hide after the evil deed was done. The stoning became such a problem that anybody with a new or expensive car took the longer but safer route to avoid the stone-throwers. The stones they threw were not large – about half the size of a man's fist – and did not do much damage, except chip the paint or break a windshield if the vehicle was unlucky enough to be travelling fast at that time.

Slow-moving trucks were seldom targeted since they could stop quickly and the driver could give chase, although no stone-thrower had ever been caught.

Clary had been warned about this danger, and was advised to take the longer road to Dar es Salaam if he valued his car's paint. He ignored the warning and went for the good new road. Just before he reached the hilly section, he loaded his 9.3mm with solid bullets and gave it to his passenger to hold.

The Land Rover was running well on the new road when the first hail of stones clattered with loud thumps onto the car's hood. Clary braked hard to a stop, jumped out, grabbed his rifle, and proceeded to fire all six rounds into the forest after the fleeing stone-throwers. He purposely aimed high so as not to hit anybody, but low enough so that his solid bullets whined and ricocheted through the treetops to instil maximum angst amongst the fleeing natives. He then reloaded the Mauser, gave it to his grinning helper, and sped on until the next shower of stones battered his car. Again, he braked hard, jumped out with his gun, and then noticed a group of smirking Zigua youths standing on top of a high, steep embankment, taunting him to try to catch them. Clary fired the first shot into the embankment just below where they stood. Then before he could fire the next shot, the group had disappeared into the forest 20 yards behind them. He did not realise that a human being could move faster than greased lightning, as these young men had just done. He fired another four shots high into the trees towards them, and was now certain that none of them would ever touch a stone again in their lives. He reloaded and motored on, however, there was no more stone-throwing along the way.

A year after this incident, Clary was talking to the Indian truck owner who had previously warned him about the stone-throwers.

The truck owner said, "I don't know what the traffic police have done, but all stone-throwing has stopped on the new road. There has not been an incident this year and traffic is flowing again."

Clary could not resist telling this Indian that it was not the police but rather he himself who had stopped the stone-throwers. He then proceeded to explain what he had done, and left the Indian rolling on the floor with laughter after hearing his story.

A vast stretch of Miombo bushland known as the Selous existed some 80 miles southwest of Dar es Salaam. It had been purged of people by German colonialists who intended to form a human-free buffer zone between the coastal inhabitants and inland tribes to stop the spread of sleeping sickness, a deadly parasite carried by tse-tse flies. The zone was declared a game reserve, the first in East Africa, and was prescribed to remain devoid of human interference of any kind. Its purpose was to let nature run wild.

Clary's request to visit this reserve was denied, simply because no roads existed that went that way, and there were no footpaths nor any maps of the place. Also, nobody had visited this area since the end of the First World War.

At the very least, Clary was determined to visit the extreme south of the country which bordered on Mozambique. An infrequently used road ran to the last border town in Tanganyika, where an unreliable wooden ferry could be used to cross over the Ruvuma River into Mozambique.

After arriving in Mtwara on the Indian Ocean – the last border town before crossing into Mozambique – Clary intended to repair and resupply his Land Rover here, as well as gather information from the game rangers about conditions and game species in this region.

The town boasted a quaint thatched roof fishing club, situated at the little port, where the colonial administrators of this district gathered every evening to drink and socialise while complaining about their lot in this god-forsaken place. Here, Clary lapped up a mine of useful information about local conditions.

One regular visitor to the club was a mysterious old man who lived in a well-built house on a small island a mile away. He was not married and had no job, yet received a regular monthly income from England. He was tall and handsome, with a fine crop of hair even in his old age, and he carried his head high. He was an amicable person who never talked about his past life and refused to answer any questions about it.

Many years after his death, it was rumoured that he was an illegitimate child born of a liaison between King George of England and a Buckingham Palace chambermaid. It would have been a terrible scandal for the respectable British monarchy at that time, if this birth had come to light. So, the mother and baby were secretly sent away to East Africa to live. They were forced to spend the rest of their lives in exile and silence, in return for an ample annual stipend from the government. The mother died soon after arriving in Africa, and her son was never allowed to return to England.

An unmaintained, very poor bush track ran westwards from Mtwara through the wild Miombo bushland for 150 miles to a mission town at Masasi. Clary intended to drive this track because it ran through some very interesting game country, and it was only ten miles inland from the Rovuma that demarcated the border between British-administered Tanganyika and Portuguese Mozambique. Since he had a reliable four-wheel drive Land Rover, which he had reloaded with extra food, essential spare parts, and petrol, he took this road without heeding any warnings that it was un-serviced.

Travelling over the rough road was agonisingly slow, and the humidity of the air in the car was unbearable, in spite of having the vents open. The biting tsetse flies streamed through the open windows and were a constant menace. Clary hoped to stop at various settlements along the way to get first-hand information about local game conditions, but to his surprise, they passed through one deserted native village after another. Some had been so hastily abandoned that cooking pots, which were a valuable possession for the natives, were still sitting untouched on their three firestones in the round mud huts. All around the empty huts grew unkempt stands of maize, beans, tomatoes, manioc, banana, and paw-paw trees, sprouting ripe fruit, some of which Clary and his helper harvested for themselves as no one was about.

One strange feature on some huts was that sections of the thick grass roofs had been ripped aside, as though someone had been trying to enter through the roof. The damage had not been caused by elephants, as they would not rip the dry grass off huts, and they normally kept away from villages, except when raiding maize fields at night. Despite the abandoned villages, the area they passed through looked like fertile farmland and was magnificent game country, as evidenced by thick green grass everywhere, interspersed by trees full of wild fruits. All the waterholes they passed were clean and full, and the streams they crossed ran clear. Wild flowers bloomed along the roadside as if in a country garden, while colourful birds flitted about and called to each other amongst the trees. But, oddly enough, they saw no game, nor any spoor of any animals at waterholes, nor were there tracks criss-crossing the road. Nothing except birds, snakes, and lizards inhabited this paradise. Why was there no game in such a perfect place? Clary could not think of a reason.

The road was mostly overgrown with waist-high grass growing in the middle, and it was washed away by rain in places, slowing their progress to a crawl. They camped the first night in a clearing by the roadside, but as it was already late, they did not put up a tent, opting instead to sleep on their beds under the stars. Clary ate some cold meat on rye bread and gulped down a warm beer. They did not light a fire, because it could have attracted lions to their camp. The next day, they travelled on through more abandoned plantations, where they were able to stop and harvest a few maize cobs.

Before crossing a stream, they stopped the car to have a break from driving and brew a cup of tea. They were also forced to clean out the radiator grille, since it had collected so many grass seeds that the engine was beginning to overheat. Except for a fleeting glimpse of some unrecognisable animal disappearing through the tall grass, they had seen no wildlife on the whole trip.

The second night was spent much like the first, sleeping under an open starry sky. At sun-up, after a breakfast of porridge with fresh fruit, Clary and his helper drove on through more lush, wildlife-less country.

By late afternoon on the third day, they broke out of the Miombo forest and abruptly entered the small mission town of Masasi. They drove on to the mission station where they hoped to find accommodation for the night. A very startled Catholic priest, dressed in his white robes, met Clary at the mission entrance. He did not expect Europeans to willingly visit this town in the middle of nowhere, so he was surprised and delighted to meet a stranger. Of course, he had a place for the night and a meal, and even had some petrol to spare.

Clary gave his helper some money and then sent him into the town, where he was warmly welcomed by the news-starved locals, who plied him with food and drink and questioned him all night about news from the rest of the country. Clary ate a good, hearty, simple meal with the mission staff in their basic furnished dining hall. They were all intrigued to hear his stories of hunting and about his adventures upcountry, though they were horrified to hear that he had just spent two nights on the bush track to Mtwara. Didn't he fear the man-eating lions in the area?

Clary was surprised at this question, but said he feared as well as respected all animals and took precautions wherever he went. *Why were they asking about lions?* he wondered.

Chapter 42
The Man-Eaters of Mtwara

As Clary pondered the priest's question, a long-time resident priest explained their preoccupation with lions, and told Clary the reason why many villages had been so hastily abandoned and remained deserted.

There had always been a few settlements along that stretch of road, because it had been an Arab trading route in the slaving days. At first, the area was only accessible by footpaths, until the British graded a passable road connecting the villages with this mission station and the administrative centre at Mtwara. When the colonial government decided to expand the tse-tse control belt, created by the Germans, to include land farther south of the Selous, they forcibly removed all the inhabitants in that area and resettled them in new locations along the new road.

The ground was very fertile, and water was abundant everywhere, with plenty of fish in the Ruvuma River not far away. Also, this far inland from the river, there were hardly any mosquitoes or tse-tse flies to worry about. At that time, an abundance of wild game roamed the region, which the Makua and Makonde natives were permitted to hunt for food. These new settlements by the road thrived and prospered on this fertile ground. However, there were simply too many people killing too many animals to sustain the wild meat supply.

The newcomers' usual method of hunting was to set long lines of wire snares that caught any and all animals passing through. This included young ones and inedible species such as hyenas and monkeys, which, when caught, were tossed aside like bits of rubbish. The good meat was carried back to the village, where it was dried in the shade and stored in their homes for future use. Any excess meat was transported to Mtwara, where it was sold at a good price in the market and was a welcome alternative to fish for the local people.

Very soon, there were too many hunters taking too much game, and the animal populations rapidly decreased. Within a few years, the wild game all but disappeared from the region. However, it was not only people killing and eating the game, but lions and leopards, too. When no more game remained to prey on, the starving lions started hunting people, and were quite successful at it. The fatal lion encounters forced the villagers to venture out of their compounds only during the day, armed with muzzleloaders and in big groups to deter lion attacks.

This tactic kept the lions at bay for a while. However, there was still nothing for the lions to eat, so they started to stalk villagers at night. The lions discovered that they could jump onto the roof of a hut, scratch the grass away, leap in through the gap, grab a screaming native, then jump out again and drag their victim into the long grass to share with the rest of the pride. These lion attacks were reported to Mtwara, where the overworked and understaffed game department would dispatch several rangers to deal with the killers. After the rangers had shot a lion or two, they declared the problem solved, and returned to Mtwara. However, the lion attacks continued.

To rectify this problem once and for all, a troop of 20 armed rangers was sent out by the game department from Mtwara. They were told not to return until the problem was well and truly solved. However, the real problem was that so little game was available for the lions that they had to hunt whatever they could find, and that often meant human beings. At first, the rangers went on patrols by day, hunting the lions and shooting quite a few of them. However, it was not enough to deter them. The rangers also stood guard at night to protect villages from attacks, but in the dark, they merely shot ineffectively into the long grass whenever a lion roared close by. It became a cat-and-mouse game, with the cats winning.

There were not enough rangers to defend every location, so lions continued the offensive in the unprotected villages. The rangers tried to anticipate which place would be raided next, so that they could protect it, but they very seldom got it right. As they later discovered, a clever lion pride would approach a village at night and roar close by. If a ranger fired at them, they would leave and go to the next village to do the same. If no shot was fired, it was safe to go in for the kill and drag out another poor, screaming victim.

In order to avoid the lions, some of the smaller outlying farms were abandoned, and their inhabitants fled to larger villages where they could be better protected. In this way, all the expanded settlements now had armed game rangers for protection. When a lion roared close to a village at night, they were inevitably shot at, so they stopped roaring. Instead, they would wait silently close to some huts until morning when the people got up and came out of their homes to start the day.

When one of the inhabitants went to relieve themselves in the bushes, or fetch water from the well, or walked too close to some grassy patch that concealed a waiting lion, death would come swiftly and silently to the careless one. Often a victim's absence was not noticed until it was far too late to save any parts of him. One game ranger became a victim himself, when he fell asleep at his post early one morning. Only his loaded rifle, his boots, and a lot of blood were found in the long grass a few yards away from his post.

The rangers were often required to escort groups of people as they walked along the main road to the next village to trade goods. Late one afternoon, a group was returning home when, at a place where the thick grass grew high on both sides of the road, a lion growled deeply and menacingly on one side. The startled rangers stood with guns ready for the expected assault.

A young man in the group panicked and ran away through the chest-high grass towards a big tree set back on the opposite side of the road. He had only gone a few yards when a lion pounced on him. Fortunately, the big cat bit into the bundle of manioc that the man was carrying on his back. He screamed as the lion pinned him to the ground. Just in the nick of time, a ranger ran up and shot the lion through the head, sending half a dozen other lions fleeing through the high grass around him. The young man was lucky to get away with only a few scratch marks on his back.

The cunning lions also set up ambushes to catch people, just as they did with wild animals. To ambush wild game, a male lion would go upwind of a herd then roar deeply, frightening the panicky animals downwind, right into the jaws of the waiting pride. When they started ambushing people in the same manner, it was the last straw!

The rangers went back to the department headquarters in Mtwara and told their stories of these invincible lions. The government had no alternative except to relocate all the communities to safer neighbourhoods far away from that area, until the situation was brought under control. Every available vehicle in Mtwara was sent out to collect the villagers as quickly as possible. The inhabitants were given only a short time to pack their belongings and get onto the trucks. Then they were trucked to safety at another location close to Mtwara.

Now Clary understood why some of the grass roofs were scratched away, why some cooking pots still lay on the stones, and why the fields had remained unharvested.

Chapter 43
Becker's Lion

The old priest recalled an even more frightening story about these lions. A young, cocky South African named Becker, who had been hunting in the area, heard that lions here were on the vermin list and a reward was given for every lion killed. So, he decided to go lion hunting to obtain the reward. As proof of a kill, he had to hand into the wildlife department a lion's tail for each one claimed.

Becker had a short-base Land Rover, jungle green with a hardtop roof, which he used for his hunting trips. He carried the minimum amount of equipment to survive, which meant sleeping in the open under the stars, eating whatever he shot, or trading game meat for vegetables at plantations along the way. He always brought along his African cook to assist in camp. On the fateful day, they sped through one recently abandoned village after another. They were hoping to trade some meat for a few fresh vegetables at one of the villages, but instead ended up helping themselves to whatever they wanted from the deserted fields.

They stopped for the night by a small, clear stream near another deserted village. While finishing his supper just after dark, Becker heard a noise very close by. Shining a flashlight beam there, he saw a lioness jump away into the tall grass and disappear. He thought nothing more about it, suspecting that she had been attracted by the smell of game meat in his car. A short time later, she came back and could be heard circling the car. Becker picked up his rifle, gave his flashlight to the cook, and told him to shine it at the noise. The big yellow eyes glowed brightly in the flashlight beam as Becker fired. However, the lioness was quick off the mark, and the bullet missed its target. He fired a few more shots her way in an effort to scare her off permanently, but to no avail. She came back again.

Becker and the cook realised that they were being hunted and the lioness was not quitting. In fact, she was getting bolder as she stalked them. The two men hastily threw everything into the back of the Land Rover and drove a few miles along the road, then off onto a side road for a few miles, expecting to be out of harm's way. They parked the hunting car, front first, deep into a heavy thorn bush that also protected both sides of the vehicle from attack. The side opening rear door was the only way for them to get in or out. This back door opened onto a long, clear patch of ground that afforded a good view of any animal that approached from that way.

They built a very large fire by the back door of the vehicle which lit up the surrounding field almost as if it were daylight. To be on the safe side, the cook slept well protected under his blanket across the car's front seats. Becker slept fitfully in the back on a thin, kapok-filled mattress with his rifle beside him and the back door slightly open to let in some air.

At some point before daybreak, he woke up from a heavy jolt to his body, and could see stars above him and smell a very strong lion odour. He realised that he was being dragged along the ground with his mattress by the lioness, who had grabbed his shoulder together with the thin mattress. He had woken up as he hit the ground. Fortunately, he still held his rifle under the blanket, so he pulled it out with his free hand and, aiming her way, fired blindly at his attacker. The lioness let out a ferocious bellow of anger, dropped him and the mattress, and jumped away to one side.

The cunning lioness had waited until the men in the car were fast asleep then sneaked in behind the smouldering fire, grabbed one of them by the shoulder along with the thin mattress, and pulled them from the back of his car. Becker was bleeding from his left shoulder as he sat there stunned. There were no broken bones, since it was only a flesh wound, though it hurt like hell. The cook had woken up with a start on hearing the shot and immediately grabbed the flashlight, shining it towards the lioness, but she was not to be seen. He took the last sticks of firewood and stoked the dying embers into a roaring furnace.

Becker walked into the field a little way from the car with his rifle, while the cook shone the powerful flashlight around, but there were no menacing eyes to be seen. He felt that perhaps he had injured her quite badly and she had gone off to die, although he found no blood on the ground except for his own.

Both men went back to the car and sat inside with the back door closed while Becker dressed his bleeding shoulder. The cook shone his flashlight outside through the closed window, and Becker sat ready with his rifle in hand in case the determined cat came back. Dawn broke a few hours later with no sign of her return. When the sun was well up, the two men stepped out of the car and walked onto the open glade and around the car to look for signs of the lioness. There were none at all, so she had definitely left the area.

Lions are night hunters, as during that time they are almost invisible to their prey, but during the day they are more visible, so they prefer to sleep at that time. Becher thought she would not return in daylight, and as neither of the two men had slept very much during the harrowing night, he thought it safe to have a little sleep before driving away. Becker's arm was beginning to swell up, and hurt quite a bit whenever he moved it, so they wanted to rest only for a short time.

The cook fell asleep on his front seat bed, while Becker slept on his mattress with the back door open to let in some cool air. Sometime later, Becker was jolted awake by a hard thump to the back of his head. The lioness had come back. This time she grabbed him by the same injured left shoulder, except without the mattress, then pulled him out of the car and started dragging him away into the long grass to kill and eat him. His gun was still lying in the car next to his mattress. He screamed at the top of his lungs and tried to punch the lioness in her sides, but she took no notice and just growled angrily through clenched teeth.

On hearing the screaming, the cook woke up, and when he saw Becker being dragged off towards the long grass, he grabbed the only weapon he could find, which was a burning log from their campfire. Disregarding his own safety, the brave cook ran at the lioness, yelling and waving the burning log at her. She immediately dropped her prey and turned to confront her attacker, but the cook did not stop. He ran towards her as she crouched over her intended meal, snarling menacingly. When he was just a few feet away from her, she rushed at the fearless cook and opened her wide mouth to bite, so he thrust the burning log into her open maw, scorching her delicate skin. She yowled in pain, spitting out hot coals as she spun around and bounded into the high grass.

The courageous cook scooped up his boss, and the two men hobbled quickly back to the car and locked themselves in. Becker's lacerated left shoulder was now seriously injured and bleeding profusely. He fetched his meagre first aid kit from behind the front seat and, with the help of his cook, proceeded to clean and bandage the lacerations as best he could, but it was imperative that he get to a hospital very quickly before septicaemia set in. Their dilemma now was that the cook did not know how to drive, and Becker's left arm, which he used to change gears, was crippled and unusable.

The Land Rover was a right-hand drive car with a manual gear shift between the seats. By leaning over and using his right hand to engage the gear, and then using the same hand to steer, Becker managed to get the Land Rover into first gear and drive very slowly back to the main track. They spotted the persistent lioness trotting after them, although she kept a safe distance behind. She had tasted blood and was not about to give up easily. The nearest town where Becker could be treated was at a Catholic mission and clinic in Masasi, more than 50 miles away. At such a slow speed in first gear, it would take ten hours to get there. However, they would run out of petrol before they got halfway to Masasi, if the lioness did not get them first.

In his poor condition, Becker was not able to teach his cook how to drive, but he could show him how to change gears on the run while Becker steered with his good right arm and operated the brake and clutch. With a little practice and a lot of patience, the cook managed to select the correct gear most of the time, and they were able to lurch along the track at a reasonable speed. At one muddy stream, the Land Rover got stuck when the cook selected the wrong gear. However, by using the four-wheel drive gear shift, they got out of the mud and went on their way. At another stream crossing, water splashed up onto the distributor and spark plugs, stalling the car midstream. There was nothing they could do except open the hood and wait for the hot engine to dry out. It took 20 minutes to dry, and during this wait, they kept a lookout behind them but saw no sign of the lioness. Hopefully she had given up her chase by now.

The rough road and stifling humidity in the closed car were taking their toll on Becker. He was weakening from blood loss and becoming delirious. They just made it to the Masasi Catholic mission before he passed out. Becker's wound was cleaned and doctored competently, because lion, leopard, and hyena bites were quite common in this district, so the doctors and nurses had a lot of practice in treating such injuries. He spent ten days at the mission recovering from his injuries, and was forced to repeat his lioness story endlessly during his recuperation for the benefit of the police, the game department, and anybody else who demanded to know the facts first-hand.

The cook, who was holed up in town while Becker recovered from his injuries, also had to repeat his side of the story endlessly to the local people in the shops and bars, but only did so if the enquirer put a glass of local beer in his hand. Becker never regained the full use of his left arm, and could not lift it above shoulder height. However, he had survived a lion attack twice, and that certainly was more than some dead lion attack victims could boast. After he returned home, he paid for his faithful cook to learn to drive a car and shoot a rifle.

After hearing these stories, Clary left Masasi with a renewed respect for lions.

Chapter 44
The Great River

On his way north, Clary intended to cross the great Kilombero River on a ferry that had been in continuous operation since German times. The ferry was a tribute to their engineering skills. Clary thought it would be a good idea to spend a few days exploring the river and its environment to learn more about it and its potential as a hunting ground.

On the drive through the lush green country towards the Kilombero, Clary could not help noticing the government's futile attempt to string up a telephone line to the Masasi post office. The English telephone technicians who had been tasked with putting up the first line had very little idea of African conditions and the habits of wildlife. Their first attempt was to simply string the copper telephone wire through the trees at head height. Not even one call went through on this line, as every passing animal taller than an English engineer's head ripped it to pieces. Even as the repairmen were busy splicing the broken wires together, the line was ripped out of their hands by the next tall animal along the line.

Their next attempt was to string the line through the treetops, above an elephant's reach. A few calls on the line were made before elephants, who like to eat the branches of succulent trees, pulled down these branches, some of which were holding telephone wires.

The third attempt saw the telephone wires strung onto high, wooden poles out of reach of local fauna. Termites love old wood, especially old dry wood stuck in the ground for them to chew on. Within a year, most of these poles fell over when their insides were eaten away by termites. Wooden poles coated with tar to ward off termites were tried next. They lasted until the rainy season arrived, which soaked the ground around the poles into soft mud and caused the wobbly poles to collapse one after the other like dominoes.

One last attempt was made to keep a phone line up and running. It called for the engineers to string a line on termite-proof steel poles on another route over hard ground that did not get waterlogged and soft during the rainy season. However, this new route crossed a region where giraffes made their home. It was not long before the line was down in too many places to keep repairing, so it was abandoned in favour of the radiotelephone that did not require long wires through the bush. Many years later, an experienced local engineer developed a high, stable, triangular steel structure on which to string the phone lines. That system worked well and lasted a very long time, and so the telephone replaced the overworked radiotelephone system, which was the standard method of communication with outlying towns at that time.

Clary stopped at Ifakara – a small, well-developed town on the bank of the Kilombero River – where he spent a few days exploring up and down the river. The local Wahehe natives used 40-foot long dugout canoes made from African mahogany trees that were felled nearby. They used these crafts to pole along the river to catch an abundance of fish, which they sold in the local market.

Clary hired one of these canoes, with its experienced and knowledgeable crew, to take him up and down the river in his search for game country. On both sides of the river and a mile or more inland, grew two-inch thick and 10-to-14-foot high elephant grass. Its long razor-sharp leaves were able to make deep cuts into bare human arms and slice heavy denim clothing into ribbons. Whole herds of elephants could live and take refuge in these reed beds and never be found. Hippos, who come out of the river at night to graze in open glades, made tunnels through the grass with their big, bulky bodies. These tunnels were also used by buffalo and other game to move between grazing grounds.

Image 18: 40 foot canoe on the Kilombero River poled by expert boatmen who knew how to avoid the hippos and crocs.

Along the few sandbanks, the exploration party could see prodigious crocodiles sunning themselves as the boat went past. The boat crew said that despite the abundance of fish in the river, these crocs caught careless people on a regular basis, so they kept the boats away from the banks. The crocodiles had been hunted by some Europeans in motorboats with high-powered rifles a few years previously, but the crocs had quickly learned to slip out of sight at the sound of an approaching outboard motor. However, they had no fear of canoes being poled silently in mid-stream.

The crew poled the long boat until they reached a fork in the river, where Clary chose a smaller side arm to explore. About halfway up the stream, where the water flowed more slowly, they heard a deep, rhythmic rumbling sound emanating from somewhere in the 12-foot high elephant grass growing on the banks. Curious as to the source of the sound, Clary made the men pull the canoe onto a clear sandbank and stepped out to listen.

Just then, his boatmen started talking rapidly to each other in alarmed tones in their own dialect, which Clary could not understand. They urged him to get back into the boat quickly and get out of here. His curiosity was now so piqued that he was determined to find out who or what was making such an awful din. Then one agape boatman explained in a solemn, subdued voice that it was the sound of a devil who lived in the densest parts of the grass. He only made this rumbling noise when someone came close to his sleeping place, and he was angry. Some fishermen had seen a place of flattened grass as big as a house where the devil had rested, yet nobody had actually seen him.

Clary did not believe a word of it. He smiled at them, waved his 450 rifle in the air, and told them that his gun would protect him from any devil, even one the size of a native hut.

Listening carefully for the perturbing sound to locate its direction, Clary checked that both chambers of his gun were loaded, closed it with a resounding "thunk", and started walking towards the noise, leaving his frightened boat crew shaking their heads in disbelief at the stupidity of this white man whom they did not expect to see alive again.

However, one man figured that if the devil did come after them, his own chances of survival were better with an armed fool than with a boatload of scared men, so he followed Clary, dogging his heels closely. The rumbling sound became louder as they pushed their way closer through the dense, razor-sharp grass. The man at Clary's side was wide-eyed and trembling with fear when he suddenly stopped and thrust his skinny black arm forward, pointing at a huge, unclear mound just visible through the high reeds.

Clary held his gun ready and edged closer to the heaving mound, then circled around to where the noise was coming from. When he was 20 feet away from the noise-maker, he turned and smiled at his terrified companion and said, "Tembo!" (elephant!). Moving closer still, he saw that the mound was a sleeping elephant lying on its side against an anthill. It was snoring. His companion smiled and was visibly relieved that they had not stumbled on a sleeping devil.

Just then, the snoring stopped, and the sleeping giant started to get up. However, it takes a few long seconds to move five tons of muscle and bone against gravity from a prone position to an upright stance. These few moments were just enough time for the two fleeing humans to make a safe getaway.

Back at the waiting canoe, the brave African devil-chaser described to a captivated audience in exact detail how he and Clary had risked their lives to discredit the myth of a devil, which was in fact, only a snoring elephant. The African had such a genuine, heartfelt laugh that it infected everyone who heard it, including Clary. They all laughed so hard after hearing this story that they were unable to get into the canoe and pole away.

Quite a few side arms on this river branched off to where one could pole up silently to large open glades and find plenty of game. Since Clary had taken his 450 Express rifle with him, the boatmen felt protected, and they agreed to take him by canoe along a stream through the elephant grass to a large short-grass plain that they knew of.

True to their word, it was teeming with game. Buffalo by the hundreds lazed on the ground, chewing their cud. Zebra, wildebeest, kongoni, waterbuck, and impala drifted about grazing or were lying in small groups on the short green meadows. It was an animal's Eden. However, as Clary approached, the animals stood up, stared for a minute, and when the first one ran for cover, so did the rest. Within a few minutes, the ground was clear of wildlife, save for a few complaining plover birds. These animals had obviously been hunted before, as they had a fear of people.

"Yes, they are hunted by some people with muzzleloaders who get tired of eating fish every day", confessed a boatman. "There are many open plains like this on the river, and each one has just as much game as this",

"What about elephants with big tusks?" asked Clary.

"Oh, yes, I have seen many elephants with tusks longer than I am tall. I have seen a tusk so heavy that one strong man cannot lift it. It was shot by an Arab", said a crewman. "But", he went on, "you cannot hunt elephants in this thick grass. It is madness. You must wait until they come out into the dry forest lands."

"Why do the elephants come out if they have all the food and water they need in the grass?" Clary wanted to know.

"When elephants have wet feet, they start to rot and hurt if they stay too long in the water, so they must come out onto dry ground at night to dry them", answered one of the men, who was obviously knowledgeable about hunting elephants.

They poled back home, arriving in Ifakara just as news of a hippo attack that had killed a woman was making the rounds. It seems that a local couple had gone to check their fish traps that they had set at a stream coming off the main river. As they returned home on one of the many hippo tracks through tall grass, they had been charged by a large hippo. The man threw himself against the wall of grass as the hippo ran past him, and was unharmed. However, his wife ran along the hippo path trying to get away, but she was trampled to death under the feet of the two-ton animal. Hippos usually don't attack on purpose, unless wounded, but when they are out of the water grazing and get surprised by someone, they run straight for the safety of the river, mowing down anyone, man or beast, in their path.

Clary learned that hippos killed more people than crocodiles, buffaloes, and elephants combined, on this stretch of the river. Many years before, a government organised hippo-culling programme that was intended to reduce the number of animals in the river, had been a total failure because more animals were maimed than killed, and a wounded hippo is deadlier than a wounded buffalo. So, the cull had been stopped and the hippos left in peace to trample anyone getting in their way.

After leaving the Kilombero Valley, Clary continued his tour on the good road to Iringa, where he had heard about a place called Ruaha that was rich with game. He camped at the great Ruaha River and walked along its banks, which were a buffalo and elephant utopia. He was never out of sight or sound of these animals during the whole time. Magnificent greater kudu herds were everywhere. Majestic sable antelope, sporting curved black horns like scimitars, wandered along the edges of open glades. Herds of wildebeest and zebra came in a never-ending stream to drink at the river. The tall giraffes seemed to peer down on shorter creatures as though they were low-life. It was a joy to see the herds of eland and impala taking no notice of passing humans. Even the big ostriches hardly gave him a passing glance.

But for Clary, this game nirvana had two drawbacks. Firstly, this sector was about to be made into a game reserve, which meant restricting all hunting activity – and rightly so, he believed. Secondly, it was a very long way from his farm in the Usambara Mountains. It was at least a three-day drive and, with a heavy truck, perhaps a four- or five-day journey, which was too long to be on the road. He left Ruaha with a feeling that East Africa had many regions that were still a game Eden, and believed they should be protected to stay that way for ever.

Along the main road to Dodoma, Clary left the main road and followed a dirt track that branched off into the bush. He drove a few miles along it just to see what was there. He came to a dry riverbed with a few pools of stagnant water that were being used by all manner of game, big and small. While walking along the riverbed, he saw that the game fled into the surrounding thickets at his approach. It was a sure sign that they had been hunted here, but judging by the amount of spoor around, they had not been overhunted.

At noon, he went looking for a shady place in the riverbed to have a rest. He came across a tree growing right on the bank with some of its exposed roots hanging over the riverbed, forming a cosy little shady spot underneath. A perfect resting place, he surmised, but to his horror, he accidentally flushed out a half dozen small crocodiles that had taken refuge on a shelf under the tree roots. Unknown to most hunters at that time, crocodiles living in semi-permanent rivers, such as this one, sometimes sheltered in riverbank hollows during the dry season, waiting for the water to return in the rainy season. After Clary had disturbed them, these poor creatures would have to find another safe place to rest until the next rainy season arrived.

On his walk back to his car, Clary passed a hunter's camp hidden under shady mimosa trees, so he called in to pay his respects, as was customary for hunters to do. He introduced himself to the hunter, whom he did not know, because the man was from Kenya. Clary also met the client, Ernest Hemmingway – a reporter – whom Clary had never heard about at that time. They had a talk about hunting, and game in general, over a cup of sweet tea, then parted ways.

Chapter 45
MMBA?

After being on the road for five weeks, Clary finally returned home to his farm, wife, and children. June had run the farm so well that it was not only paying for itself but was making a small profit. This was good news, as it meant Clary could leave the farm safely in June's care and get back to his beloved bush country to hunt again.

A month before, while passing through Dar es Salaam on his way south, Clary had stopped at the government map ordinance office to buy a complete set of survey maps for Tanganyika. The maps had not been available during the war and shortly afterwards due to the fear that they could have been used by the enemy. He bought a set of the expensive and durable cloth-backed maps in a protective leather-bound cover. The map office clerk requested that while using them, Clary should make detailed corrections of any errors he found in the maps. In addition, any new tracks, waterholes, river courses, or new villages that he found should be added. The alterations were to be marked on a sketched copy of the map and sent by post, addressed to the chief surveyor's office, where they would be verified and included in the next map printing.

Before Clary left the map office, he asked about an abbreviation that he had noticed on the maps that puzzled him. What did the letters MMBA mean? As these letters were printed over his favourite hunting grounds of the south Maasai steppe, he was curious to find their meaning. However, the chief surveyor had no idea what they stood for, and there was no explanation in the legend.

Clary suggested they could mean "Main Maasai Bush Area". The chief surveyor accepted this explanation, although he too was now curious to know the real meaning, and would pursue the matter. Like all maps of East Africa, these had been printed in England, so he would ask the English printing office for an explanation. Some weeks later, the printer in England replied that the surveyor of this sector had retired to England many years ago. His present whereabouts were unknown, but they would endeavour to find him.

While using these maps, Clary had diligently marked in any new villages that had sprung up since then. He marked in waterholes he found and his self-made tracks, as well as open plains he had discovered. He included waterholes in his locality, and his private Ruvu river crossing.

Months later, while he was in the Dar es Salaam map office handing in some map corrections he had made, Clary asked if they had finally found the real meaning of MMBA. To his surprise, the officer said yes! They had managed to locate the retired surveyor through friends of his who still worked at the map printing office.

This is the story he told them.

The man was now living in a small English village, thoroughly enjoying his retirement, and had no intention of ever setting foot in Africa again.

He had come to Africa as a land surveyor and had been tasked with surveying all that part of Tanganyika south of Kilimanjaro known as the Maasai steppe, right down to the far south, as far as the Wami River. The English surveyor was assigned eight porters to carry very basic camp equipment, plus food and water, and surveyors' instruments, as well as a rifle for protection and to supplement their meagre food rations with game meat.

Every morning, he and his porters got up, ate a meagre breakfast, packed their belongings, and trudged through stifling heat, unrelenting thorn scrub, annoying swarms of flies, and snorting wild animals, to the next high ground to take their survey readings. They camped for the night wherever the last reading was taken. This routine repeated itself day after day, week after week, and monotonous month after monotonous month, without a break, except for a day off in camp on Sundays. They used this day to wash their accumulated pile of dirty clothes and repair broken equipment.

Each time the English surveyor climbed a high hill, he looked out upon nothing but endless miles and miles of uninhabited bush. Then, one last time, he climbed a hill and realised that there was nothing to look forward to for the next few months except to survey more hot, dry, tsetse-infested, inhospitable, uninhabited, useless thorny bush. Exasperated with what he saw, he scrawled MMBA over this un-surveyed area on the map. The letters, he said, stood for Miles and Miles of Bloody Africa.

With that, he packed up his camp for the last time and walked back to civilisation. He went straight to the chief surveyor's office, resigned from his job, effective immediately, and flew back to England for an early retirement to enjoy, as he said, green, green grass everywhere, rain showers, winter snow, fresh farm fruit, meals on China plates, cosy pubs, and where he would meet nothing that bites, stings, or charges.

Finally, Clary discovered the true meaning of MMBA.

Chapter 46
Elephants Are So Big

With the farm running well, Clary wrote letters to safari agents in America asking them to find clients who would book safaris with him. He transported all his safari equipment to the Ruvu River campsite and built a new camp by the river at a different location from his first camp. The new site was larger and spread out under tall mimosa, wild fig, and sausage trees. It stayed pleasantly cool even during the hottest part of the day, since a constant breeze blew off the river. The dining tent looked out over the slow-flowing Ruvu River. Liberal use of plaited grass partitions between sleeping tents and the kitchen area gave the camp a sense of privacy and luxury. Parallel to the dark green riverine forest and the thick bush beyond, stretched a four-mile long, 300-yard wide open grassy plain where guinea fowl, spur-fowl, bustards, and doves came each morning and evening to look for insects and scratch amongst the tufts of grass for seeds. Thick, heavy Commiphora woodland, interspersed with Acacia thorn trees, black terminalia trees, cordia bushes, and the terrible wait-a-bit thorn shrubs, dominated the land beyond the plain.

Clary wanted to make another camp 30 miles inland at the foot of a small hill marked on his map as Lamwe Hill, where there was a large waterhole. At first, he was hesitant to put a camp here because the Maasai, with their huge herds of cattle and goats, were just starting to move down from the north into this part of the country. So far, only two Maasai families had arrived, although more would undoubtedly follow. He decided to risk setting up his camp anyway, although none of his employees was willing to stay alone in the camp, even for double pay and with a rifle to defend themselves, because the reputation of the Maasai as fearless men who fought lions for fun still frightened the local natives. Clary built the camp anyway, using some of the older tents and equipment, but had to leave it unattended when it was finished.

One of his first clients in the new locality was a Mexican and his assistant who had booked a 30-day hunting safari for the purpose of shooting a big tusker. The client had insisted on a written guarantee of success for shooting an elephant, otherwise he would not pay for the safari. Clary was desperate for safaris, not only for the money but also to spread his reputation around international hunting circles in order to attract more hunters. He signed the guarantee for the Mexican and sent it off, but demanded a cash down-payment before the safari started. The Mexican agreed to that condition and booked the safari.

The client and his young assistant, who acted as interpreter, arrived at Tanga aerodrome by air from Nairobi. As usual, Clary was there to meet them and clear their guns and ammunition through customs. However, a small problem occurred at the aerodrome. The client was carrying over 2000 dollars in Mexican gold coins to pay for his safari. The dilemma was that customs duty was payable on imported gold, but not on gold currency. While the chief customs officer read through his rule book, trying to decide if the coins were duty-free or not, Clary came to the rescue and explained that these gold coins were standard currency in Mexico, and his client was simply paying for his safari in

Mexican currency. So, no duty was levied, and the Mexican was allowed to go.

Nevertheless, the client, who carried a fortune in gold in his briefcase, was taken to the local bank and locked inside until the bank manager could be located in town with a businessman. He had to come and open the large steel safe to lock up the coins. When the flustered manager arrived, he insisted that each coin be weighed on an accurate scale borrowed from a local goldsmith to determine its cash value, as he did not trust Mexican banks or believe them to be honest institutions. In addition, there was not enough cash in the bank to buy the gold, so the manager agreed to keep the gold coins in his safe until the safari ended, at which time he would give Clary sufficient coins to cover the amount owed, and return the excess to the client when he left the country.

The safari started at the new luxury Ruvu River camp, where the clients could get used to African hunting by pursuing small game before tackling the larger, more dangerous animals. The Mexican client was unhappy with this arrangement and insisted that they immediately start elephant hunting. He said that the other animals on his licence were of little importance to him, so he could hunt them after he had shot his big elephant.

The Mexican went on to explain, through his interpreter, his obsession with elephants. As a young boy, he had been fascinated by them when his father took him to a circus with performing elephants. They were Indian elephants with small bodies and tiny tusks, though they were still impressive giants. Then, when he was older, he went to visit a zoo in the United States and saw for the first time an African elephant with big, shiny tusks. The tusks mesmerised him so much that he could not forget them. He now desperately wanted to have a pair of elephant tusks for his living room, to remind him of his youth. He had taken up weekend hunting in Mexico, but had been too busy building his business to consider an African safari. Now, however, he had handed over his company to his sons and had time to hunt in Africa. Clary understood his feelings very well, as he too had had a similar fascination with elephants when he was young.

The next day, they loaded the truck with provisions and equipment for ten days of hunting, and lurched along the rough track to the Lamwe Hill camp. On arrival, Clary was pleasantly surprised to find the camp still standing and intact. On closer inspection, he saw that the Maasai had been to the camp and walked through it, but had not touched a thing. A lion and a few hyenas had ambled through, as had a few mongooses, but nothing had been eaten or damaged.

On the first morning at Lamwe camp, Clary, the Mexican, and his assistant, climbed up the nearby hill to view the area for signs of elephants. As luck would have it, they spotted a big lone bull elephant feeding peacefully a few miles away in a fairly open woodland. From the hilltop, they were unable to see its tusks clearly due to the thick bush, so they would have to get close to the bull to determine the size of his tusks before shooting him. Quickly they gave chase. The wind was in their favour, and the going was easy until they got close to the elephant.

The Mexican had a beautifully engraved English double-barrelled rifle in 470 calibre, which he had bought especially to shoot his elephant. He now took it out of its leather carrying case, loaded it and, with a big childish grin said, "Let's go get my elephant"

Clary led the way with his client at his heels, followed by the young assistant and two trackers. They stalked quietly to within 40 yards of the feeding giant, then Clary went forward on his own to assess the size of its tusks. It was a 90 pounder, an excellent trophy. He waved to the others to come up, then he took the client in closer for the kill. At 20 paces, the massive elephant stood broadside to them, but the client could not see it due to the heavy brush. Very slowly, Clary took the client five paces closer. Then the elephant sensed danger, stopped eating, and stood listening, his great bulk still broadside to the hunters and its upper body obscured by a bush. Everyone froze. Half a minute later, the giant started chewing again.

Clary moved his hand slowly and pointed at the elephant 15 paces away, but the client was unable to see it. Clary was puzzled as to why the client could not see an animal as big as a house in front of him. The client kept moving his head from side to side trying to find the animal. Suddenly, Clary realised that the client was actually looking underneath the elephant's belly at the bush beyond. He gingerly took the man's hand and pointed it up towards the elephant's head, just as the bull took a step forward and came into plain view.

The client's eyes widened to saucer size then he dropped his rifle and staggered backward, stumbling over sticks and bushes as he barged his way back through the thicket. He ran past his assistant, passed the trackers, and just kept going. Clary was confused at this turn of events, yet had to stay where he was and keep his gun on the elephant in case it attacked him. Sure enough, first it turned towards him and was about to charge, but then quickly spun around and walked rapidly away.

The trackers caught the fleeing client, who was going the wrong way, and led him into camp where everyone was waiting.

Clary tried to calm the nervous hunter by saying, "Come and sit down, have a whisky, and we can talk about your elephant".

"No, no, I just realised that I have very urgent business back home that I must attend to", said the Mexican, as he rushed into his tent and started packing.

He came out a few minutes later, walked over to the car, and said in an angry voice, "We must leave immediately. Right now." Then he got into the vehicle and sat in the front seat, staring straight ahead, waiting impatiently.

Clary tried to reason with him, but the client briskly cut him short and insisted they leave immediately. Clary grabbed his briefcase with all his documents, while the assistant grabbed his own bag, and they drove away. On the drive back to the Ruvu River camp, the Mexican refused to talk about the incident, and only repeated his urgent need to return to Mexico.

While Clary was refuelling the car at the Ruvu camp, readying it for the long drive back to Tanga, the nervous client still refused to talk to anyone, not even his young assistant, and impatiently urged more haste.

On the road to Tanga, the Mexican kept repeating, "They are so big. They are so big."

Then the truth dawned on Clary, as he realised that the poor man had been scared out of his wits when he looked up and saw the huge animal towering over him.

The Maasailand elephants are bigger than most, and can measure 14 feet at the shoulder and weigh seven tons or more. A grown man can easily walk between the front legs of an African elephant and not touch its belly with his head.

After Clary told him that there would be no refund for this safari, the client agreed to let his assistant finish the safari and shoot all the game on his licence, including an elephant. His assistant could use the gold coins in the bank to pay for everything and carry the rest back to Mexico.

Fortunately, they arrived in Tanga in time to catch the last scheduled flight back to Nairobi, from where the client could catch another international flight back to Mexico.

Later on, during the safari with the assistant, the young man said that his boss had never seen an African elephant up close. In the zoo in America, the animals were down in a pit, so they looked small from above, and the Indian elephants which he had seen at the circus were only half the size of a fully grown African bull elephant.

The Mexican's assistant was just as scared of African game as most men are, though he had full trust in Clary's hunting knowledge to keep him out of danger, and followed him trustingly through thick and thin. He had a very successful and enjoyable safari, shooting every animal on his boss's licence, as well as a good elephant. When the assistant returned to Mexico, he wrote Clary a letter of thanks and said that although he would love to hunt in Africa again, he was not a rich man and could not afford the high safari fees. He added that his boss had no intention of ever returning to Africa, and had given up hunting altogether.

Chapter 47
Rhino in the Sisal

Clary had a British friend who was manager of a sisal estate that was expanding rapidly and was grading access roads throughout the estate to connect the outlying plantations with the central factory. The estate was close to the Ruvu River, so Clary had permission to use their graded roads to get to and from his camp, which substantially cut his usual travel around the estate.

He would occasionally call in on his friend to offer him some game meat, and have a chat and a drink or three. The manager had been a game warden for a while but gave it up for a much better paid job as sisal estate manager, although he missed being out in the bush.

One day while the company was clearing some large acres of bushland in order to cultivate more sisal, a young, fully-grown rhinoceros was flushed out of its habitat. The bush-clearers left a patch of bush that was not suitable for sisal cultivation in the middle of the estate, so the young rhino took refuge in this patch, although it was far too small for a rhinoceros to live a normal rhino life. The rhino often chased unsuspecting passers-by from its patch, scaring the daylights out of them and eliciting complaints to the manager. However, it had never poked its small horn into anybody – at least, not so far. The Greek estate owner told his manager, Clary's friend, to have this animal shot immediately, before it gored some innocent person to death. However, the British manager, being a former game warden, refused to do so. He knew that rhinos were one of the easiest animals to tame, so instead of killing it, he captured it by setting up a walk-in trap.

Firstly, he had a large rhino-proof stockade built close to where it lived. Then he had a big, muddy waterhole dug inside the stockade, and a sturdy concrete-covered shelter built. Finally, he had bales of fresh green grass thrown in. Now it was only a matter of time before the rhino smelt the fresh green grass on one of its nightly forays and walked into the trap. Then a waiting guard closed the thick wood and steel gate behind the animal, trapping it inside.

Every day after that, the manager would go to the rhino enclosure with a bale of fresh grass, or sometimes stalks of sweet sugarcane, talk to the animal in a calm voice, then throw in the food so that it associated his voice with food. He also made sure that its private waterhole was kept full of water, as rhinos like to wallow in cool mud when the sun gets hot.

At first, the rhino ran wild, butting the enclosure sides with its front horn and trying to escape whenever it saw someone looking over the walls. By the end of the first week, it had calmed down, and no longer ran wild when it saw a person. Instead, it would come to the wall expecting food to be delivered.

By the second week, the manager could stroke it from behind the enclosure walls. In the third week, the brave manager could go into the enclosure and pet the young animal without it becoming aggressive. After the fourth week of captivity, anyone brave enough to take a chance was invited into the enclosure to bring an armful of food, or just to pet it.

Once the rhino lost its fear of people, the enclosure gate was opened, and it was free to ramble all over the sisal estate. It usually stayed close to its refuge, returning every day to its enclosure, where it wallowed in its mud bath or rested in its covered shelter. The estate workers lost their fear of it and became used to seeing it around.

The rhino's favourite hangout was the manager's house, which sat on a hilltop with beautiful views over the estate. It was surrounded by a lush green lawn with jacaranda and mango trees growing in the garden, as well as delightful red and white bougainvillea bushes covering parts of the house. There was always a treat waiting for the rhino at the house, or lush grass to nibble on and a few fallen mangoes to eat. Yet for some unfathomable reason, the rhino took a dislike to the manager's African cook and would charge him on sight. Perhaps the cook had teased or beaten the rhino when it was still in its enclosure, or annoyed it so much that it had not forgotten the bad treatment. He was a very good and reliable cook, so the manager's wife refused to let him go in spite of his perilous situation.

Whenever the rhino was around the house, which was often, the cook was ordered to stay in his living quarters or keep out of sight and smell of the rhinoceros. The manager's house – a typical one for that time – was a long, concrete block building with a red corrugated iron roof. It had a sitting and a dining room at one end, and bedrooms and baths at the other end. The kitchen was in a separate building, 20 yards away from the main house. The kitchen was a small, square, concrete block hut covered by the same ugly tin roof as the main house. It had one wooden entrance door, a window on one side, and a tiny back window above the wood-burning stove to let smoke out.

The servants' quarters, built 50 yards beyond the kitchen, housed the cook, and also a housemaid and the gardener, both of whom were on good terms with the rhinoceros. The gardener and housemaid warned the cook whenever the rhino was spotted lurking about the garden, and sometimes they distracted it with food to keep it away from him.

One weekend, Clary and June were invited to stay overnight at the manager's house for a party on the Saturday afternoon. The party was a resounding success, except that much to the partygoers' disappointment, the renowned rhino did not appear for the guests to pet. The next morning, being a Sunday, was a day off for the housemaid and gardener; only the cook had to work.

Around nine o'clock in the morning, the cook came into the sitting room carrying a pot of freshly brewed tea for the hosts and their four overnight guests. He then took their breakfast orders for eggs, bacon, sausages, fried tomatoes, and toast with jam, and went off to the kitchen. It took him an hour to prepare the large breakfast order, put it on a trolley, and push it towards the main house. But before he made it halfway there, hosts and guests heard loud screams of panic that broke the Sunday morning calm, followed by huffing and puffing and thundering feet, and the crashing sound of breaking China.

The tame rhino had seen the cook and charged him as he tried to push the breakfast trolley between the kitchen and the house. Everyone rushed outside, where they were confronted by freshly fried eggs, bacon, sausages, tomatoes, and toast scattered wildly over the lawn, and one demolished food trolley lying on its side in a pile of broken porcelain. The cook had taken refuge in the kitchen and was screaming for his life as the irate rhino, puffing menacingly, was stuck in the doorway trying to get at him.

Four weak guests tried pulling the one-ton rhino by its short tail away from its course of action. They even tried thrusting sticks of sweet sugar cane through the open window to stop its pursuit of the cook, but to no avail. A quick-thinking guest, realising the cook was in dire straits, took a spade and smashed the little kitchen window above the stove, then attached a rope to its frame. The three other guests pulled hard and tore the window frame out of its moorings together with a few bricks, making a hole big enough to extract the hysterical cook, unharmed.

The trembling cook was overjoyed to be freed, and demanded to be driven immediately by car to the next bus stop in a distant village. He was determined to leave this place without delay, and he vowed never to return. The starving guests were forced to go to the local clubhouse for their breakfast, but all agreed that they had a marvellous conversation topic. When Clary and June went back to the manager's house after breakfast to collect their belongings, they saw the rhino calmly ambling through the garden with the kitchen door frame around his middle!

Chapter 48
A Frenchman Tastes a Safari

A fellow hunter had booked two safaris, one after the other, then realised that he would be unable to manage both safaris. Knowing Clary's good hunting reputation, he asked Clary to take one of them.

Clary very gratefully accepted the safari, which was with an upper-class Frenchman and his wife. They, or rather he, wanted to hunt East African game. The Frenchman had hunted all over French-speaking West Africa with professional French hunters, and now he wanted to hunt with a renowned East African professional, and compare them.

To ensure they had a successful safari, Clary went out of his way to outfit the camp with all the luxuries he could afford, including champagne, fruit liquors, and an assortment of alcoholic beverages for every taste. He even bought new linen bedsheets, carpets, fancy tablecloths, and expensive perfumed soap. Italian spaghetti, cheese, and hard German sausages were the only edible luxuries available in Tanga, so he bought a supply of these items, as well as exotic Indian spices. He also bought an assortment of luxury imported English tinned goods which he purchased in the local shops. He hoped his safari cook could conjure up enough exotic, tasty meals from all this food to impress his French guests.

Clary met the Frenchman, Claude, and his attractive "wife" Marie, plus their large pile of suitcases at the aerodrome. The "wife" was less than half Claude's age and, in fact, was his mistress. As Clary learned later, this state of affairs was very common in France and accepted as normal by Claude's much older real wife.

There was an easily hunted area rich in game that Clary had explored several years previously at a place called Mkomazi. And this was where he decided to take his new clients.

The big Dodge truck, overloaded with all the equipment, bumbled along the track and was quite a bit slower than the Land Rover hunting car that carried Clary and his guests. So the clients had to wait patiently for an hour at the bare campsite for the truck to arrive. In the meantime, some little animal would have to give up its life to feed 15 hungry people that night.

Clary left his guests in the Land Rover, walked a few hundred yards onto an open plain, and shot two dainty Thomson's gazelles. He intended to shoot only one, but a second animal was so close behind the first one that the single bullet killed both. Clary was unconcerned about the second kill, because none of the meat would go to waste.

The old, dusty truck finally lumbered into the campsite and the travel-weary crew laboured to get the equipment off-loaded and a basic camp set up before nightfall. The experienced men just managed to set up before dark. However, before they could rest their tired bodies, they still had toilets to dig, showers to erect, water to fetch, and firewood to collect. Excepting the firewood, Clary decided the other chores could be done the next day.

That evening, as the guests sat by a small fire with drinks in hand, the attractive French girl stood up and looked around in a confused way.

When Clary asked her what she was looking for, she replied, "Where is the toilet?"

He was taken aback by this statement, but then realised she was serious, so he said, "Just a minute, I'll show you."

He took a roll of toilet paper from a supplies box, pressed it into her hands, swung his arm in a wide arc from left to right, and said to her, "The whole of bloody Africa".

On the first night and on all subsequent days, the cook and his helper did their best to provide meals as delicious and exotic as possible. A different dish was provided at each meal, and Clary believed the offerings were very tasty. The finicky French couple thought otherwise and always had a negative comment to make, comparing this camp concoction to real camp food served in West African hunting camps.

"Over in French Africa", Claude elucidated, "at all meals, except for breakfast which was black coffee and a croissant, an appropriate wine was served, and the meal was finished with three types of cheese and biscuits. Bread was mandatory and baked fresh every morning. The cook fried the dry game meat in beef or pork fat to enhance its flavour. Or it was sautéed in red wine with herbs."

Claude continued, "Vegetables were bathed in cream or butter sauce. Olive oil and vinegar for leafy green salads were a must. Fresh fruit was steamed in liquor and served with hot chocolate sauce. Any West African cook worth employing could make crêpes Suzette in the bush on a hot tin plate over open coals. Coffee was the only drink for morning, noon, and night, not tea. Tea was for English gentlemen and ladies, not Frenchmen", he concluded.

Despite their criticism of the food, the couple ate it all good-naturedly and put the experience down to a safari adventure.

They had not seen any elephants in the area, only some old tracks, and Claude was a bit concerned that he may not get to shoot an elephant. So one day he asked Clary if there were any of the big animals here.

"Yes, of course they are around here. We just have not been in the right place to see them", Clary answered.

As proof of their presence, early the next morning there were some huge elephant turds right outside the French couple's tent. A lone animal had walked right through the camp at night without tripping over a single tent guy rope. It had stopped in front of the client's tent to leave a message then continued on its way. No one in camp had heard it.

Since Claude was keen to shoot a lesser kudu, which was rarely seen in that area, Clary decided to make a fly camp far away from the main camp for three nights. He took the truck with just enough equipment for a very basic camp. Given that it was probably too rough for Marie, she stayed in the main camp to relax and watch the local birdlife through a pair of binoculars. Clary gave orders to his remaining staff to cater to all her wishes while he was away.

The drive to the fly camp was through dull, dry thorn country without roads or tracks, so they used elephant trails to bash their way through dense thickets to find a waterhole where they could camp. Game trails usually led to waterholes, so it was fairly easy to find water by following a trail, although they needed a waterhole with sufficient water in it to last them a few days. They eventually found one with blue-green water which had elephant manure floating in it. The disgusted Frenchman could not believe that Clary intended to touch that contaminated water, but was assured that after clearing, boiling, and filtering, it would be safe for washing and cooking. For drinking, they had brought two jerry cans of clean water from the main camp.

There was only one tent, which Clary and Claude shared. The dining room, with a table and two chairs, was a canvas sheet strung between four trees. The four camp personnel had to sleep on their thin rubber mats under the truck or on the hard ground in the open.

Clary was a little worried about his staff's sleeping arrangements because he had seen a lot of lion spoor at the waterhole, but there was little he could do about it now. The first night, the camp was bathed in the glow of a clear full moon shining down from a cloudless sky. Clary kept both tent flaps open to let a cool breeze blow through while they slept.

About 4am, he awoke instinctively, as he sensed something was wrong. He looked out through the open flaps at the brightly lit camp which was still immersed in the glow of the full moon low in the night sky. He saw a big, black-maned lion sniffing at something lying under the truck. To his horror, he realised that it was sniffing one of the workers, who was still fast asleep. Clary always slept with his rifle close by, and now he grabbed it and aimed towards the lion, but he dared not shoot for fear of hitting the sleeping man. Then came a loud cry of pure angst from under the truck.

The lion growled and sprang back as the shocked man jumped up, hit his head on the hard steel chassis, and knocked himself out, falling back where he had lain. The lion walked up to the unconscious man, sniffed him curiously, then ambled off into the bush. The other three men had been asleep on the bed of the truck, and they remained fast asleep throughout the entire incident.

Clary went over to the unconscious man just as he was recovering consciousness. The poor fellow jumped up, screaming, "Simba. Simba", meaning, "Lion. Lion". Then he quickly climbed into the truck's cab, where he cowered in the footwell for the rest of the night, shivering with fear. He had a nasty lump and cut on his forehead that was bleeding, but adamantly refused to come out of his hiding place to get the gash cleaned and bandaged.

At seven o'clock the next morning, when the sun was well up, the frightened man still refused to open the truck door in spite of assurances from his comrades that it was safe, and the lion had long gone. Eventually, he agreed to open the truck door to let Clary attend to his wound, but only if he was taken immediately afterward to a village where he would be safe.

The good-humoured Frenchman, laughing at the latest incident, agreed to relax in the fly camp until Clary returned later that day. Clary drove the worker, who clung white-knuckled to his seat, to the next village where he could catch a bus home.

Clary was back at the fly camp that afternoon just in time for a kudu hunt. After an hour's walk close to camp, Clary spotted three of the elusive males feeding along a row of trees. Their fawn striped coats blended in so well with the surrounding thicket that Claude could not spot even one of them. Try as he might, the client just could not see the animals until, sensing danger, they ran off.

"Alors! They are grey, not red!" Claude uttered.

He had been looking for red animals in the bush because his poorly illustrated French gamebook showed kudus with red coats. The two hunters both laughed at the error. Clary laughed at himself for not describing the kudus' colour, and Claude laughed for not asking. However, the day was saved on the walk back when they came across an old lone male walking towards them near a tangled stand of bush.

They waited until the animal was 30 yards away, then Claude fired a perfect heart shot. The camp was so close that the personnel heard the shot and came running out to help carry the kill back. Now that they had a kudu, Clary suggested that they pack up right away and go back to the main camp, and Claude eagerly agreed. The staff were delighted at this news, because they did not want to be there if the lion from last night returned and was hungry enough to eat someone.

The hunting party made it back to the main camp before 9pm and, after a quick meal, the Frenchman and Marie disappeared into their tent, ostensibly with urgent matters to discuss.

About half an hour's drive from camp was a small settlement where goats and dogs were regularly being taken by an old male leopard. Very likely it was too slow and frail to hunt wild game for itself, so it started to catch easy prey from nearby villages. A game scout, who was out checking on hunting camps for legality and compliance with game laws, alerted Clary to this leopard, saying that the villagers had been complaining about it for quite a while. The warden had asked that it be dealt with, meaning that it be shot by a scout. The game scout suggested that the French hunter shoot it, as he had a leopard licence, and the villagers reported that this was a big male so it would be a good trophy. Claude was happy to oblige.

The hunters made a trip to the village and found that the people were very pleased that someone was going to rid them of this menace. Leopards move about and hunt at night, so the only sure way to shoot one at night is with the aid of a flashlight. However, shooting at night with artificial light was illegal, so the only other way was to hang a bait in a tree and wait in a blind nearby, hoping the leopard would come before dark to get its free meal. If the piece of meat is large enough and the cat finds the bait, it will eat half of it in one night, although it usually comes too late to see it and to be shot on the first night. However, it will come early the next evening, when it is still light enough to see, to finish the rest of its meal.

Claude shot a kongoni, took one back leg to hang up with a stout rope in a tree as bait, and took the rest back to the base camp.

Clary explained his leopard-hunting plan to the villagers and warned them to keep away from the big tree where the blind was situated. Early the next morning, they went to check on the bait and saw that the whole leg had been taken away, bone and all. This was definitely a big, hungry leopard that had come here. They dashed back to camp and collected the other kongoni back leg for bait, hanging it with double ropes in the same tree.

Clary thought the leopard would have eaten so much the previous night that it would not return tonight, so did not sit on the bait. The following morning, the bait and ropes were gone again. Perhaps two leopards were feeding off this bait, one male and one female, which could explain why so much meat was being consumed, concluded Clary. This time, he hung up the entire front quarter of the kongoni, tying it well with thicker ropes. However, Clary and Claude had returned too late from an afternoon hunt to sit up that night. Again, the following morning the whole carcass was gone, including the stout ropes. Clary was shocked that two leopards could consume so much food in such a short time and be hungry enough to chew through the strong ropes.

He thought there were only two possible explanations for this. The first one was that the female had half-grown cubs to feed as well as herself and her mate, or the second one was that a tree-climbing lion was helping itself to the meat before the leopard arrived. The hard, stony ground under the bait tree made it impossible to ascertain which animal was taking the bait. Clary thought it was very unlikely that a villager had taken the meat, because they were keen to have this leopard, this killer of their goats, removed.

Clary was determined to find the answer, so he asked Claude to shoot a warthog that afternoon, which they then hung whole in the tree. Then Clary and Claude drove their car a mile away, left it there, and came back on foot to hide in the blind and see who turned up. Half an hour before dark, they heard a commotion as something climbed up the tree. The hunters saw two men in the tree who were busy cutting the ropes to get the bait down. Without hesitation, Clary fired a shot into the tree trunk just above their heads.

The two villagers hit the ground running and screamed, "Don't shoot, don't shoot" in Swahili, as they disappeared in a cloud of dust towards their village.

The next day the culprits came forward and admitted that every evening they had waited until just before dark and left the village unnoticed. When no car was in sight, they climbed up to the bait, cut it down and ran away with everything, including the ropes. They claimed they were just hungry for meat.

The leopard never appeared again, and no more goats or dogs disappeared from the village. Leopards become weak and slow in old age and are unable to hunt. They are usually killed by hyenas or lions before they can die a natural death. The old cat who had been robbing the village had probably met his fate in this way. Whatever the reason for his disappearance, the village animals were safe again.

At least twice a week Marie insisted on having a bath in front of the evening campfire, while the men sipped their after-dinner drinks. The bathtub was a two-foot-high rectangular canvas basin supported by a foldable wooden frame. It was placed right beside the campfire and filled with hot water. To take her bath, the young lady stood by the warm fire, stripped naked, placed her clothes on a chair, stepped into the bathtub, and sat down in the shallow water, all the while keeping up a conversation with the two men admiring her sensuous form.

Marie never showed any sign of embarrassment or shyness, even when she noticed the African camp labourers ogling her from their quarters. One of the trackers told Clary that Marie's behaviour was not good for morale, given that the camp had 12 men who had not seen their wives for weeks. Despite these complaints, Marie insisted on having her twice-weekly bath, so Clary put a tarpaulin around the bathtub whenever she bathed.

The safari was a huge success for Claude on the grounds that he enjoyed the hunt for each animal as if it was a brand-new adventure for him. Marie had fun showing the camp cook how to make crêpes Suzette and other French dishes, using a blackened skillet balanced on three stones over a smoky fire. Before the safari ended, Claude admitted that there was a much greater variety of game in East Africa than he had seen in French West Africa. However, he iterated, camp food was definitely superior in West Africa.

Overall, though, Claude was very happy with his safari, and Clary was immensely pleased that it had gone so well.

Chapter 49
Charged by a Dik-dik and Co

Clary had been back on the farm only a short time when the next safari was due to begin. This time it was an American banker named Walter, who was after a big elephant but also wanted to hunt all the other game on his licence during his 30-day safari. Clary's favourite hunting ground, the South Maasailand, was the perfect place to shoot most of the game his client desired. Walter was in his seventies yet still fit enough to walk for a few hours through the bush. He still hunted in the United States during the summer, so he had retained his shooting skills, which pleased Clary as it meant fewer wounded animals to follow.

They started the safari at Lamwe Hill camp, next to the waterhole. Every morning, Clary and Walter walked the three hundred yards to the waterhole and circled it to see which animals had come to drink during the night. There were a few other waterholes scattered throughout the area, so the game was not restricted to using only this waterhole. If they did not find any tracks worth following, they climbed Lamwe Hill to view the surrounding country through binoculars and look for elephants and other animals.

Every day they saw groups of elephants and an occasional lone bull in the thicket below the hill. They spent an hour on the hill trying to determine if any of the elephants carried big ivory, but due to the heavy bush, they very seldom got to see the tusks. If one elephant looked like an old bull, whose age was determined by its size and its wrinkled skin hanging on a low-sagging back and protruding bones, they would go down after it on foot. If none of the elephants seemed to be worth following and if no other game of interest was spotted, the hunting party walked back to camp and took the hunting car to search another sector.

There were only two of Clary's self-made roads in this quarter, so they would drive for a few miles, park the car under a shady tree and, depending on the prevailing wind, hunt in a wide circle for an hour or so, before arcing back towards the car. They never failed to see animals on these walks, but they only shot the good trophy animals. Determining if an animal carried large enough horns to make it worthwhile shooting before it got wind of the hunters and fled, was an art that Clary had mastered very well.

Alas, old Walter was seldom quick enough off the mark to shoot before it was too late. So, Clary made a light, portable tripod from three long sticks bound loosely with string near one end to give Walter a stable platform from which to shoot. A gun bearer carried the tripod and set it up whenever they saw an animal, even if Walter did not want to shoot. It worked so well that Walter was able to shoot accurately from a fairly long distance. He became so dependent on the tripod that he insisted on having it available all the time, even when in thick bush where a quick freehand shot was usually required.

One day Clary embarrassed himself in front of Walter and the gun bearers when he stumbled on a mating pair of ratel – a very vicious, black and white, fearless skunk-like animal with short legs. On being disturbed, the male rushed at the hunters, baring its sharp teeth and grunting as it came at them. Clary kicked the ratel in its face with his heavy boot, sending it flying several feet through the air. The little creature picked itself up, turned around, and came charging back.

Fortunately, they cannot run fast. This time, Clary ran to an anthill and jumped onto it as the enraged little devil chased him. It was a determined creature and climbed up the anthill after Clary and almost bit into his boot. Fortunately, a large fallen tree happened to be nearby, so Clary made a dash from the anthill and climbed onto a limb high enough to be out of reach of the furious animal. After snarling and biting off a few pieces of bark from the trunk to show who was boss here and who had won this fight, the ratel ran back to its waiting mate, and they disappeared into the brush to continue where they had left off. Both the gun bearers and Walter, who was standing farther away, were laughing hysterically at what they had just witnessed. A fearless professional hunter, armed with an elephant gun, was being chased by an animal no bigger than a cat.

"Next time I will shoot the little bastard", said Clary, blushing with embarrassment.

They continued walking through the bush slowly and silently, taking into account the wind direction so that they could adjust their route to keep into the wind as much as possible. From time to time the lead tracker pointed out well concealed game standing motionless in the bushes for Clary to judge as a trophy, only to be told that the animals were either immature or had already been collected.

On the walk back to the car, they broke out of the thickets onto a long, narrow, open plain, where a few oryx grazed at the far end. Thinking that there might be an old male with long horns in the herd, Clary took over the stalk, keeping the oryx in sight but staying hidden by bushes as they crept along the fringes of the plain. Suddenly, some movement in front of them caught Clary's eye. They had unwittingly blundered into a small group of zebra that ran out onto the plain, alerting the peaceful oryx of danger.

Just then, one zebra broke from the group and came running their way. Presumably it was being chased towards them by a predator, so Clary unshouldered his rifle, ready to shoot. However, although he crouched low to look under the scattered trees, he could not see what was chasing it. Just then, he realised that the zebra had its head and neck thrust forward and its ears laid back, and it was coming straight for him. It was charging him! Aghast at this incredible revelation, he was so stunned that he stood there dumbfounded, unable to react.

When the zebra was six yards away and opened its mouth to let out a shrieking bray, as well as reveal a set of big yellowing teeth, Clary came to and shot the charging animal through the head, jumping to one side at the last moment to avoid the falling beast. It had been so close that there were black gunpowder burns on the front of its face. The dead zebra turned out to be a female that had most likely had an encounter with wild dogs, because her underbelly and lower legs were badly bitten, a sure sign of a wild dog attack. The poor animal must have been in agony from its festering lacerations and would have chased any intruder. They left the zebra where it lay for the local scavenges to clean up.

On the drive towards camp, a little dik-dik ran out onto the road about ten yards in front of the Land Rover. It looked infuriated and charged the car. They heard a soft thud and felt a tiny jolt as the little animal hit the front bumper. It was hard to believe that a foot high, 12-pound dwarf would dare to tackle a one-ton car. When the hunters stepped out to see what had happened, they saw a small animal lying on the ground in front of the car, stunned but alive. It had hit the car's steel bumper with its three-inch horns and broken them off at the base. This was the fifth time that Clary had been charged by a dik-dik. A tracker took out his knife and slit the brave little animal's throat, then put it in the back of the car for camp meat.

"Does every animal in Africa charge?" asked Walter in amazement.

"Everything in Africa either bites, stings, charges, or overcharges", replied Clary, with a smirk on his face.

One morning, from the top of Lamwe Hill, they saw in the distance what looked like a lone bull elephant that was worth a closer look. After watching it for a while to estimate its route and walking speed, the hunting party headed down the hill after it. On the way through the bush, they spooked a few unseen animals and the odd dik-dik, with Walter wryly remarking that they were lucky not to be charged by them.

The trackers picked up the elephant's spoor a little later and began tracking the big animal. It was moving at a slow pace, feeding as it headed for dense bush to rest before the heat of the day set in. At one place, the elephant had walked up to a giant baobab tree and walked around it, yet they could not find any tracks leading away from it, only its footprints leading up to the tree. The gun bearers searched all around the field but found no tracks leading off.

Clary embarrassed himself once more by walking around the tree while looking up into the branches.

When Walter asked him what he was looking at, Clary said, "I was just looking to see if that darn animal was up in the tree because it hasn't left this place yet, as far as I can see!"

Walter burst out laughing, although Clary had meant it seriously. Even the gun bearers started laughing when they were told the joke. Clary turned a little red in the face when he realised the stupidity of his remark.

By carefully following the spoor, one of the gun bearers finally noticed that the elephant had followed its exact footsteps back the way it had come. A hundred yards farther on, they saw where the animal had turned off its tracks and gone back into the thick bush.

Tracking was getting difficult in the heavy brush, but since they suspected the animal to be close at hand, they cautiously continued the hunt, testing the wind whenever they sensed it shifting direction. By the time they caught up with the elephant that afternoon, it had already rested under some trees and was moving slowly through open, short scrubland. They could see its enormous back protruding above the bushes, but could not see its tusks. They followed closely behind, keeping track of the blowing wind all the time.

When their quarry was 50 yards away, it stepped into an open glade. Nobody moved as the huge elephant stopped at a greenish bush and tore off a branch to stuff into its mouth. It had a pair of short, thick tusks that were evenly matched, although too small to make a good trophy. There were bigger elephants than this one to be found, so they all stood in awe for a time, admiring this magnificent creature before it wandered off, still unaware of the hunters' presence.

Before Walter asked, Clary anticipated his question and said, "Elephants have very good hearing, an excellent sense of smell, and good eyesight, except they seldom look around, unless some movement close by attracts their attention. As long as you keep 40 yards or more away, out of the wind, and keep still, it will not notice you. You can watch him all day like this."

It was a long and tiring hike through the dry bush back to camp, but they made it in just before sunset and in time to have a cold shower and an even colder beer or two or more by the crackling campfire.

Walter was getting worried that he might not get his big elephant and was contemplating shooting any reasonable sized tusker that they came across. They had seen elephants every day and had followed a few potential ones, but none had turned out to have trophy-sized tusks. There was one place they had not hunted yet where Clary reckoned they had a good chance of seeing a big elephant. He persuaded Walter to hold off on shooting a small tusker until they had searched this new region. However, it would mean a basic fly camp for a few days. No luxuries at all could be carried on this short trip, as they would have to pack the minimum of equipment plus four camp staff into the faster Land Rover instead of the much bigger, slower, Dodge truck. It would be a tight fit, but manageable.

Clary had not been to the waterholes at Losira for many years, after his shocking betrayal from the Kenya hunter, so he was not sure what to expect or if his old tracks leading that way would still be visible enough to follow. Even so, he was determined to go and see for himself.

The going was rough as they followed the overgrown tracks through the tangled bush. They lost their way a few times when well-used game trails crossed their track and led them in the wrong direction. Old tree stumps that his road builders had left standing years ago guided them back on track. Having to clear off masses of twisted vegetation left by passing elephants caused the most delays. Eventually, they arrived at the Losira waterhole and were pleasantly surprised to find it full of clean water.

About 100 yards from the water's edge were some flat rocks and stunted trees where they set up their fly camp. From this vantage point, they had a good view over the water and the surrounding 200-yard wide grassy plain with its few scattered Terminalia trees

While the workers set up the small camp, the two hunters scouted the other waterholes to look for tracks and see what game was drinking there. There were signs that large numbers of game used these waterholes almost daily, as did a few elephants. Hunting here looked very promising, especially when they came across a pride of lions waiting for nightfall to start hunting. The first night, everyone was too tired to stay awake and watch what game came to the water to drink, but from the constant bickering of the local plovers, it seemed that there was traffic throughout the night.

After an early cup of hot sweet tea, Clary and Walter walked around the water's edge and were happy to see that a few lone elephants had drunk there during the night. Walter was eager to start tracking the biggest of the elephant spoor, but Clary said no, making the feeble excuse of wanting to look at another potential elephant area first. In reality, he could not contain his niggling curiosity to know the fate of his "private" hunting paradise on the Kitwai plains.

There had been no space in the car to carry extra petrol to the fly camp, so they had to use the car as little as possible. However, for Clary, seeing if his ravaged land had miraculously recovered from its devastation was paramount for his sanity, so he just had to make the trip.

The Kitwai plains were beautiful, with their endless fields of tall, swaying, yellow grass. A few ostriches strolled about, pecking at grass seed heads. A small mixed herd of wildebeest and zebra trotted away in a cloud of grey dust at the sight of an approaching vehicle, and as he feared, a large herd of Maasai cattle were grazing at the far end.

The big herds of game that roamed here in bygone years had been so decimated and scared by the Kenyan hunter that they had not recovered, not even to one-tenth of their previous numbers. Clary had seen enough. He had hoped that if the game was left unmolested for several years the herds would recover. Regrettably, it was, as he had feared, gone forever. It would remain a Garden of Eden only in his memory.

On the drive back to the fly camp, Clary, with a heavy heart, described to Walter in vivid detail his lost paradise and the man who was responsible for its destruction. By the time they reached camp, Clary had completed his story and had tears of sadness in his eyes. Walter was silent with respect for his sensitive big game hunter. They stayed in camp for the rest of the afternoon while Clary brooded quietly in his camp chair with a warm whisky in his hand.

They had a plan for that night, which called for sleeping until midnight, then getting up to watch the waterhole to see if any big elephants came to drink. The old bulls tend to come to water after midnight but before dawn to drink. If one carried tusks big enough to be worth hunting, they would wait until morning and follow its track into the bush where, hopefully, it would spend the day feeding and resting.

When all was quiet, the whole camp was unceremoniously awakened before midnight by the screeching and trumpeting of a herd of about 15 elephants at the waterhole. A few unruly youngsters who were making the most noise were cavorting playfully in the water. A three-quarter moon was just coming up behind the tree line, bathing the herd in a silver sheen of eerie light. Moonlight and starlight danced on the water to the rhythm of waves created by the romping little giants. It was a joy to behold such a rare scene in the wild, and the whole camp watched in awed silence.

After the elephant herd departed, Clary and Walter wrapped themselves in woollen blankets against the chilly night air and sat for the rest of the night on camp chairs observing the goings-on at the waterhole and listening to the mysterious sounds of the wild.

They heard the "WHOU" of wandering hyenas and the distant roar of a male lion.

"Do you know what a lion is saying when he roars?" asked Clary. Not waiting for an answer, he continued, "He is saying, 'Whose land is this? Whose land is this? It's mine, it's mine, it's mine.' Listen carefully the next time you hear one roaring."

Occasionally the duo dozed off, but they were always awakened by the plovers who complained loudly whenever an animal came too close to the little birds at the waterhole.

One after the other, three bull elephants came to quench their thirst. They were all old bulls with wrinkled hides and concave backs, but they did not carry ivory big enough to make them worth following in the morning. The biggest was a 75-pounder, which was big yet not quite big enough, as Clary knew they could find a bigger one.

By 5am, they did not expect any more visitors, so the hunters left their uncomfortable camp chairs and went to bed, where they slept soundly until mid-morning. Upon waking, they had a frugal breakfast of fire-blackened toast with jam and very sweet tea, then went to check the other two waterholes, where they found fresh elephant spoor at each one. Although the footprints were big, indicating a fully grown animal had made them, the sole imprints in the mud were rough and not smooth, which indicated a younger animal.

As they returned to camp, they saw in the distance a small pride of lions with a very big black-maned male amongst them. Walter had a lion licence and wanted to hunt it. However, Clary warned him that if they fired shots now, any big tuskers within hearing range would leave this territory for quieter and safer places, so they let the lion live.

They spent the rest of the day in camp with binoculars, watching the herds of game coming to the waterhole to drink, and admiring the little plovers dive-bombing any animal that came too close to their nest. In the late afternoon, a pride of lions appeared out of the long grass, scattering the startled wildlife. Luckily for the game, the lions were thirsty, not hungry, so after leisurely lapping up a sufficient quaff of water they swaggered back into the long grass from whence they came.

For the second night in a row, the hunters sat up from midnight onwards watching over the waterhole. Another five elephants came to drink at various times in the night. In the moonlight, the silver-grey behemoths with their shimmering white ivory tusks were easy to see as they sucked up trunksful of water to squirt into their mouths or drench their dusty backs. Clary estimated the first and biggest elephant to be an 85-pounder, with the rest being just slightly smaller. The last elephant to appear just before dawn was a 70-pounder. Walter was frustrated that they had not seen a 100-pounder, which was what he wanted, or one even close to that size. He was worried that he might not get to shoot an elephant, so against Clary's better judgment, Walter decided that they go after this last elephant, saying that at least a 70-pounder was better than a zero pounder.

An hour later, just as the moon was going down and red dawn streaks appeared on the eastern horizon, they left camp, picking up the last elephant spoor just beyond the waterhole. It was easy to follow the tracks through the open ground until it entered the jungle at the far end of the plain. Here the hunting party were forced to wait a while for the sun to peek over the treetops so that there was enough light to follow the spoor through the bush. Fifteen minutes after entering the thicket, they heard the sound of breaking branches ahead, not too far away. Walter was still adamant that he wanted to shoot this elephant and accepted the risk that if they saw a larger one later, he would not be permitted to shoot it.

The hunters went in for the kill. They glimpsed the animal through the trees some 80 yards away, just before its arched shoulders appeared over the top of low, scrubby bushes on the edge of slightly open ground. They knew it was the same one they had seen at the waterhole two hours ago, due to the dry water streaks on its back.

They found good cover so that they could creep within easy shooting distance of the elephant. At about 40 paces, Walter rested his .375 calibre Winchester rifle on the tripod and was able to place a perfect heart shot. There was no need for Clary to back him up with his 450 Express, as the mortally wounded elephant ran almost 200 yards before it fell to the ground and died.

The trackers congratulated Walter for a clean kill on a big elephant, and a gun bearer cut off the animal's tail, presenting it to him as proof of ownership. It was an old bull elephant, beyond breeding age but still enjoying its last years of living alone in the bush, where it had likely been born and lived for the last 65 years.

Regrettably, there were no communities nearby who could take all this meat, and the Maasai did not eat game meat, only their own cattle. On the other hand, it would keep lions, leopards, and hyenas fed for many days, sparing the lives of some other animals who would otherwise fall prey to these predators. Vultures, flies, and insects would devour whatever the scavengers left. Only the largest bones would remain for a few years until, bleached by the merciless sun, they too would disintegrate and return to the earth as calcium to renew the circle of life. Nothing was ever wasted in the jungles of Africa.

After hacking out the tusks from the mighty skull, the hunting party carried them back to camp to be weighed with a simple but accurate spring scale. The tusks were not 70 pounds each, as Clary had estimated, but rather 90 pounds a side. He could not believe it and insisted on another weigh-in, which still showed 90 pounds each. Clary realised that if this elephant, which he had thought was a 70-pounder, was in fact a 90-pounder, then all the others must have been bigger too, some definitely more than 100-pounders.

There is a distorted sense of perspective when looking at animals in the moonlight, especially estimating the size of elephant tusks, which Clary was not aware of since he had never before hunted elephants in moonlight. Walter listened patiently to Clary's explanation of his mistake in misjudging the tusk size as he embarrassed himself for the third time on this safari. However, Walter now had his big elephant and was satisfied, although a 100-pounder would have been nice.

All day long, vultures came from miles away to swoop down and take part in the free feast of elephant meat. Vultures have binocular eyes and the ability to spot blood on the ground while flying high through their territory. Whenever they see blood or an animal lying on the ground, they circle for a while to check for the presence of predators nearby, then they fly down, with wings half open and legs slightly out, to land a safe distance away, either on the ground or in a tree. Another vulture, flying through its own territory, will see this manoeuvre and come over to investigate. It will circle a few times, assess the situation for itself, and fly down with wings and feet in landing position to join those already waiting.

Vultures miles away can see their circling comrades, so they also fly over to have a look. Many more miles away, other vultures cannot see their mates circling high or in the trees, but they notice their neighbours flying fast in a straight line, heading for some distant location, and they simply follow them. All the vultures in neighbouring territories are always watching each other's every move. When one acts like it has found food, the others fly over to look. In this way, they have the whole of Africa as their dining table.

Hyenas usually spend the day resting in a cool, shady place and only move about at night to scavenge for food. However, when they see vultures flying purposefully in one direction or hear the whistling of wind in wings of a fast-flying vulture, they will also head in that direction because they know there is food to be had. Hyenas have understood vultures' behaviour for thousands of years and have benefitted greatly from this understanding. In addition, hyenas have a superior sense of smell, and when the wind blows towards them, they can scent a dead or wounded animal from many miles away.

Lions and leopards prefer to kill their own food but, being opportunists, they will come to scavenge on any meat they smell. They will also investigate if they hear the ghoulish laugh of hyenas feeding on a kill. In this way, the whole jungle kingdom of carnivores is informed about where there is food to be had.

While the hunters were sitting that night by their crackling campfire, listening to the cacophony of hyenas and jackals telling each other about the mountain of free meat to be had, there was a roar from a male lion behind camp. Clary and Walter jumped up and reached instinctively for their guns.

"I would like to get a black-maned lion. If there is a good one, can I shoot it?" asked Walter.

The moon was big and bright that night, and although game laws do not allow hunting at night or using artificial light to shoot game, Clary reasoned that it was so bright that it was as good as day, so there was no need for a flashlight.

They did not even have to walk too far out of camp to find the roaring lion. It stood 70 yards away on a flat rock, silhouetted against the night sky. It was a magnificent old black-maned lion, just standing, side-on, with its huge head turned towards the camp.

"Take him right on the shoulder", said Clary, standing ready with a five shot .375 calibre rifle.

Walter took his .375 Winchester and did not wait for his tripod to be set up but instead fired immediately, hitting the animal too far back and too high on the shoulder. The lion went down from the impact of the first shot, then got up and immediately charged, growling menacingly as he came on in great bounds towards the hunters.

Clary now realised they were in a dangerous situation, so he fired repeatedly and hit the charging lion three times, eventually killing it at 15 paces with his fourth shot.

Surprisingly, Walter did not fire a single shot at the charging lion, yet he turned to Clary and said, "Lucky I got it with that last shot. My gun's empty."

Clary was totally confused by this statement, but then noticed four unfired cartridges lying on the ground at Walter's feet. The client had somehow hit his gun's safety catch "on" after his first shot, and the blasts from Clary's four shots had given Walter the feeling of having fired four times, although he had simply ejected unfired cartridges at each shot. Clary now realised what had happened and said nothing to Walter. He reloaded quickly and moved back to the safety of their camp.

The rest of the lion pride were growling and snarling as they prowled menacingly behind the dead lion, and the hunters did not want to provoke them into an attack. When the situation calmed down and the intimidating lions left, Clary spoke to the gun bearer in Swahili, telling him to pick up the full cartridges secretly and replace them with the empty cases that Clary handed to him. He did not want to disappoint Walter, so he let him believe he had killed this lion with his last shot. It was a magnificent dark-maned lion, one of the best Clary had ever seen.

The best maned lions are found where it gets cold at night and where there is grassland for them to roam, like the conditions here. In heavy thorn bush country, thick manes get thinned out when the lions walk through the thorny bushes.

The crew carried the dead lion into camp, where the skinner skinned it out that night with the aid of a flickering, pale, kerosene lamp. A gun bearer watched over him, occasionally throwing stones at nosy hyenas to keep them at bay. By midnight, the skinner had completed his fine work, salted the skin and skull, and put them in the Land Rover to keep them safe from hungry hyena jaws. The once majestic lion's carcass was unceremoniously dumped a few yards from camp, where it was immediately seized upon by hysterical, sniggering hyenas, torn to shreds and devoured in a wild frenzy of guzzling.

No elephants came to drink at any of the waterholes that night, and the plovers were silent. News of danger travels fast and in mysterious ways in Africa. The next morning, they found no evidence of the lion carcass, for the scavengers of the night had done their duty well.

Now that Walter had his big elephant, there was no reason to hunt here any longer, so the camp was dismantled and packed into the Land Rover. However, the long tusks would not fit anywhere in the car, so they were wrapped in a canvas flysheet to protect them from chafing and tied to the car roof. Before they drove away, Clary made a last inspection of the campsite to remove any evidence of human activity, except for the dead fire and footprints.

They arrived at the Lamwe Hill camp late at night and did not bother to unpack the Land Rover or even have something to eat. Instead, everyone went to bed and was asleep in no time.

The next day, Clary could not find a reason to continue the hunt from this camp. All the remaining game on Walter's licence could be hunted from the more comfortable Ruvu River camp.

Before travelling on, Clary ordered his crew to leave the Lamwe camp intact, except to take all the perishable food and the trophies and load them onto the Dodge truck. They were to drive the truck back to the Ruvu camp the following day.

This safari was to be Walter's last one in Africa. Soon after his return to the United States he had a stroke and was hospitalised. When he was discharged, he was unable to hold or shoot a rifle due to his paralysed right arm. Even with the use of a steadying tripod, he was unable to shoot.

His days of hunting to shoot a single trophy were now over. However, he had a lifetime of memories of each and every animal he had chased. He could relive his past safaris from the comfort of his specially designed trophy room, where the mounted heads and cured hides of his animals were displayed in an orderly row on the walls and along the floor. Each mounted head on the wall and each skin on the floor was not simply a souvenir of a killing spree in the African bush, but had a unique story of adventure attached to it, which

Walter could relive and recount in minute detail to a listener. Even many years later, one look at the lion skin rug lying on the trophy room floor would conjure up the scene of the Losira waterhole in the silvery moonlight, while the magnificent king of the jungle stared down at him from his rocky throne.

Chapter 50
Wife and Kids on Safari Spell Trouble

After the safari with Walter, there was a long period with no bookings. Money was running out far too quickly, forcing Clary to hunt for a large enough elephant to make ends meet on the farm and pay for upcoming expenses. He could still buy two elephant licences for himself this year but only one for June, as he could not afford a second one for her. He hoped that tusks from three good elephants would bring in enough money to pay all expenses for the rest of the year.

The Lamwe Hill camp was still set up, so it was only a question of buying adequate food and fuel to get it up and running. It had been very dry in July in Maasailand, so all the game, including elephants, stayed within two days' walking distance of water. The waterhole at Lamwe was still a quarter full, though it was dwindling quickly due to all the thirsty creatures drinking there.

On this safari, June insisted on bringing their four young children to the camp instead of leaving them with a nanny back on the Malindi farm. Clary would be up early every morning and out of camp long before the noisy children were awake, so he did not object to them coming along.

The routine for Clary was the same every morning. Get up at 4:30, wake up the cook and his helper, and the gun bearers and trackers. Clary would wash in front of his tent in a basin of cold water, then shave in the same water. At 5am he was served a refreshing mug of hot, sweet, milky tea as he sat in the open by last night's smoky fire, mentally planning today's hunt. Twenty minutes later, a standard English breakfast of two fried eggs, two pieces of bacon, two pork sausages, some fried tomatoes, and a pile of toast awaited his attention in the dining tent.

At 6am, when he had finished eating and just as it was getting light, his gun bearers and trackers assembled in front of the mess tent. They would check that the guns were there with the correct ammo, the water bottles were full and not leaking, the emergency rations of biltong were packed, and the very important first aid kit with a box of matches was in a backpack.

When all the equipment was in place and order, Clary called a "Twende", meaning "let's go", and they all silently walked out of camp.

The first stage of the hunt was always to hike up nearby Lamwe Hill and spy out the country below with a pair of powerful binoculars. If no elephants were spotted, Clary consulted with the trackers as to which way to go that morning.

One morning from the top of Lamwe Hill, Clary saw three bull elephants quite far away that looked as though they carried big ivory. He decided they were worth investigating. At this dry time of year, the thick bush had withered to brown clumps of foliage, making it fairly easy to walk through the thickets.

Edible vegetation for hungry herbivores was scarce, so feeding animals became aggressive with each other whenever a competitor got too close. Screeching, trumpeting, squealing, and grunting of various game animals could be heard throughout the patches of bush, giving away the position of each species.

Clary heard the three bull elephants complaining loudly to each other long before he got close enough to see them. All three were close to each other, vying for the same fodder, and they kept attacking one another with angry, vicious charges, throwing up clouds of fine red dust at each assault that made it difficult to discern their tusks.

He moved closer to them, then suddenly the wind changed and blew straight from him towards the elephants. Their trunks went up, testing the air to get a better sniff of the scent of danger. Almost as one, the three bulls turned directly towards Clary and charged headlong. Their heads were down, with their trunks rolled up under their chins. This was a real charge, not a mock attack to scare someone away, although it was unlikely that they had seen him hidden behind the bushes, but rather only scented him.

There was no place to run and hide out of the wind and no time to escape the onslaught, so when the three elephants were 40 paces from him, Clary stepped into the path of the oncoming behemoths, raised his 450 double rifle, aimed at the third wrinkle in the middle of the central elephant's head, and fired. A jet of yellow flame shot from the gun muzzle and a loud bang shattered the air. A puff of dust flicked off the middle elephant's forehead indicating a hit, but it did not drop dead. All three animals wavered a little, and then rushed on at full speed.

They would be on top of Clary in a few seconds, and he only had one cartridge in the gun but three charging elephants to deal with. He could see the whites of their angry eyes as he aimed his last shot at the left bull's forehead and fired. Immediately, two mighty bulls fell over to the left, sending up a cloud of red dust as they slammed into the dirt not ten paces away from where Clary stood, rock steady, hurriedly trying to reload his empty gun. The third bull veered off to one side as its mates fell. It angrily eyed Clary, who was still fumbling with his empty gun as it thundered past him and continued running into the thickets beyond.

Clary gaped around him, visibly shaken, trying to comprehend what had occurred. His mind was piecing together the events slowly. He concluded that his first shot to the brain had killed the middle bull elephant, but it had been carried forward by the others on each side of it. His second head shot to the left bull had killed it, too, causing both animals to fall over. His faithful gun bearer Timoteo, who had stayed right behind him the whole time, agreed with Clary's scenario of the events. The other two men had run away to hide safely until the elephants were gone. They slowly emerged from their hiding places and came over to admire the two fallen giants.

Clary was disappointed, because the ivory was not as heavy as he was looking for, but it was still in the 50-to 60-pound range. As he still had one elephant on his wife's licence, he was determined that it would be a very big heavy tusker.

It was going to be an all-day job to remove the tusks from both elephants, so the group returned to camp to prepare the axes, pangas, and knives for the task.

Back in camp, while thinking about the triple elephant charge, Clary was not content that he had been unable to pull out the cartridges from his breast pockets quickly enough. His fumbling while trying to load his gun had scared him. He would have to practise pulling out two cartridges at a time from his pockets and ramming them into the gun's chambers. When he could reload his double rifle without fumbling very quickly, he was content with himself. Nevertheless, he continued to practise this skill each time he went hunting.

The next day, Clary took June and the children with him in the Dodge truck to let them see an elephant up close and show them what his job as a hunter entailed. They took some pictures as Clary explained to his three children the anatomy of an elephant. Then it took Clary's men six hours of hard work in the blazing sun to remove the four tusks and carry them to the truck.

The Ruvu camp offered good fishing, entertaining Sykes' monkey antics in the overhead branches, butterflies and birdlife to observe, and was a cooler, more interesting place for his family to stay. And at this dry time of year, there was an abundance of game coming down to the river, including large herds of elephants. However, it was in the Lamwe Hill area where the big elephants preferred to feed. So, the family was forced to stay in the boring, dusty, dry Lamwe camp until Clary shot the third elephant.

June became bored sitting in camp for days looking after her unruly brats, so one morning she decided that she wanted to join Clary on the day's hunt. She felt confident that her children would be safe in camp with the caring African staff.

It was already late morning by the time Clary, June, and the trackers climbed Lamwe Hill to spy out the bushland below. Since the three elephants had charged Clary a few days before, no more lone bulls had been seen in the area. Clary was hoping to spot a bull just passing through this stretch, but saw only a few scattered small herds of elephants with squealing young ones. A few vultures could still be discerned, circling far away over the remains of the two elephant carcasses. There seemed no point in hunting here today, so Clary decided that they would drive to another lookout hill four miles away to check out that sector. However, before they left, Clary and June happened to look down from the hilltop at their camp six hundred yards away.

Clary saw a big red cloud of dust to the east of the camp where the trees were short and the bush less dense. The dust cloud was thrown up by a herd of about 25 elephants walking at a fast pace towards the waterhole which was close to camp. Their route would take them through the camp, just where he noticed the children playing amongst the trees. June saw the elephants, too.

She suddenly stood up and screamed, "My babies, my babies!" Dropping her binoculars, she took off running down the hill for all she was worth, still shouting, "My babies are down there."

Startled by the sudden commotion, Clary looked up and saw June disappearing down through the thorny bush.

He shouted to her, "You don't have a gun, you stupid…" He suppressed the last word under his breath, then ran down the hill after her with his gun in hand.

Her route was easy to follow. He found bits of shirt sleeve hanging on thorns, a torn-off jacket pocket, and June's hat caught up in a bush that she had just dashed through. He could hear her crashing headlong through the bushes, still crying, "My babies, they're alone down there."

Dishevelled and panting like a sprinter, June burst into camp just as the first elephants walked through the clearing towards the children's playground. She had no time to dash into the tent where a spare .375 rifle was stored, so she grabbed a white towel drying on a washing line and raced towards the confused elephants, waving her towel and shrieking, "Get away from here! Get out of here."

The first elephants stared at her and started growling and trumpeting loudly as she ran helter-skelter towards them. One old female was about to charge June, but changed her mind, turned, and ran back the way she had come, bumping into the other animals and causing confusion and panic amongst the milling herd.

June spun around and dashed to where her children were standing staring at the elephants. She grabbed one-year-old David from his cot and shouted to her other offspring to follow her and get into the Dodge truck. By the time Clary arrived at the camp, wheezing and breathless with his 450 Express rifle at the ready, he encountered trumpeting, confused elephants crashing about all over the place except, thankfully, not through any tents. He waited until the milling herd sorted itself out, while June and the children watched from the safety of the truck.

Ten minutes later, screeching elephants could still be heard in the distance as they fled to look for a quieter drinking place. Clary gave June a stern lecture about her maternal behaviour, using words like "fool", "killed", "stupid", and "dangerous" many times, but was answered with, "At least my children are safe."

In the end, Clary had to take his gun bearer, Timoteo, out beyond camp and teach him all about guns and how to shoot. After a few practice shots at a tree with the tiny .22 long rifle, then more practice with the .375, he became skilled enough to shoot straight and to hit his target rather than someone nearby. Timoteo could now be an armed guard for the camp whenever Clary and June were away. Not only did Timoteo later become an excellent marksman, he proved to be a fearless and reliable gun bearer, too.

Another incident near camp showed just how dangerous elephants could be. Early one morning before Clary went off to hunt, some Maasai warriors came into camp to ask for help in locating one of their women who had gone into the bush the previous evening to look for her lost goats. She had not returned, so the Morani (warriors) feared that she might have been killed by lions.

The Maasai were not afraid of lions, and defended their livestock against any attacking animal. They hunted lions for sport. Whenever a young man had to prove himself a warrior, he had to hunt and spear a lion. However, there were also many buffaloes and elephants in the bush, and they preferred not to tangle with one of these creatures so they sought help. Clary and June, together with some trackers and the Morani, made up the search party. They went with the Land Rover along the rough road towards the Maasai boma to look for circling vultures, who were usually the first to spot a dead animal or person. Along the way, they noticed a few vultures sitting on a tall Acacia tree waiting for one of their bravest to fly down to investigate a possible meal.

Hidden between some broken trees, the search party came across the smashed body of the old Maasai woman, lying in a pool of dark, dried blood. Iridescent blue bottle flies buzzed around the mangled body, laying lily-white eggs in exposed wounds. Fat, squirming maggots had already started devouring putrefied parts of the old Maasai. All the broken trees and the gouged earth pointed to an attack by an enraged elephant. The search party surveyed the scene and surmised what had happened.

While looking for her goats, the old woman must have startled an elephant in the thicket. It had chased her as she tried to dodge left and right in between big trees. It caught her from behind, threw her high in the air, and she landed in a tree. She must have still been alive, as she had been able to jump from the tree and start running again. Sadly, the elephant was faster. It grabbed her again and smashed her old, frail body against a tree. It then picked her up once more and threw her to the ground, like a rag doll, at least four times, breaking every bone in her body. However, its rage was still unsatiated. It gored her lifeless body with its tusks again and again, then threw her across the ground to where she now lay.

Still not satisfied, the enraged elephant attacked the bigger trees it saw, breaking off large limbs, and then it uprooted smaller trees and trampled them into the hard red earth, as though they too were responsible for its anger. Finally, it left the battlefield, going back the way it had come, still raging, and tearing off tree limbs as it went. Clary's suspicion that this was the work of a female elephant that had just lost her calf was confirmed a day later, when he was investigating a gathering of vultures and found a very young dead elephant not far from where the Maasai woman was killed.

To perform their last rites for the old woman, the Maasai would straighten out her remains into a proper body shape, turn her to face the rising sun, cover her with a few green branches, and leave her where she lay, for the hyenas to devour that night. On hearing the news of the old woman's demise, the rest of the tribe back at the Maasai boma, would mourn her passing at a gathering of old folks, who would drink gourds of Sauer honey beer while telling her life story over and over again. By tomorrow, she would be eaten by hyenas, her existence would slowly fade from memory, and life at the boma would go on as usual.

Clary had given orders to his men not to let the Maasai into the camp, in case they caught a deadly disease such as chickenpox or smallpox from one of his staff. The Maasai were to wait outside the perimeter until someone came to bring them into camp.

Late one morning on a non-hunting day, a camp labourer came to the dining tent where Clary was busy writing his diary to advise him that a group of Maasai with a very sick man were waiting at camp's edge. Clary stopped what he was doing and took one of his Ndorobo trackers who could speak Maasai to act as an interpreter then walked over to the waiting men. They had carried one of their sick warriors several miles through the bush on a cowhide stretcher. The sick man was barely conscious and breathing in feeble little gasps. He was covered from head to foot in open, bleeding sores.

To Clary, it looked like an extremely serious case of chickenpox. They begged Clary to take the sick man by car to a hospital, because this man was their chief's son. However, the nearest clinic where this man could possibly get help was on a sisal estate about six torturous hours' drive away, over bumpy bush tracks. The nearest hospital where he could get proper treatment for his condition was more than a day's drive away. This sick warrior would not survive even three hours on a torturous car journey.

Clary told the waiting warriors that there was no hope of saving this man's life. They answered by saying that if he would not drive the sick man to the hospital, they would carry him on their own through the bush until they reached a place to get help. If he died on the way, they would bury him in the bush at that spot. A chief and his male children have the privilege of being buried in a grave when they die, and not being left out in the bush for the hyenas to devour.

Clary felt helpless and ashamed that he was unable to assist these brave men. Then he remembered some new medicine in camp that might help to keep the injured man alive long enough to get him to a hospital.

A previous hunting client had brought with him a new miracle drug called penicillin. He had not needed it on his safari, so he left all of it with Clary, and gave him complete instructions of how and when to use it. Perhaps it would work on this dying warrior, mused Clary. Now seemed like a good opportunity to try it out.

He fetched his new wonder drug from his little steel medicine box, read the accompanying instructions, and prepared a hypodermic syringe with a very large dose. It was impossible to find a small patch of clear skin on which to inject the antibiotic penicillin, so he pushed the needle deep down through a sore, injecting the man with a massive overdose. Then, to help heal the man's bleeding sores, he covered him with soothing calamine lotion. Clary warned the carriers that his medicine was very powerful, more powerful than a lion, but even so their sick man could die soon. However, if the medicine worked, he might live a long time. Only God knew.

They readily accepted those fateful possibilities as the will of God, picked up their charge, and left. As the warriors carried their burden back to the boma, the Ndorobo tracker said to Clary that he had never seen such injuries before, and it was very unlikely that he would survive very long.

Four days later, a lone pale Maasai warrior came and sat under a tree on the outskirts of camp and waited. When Clary got back from the morning's hunt, he sent a tracker to the waiting man to ask what he wanted. The tracker ran back and said it was the sick man from a few days ago, coming to thank Clary for saving his life.

Flabbergasted, Clary went to see for himself, as it seemed impossible for the sick man to be healed of such severe injuries in only four days! The man sitting under the tree was almost white, and covered all over with pinkish, round blemishes where new skin was growing. It was definitely the same sick warrior from a few days ago. He had walked all the way from his boma unaided, and except for his sore feet, he was fine. Just to make sure that he made a full recovery, Clary gave him another, much smaller dose of penicillin, and took him back to his boma in the Land Rover. The warrior made a remarkable recovery, and in subsequent years, Clary could easily recognise his patient due to his pale complexion and his rough, pockmarked skin.

While out hunting with the Land Rover for some game meat to feed the camp, Clary suddenly stopped when he spotted some strange black and red animals walking through the open bushland. They were cattle, just walking and grazing peacefully with no one looking after them, which was very unusual.

A Maasai's wealth was measured by the number and quality of his cattle, and each calf born was given to someone in the boma. They rarely sold any cattle, except during severe droughts or if they needed money to buy a blanket or spear. Otherwise, the Maasai shunned money. Cattle were kept in one big herd by the Maasai and were never allowed to graze alone, as they would be easy prey for lions. Thinking that these cattle had been accidentally separated from the main cattle herd, Clary drove past the Maasai boma to inform the herders where they could find their lost cows.

A Maasai boma is a large circular thorn enclosure built to keep their cattle safe from predators during the night. It is ten feet high and ten feet thick, and built of densely packed thorn bushes. Arranged around the inside perimeter of the boma are dung and mud-covered wattle huts where the Maasai sleep. The cattle are kept in the centre of the boma, and the goats, which are much fewer in number, are kept in separate enclosures close to the sleeping huts.

Clary saw men and women dragging thorn branches, freshly cut poles, and lengths of bark rope towards one side of their boma, where other Morani were using the material to patch a broken section of the fence. After a gun bearer managed to talk to a busy Maasai, he returned to the car and told Clary what had transpired. The previous night some lions had come around the boma to harass the cattle. The Maasai Morani heard them, got up, stoked their fires outside the huts to a bright yellow glow, and walked amongst the cows, talking and whistling to keep them calm so that they would not panic and stampede.

Then a male lion roared, dangerously close to one side of the boma, and permeated the air with the strong stench of his urine. The cattle became agitated and shuffled about. Then the men picked up burning logs and walked amongst the cattle to provide some light for their animals, as that tended to calm them. They continued touching, talking, and whistling to the animals, trying to keep them quiet. For 15 minutes, they repeated reassuring words to their cattle and managed to keep them calm. However, the lions were not about to give up so easily.

They started circling the boma very closely, looking for a weak spot. They tested the strength of the impenetrable enclosure in a dozen places, only to be driven off by burning logs and long sharp spears thrust at them, while frenzied men shouted from the other side. By now, the milling cattle were almost in a panic. They stomped around inside the boma, running into each other and bellowing with fear. Some frightened cows tripped and were trampled by other terror-stricken animals.

There was one entrance for all the cattle to enter the boma, and once they were all in, this entrance was closed off by a whole thorn tree dragged into the opening. The agitated cattle had repeatedly knocked this big thorn tree aside, and now there was a breach just large enough for a lioness to break through.

One female saw the gap and leaped into the boma, growling and slashing with her sharp claws amongst the terrified cattle. The lioness forced the cattle to rush headlong into the boma walls, eventually breaking through them, and they fled wildly into the dark night towards waiting hungry jaws. The lioness rode to freedom on the back of a bucking, panicked cow. The lions now had a plentiful supply of easy meat for at least several days, if not longer. Only half of the cattle herd could be rounded up and saved during the night; the rest were lost in the pitch-black darkness.

In the morning, the Maasai discovered that ten cows had been killed and partially eaten in the night, while a few more had died of fright or been trampled to death in the stampede. The Maasai would never be able to find all the missing animals, because cows have no homing instinct, so they would wander aimlessly until they fell victim to lions, leopards, and hyenas.

In most herds, the most valuable and the leader cows were fitted with bells so that they could be located easily if they strayed away from the main herd, but if a group of cows got lost without a bell cow, they were unlikely to be found. Bells on the cattle also warned other animals that there were humans around whom they would try to avoid. In the north of Maasailand, however, the Maasai realised that lions listened for ringing cowbells. The bells actually attracted the lions who were always on the prowl to snatch a cow, so the bells were removed.

Early that morning, most of the warriors had gone out to look for the remainder of the lost herd, with hopes of bringing them back. The rest of the tribe, including women and children, were tasked with repairing the boma. The Maasai would search for their missing cattle for about three days, after which there would be very little chance of finding any alive, so they would abandon the search. Then they would take revenge on the lions by organising a hunt. The warriors would strengthen their physiques by slaughtering a cow and eating plenty of fire-roasted meat, and bolster their spirits by singing and jumping in the air as high as they could with their feet together, while gripping their long-bladed steel-tipped spears with which they would kill the lion. Clary was familiar with the Maasai from his previous encounters with them, and he knew that within a few days, the hunt would start and a male lion would be impaled by a Maasai spear. This was their time-honoured practice of revenge.

Clary informed the people where he had spotted their cattle and hoped they could gather the animals before the hyenas and lions got to them first.

One afternoon, Clary became very annoyed when he arrived in camp after a particularly hard day of hunting. Not only was the camp overrun by cattle, but also half the inhabitants of a Maasai boma were sitting around under the trees in their finest beads, chatting to each other as though they were at a party. He soon discovered that they had come to buy one of his children!

He found June hiding in one of the tents with the baby and her other three children, holding a loaded .375 in her hands. Clary demanded to know what was going on, and June sheepishly told him that a few days ago some Maasai warriors had come to the camp out of curiosity to see what they did in camp all day. The warriors, with their red blankets tied over their shoulders and carrying their long spears, had spent the time watching camp life. In particular, they were very interested in the children playing games around the tents. One Maasai warrior who could speak Swahili asked June if she would sell one of her children to him.

"Of course", she had joked, "take them all."

The warrior said he only wanted one of them, and he would pay 30 cows for him. The Morani then left camp, and she thought nothing more of it.

This morning, half the men and women from the Maasai boma, along with a large herd of cattle, arrived to make the trade. The chief himself took June on a tour of the cattle and explained to her which were the best animals to choose, which ones had calves, which ones gave the most milk, and which ones were strong. Then he pointed to Christopher, June's second oldest child, and said he would take him in exchange for the 30 cows and raise him personally as his own son.

That was when it dawned on June that he was serious about buying one of her children. She was terrified at the consequences she had unknowingly brought on herself, and in a trembling voice she said to him, "No, I don't want to sell any of my children. I was not serious about the exchange."

The chief became angry and told her that she had agreed to the sale a few days ago, and after consultation with his sub-chiefs, he had also agreed to the purchase, so there was no going back now. Shaking with fear, June stood her ground and stared at him, repeating her "no" again.

The infuriated chief strode back to his warriors, and after a long, heated discussion with them, he stalked back to June and said, "We have agreed to 50 cows now, but no more."

On hearing that, June knew there would be ructions, so she grabbed her children, ran into her tent with them, loaded the .375 rifle, and waited for trouble to start. She ordered one of the camp employees to tell the Maasai to go home as she was not selling any children for any number of cattle. The proud Maasai stood their ground and refused to go away until the transaction was completed for the white child.

So, a dangerous and delicate stalemate ensued until Clary arrived. He pointed out to June that if the situation had flared out of hand, there were 25 armed warriors out there, but she only had five shots in her gun.

The Maasai were a fearless, independent-minded people who did not recognise any governments, borders, or laws, except their own. They fought and defeated every tribe that opposed their expansion southward from ancient Egypt along the Nile as they sought new grazing lands for their cattle. Fighting fearlessly was second nature to them. One puny little white woman with a gun was a joke to these warriors. Their word for fear was the equivalent of "little girl". They had no word for a coward; that concept did not exist in their culture.

Had June fired a single shot towards them to try scaring them away, they would have attacked and slaughtered every single person in the camp, including the children. Bargaining deftly with the chief was the only way out of this delicate situation now.

Confronting the annoyed chief, Clary explained to him that he would not be able to look after a white child in the bush, because it could not live like a Maasai child. The chief shook his head and asked why it was possible for a white person to look after a Maasai child in a town but not the other way around.

He went on, saying", The European missionaries come to our bomas and tell us that we must send our children to school so that they can become wise to the new world. When we say no, they tell us that the government wants every child to attend a school and that it is good for everyone. We still say no, but they tell us to give them only one child to educate, and they will bring him back in the rainy season to show us that he is clever." He continued, "So we give them one, and the missionaries go away and don't bother us again".

The chief had a point. He did not understand that it was for the good of the Maasai to be educated in the modern world.

Clary had a tense situation on his hands that required skilful handling so as not to end in a bloodbath on both sides. Suddenly, he had a bright idea. He agreed to sell Christopher for 50 cows, on condition that the chief promised to look after Christopher in the same way he was accustomed to being cared for, or he would die.

Clary then took the smiling, happy chief on a camp tour, explaining how a European child has to live.

"He must wear soft cotton clothes like this", letting the chief feel a little cotton shirt. "He cannot wear goat skins, because his white skin is delicate, not strong like a Maasai."

"Yes, I will get some cotton clothes for him from the Arab shop", said the chief.

Clary went on, "He must sleep on a soft bed with clean sheets, like this", inviting the chief into the children's tent to feel the soft mattress and pillow.

"Yes, I will exchange some cows for a nice bed for him", answered the grinning chief.

Next, Clary took the eager chief into the dining tent, letting him taste some cheese, a raw potato, a green tomato, some uncooked cabbage, a teaspoon of vinegar, and to top it off, a red hot chilli, all of which the man spat out in disgust.

"He must have food like this every day, as he cannot live on blood and milk like a Maasai boy", explained Clary to the chief, who was no longer smiling.

Clary's ruse was working. The chief was fast losing interest in the white child. They went on to the food boxes full of imported English tinned foods, glass jam jars, and packets of oats, flour, and maize meal.

"This is the food you must get for him every week", continued Clary.

The chief's eyes almost popped out of his face as he looked at the full box of food. "Every week he eats this much food?"

"Yes", said Clary, "and when he is older, you must send him to school so he can learn to read and write like this". Clary picked up a coloured fairy tale picture book.

"But why must he learn to read and write? He will be a chief like me when he is ready to take over. I can't read or write", cried the chief in a disappointed voice.

"Because he must learn to drive and repair a car like this one, so that your people can get to market or a hospital when you get sick", Clary replied, leading the chief over to the Land Rover and throwing open the engine compartment for him to look inside. By this time, the chief was totally disenchanted and was shaking his head vigorously as he backed away.

"Don't forget, he must have a hot bath every day!" shouted Clary at the departing figure.

"Oh, and he must wear a hat in the sun all the time."

The chief stormed over to his waiting warriors, and in vociferous tones explained to them the fragile nature of European children and why he was not going to have one of those weaklings in his boma. He ordered his womenfolk to drive the cattle back to the boma as he and his disgusted warrior stomped away.

When June plucked up enough courage to venture out of the tent, Clary said, "Do something asinine like that again and I will sell you to the Maasai for one cow!" June didn't answer.

Just in case the Maasai came back, now was a good time to leave quickly and drive back to the Ruvu River camp, even without that one last big elephant. They would have to find another place for good elephants.

It was pleasant to be back in a cool, shady camp where eager young children could catch tasty fish every day. It made a welcome change from the usual fried, boiled, or roasted game meat.

The next day it rained and put a stop to all fishing activities. It was not unusual for it to rain at that time of year, but it was unusual for it to rain so heavily. Soon, the little Ruvu swelled its banks and spilled over into the camp, causing it to flood. Only the sleeping tents, which were on higher ground, were safe from the rising water.

Fortunately, all foodstuffs in boxes had been placed on tables made from green log beams, so only items on the lower ground got soaked.

When the rain stopped the next day and the sun came out and the water receded, wet items were strewn over the drying ground on mats of palm leaves or hung on washing lines strung between convenient trees, giving the campsite a carnival look.

By late afternoon, everything was bone dry and put away carefully so they did not get wet in the next rain. Then the insects and other crawling creatures had to be forcibly removed from their hiding places in clothes, beds, and even smelly shoes, and were allowed to scamper away into the undergrowth.

In the evening after a heavy rain, the wet forest floor gave off a pleasant, pungent, fungal odour of decaying wood and rotting leaves. Rising steam condensed on overhead leaves, so that water droplets constantly fell back to the ground throughout the forest. It was a pleasant time to relax in camp.

That evening, when the tired children were fast asleep in their beds, Clary sat under the eaves of the mess tent, enjoying a few after-dinner drinks as he listened to the soothing tapping of falling raindrops on wet canvas. June lay a few yards behind the tent in a grass-walled enclosure, having a long hot bath in the canvas tub.

Still on his third whisky, Clary noticed a totally naked, wet, pink woman run past him and pick up the hissing kerosene pressure lamp standing some yards away.

"There's a bloody great big snake next to my bath!" June hissed in a very annoyed voice.

Slightly taken aback, Clary put down his glass and ordered a kitchen helper to fetch the 12-bore shotgun and box of ammo from his tent, while he looked for a covering for his naked wife. The grinning helper who had noticed June running about naked, handed Clary the gun and ammo and retreated hastily.

Clary loaded the gun, then took the lamp to search behind the grass enclosure, where he discovered a six-foot cobra slithering around chasing rodents. It quickly disappeared into the undergrowth as human footsteps approached.

"It's gone, you can get back to your bath", said Clary.

"Not likely. If it's not dead, it will come back", replied June, and then explained what had happened.

"I was just beginning to relax in my hot bath when I heard something scraping alongside the canvas tub. Next, I see this cobra's head, a foot away from my face, looking straight at me over the bath rim. I dared not move my lips to shout. I tried flicking water at it with my fingers, but it flared its hood at me. I lifted my foot out of the water and wiggled my toes in an attempt to attract its attention; it turned towards my toes and was about to strike them, probably thinking it was a rat in the water.

"So I very quickly pulled my toes under. Now I had to just sit there, not moving a muscle for at least five minutes until it went down and crawled away towards my little hurricane lamp, close to the bath, where moths were fluttering about. That's when I got out of the other side of the bath and ran here." She continued, "I'll finish my bath tomorrow in daylight, when I can see the blighters. Get me a stiff gin and tonic. No, make that a double."

It was only later that Clary realised it had been a mistake to ask one of the kitchen helpers to collect the shotgun from the sleeping tent and bring it to him there under the eaves. He was about to learn the hard way that he should have done it himself or asked a senior staff member to do it.

As the droplets off the trees gradually ceased their music, Clary yawned, downed the last drop of whisky from his glass, and headed for the sleeping tent, gun in hand, while June decided to stay a bit longer to finish the last of her G and T.

There was a low flame burning in the hurricane lamp by the sleeping tent. Clary picked it up and turned the wick up to give off more light so he could see to unzip the tent flysheet. To his surprise, the fly was already unzipped and open.

It must have been that kitchen helper who forgot to zip up after collecting the shotgun. I must remember to advise the camp staff to keep all tent zips closed at night, he thought to himself.

He entered the tent, holding the lamp in one hand and the gun in the other, then turned around, put the lamp down and reached up to pull the zipper down to close the flysheet behind him.

He picked up the lamp again and hung it on a wire hook bent around the ridgepole. He turned around and saw her in his bed. She was black as night and very beautiful. Her head was resting on the white pillow, and her dark eyes sparkled in the lamp's light. She started to wriggle her long, lithe body under the thin blanket. *She must have snuck in through the open flysheet and crawled into my bed*, he thought.

Clary stared at her in dread as he slowly brought the shotgun up to his shoulder and fired. A blinding yellow flash illuminated the interior as a mighty "boom" shook the canvas tent like a flimsy piece of cloth in a high wind. Her delicate head was blown to pieces, and her lifeless body writhed in death. Clouds of feathers from his demolished pillow floated down gently over the gruesome scene. He reached over to his bed and threw back the blanket to reveal the remains of a deadly black-hooded cobra. He picked up her lifeless body by the tail and dragged her outside, depositing her on the dark earth.

The shot had abruptly awakened the whole camp. Some men took to the trees in panic and did not come down until the area was declared clear and safe. Others ran to shelter in the truck cab, while a few curious souls came timidly to the tent with lamps to see what was going on.

Clary was livid with rage at the staff member for leaving the tent zipper on the flysheet open. He vented his anger on all those present, calling them every evil name he could come up with. The guilty man responsible for the mistake was one of those workers high in the trees where he was able to avoid Clary's wrath.

The children had woken up but soon fell asleep and only enquired about the commotion the next morning.

June's only comment on the matter was, "Now I can safely have my bath behind the tent again."

The mangled snake's remains were tossed into the river for fish food. A spare folding bed and mattress replaced the blood-splattered one. A new pillow was found, and clean white sheets and a blanket made the bed ready. The back wall of the tent was cleaned of snake fragments, so ants would not be attracted during the night. And a large hole in the tent was temporarily patched with tape, then everyone went back to bed.

June took extra care as she pulled back her bedcovers but nothing suspicious was revealed. The snake incident would be the main topic of conversation in camp for a few days until another terrible event replaced it.

Chapter 51
Boy Overboard

A boating accident on the Ruvu brought home the dangers that lurk in unexpected places.

Mr. Wilkins, a wealthy Englishman, owned a very large sisal estate just a few miles away from the Ruvu River. His 13-year-old son James, who was schooling in England, came to Tanganyika to spend his summer holidays on the estate with his father. The old man had bought a new aluminium boat and outboard motor that he intended to take on a boating trip down the Ruvu River. He also bought a .22 rifle with a five-shot magazine and a 12-bore shotgun with which to do some bird shooting along the way.

Taking his son and three boatmen, Mr. Wilkins trailered the new boat with his Land Rover to the river and launched it at an upstream site. From there, they planned to motor leisurely downriver for 30 miles to a native village, where their Land Rover and driver would be waiting for them. On the boat ride, they could expect to see plenty of wildlife along the riverbanks, as well as hippos and crocs in the river. They planned a stop on the journey to eat a sumptuous lunch, which they had brought with them, and perhaps a little bit of bird shooting in the surrounding terrain.

The boat party left the launch site in the morning and headed downriver. The Land Rover and driver were sent off to wait at the rendezvous village 30 miles downstream.

Young James was allowed to hold the loaded .22 rifle just in case his father needed it to shoot a duck on the water.

The boat engine purred gently as they rode leisurely down the river, enthralled by the beauty of a lazy African river and its diverse flora. The African boatmen, with their keep eyesight, pointed out sunning crocodiles and curious monkeys staring down at them for high trees, although being village folk they could not name them. They even surprised a buffalo or two ambling along the riverbank.

About halfway through the trip, just after a long bend in the river, the boat driver noticed a large tree had fallen three-quarters of the way across the channel, blocking their passage. There was a clear passage around the obstacle to the left that the boatman steered towards. But while trying to manoeuvre past the fallen tree, the unskilled boatman misjudged the strong current and the boat slammed sideways into the tree.

For a few seconds the little engine screamed as the driver gunned it to try to extricate the boat. It was too late. The strong, fast flowing current pulled the boat underwater, dragging everyone with it. James resurfaced beyond the fallen tree and managed to swim to the nearest shore. He climbed out on the right bank, still clutching the .22 calibre rifle. The three boatmen, who could not swim, were swept down the river into a bend where the water was shallow, and they managed to clamber out onto the left shore. However, there was no sign of Mr. Wilkins.

James stood alone on the bank, waiting for his father or the boatmen to come out. He did not know what to do or where he was, except that this was the Ruvu River. He called his father's name repeatedly while walking downriver, but received no reply. The boatmen heard James calling and shouted to him from their position on the opposite bank.

Unfortunately, James could not understand Swahili, the local language, and the boatmen could not speak English, so they could not understand each other. None of them had any bush experience, as the boatmen had only worked on motorboats in Tanga harbour, and James had never been to Africa before.

Everyone seemed clueless about what to do next as they sat on the bank, shivering from the cold in their wet clothes. There seemed no way for anyone to cross over the river to join up. Finally, James, taking charge of the situation, pointed downstream and indicated to the men that they should do the same. He started walking downstream on his side, and the boatmen did the same on their side until they came to some rocky rapids where they found the capsized boat. It was empty, twisted out of shape, and its transom had been ripped away together with the outboard motor, rendering it unseaworthy.

Feeling confused and helpless about what to do now, they sat down on the grassy bank to think things over. James hoped that his father would emerge from the river and take charge of the situation, but he did not appear. James knew how to shoot a .22 rifle, but it was only a bird gun with five rounds of ammunition in the magazine. He was not brave enough or stupid enough to continue walking on his side of the bank, through the wild animal-infested riverine forest alone.

Their only hope was that the driver of the Land Rover would come looking for them when they failed to arrive at their destination in the village. However, that could mean many hours or even days of waiting, while hungry and cold in a dangerous place. They were in a terrible predicament.

Clary was writing his diary in camp late in the afternoon when he heard a car approaching. It was very strange to hear another vehicle on this side of the river, and even stranger at this time of the afternoon. When the worried driver came into camp and told Clary about the river trip that was long overdue, Clary expected the worst. He knew there were too many rapids and rocky outcrops on this part of the river to afford safe passage by boat, especially with inexperienced boatmen.

Since no boat had passed his camp, Clary reasoned it must still be farther upriver. He knew the river well from his crocodile hunting times, and knew where the dangerous rapids and rocks were located. He sprang into action immediately, as night was rapidly approaching, and the darkness would greatly hamper a search effort.

He jumped into the big Dodge truck with six of his best men and drove along one of his tracks that ran parallel to the river, until he came to a dangerous spot. Here he turned towards the river and bashed his way in first gear, through the tangled bushes to the rapids. He switched off the noisy engine and shouted out Wilkins' name, then waited in silence.

When no reply came, he drove on to the next spot and did the same. At the third rapid, he found James still holding the .22 calibre rifle, and shivering from cold and fear. The boy was in tears and unable to speak. He could not comprehend why his father had not come for him.

Clary sent his men up and down the river to look for James' father, while he devised a plan to rescue the three frightened boatmen from the opposite bank. To rescue them, he tied a stone to one end of a rope and twirled it over his head until there was enough momentum to fling it across the river. He ordered a boatman to tie the end to a stout tree while

Clary did the same with his end. He attached two empty jerry cans to the rope to use as floats, which the boatmen pulled over. Then one man attached the jerry cans around his chest and pulled himself, hand over hand, across the river by the rope. When he was over, the jerry cans were sent over to the next boatman to use. In this way, Clary managed to pull them all over to safety.

Before it got too dark, Clary called off the search for Mr. Wilkins and recalled his men to the truck. Everyone piled into the Dodge for the sombre drive back to camp.

James and the three hapless boatmen were given dry clothes to wear while their wet ones were hung by the fire to dry. Then they were given a hot, nourishing soup to eat while they warmed themselves by a crackling fire.

James tried to put on a brave face, but the worry about the fate of his father showed through. Overcoming his sorrow, He tearfully told Clary what had happened and how the boat trip had started so enjoyably and peacefully along the slow flowing river.

"Even the fallen tree across the river seemed nothing more than an inconvenience to the trip. When the boat driver revved the engine at full power to back off from the tree and the boat didn't move, I knew we were in trouble", said James, as his eyes welled up in tears.

He was able to finish the rest of his story so that Clary had an idea of where to search for Mr. Wilkins the next day.

Clary insisted that it was best if James and the boatmen return to the sisal estate that evening so that they could sleep at their homes. The Land Rover driver was instructed to drive them home then report the incident to the police and request them to organise a search party for tomorrow.

The next day, a contingent of 20 men arrived early at Clary's camp to continue the search. With the help of Clary's knowledge of the river, Mr. Wilkins' body was found a few miles downstream from the accident site, trapped by a rocky outcrop in the river. It looked as though the capsizing boat rails had hit Mr. Wilkins' head, rendering him unconscious as he was sucked underwater and drowned. Luckily, he had not been found by the many crocodiles in the river, so his body was untouched.

Clary was given the mangled boat as a gesture of thanks for his assistance in rescuing the survivors. He repaired it and got 35 years of good use out of it. Nothing else from the boat was ever salvaged - not the new outboard motor, nor a new Purdy double-barrelled shotgun in its wooden case, which had never been fired.

Sitting in a camp chair by the slow flowing, green Ruvu river a few days after the Wilkins incident, Clary could not help thinking about how many people had lost their lives here.

More than 500 Zigua villagers had been taken by crocodiles. Perhaps another hundred had been drowned when their flimsy canoes had overturned in the river. Floods had swept too many to count into the river and drowned. Along its banks, people had been bitten by snakes, gored by buffaloes, and attacked by lions, leopards, and hyenas. Countless thousands had died of malaria that was rampant along the lower reaches of the Ruvu.

And a few days ago, this gentle river had claimed another victim – Mr. Wilkins.

Oh, you silent and dangerous life-giving liquid, how many human lives have you taken and how many more will fall into your tranquil depths and be gone? Will I be the next?

These thoughts ran through Clary's whisky clouded mind as he sat contemplating the death of Mr. Wilkins.

Chapter 52
Eating a Missionary

After the Wilkins tragedy, Clary and June became increasingly aware that time was running out on their last elephant licence, which would expire in less than a month. To make matters worse, June was now six months pregnant, and that meant more expenses coming their way. That third elephant was vital if they were to get through the next three or four months without financial difficulties.

Clary knew of a hunting ground just south of the Usambara Mountains where there was a very good chance of finding a big elephant at this time of year. He knew from previous years of hunting there that it would be hot and dry, so the herds of elephant cows and their squealing young would have gone off to greener pastures, leaving it open for the lone bulls to savour. It would be a long, uncomfortable ride in the go-anywhere Dodge truck, over rough roads to get there, and it would entail a fly camp for a few days. Water sources in that area were scarce, which meant bringing in their own drinking water. The bush around there was very thick, impenetrable in places, and the hard stony ground would make tracking difficult. It was also extremely hot at midday because the nearby hills blocked any cooling breezes coming down from the forested mountains.

They travelled for four gruelling hours over dusty tracks to the hunting ground, where they found an unpleasant shade-less campsite amongst the camel thorn trees. They made camp there because it was as far as they could bash their way through the thick bush with the old Dodge truck before it stalled. The camel thorn provided some shade during the day and the ground was stony, but at least the tent could be pitched on flat ground. However, it was only a mile off an old survey track and not far from a Digo village where they hoped to get water if there was enough to spare. And with luck, they could engage a honey hunter from the village who knew the area well to be a guide.

As they had expected, hunting was hot, hard, and tiring. June was suffering in the intense heat, carrying her heavy, swaying stomach through tangled brush, yet she never once complained. She suffered constant bites from tsetse flies, and sweat bees swarmed around her eyes during rest stops for a sip of warm water. In spite of the tough conditions, she kept going without complaint. None of these conditions fazed the local guide as he walked along at ease, occasionally slapping at a biting tsetse fly on his arm. At rest stops, he let the tiny sweat bees drink the sweat off his brow and waved them off only when too many got near his eyes.

From midday until about three o'clock in the afternoon, it was so pressingly hot that none of the hunting party could move anywhere. Even sitting still in the sparse shade caused them to sweat profusely.

One morning, the local guide who was leading the hunters stumbled into two dozing rhinos, who jumped up and immediately stormed towards the intruders. Rather than shoot the animals in self-defence, Clary shouted, "Rhinos! Run!" which everyone did with newfound energy.

June, who was last in line with her gun bearer, whirled and ran back the way she had come, heading for a large tree with low hanging branches. She managed to clamber up into the branches, just high enough to be out of the rhino horn's reach. Just then, her gun bearer ran up to the same tree, dropped the rifle on the ground, and climbed up after her. He not only ignored June's plea to bring the rifle with him, but climbed right past her into the small swaying branches above. Eventually, the snorting rhino sounds subsided into the distance, and it was safe for the humans to come out of hiding.

On the ground, after hearing June's account of the story, Clary confronted the frightened gun bearer about his actions. It transpired that he had never worked before as a gun bearer but needed a job, so he had lied about his experience in his interview for the position. He was quite happy to be demoted to the safe position of kitchen helper in camp and not have to confront these monstrous, twin-horned, pre-historic relics again, or trudge all day in the oppressive heat.

The ground was so hard that successfully tracking a faint elephant spoor required a careful eye for the smallest details. Distinguishing new spoor from old, then finding the correct spoor to follow when the elephants crossed paths, was a painstaking task that wasted valuable hunting time. Clary, with his years of hunting experience in such conditions, did an excellent job of sorting out the various old from new spoors, and kept the safari on track.

One morning, Clary went without his wife to the local village to fetch water and hire another gun bearer for June. While waiting for his men to haul up buckets of water from the well to fill the 50-gallon steel drum, Clary paid a visit to the Digo chief and gave him some prized tobacco as a gift for taking his water.

When asked about elephants with large tusks, the chief said that his men did not venture far from the village so would not know. He suggested that Clary visit a local medicine man who lived in the hills above the village. He did not go out except up into the hills to collect plants for his medical concoctions. But he could use his magic to predict where these big animals with big teeth would be found.

Clary never believed in sorcery, black magic, or any sort of hocus-pocus, but perhaps this African witch doctor who had lived here all his life knew where to find big elephants. *It was worth a try*, he thought.

The medicine man lived only a half hour walk along a dusty footpath up the hill from the village. When Clary arrived, he saw that the primitive wooden hut was decorated with various bleached white bones, animal skulls, dry skins of unknown origin, and bunches of dried plants hanging from the grass roof. The inside stank heavily of old smoke, unwashed bodies, and pungent wild herbs.

The sorcerer was younger than Clary expected, although his dirty clothes and unkempt appearance made him look older. Clary greeted the doctor in Swahili at his front door, and was invited in to sit at a smoky little fire. He explained in Swahili that his wife was expecting a baby and needed money so that her new-born would have a good start in life. He went on to explain that only an elephant with very big tusks would bring in enough money for his baby, so he asked where he could find such an elephant.

The witch doctor rubbed his stubbly beard, deep in meditation. Then he reached for a big leather bag behind him, shook it several times over the fire, and emptied its contents onto the bare earthen floor. There were stones, animal teeth, small jawbones of rodents, pieces of horn, tiny hooves, roots, burned sticks, and a myriad of other unrecognisable artefacts.

He studied them for a while, grunting on occasion, nodded his head a few times, then closed his eyes and uttered a few words under his breath.

"Yes, I see a big elephant", he said. "In four days you will find him, but you must have some magic from me."

"What magic can you give me?" asked Clary excitedly.

The man picked up a smaller leather bag and threw its contents to one side of the first items. There were more unrecognizable objects, although they were smaller than the first lot. Again, the witch doctor studied the items carefully, then picked up what looked like a dried stick, broke off an inch-long piece, and handed it to Clary, telling him he must eat it now.

At first, Clary was reluctant to do so, thinking it might be poisonous, but said he would eat it later in camp. However, the witch doctor insisted that he must eat it now before he left the hut, otherwise he would have very bad luck. Clary realised there was no way out, so he timidly bit off a piece and chewed it. It was very dry and brittle, like an old piece of wood. It had a salty and not unpleasant taste to it, so was probably not poisonous. He chewed the rest and swallowed it.

"Now you will find your big elephant. Give me ten shillings", demanded the good doctor for his services.

Clary knew that ten shillings was almost a month's wages out here and far too much, but he paid up anyway, with ten new, shiny one-shilling pieces, which pleased the witch doctor very much.

As Clary walked back to the village with his guide, he realised that all the descriptions and stories he had read about witch doctors in Africa were true, as he had just witnessed it for himself. Whether their predictions came true or not would soon be proved, one way or another.

Back at the well, he found the water drum full and everyone ready to drive back to camp. On their return, June demanded water for a shower. Cold water would do, as long as it was wet; she had not washed for three days, and even the hyenas were avoiding her, or so she said.

While June showered behind the tent under a canvas shower bucket hanging over a branch, Clary sat on a log close by and told her about his visit to the witch doctor and how he had assured them of a big elephant in a few days.

"Hand me my towel and stop talking nonsense", she answered testily.

Four days later, when they had just returned from another tough and unsuccessful morning hunt without even seeing an elephant with tusks bigger than toothpicks, June had had enough of the heat, these tsetse flies, and all the sweat bees. She demanded that they head back to civilisation without her bloody elephant. For once, Clary was in full agreement with her.

"Pack up the camp, we're going home", said Clary, as cries of joy went up from the disillusioned and weary workforce.

They were loading the truck when a gun bearer said that he had just heard some branches breaking, as if an elephant was feeding not very far away.

Clary was reluctant to stop loading now, but decided to follow his instinct, so he gave his men a ten-minute break while he went to look for the source of the noise. He picked up his faithful 450 double and walked towards the noise of breaking branches. He stopped dead in his tracks a hundred yards on and could hardly believe his eyes when he spotted a 90-pounder feeding slowly in a stand of bush, barely 300 yards from camp. He quickly sent his tracker back to tell the staff to extend their ten-minute break in silence and to get June, because by law, she had to be the person who shot the animal on her licence. June was so worn out from the morning's hunt that at first she did not want to move, until she was told that the elephant was a 90-pounder.

"Why didn't you say so in the first place?" she demanded, grabbing her .375 and following the tracker back towards the elephant.

It had moved a short distance farther on, which meant that June had to run across a 30-yard stretch of open ground to reach Clary, during which time she would be in full view of the elephant. Clary made motions to her like an animal to indicate that she should get down on all fours and crawl over to him like a walking impala.

June rolled her eyes skywards, got down onto her hands and knees, and acted her "sauntering impala" role very well, while the elephant watched her curiously the whole time without becoming alarmed. It was then a short stalk behind some bushes to get close enough to shoot.

She sat with her knees up so that she could rest her arms on them to steady her aim. At 40 yards, she could hardly miss such a huge target. She fired the .375 from a sitting position, easily piercing the giant's heart. Clary was ready with his 450, although there was no need for a second shot. The imposing elephant ran less than 100 yards before it fell over and died. The tusks from this elephant alone would pay for all the children's school fees, plus their new clothes, and the hospital fees for a newborn baby, and there would still be money left for other unforeseen expenses. With careful planning, they could hold out for six months on the income from the sale of their six elephant tusks.

The overworked camp staff had to partly unload the truck so that Clary could drive to the nearby village and collect a party of men who would camp here by the elephant and butcher all the meat. The rest of the natives would follow on foot. Clary explained to the Digo villagers that they could have all the meat for themselves. However, they must keep the tusks for him until he returned to collect them.

It was almost a week before Clary had time to return to this little village to collect his tusks. However, besides collecting his ivory, he wanted to see the witch doctor again to ask for more magic sticks. The doctor was pleased to see Clary and gratefully accepted his gift of tobacco. He was not surprised that Clary had shot a very big elephant. After all, the man declared, he had ordered it to happen.

In spite of Clary's request, the doctor would not part with any of his magic sticks. As he pointed out, they only worked with his spell attached to them. On their own, they were useless. Still, Clary insisted on knowing what it was that he had been given to eat to ensure he shot his big elephant.

"Oh", said the witchdoctor, "that was a dried piece of a German missionary who we killed in the mountains during the war years. He was a man of God with much power."

Clary was deeply shocked. He stood up silently, and without saying a word, walked back to his car and drove home. He never mentioned the incident to anyone, not even his family, until many, many years later. But that is another story.

Chapter 53
The Farm Gone and School Scandals

Clary and June travelled with the children to Tanga to sell the ivory and give the children a short seaside holiday before they went back to school. The truck carried all the camp equipment and the camp labourers to the farm at Malindi to await Clary's arrival so that they could be paid.

Clary had left the farm in the care of a retired British army major before he had gone on this latest safari.

When Clary and family arrived back at the farmhouse, they found it deserted except for their old faithful cook Rajabu, who greeted them and told them that all the farm labourers had left as they had not been paid. The Dodge truck had been offloaded and parked at the back of the farmhouse, and the camp staff had gone to the village.

Clary and June took a walk around the farm to see the state of affairs for themselves. The few farm cows looked weak and skinny in their grassless enclosure, because nobody had taken them out to graze. Most of the chickens had died from a virus because they had not been moved to a clean run next door. And those that had survived looked scrawny and about to die. Clary's prize pigs, for which he had received top prices, looked lean and lethargic. The 12 acres of vegetable fields that yielded sufficient income to keep the farm profitable, had been neglected, and were overgrown with weeds.

The farm was in a derelict state. Their hearts sank lower as Rajabu narrated how the cedar wood trees were being cut down and taken away, the wattle bark trees harvested to sell as firewood, and even whole beehives carried away and sold.

As he spoke, more details of the total neglect emerged. Only the farmhouse and stores had been untouched, because he had been here all day and night.

The retired major, hired as a caretaker, had only spent a few days on the farm, then moved into a hotel in Lushoto, 35 miles away. He had driven up only twice per month to check on farm matters for an hour or so. All the money Clary had given him to pay the farm labourers' wages and buy feed for the farm livestock had instead been used to pay for his hotel stay and huge bar bill.

When Clary confronted the major at the bar in the Lawns Hotel, the man said that although he had done a good job of minding the farm, it was the useless farm workers who were lazy and good for nothing who were the cause of all the neglect. Clary had never been more furious in his life. If the bar had been empty, he would have punched the man's face into the back of his head.

To add insult to injury, the major demanded his full salary for the last two months, saying that the money he had been given had only covered his hotel stay and not his other expenses. Clary left the hotel bar immediately before he committed murder.

After paying off all the farm labourers and selling the few remaining pigs, cattle, and the few surviving chickens, ducks, and geese for whatever price he could get, there was not enough money to start farming all over again, even taking into account the sale of the ivory.

Their only hope of making money was to use the resources that remained on the farm, such as the wattle bark and the cedar trees. There was an orchard at the front with fruit trees that, after pruning and clearing, would soon start to bear fruit.

They would have to hire some farm labourers to clear the fertile vegetable fields and replant them with quick growing crops for market.

However, these measures would only keep the farm going for a short while. Now more than ever Clary would have to secure more hunting safaris to earn a living. His reputation as a successful hunter had spread rapidly after each hunt, which attracted new clients his way.

After sending letters to some of his old clients and a few reputable safari agents, business started to pick up.

The roads all over the territory had been improved so much that travelling times between towns was now cut in half. Newly constructed roads through rugged bush country, built to increase the goods trade between towns and villages, also gave easy access to new hunting grounds. Clary could use these roads to his advantage by allowing him to hunt new places and reduce driving times when hunting several different areas on one safari.

While Clary ran the safaris, June stayed at home where she could not only run the farm but also organise the safari logistics and answer correspondence from potential clients.

Only the rambunctious children disturbed the smooth running of the farm and the safari business. Therefore, except for the newborn baby, the three other children – aged five, six, and seven years old – were sent off to boarding school at Kongwa.

Kongwa was a small village located in the middle of a vast, desolate, dry, and almost uninhabited bushland. Its light red soil was ideal for growing peanuts but not much else.

Three years before the school was established, the government started a massive scheme to grow peanuts there, which would supply Britain and its colonies with cheap, healthy, peanut oil. It was the grandest, most expensive agricultural scheme Britain had ever undertaken, costing millions of pounds. Unique bulldozers were designed so that they could be linked to each other by long chains, and could drag massive chains and balls behind them to clear thousands of acres of bush as quickly as possible. Tractors, wielding long metal spikes, had to be constructed to push over mighty baobab trees. Fires were lit and kept burning day and night to get rid of the mounting piles of cleared brush. The largest Caterpillar tractors available were bought to till the red soil with the biggest ploughs ever made.

A whole town had to be built on this nowhere land to house the thousands of people expected to find work here. Ample uninhabited land to build this spread-out town was available, so blocks of apartments were constructed half a mile from the offices. Huge storage sheds capable of holding thousands of tons of nuts each were erected farther away. A clubhouse, swimming pool, church, and cricket playing fields were a must for any modern town, so they were built and scattered haphazardly about the area.

This whole expensive scheme had one major drawback, however. Huge fields of peanuts that were eventually planted did not grow very well. In most of the cleared land, the light red soil that peanuts favoured was only a few inches deep, below which were rocks and sand.

Had the highly paid agricultural experts from England bothered to ask the local natives about peanut growing, they would have been advised that they only grew in small fields where the red topsoil was deep. However, the experts did not ask the locals.

The whole plan was not only a failure, but an enormous failure – one of the most expensive failures that the British government experienced in Africa.

Attempting to salvage something from this failed scheme, the government turned Kongwa village into a boarding school for colonial children of both sexes. It was here that Clary and June dumped their children, while he hunted and she ran the farm.

Since the school was situated in such an isolated place with only one road passing by, it became an ordeal for all the pitiful children to get to the boarding school at the beginning of each term.

The journey for Clary's three children started very early in the morning when they were driven from the Lushoto farm for two-and-a-half hours down the mountain roads to Mombo, where a special school bus with hard wooden bench seats and barred windows was waiting for them. Here Clary and June said goodbye to their kids and put them on the bus for a six hour, 250-mile torturous trip to Morogoro, with only one pit stop. They arrived at Morogoro in the evening and immediately boarded a special train for the 12-hour overnight journey to Dodoma, where they disembarked at six o'clock in the morning, bleary-eyed from lack of sleep.

They were given no food or water throughout the whole journey, because parents had been advised to supply these to their offspring before they started the trip. In Dodoma there were special buses waiting to take the children on a three-hour ride to the village of Kongwa. Arriving at the Kongwa bus station, the children were herded into age groups, with boys separated from girls, for the final half hour bus ride to the school.

Upon arriving at the school, they were met by stern teachers in black coats, who assigned each of them to a dormitory for the coming term. In the dormitory, they were allocated a bed and a shelf for their clothes. After unpacking their suitcases and putting their clothes in their allocated shelf, they were herded into groups for the 15-minute walk to the mess halls. Here they were given a frugal evening meal, their first in two days, and marched back to their dormitories to sleep.

Early the next morning school started.

For Clary's five, six, and seven-year-old children, it was an epic journey, never to be forgotten. Even after arriving at school, their trials were not over. Leopards, hyenas, and the occasional lion prowled through the school grounds at night. This meant that all the children had to walk in groups from the dormitories to the mess hall, a quarter mile distant, as they went to and from dinner each evening.

Snakes, lizards, scorpions, and centipedes usually crawled away at the approach of trampling little feet, so they were not considered a threat. Hyenas tended to steal shoes left outside the dormitories, so any child losing a pair of valuable shoes was beaten by the housemaster with five hard whacks of a thin bamboo cane and told to have another pair sent from home.

During the daytime, when predators and scavengers were resting in the distant bush, it was safe to walk around the school compound, and on Saturday afternoon and all day Sunday, when no classes were held, pupils were free to go anywhere, although they were not permitted to venture more than one mile from the school. Since there was no supervision of pupils by the lazy teachers on the weekends, children ignored the one-mile rule and went wherever they liked.

Students had great fun on weekends chasing baboons up and down the hills, while throwing stones at the fleeing monkeys and stalking duikers in the thickets with homemade bows and arrows. Whenever a leopard was spotted in the hills, the baboon chasing ceased as pupils ran away to pursue more mundane but safer pastimes, such as chasing snakes. Leopards were heard prowling around the school dormitories almost every night, but they only wanted to seize the teachers' dogs from in front of their quarters.

The problem of dog snatching was solved when the headmaster forbade teachers from leaving their dogs outside during the night. He insisted they had to be kept in the house. By the time this rule was issued, most of the dogs had been eaten anyway, and those that had not been taken were too timid to venture out without their masters at their sides, even in the daytime.

When boredom sets in, as it did on many an occasion in Kongwa, young people will do stupid things.

One of these was a dare, where three 11-year-old boys decided to "escape" by running away from school to see if they could make it home on their own. This dare was a major undertaking for anyone, as it entailed a journey of several hundred miles before they reached home – most of it through game-rich, uninhabited country.

So, after breakfast one Saturday morning, the three of them left the school compound carrying some water and a few slices of bread that they had saved from the breakfast table, and hiked through the bush for several hours until they reached a well-travelled road where they hoped to hitch a lift from a passing car. Unknown to the escapees, however, on weekends there was almost no traffic on this road. So they were forced to walk along the road for hours without seeing a single vehicle.

After darkness fell, they saw the headlights of an approaching truck – the first vehicle to come along that day. Two of the boys became frightened and ran into the bush to hide, while the third one flagged down the rattling old truck. A young white boy alone in the middle of the bush at night caused quite a stir amongst the Africans in their truck. They questioned him for a time about what he was doing here and where he had come from. The Africans wanted to be certain that they would not be arrested for abduction or kidnapping a white boy if they took him on board.

They accepted his excuse that his bicycle had broken down far away down the road, but could not believe that he intended to walk tonight to the next town of Dodoma, 75 miles away. They took him with them, and on reaching Dodoma three hours later, they drove straight to the local police station where they turned him in. An astounded policeman, after hearing the Africans' incredible story of finding a little European boy at the roadside, took the scared, dirty, dishevelled boy into an empty cell and let him fall asleep for the night on a thin, soiled, bare mattress.

After the boy admitted that he had come from Kongwa school, the policeman tried to phone the school, but there was only one line that ran to the headmaster's office, and it was unattended on weekends, so he gave up. The next morning when the duty sergeant came in, he was extremely angry when the boy told him the story of the dare. The duty sergeant phoned the school but there was still no reply, so he was forced to send a police car to the school to return the delinquent runaway.

The other two boys, who had run off when the truck approached, had spent an uncomfortable night sitting high up in a thorn tree. They believed they were out of reach of predators, but learned later at school that leopards could run up trees like theirs in two bounds. They had finished all their food and water the previous day and were ravenously hungry and extremely thirsty. One of the two boys had decided to try walking on the road back to school, while the other one kept walking on the main road towards Dodoma, still hoping that a car would come by.

The police car picked up one boy trying to flag them down, then found the other one a few miles farther along the school road, sitting on the edge and crying his eyes out from hunger and thirst. When the police car arrived at the school with the three runaways, the headmaster was flabbergasted by the story he heard, and had had no idea that any boys were missing. In fact, they would not have been missed until Monday morning, when classes started.

As punishment, the three boys were locked up in the school laundry room for the night and given only dry bread to eat. Fortunately, a water tap in the laundry room was available, with clean drinking water. The next morning, each boy was beaten with six strokes of the cane in front of the senior class, told never to do such a foolish thing again, and sent back to class with very sore behinds.

A more serious incident occurred several months later. One Sunday, some senior boys tried to blow up the school – not the whole school, just the classrooms – so that they could have a few days off from classes.

Several miles from the school was a stone quarry that was in operation only a few months each year. The rest of the time, it was left idle and unattended. A windowless reinforced concrete storehouse, ten feet by ten feet with a solid concrete roof, had been built at the quarry to store the dynamite and blasting caps. The dynamite for the quarry had to be transported by special trucks from Dodoma, so a whole year's supply was ordered each time and stockpiled in the store. This dynamite bunker had a solid heavy iron door locked with a hardened steel padlock.

It was so massively built that it was impossible for anybody to break into it, with the exception of two Kongwa school pupils with a bit of common sense. They discovered that although the door hinges were made of thick steel, the large centre pins on the hinges could be hammered out using a rock and large nail. So, they knocked out the hinge pins, shoved the steel door to one side, took two sticks of dynamite and one blasting cap, went to the other side of a small hill, and set off the dynamite to see if it worked. One of the boys had seen his father use dynamite on their farm, so he knew how it was handled. They discovered that it worked very well indeed. Returning to the storehouse, they took six sticks of dynamite and two blasting caps, which they concluded was sufficient to blow up the school. Then they propped up the steel door over the door entrance and set off for the school classrooms.

It was a Sunday, so there would be nobody to see them at the classrooms, which were half a mile from the dormitories and teachers' living quarters.

Unluckily for the boys, while walking towards the school with dynamite in hand, they were passed by one of the school kitchen helpers riding his bicycle to work. Luckily for the school, this kitchen helper worked part-time at the quarry, so he knew what dynamite looked like and how dangerous it was in the wrong hands. He pedalled as fast as he could straight to the headmaster's house, where he reported what he had seen.

The astounded headmaster could hardly believe what he had been told, but knowing that children are capable of many foolhardy exploits, he quickly roused three other teachers from their afternoon siesta and laid an ambush near the school. They were not disappointed. The teachers caught the two boys red-handed when they were at the classrooms, holding the dynamite with the caps already attached.

The two pyrotechnicians were "arrested", taken to the lockable laundry room, and locked up there for the rest of the day and night. The furious headmaster immediately went to his office and telephoned the boys' parents to demand that they collect their offspring from school this very day or from the police cells in Dodoma tomorrow.

Word of the failed act of sabotage spread like wildfire throughout the school, and by evening, everyone knew about it. Most of the boys were disappointed that it had not been successful.

At the school assembly on Monday morning, a scowling, red-faced headmaster reprimanded all the students for not reporting the two miscreants to a teacher before they attempted their deed, and said they were just as responsible as the two bombers for this wickedness. However, the two expelled pupils had the last laugh, because some years later the school was in such a bad state of repair that most of it collapsed, and it was abandoned.

One last event completely confirmed the school's poor reputation as a place of learning.

The girls' dormitories were a long block of ten adjoining rooms, with five pupils to each room, for a total of 50 girls. At one end of the block was a headmistress's flat.

Three senior boys came up with the impertinent objective to sneak into the senior girls dormitories at night and entertain them. And their fiendish scheme worked for quite some time.

The three boys arranged that around midnight on Saturday nights a girl in one flat would open the locked dormitory door to let boys in. Then each one would slip into the bed of any girl willing to be fondled. They went from bed to bed and from room to room each Saturday night without the headmistress being aware of the shenanigans happening right under her nose.

This mischief went on for several weeks. However, one ugly fat girl was never fondled by the boys, due to her looks, although she wanted it. So, she complained about it in a letter to her mother. The mother was shocked that such a thing was occurring in the school, so she reported the matter in a strongly worded letter to the headmaster, and demanded action. The dumbfounded headmaster was furious when he read the letter, as was the dormitory headmistress when she was informed of the matter.

However, in order to catch the culprits in the act, they had to watch and wait for them in secrecy. They knew from the fat girl's mother when to expect the senior boys to appear. So, the next Saturday night, the headmaster and two senior teachers hid behind the girls' dormitories until they heard happy giggling sounds from inside one room. They ran around to the front door, dashed in, switched the lights on, and caught all three senior boys in a compromising situation. The boys showed no remorse for their actions, but were true gentlemen as they freely admitted their guilt without reservation and protected the girls' reputations by refusing to name the ladies with whom they had slept.

The boys were marched off to the laundry room and locked in there for the rest of the night. And they were collected by exasperated relatives the next day. At the Monday morning school assembly, the headmaster did not utter a word about this incident, although all the pupils knew about it and smirked behind their hands.

When Clary and June heard these stories from their children, they were reluctant to send them back to the Kongwa school. However, there were no other affordable schools in the country, so they sent the two oldest boys off to England, where education was free, and enrolled one child for one more year while they made plans for further education in England.

Chapter 54
Mau Mau Attack

One night, when Clary was hunting far away in Maasailand, the farmhouse was attacked by the Mau Mau. June was there with her one-year-old baby, a nursemaid called Jeanette, and the three young boys, who were seven, eight, and nine years old.

There had been warnings about them on the radio and in the local newspapers, but these incursions were occurring far away in the lowlands, not up here in the mountains.

There were at least eight Mau Mau gang members that raided the farm that night, and all were armed. Three had rifles and the rest carried heavy axes, pangas, and bows with poison arrows.

They came just after 7:30pm when the nurse had put the children and baby to bed, and June was sitting at a table in the sitting room catching up on some accounts.

The terrorists walked up the front driveway where they were set upon by the farm dogs. The men fired at the dogs, missing them all but sending them fleeing for cover. The faithful cook, Rajabu, came out of his kitchen to see where all the noise came from, but couldn't see much in the dark. The Mau Mau shot at him twice as he ran for cover into the kitchen. One bullet missed, but the second one hit him in the knee as it ricocheted off the heavy kitchen table. He screamed and ran out the back door of the kitchen and into the night.

June heard Rajabu's screams and shooting and knew instinctively that the Mau Mau had arrived. She ran to the mantelpiece and put out the bright kerosene lamp, plunging the room into darkness. She grabbed her .45 calibre revolver from the table and fired two rounds through the open sitting room door into the dark to keep the attackers at bay while she ran into the adjacent bedroom, locking the heavy door behind her, and waited. There was silence for a few minutes, so she thought that she had scared them off.

She listened at the bedroom door and, hearing nobody, she opened it and dashed to the gun cupboard in the sitting room to get more ammunition for her revolver. Halfway to the cupboard, a shot rang out but missed her by inches, hitting the plastered wall right behind her. She fired her last three bullets blindly towards the intruder somewhere in the dark then fled back to the bedroom, hoping that the attackers would realise that she was still armed and would take off.

However, they were not deterred by the shots. They had the house surrounded and just needed to wait to attack from all sides. After a while, some black men came into the sitting room and tried to open the locked bedroom door. When June did not fire at them, they got braver, and one of them demanded that June open the door immediately or they would kill her. She refused, bluffing that she had a loaded gun to defend herself, although her .45 revolver was empty. They did not believe her and started hacking at the bedroom door with a heavy axe. The German-built solid wooden door held for 20 minutes before the lock gave way to the hard, hammering blows.

As the broken door opened, they jumped to the side expecting shots from June to come their way. When no shots were fired, two of the rifle-toting men, carrying flashlights, burst into the bedroom, pointed their loaded weapons at June, and yelled at her to drop the gun and put her hands up. She felt she had no choice now and obeyed them.

June was taken aback, as both men were clean-shaven, well-dressed in dark clean clothes, and wore expensive looking black leather jackets. According to a newspaper article she had read, one was called Paulo and the other Usali – pleasant first names for such ruthless killers. They were in their late twenties and looked far too young to be such dangerous criminals.

While one man held June at gunpoint, the other ran into the connecting rooms to check who was there. He found the two younger boys shivering with fear in their beds, but noticed two beds empty. He came back, demanding to know who had occupied the two empty beds in the next room.

Don't show fear or you will lose their respect and get killed, June thought grimly. She had learned this from a seasoned British soldier when he and she had been held at gunpoint by 20 bandits in the Ethiopian highlands during the war.

"They are the beds of my nurse and my oldest son, she said, trying not to quiver with fear. "They have gone to get help."

In fact, Janette and Michael had only run into the outside toilet and were hiding there in the darkness.

One of the men hit June in the chest with his rifle butt, knocking her onto the bed.

"You are lying! Our men have surrounded the house, and nobody can escape!" he shouted.

But just then, a scruffily attired man smelling of stale beer came into the room and told the older Mau Mau that the cook was not dead and had run away. They had found a lot of blood in the kitchen, which they followed to a footpath that, he was told, led to a small village several hundred yards down the hill.

In spite of his kneecap hanging on by a flap of skin, and blood flowing from the injury, the cook was able to hobble down the hill to the nearest huts and persuade a bicycle owner to take him to a mission hospital 20 miles away and two thousand feet down in the valley. The bicycle owner, who did not like the Mau Mau, said he would avoid the long, serpentine main road to the mission, and use a steeper, quicker footpath that cut the distance in half. The poor cook sat on the bike's rear steel carrier, his temporarily bandaged leg hanging free as the cyclist raced towards the mission at breakneck speed down a rocky path at night, with no lights and no proper brakes. The two men just made it in one piece in record time, but the bicycle hit too many rocks and potholes to be usable again.

At the mission, they were met at gunpoint by an armed contingent of police and army soldiers who had been waiting there for the terrorists. An informer at the next village had warned them of an impending attack. A dusk-to-dawn curfew and a shoot-on-sight order had been issued for the area, although no one outside the area had heard about the orders, and definitely not the bicycle owner.

The guards at the mission had not opened fire on the cyclists, because they heard the rattling and clanging as the bicycle sped towards them and assumed that a Mau Mau attacker would not announce his presence in such a loud way. The cook, Rajabu, while being treated for his injuries at the hospital, informed the police about the attack on June at the farm. Then another cyclist on a sound bike, with working brakes and a light, was sent farther down the valley to inform the army, where they had set up a roadblock to control all people and vehicles entering the valley. It would take the army with their trucks at least three-and-a-half hours to ascend the winding mountain road to reach June at the farm.

Meanwhile, the terrorists at the farmhouse were worried that the injured cook could have alerted the police in the valley who might arrive soon, so they decided to ransack the place as quickly as possible and get out of there. One brutal man came into the bedroom, took the empty 45 revolver from the bed, and stuck it in his belt.

Holding a lantern in one hand, he grabbed June's arm and dragged her into the sitting room, screaming at her to open the gun cupboard. She took her bunch of keys from a table and opened the wide door very slowly. The wooden cupboard had racks for 12 rifles and shelves for ammunition packets, but it was completely empty, as Clary had taken them with him on safari. June was surprised that there was not even a spare box of ammunition for her .45, which she knew should have been in there.

However, at the far end of the cupboard was a new rifle with telescopic sights in a green canvas bag, which blended in so well with the green felt interior that it went unnoticed by the brutal man. Angry at finding the cupboard empty, he demanded June give him all the money and jewellery in the house. Then he became dangerously agitated when he saw the small cash box that June gave him, as it contained only a small amount of money in coins. Pointing his rifle at her chest, he threatened to shoot her there and then if she did not give him the large amount of money that he knew all Europeans kept at home.

She told him firmly that there was no more money. And to keep him from carrying out his murderous threat, she took her handbag and emptied its contents onto the floor, pulled open all the writing desk drawers for him to peer in, went into the bedroom and opened all the cupboards and drawers, then turned to him and told him to look for money himself. Except for the few coins in her purse, she insisted there was nothing more. A large sum of cash which Clary had left in the house was hidden in plain sight in a dark wooden box on top of the wooden curtain box in the sitting room. None of the thugs noticed it or even glanced up towards it.

One-year-old David was crying in his cot next to June's bed, so she went to the cot, picked him up, and sat on the bed holding him close to her. The brutal man pointed his gun at them and demanded in a very loud voice that she put the crying child down or he would shoot her.

Enraged, she snarled, "You are going to kill us all anyway. You brutes even kill children and babies."

She realised too late that this statement provoked the man's anger even more, as he stormed over to where she sat. Fortunately, one of the better dressed men overheard this angry exchange and came into the bedroom and stopped him before he hit June.

He said, "We don't shoot women or children." And he ordered the brute to ransack every room and take everything of value, but do it quickly as they had to leave soon before the police arrived.

Using a lamp and flashlights, the Mau Mau horde, in their quest to find everything of value, ransacked the house, strewing papers, letters, books, and files all over the floor. They emptied the pantry of tinned food, jars of jam, packets of tea, sugar, flour, maize meal, and powdered milk. All the other items in paper packets which they did not know or did not want, they tore open, scattering the contents over the kitchen floor. Bottles of vinegar, mustard, and sauces, which they did not like, were purposely smashed, just out of spite. A large five-gallon stone jug of pickles in vinegar was shattered to pieces with an axe, spilling cucumbers and onions over the already sticky floor.

They took all the cutlery and any steel or silver kitchen items they found. They raided the kerosene-powered fridge, scooping out butter with their fingers to spread thickly on old bread, which they greedily wolfed down with some cold meat. They bit off a piece of cheese from a small cheese wheel, but spat it out in disgust. The mess they left in the kitchen of half-eaten food, spilled sauces, scattered cereals, sour pickles, and dried blood looked worse than if a herd of wild pigs had held a party. They looted the clothes and shoe cupboards of everything except the lady's undergarments, and even stole all the baby clothes, which they hoped to sell for a few shillings in the local markets. They took the blankets off June's bed to wrap all the clothes in them to carry away. They took the sheets to wrap the other loot and pile it on the veranda, then argued amongst themselves as to who should carry what.

June was approached by one of the well-dressed men who said, "We will come back when your husband is here, and then we will kill all of you." With that, he walked out of the house and was gone.

June sat shocked and dazed on the bare bed as she held a sobbing David to console him and try to come to terms with what had happened and what to do next. She was alive and thankful for that. David fell asleep in her arms, so she put him in his cot, took the lamp, and walked through the paper-strewn sitting room and out onto the veranda to see if any of the Mau Mau were still lurking about. It was deathly quiet and she saw no one.

She went back to her room and then into the children's room, where she saw two of her children in their beds, unharmed but shivering from fear and unable to speak. The other two beds, those of her nine-year-old son Michael and the nurse Janette, were both empty. June called out gently to them, but she heard no reply. She walked out of the open back door and called again a few times, quietly at first, then louder.

A reply finally came from the dark outside toilet. Then Janette emerged holding Michael's hand; both were white as sheets at their ordeal, although unharmed. It was a great relief to know her family was safe, but June thought that the Mau Mau had killed her cook and her dogs during the first wave of shooting.

The old German farmhouse did not have electricity. It only had kerosene lamps for light and a wood-burning stove for cooking. There was no running water. It had to be carried from a well 300 yards away and poured into empty petrol drums placed on high ground around the house. Hot water for washing came from a drum heated with firewood. There was no telephone or any other form of communication in the district with which to summon help. The only way to get help here was to drive to the next town, 15 miles away.

However, June saw that the old Ford Prefect in the driveway had been well and truly sabotaged by the attackers, who had ripped out all the wiring on the engine. Even if the car had not been damaged, it would have been dangerous to drive anywhere with the Mau Mau still around.

June could not even find some clean water to quench her thirst, because the terrorists had broken all the filtered bottles of water as well as the filter itself. There was nothing left to eat, not even stale bread. The remaining piece of cheese had been stomped into the glass shards, spilled vinegar, and dirt.

An ice-cold wind blew in through the broken door, rendering the bedroom a cold and uncomfortable place to sit. So, June ordered Janette to take the only working kerosene lamp into the children's room and go to bed, but leave the light burning to soothe their fears. She braced a chair against the broken bedroom door to reduce the cold wind and then laid down on her bed, covering herself with a dirty bedside rug. There was nothing more she could do except wait for the morning.

June did not know that her faithful cook was alive and had alerted the police and army who were now on their way up the mountain.

Far off, June could hear the deep growl of a truck labouring up the torturous escarpment track below the farmhouse, but at first took no notice of it. Then she had a dreadful panic attack as she heard the truck engine get louder and louder. To her horror, she heard the truck turn into the farm driveway and stop in front of the house.

It must be the Mau Mau returning with a truck to collect all their looted stuff and kill us, she thought.

Then came the sweetest sound she had ever heard in her whole life. It was the voice of a young British soldier calling her name. June burst into tears of joy at the sound of her name. She could not stop crying, sobbing openly as the young man put his arms around her and tried to comfort her. It was now almost 2am, six-and-a-half hours after the Mau Mau attack had begun. The army and police who turned up still had other duties to attend to that night, as well as search for the Mau Mau gang, so they could not stay long at the farm. However, before they left, they ordered four well-armed policemen to remain on guard at the farmhouse.

The next morning, two police Land Rovers arrived at the farm to take June and the children to a hotel in Lushoto where they would be safe.

After leaving June's farm, the Mau Mau gang had gone to the neighbouring farm and raided it. The lone German farmer had been awakened by the intruders as they attempted to smash in the front door. When they failed to break it down, they shot out the lock. Not finding the farmer anywhere in the house, the Mau Mau gang proceeded to lay waste to every room, breaking all the plates, cups, and saucers they found. Every glass pane in the cupboards was broken. Every picture hanging on the walls was thrown down and trampled on. They were venting their anger and frustration at not having caught the farmer at home. They wantonly destroyed his beautiful antique furniture with savage blows of their axes.

Unbeknownst to the intruders, the farmer was watching them from behind a trapdoor in the ceiling. He attempted to shoot the invaders from above, but all his very old .22 cartridges were duds and did not fire. So, he had to watch helplessly as the terrorists destroyed his home. However, he was thankful that he was not discovered, as he would surely have been killed.

After leaving the German's house with very few items of value, the terrorists raided a church in the forest that was situated between three villages. They dragged the old African priest out of his bed, and in their quest to find the whereabouts of valuables in the church, they cut him up so badly with their axes and pangas that he bled to death on the steps of his church. Before he died, the Mau Mau made him open the church so they could steal the bottles of sacramental wine and take a few coins from a collection box. Drunk and overloaded with their spoils, the Maua Mau gang disbanded for the night, each heading off to his home with his bags of loot.

The gang continued to terrorise the residents of the region for three more weeks. Then one afternoon, with the help of some courageous local informers, the gang leaders were ambushed and wounded in a firefight with an army unit, and finally captured. One died later from his wounds, while the other was tried and executed.

Two days after the attack, Clary got word of the incident through a police courier sent to his camp in Maasailand. Two days after being informed, he arrived at the hotel where June and the children were staying. He was relieved to find them all well, although still traumatised from the ordeal. June refused to go back to the farm while the Mau Mau were still at large, so they rented a big house a few miles outside of Lushoto at Magamba, which was in a very safe area. Clary promised June that he would buy a house in Lushoto after his safaris were over, but in the meantime, she would be secure at the rented house.

Chapter 55
Your Child is Dead

A few years later, another tragedy struck the family when one of the children died.

It had been four years since the attack on the farm, which was now run by a competent manager. June had refused to go back there to live, saying it brought back too many bad memories, so she stayed at the rented Magamba house. There she gave birth to twins – a boy and a girl – so she now had six children to feed, clothe, and take care of. Janette had stayed on in spite of her desire to go back home to Europe after the Mau Mau attack. She happily looked after the twins, while another English lady was engaged to look after five-year-old David. The three older children were again sent off to Kongwa boarding school. This gave June time to help Clary with organising his safaris and take a few days off to go hunting with him at the Ruvu camp.

Late one night when Clary was fast asleep in his camp bed, he heard a bicycle bell ringing. It must have been in his dreams, he thought sleepily, because there are no bicycles running around in the bush, and certainly not at midnight. But it was a bicycle bell, very faint at first, though when he lifted his head off the pillow, he heard it more clearly. Then he heard voices calling from the opposite riverbank.

Clary reached for his flashlight and, without waking June, put on a hunting jacket and went to the riverside where some of his camp staff had already gathered. Shining his flashlight beam across to the other side, he saw an African policeman in uniform standing next to a tall figure holding a bicycle.

"Mtoto ame kufa!" shouted the policeman. "A child is dead."

Clary was dumbfounded. He could not comprehend the situation. "Whose child? Which child? Where? What happened?" he shouted back, confused and frightened.

"Mr. Wilson's child, I don't know any more details", answered the policeman in a voice that Clary could hardly hear.

He ordered one of his men to pole across the river with the dugout canoe and bring the messengers across, while he woke June and got dressed. Upon arriving on Clary's side of the river, the policeman explained that he was stationed at the sisal estate and had been ordered by his superior in Mombo to come here immediately, by any means, with the bad news. This brave man and his bicycle driver had ridden hours through wild terrain inhabited by game and night predators, unarmed except for a police whistle and a two-cell flashlight tied to the handlebars to light the way.

Clary and June were in deep shock at the incomplete news, not knowing which one of their six children had died, and how and where.

"We must leave immediately for Magamba", sobbed Clary.

Without bothering to pack anything, they loaded the policeman, his bicycle driver, and the bicycle into the Land Rover and sped east out of camp, paralleling the river for 12 miles to cross the Ruvu River on a pontoon bridge. The bridge had recently been constructed by the owner of a sisal estate to explore this side of the river for additional areas to grow sisal.

As they hastily weaved their way along the bush track, a group of stampeding buffalo trying to cross in front of them almost hit their car, but with some hard braking they avoided a crash. They had been in such haste to leave camp that they had forgotten to take a rifle. The car arrived at the pontoon bridge only to find a new locked and bolted steel barrier across the bridge, and there was no one around at this time of night to ask for help.

However, the tall cyclist knew that a man in a village a few hundred yards away had been given a spare key for the barrier, but he did not know which hut the man lived in. While the tall man and the policeman went to find the key holder, Clary became very agitated at this delay. He walked over to the steel bar across the bridge to see if he could pull the barrier out of the ground with the Land Rover. The two upright steel poles had been set deep into concrete bases, making them immovable even with a powerful vehicle. Then Clary noticed that he could just slide the cross bar with the small padlock through the holding ring and push it open, which he did.

He went back to the car and drove over, replacing the cross bar in its original position, then he stopped in the village to pick up the policeman and his astonished helper, who still had not located the key holder. After dropping off the two men and the bicycle at the village where they lived, Clary and June hurried on towards Lushoto in deathly silence. Each one was deep in thought as to which child lay dead and why.

At Mombo, the Land Rover fuel gauge read empty. In their haste to leave camp, they had not only forgotten to refuel the car but also to take some money, which they kept in a locked steel box under Clary's camp bed. It was 3:30am, so all three petrol stations were closed. Clary knew that one station was owned by a Greek man who lived in a house right next door to the petrol pumps, so he had no choice but to go and wake the man up.

The petrol station and house were dark, but a dull, glowing street lamp cast a pale yellow light onto the door of the house. Clary started knocking repeatedly on the door. After a few minutes, a sleepy voice from within asked what the matter was.

"I need petrol urgently!" shouted Clary.

"Petrol is finished", answered the sleepy voice.

"I must have petrol now. It is very urgent", said Clary again.

"I said there is no petrol!" responded an angry voice.

However, Clary was not about to give up. He said, "You have some petrol in drums in your store."

"It is finished. There is no petrol." The man's voice was getting angrier.

"You must help me with some petrol; my child is dead!" begged Clary.

From inside the house came frantic movement, then a lamp was lit, and an old Greek man stood at his open door in a T-shirt and striped pyjamas.

"Your child is died? Why didn't you say so? I would have got up immediately", he remonstrated.

To the Greeks, children are a man's greatest possession, and the death of a child is the worst tragedy that can ever happen to a family. He gave Clary a full tank of petrol and a packet of biscuits to munch on, with a few warm Coca-Colas to drink. Although he did not know Clary and June, he let them have the petrol on credit, saying they could pay for it whenever they passed through Mombo again.

Clary thanked him profusely and drove away.

There was no traffic on the winding, perilous road up the mountain at this time of the morning, so Clary drove faster than was safe, even around blind bends.

Their Land Rover rattled into Lushoto just as a magnificent sunrise sent rays of shimmering light through the tall cedar trees that lined the main road to the hospital. Such a beautiful beginning to such a tragic day, mused Clary.

They stopped the car at the whitewashed hospital entrance and found the night duty nurse dozing at his desk. He led them to the mortuary and into a small, white tiled room, then quietly left.

David, barely five years old, dressed in a bright blue shirt, lay on a clean, white, starched sheet with his eyes closed, as if in sleep. His face was pale and cold as June caressed his chubby little cheeks, hoping that perhaps he might wake up or that she would realise this was just a horrible nightmare. But this was not a dream. David had drowned in a well two days ago.

There is no remedy for the heart-breaking loss of a child. A part of your spirit dies with your child and never recovers. The hurt stays dormant but resurfaces from time to time with the same intensity as the day it happened.

June and Clary went outside and sat on a green wooden bench in the hospital garden, fell into each other's arms, and cried with the deepest sadness they would ever know.

David was buried the next day. Clary, June, and two family friends attended his funeral. His tiny wooden coffin was lowered into a small grave in the little cemetery next to the local church. Clary later bought a nice, newly built wooden bungalow in Lushoto not far from the cemetery, so that he and June could come occasionally to lay a few flowers on David's unmarked grave.

All deaths are tragic affairs, and even more so when they could have been avoided. Clary heard the story of David's death from an investigating police sergeant. In the afternoon at the rented Magamba house, Janette was minding the two-year-old twins on the large front lawn while the English lady was reading a book and David played on the small fenced-in back lawn. The English woman decided to have a bath, so she told David to stay on the lawn and play there until she came back.

An hour later, having had her bath, she returned to find David gone. The household staff had not seen him, so they started a search. They found his body floating in a well on the neighbouring farmland. The well had a strong wire fence around it to keep the cattle away, but there was room for a small boy to slip underneath. The well sides were too steep and slippery for him to clamber out on his own, and it was out of earshot of the house, so had he screamed for help, no one would have heard him. The English lady, who was being paid to look after David, packed her bags that night and fled the house, unwilling to face the wrath of June and Clary. She could not explain to the police why she had not taken David to Janette on the front lawn, or asked the gardener or the kitchen help who were at the back to keep an eye on him. And why had she not simply locked the garden gate to stop David from getting out?

Her parting words to the police were, "If he had done as I told him and stayed there, he would still be alive". Out of fear of prosecution for neglect of duty, she left for England soon afterward.

David's death was the last straw for June. She could not take this life of constant hardships and tragedies any longer. It was no longer an adventurous life she was leading, but one of constant nightmares and lack of money. Soon her marriage to Clary broke up, and she went to England to live and arrange for her children to follow.

Chapter 56
Alone and Struggling On

Clary was now on his own, with no wife and no children to worry about. Although this lifted a burden from his shoulders, he felt lonely and empty without a comforting family waiting for him whenever he returned home. He still lived in his little house in Lushoto, and still owned the Malindi farm, which he would have to run himself or sell.

To try selling it, he contacted an Indian businessman from Tanga who was interested in buying a vegetable farm anywhere in the territory. Clary arranged for him to come to the farm to look it over. The English caretaker whom Clary had hired to look after the place, was keen to leave and find another more challenging job, but agreed he would stay on to show any new owner around before quitting.

Clary drove up alone one day and inspected the farmhouse, which he knew was in desperate need of renovations, which had not been done due to the never-ending lack of money. Three bullet holes from the Mau Mau attack a few years ago were still clearly visible on the kitchen walls, as was the hole in the kitchen table where another bullet had ricocheted off and hit the cook. The heavy bedroom door that the Mau Mau had hacked down had only been temporarily boarded over. In the back yard, on a ten-foot cedar pole, stood a small wooden house that had been the home of their pet baboon called Stalin, so named because he tyrannized any person and any animal who dared get close to him. He had lived his whole adult life chained to the pole, and died of old age, a fierce lonely monkey. An empty doghouse under a guava tree still had a rusty old chain attached to it. The house had been the home of Satan, a jet-black Labrador who guarded the house faithfully at night against all intruders, except the night the terrorists shot at him. He only guarded the house at night while waiting for the morning when he got fed. After his morning meal, he would run off into the forests nearby and hunt alone all day long, returning before dark to take up his guard duties. When he returned home, he was covered in leaves and little sticks, and sometimes had deep gashes from fights with unknown animals. No one ever found out what he hunted or if he ever caught anything. One evening, he did not return from his daily hunt. A search party sent out from the farm looked for three days in the forest but found no trace of the loyal Satan.

A hundred yards away from the main house stood the empty, overgrown chicken runs. They had held 500 leghorn chickens that had brought in a good, steady income from the sale of their eggs. Then a chicken pox struck, and all the chickens died within two months. The long row of 20 pigsties had collapsed into a heap of rubble. They had housed free-ranging bacon pigs that had commanded the best prices from the butcheries. Still hanging from the branch of a stout tree near the pig pens was an old Dodge tyre rim, now rusty with age. When the rim was hit with an iron bar in the evenings, it could be heard for two miles all over the farm and brought pigs, cattle, and children running home at bed time.

All the 300 fruit trees in the large orchard at the front of the farmhouse were old and sagging from neglect like forlorn scarecrows. Now they produced hardly any fruit. The farm was in a desolate state and needed an experienced man and a lot of money to get it running again. Clary certainly was not that man, and neither was the Indian businessman who arrived with his two partners.

At first, they were not at all interested in such a rundown place, but at Clary's pleading, they agreed to rent the bottom section of the farm for a pittance, as it had fertile soil to grow vegetables. The rest of the farm would be left to the local farmers to graze their sheep and cattle. Clary retained ownership of this worthless piece of land, hoping to sell it in the future.

Clary's former cook Rajabu now worked at the local mission kitchen, preparing food for the priest and nuns. He became a hero in the valley after his daring escape from the Mau Mau and the death-defying bicycle ride down the treacherous mountain to get help for June and her children. Occasionally he was asked to tell his tale of bravery at every bar and drinking place in the village, with beer as payment. At each recital, he dodged more bullets, ran faster, was wounded more seriously, and was chased farther than before. He had been given a monetary reward and a letter written in English by the district commissioner, commending his bravery. Rajabu liked to wave this letter in the face of his sceptics as proof of his bravery, although nobody could read English to authenticate his claim.

Although Lushoto was a pleasant place to live, it was too far from Clary's hunting areas and the special shops where he needed to buy safari supplies. Now that he was on his own, he was forced to outfit and run his safaris by himself, with no one to help him. Clary leased his Lushoto house to an employee of the Lawns Hotel, which was only a five-minute drive away.

Lushoto was full of memories for Clary, and he would miss it. It was where his little boy was buried. At the Lawns Hotel, he had spent many afternoons and evenings in pleasant company telling hunting stories. He remembered the time when driving out of the hotel grounds with his six-year-old son Michael in the car. Clary had driven too fast around a sharp bend with a steep downhill slope along the driveway. The passenger door sprang open, and Michael was flung out of the car and rolled halfway down the grassy slope. Clary stopped the car and came running after the boy, but he was not interested in seeing whether his son was hurt or not; he was worried about his expensive Leitz camera, which Michael had slung around his neck. Only after ascertaining that the camera was undamaged did he look to see if his son, still lying in the grass, was hurt. Except for a few bruises and scrapes, he was fine. When June heard about this incident from Michael, she became very angry, accusing Clary of caring more about his camera than his children.

"Children's injuries heal by themselves; my camera's damage won't", retorted Clary.

"You can buy cameras, but not children", answered June testily.

With the Lushoto house leased, Clary was now homeless and needed to find a place closer to his hunting grounds from where he could conduct his safaris. He went to ask old friends with property close to Tanga if they could rent him a bungalow and storage sheds for his equipment, but it seemed that everyone was struggling to make a living in this difficult land. No one had vacant buildings to give him.

Chapter 57
Charlie and His Gunpowder on the Plane

Clary could not find a new base, so he moved to his old haunt in Tanga and rented a large two-storey flat with a big courtyard. It was an ideal place from which to organise his safaris.

One of his first safaris after June left was for an American car dealer who was coming to Africa to hunt for the first time. He wanted to hunt everything he could during his one-month safari in December. Clary had bought a hand-operated reloading tool for making his own hard-to-find 450 No. 2 ammunition. With it, he could produce 50 cartridges in a day, which was enough ammunition to last him for a safari season. He reused his old brass cartridge cases, and bought the bullets and the primers from a local gun shop, but he could not get the cordite gunpowder that he needed. He knew about a more powerful version of cordite that was made in the USA and hoped that his client, Charles, could help. He wrote to him and asked if he could bring a pound of the special American-made cordite when he came in December. Of course, agreed Charles, he would be happy to do so.

Clary was waiting at the Tanga aerodrome for Charles to come out of the terminal because he was arriving on the plane from Nairobi, which had just landed. An air hostess in a blue uniform came up to him and asked if he was Mr. Palmer-Wilson.

"Yes", he replied.

She handed him a small package wrapped in Christmas paper and said, "I think this is yours", then turned and walked back into the terminal.

Clary was a bit confused by this, but just then Charles walked out and they greeted each other.

"I see you got your package", remarked Charles.

Clary, still puzzled, thought it was probably something he had ordered from Nairobi and had forgotten to collect. So he commented, "Yes, but I am not sure what it is."

"It's your gunpowder", said Charles irritably. "I'll tell you about it when we get to my hotel."

At the hotel, over cold beers half an hour later, Charles recounted his story.

"I ordered your gunpowder from my local gunsmith in Chicago, and he advised me not to let it get hot or shake it too much, as it is quite sensitive. Therefore, I wrapped it in Christmas paper to disguise it, with the intention of carrying it on my lap on the plane from Chicago to London.

"Before take-off from Chicago, an air hostess asked me what the package was, so I told her it was a Christmas present. She said, 'Yes, I can see that, but what is it?' So I answered, 'It's gunpowder.' She laughed and replied, 'Oh, you Yanks are always joking.'

"She said it looked awkward to hold on my lap, so she took it from me and said she would put it in a forward compartment and give it back to me when we landed. After we arrived at the London airport, she gave me the package, and I carried it to the customs inspector. He asked me what was in the package, so I told him gunpowder. He warned me that he was being serious and that I should answer his questions correctly. So, I said again, 'gunpowder'. He looked very sternly at me, then waved me through, thinking that he was not going to get a sensible answer from me anyway.

"The next morning, on the flight from London to Nairobi, another air hostess asked me what was in the package, so I said, 'It's gunpowder. It's a Christmas present for my hunter in Africa.' She just laughed, shook her head, took the package from me and put it in the forward cabin baggage bay. When we arrived in Nairobi, the air hostess gave me the package just as we got off the plane.

"At customs control, an Arab customs officer checked all my guns and gun permits, then asked me what was in the package, so I said it was a Christmas present for my hunter in Tanga. 'But what is it?' he persisted. So I said, 'Gunpowder.'

"He then took the package from me and said, 'You cannot import gunpowder. I must confiscate it.'

"I was stunned and absolutely livid with him. I told him I had carried it all the way from America without incident, and now he was taking it from me. He just repeated that I was not allowed to import gunpowder. I started swearing at him in my best Arabic, because I did not think he would understand. The customs officer's eyes got bigger and bigger as I swore at him.

"Then he said, 'You speak Arabic, you speak perfect Arabic.' I thought he was going to have me locked up, but he said, 'I am so happy to meet an American who can speak my language. Don't worry, I will keep the package safe for you here, and tomorrow I will personally give it to the captain of your plane to Tanga.'

"That's why the hostess gave you that package. I hope you appreciate it."

Clary laughed and said, "That is a story I will remember all my life."

"Me too", replied Charles wryly.

They started the safari at the pleasant Ruvu River camp to let Charles (Charlie, for short) get used to the African heat before they moved on to the real bush country. Every morning after a hearty English breakfast, they drove to where Clary planned to hunt that day. They parked the hunting car under a shady tree, leaving one happy tracker with nothing to do except rest and guard the vehicle while the hunting party left to search for game.

The hunters always carried water bottles and extra food rations in the form of sun-dried meat, just in case they wounded an animal and had to follow it a long way. They tried to be back at the car before noon so that they could drive to camp and spend the sweltering afternoon in the cool shade by the river. Some days Charlie was too exhausted from the heat to go on the afternoon hunt, so he stayed in camp and fished for tasty tilapia, which the cook prepared in his unique and delicious way for dinner.

On one early morning hunt, the hunting party left a new porter guarding the car while they left to find game. When they returned to the car a few hours later, the porter was nowhere to be found. After calling his name a few times, they heard his reply, though he was quite far away. When the porter finally ran up and arrived at the car, he said that some very dangerous looking men dressed in red blankets and carrying long spears had come towards the car, so he had run away and climbed a tree to hide and observe them. The strangers only stayed a few minutes looking at the car before going away, but he feared they might be hiding in the bushes, waiting for him to return, so he stayed up in the tree until Clary came back.

After the other trackers explained to him that the men were Maasai warriors walking around as they usually do, and that they were not aggressive, he felt embarrassed but insisted that he not guard the car again as he did not feel safe with these fierce looking savages around.

During an afternoon hunt for kudu, the hunters came across the very fresh spoor of a lone buffalo. It was going in the same direction they were, so they followed the tracks for less than 200 yards before coming upon it. It was an old bull buffalo with a good head of horns, so they stalked to within 30 yards of the big animal. Suddenly, it lifted its head and stopped chewing, as it sensed the presence of danger.

Clary had to make a quick decision before it fled, so he said, "Charlie, it's a good one, shoot".

Charlie was nervous about being so close to such a large animal so he aimed and shot too quickly, hitting the buffalo too far back to kill it. Clary also fired a quick shot as it ran through the bushes, but he also hit it too far back. The crippled buffalo swung around at Clary's shot and came charging straight at them, tossing its head up and down as it bore down on them. When a buffalo charges, it will not stop until it kills you or you kill it. There is no other outcome.

Charlie fired at 15 yards, hitting its shoulder, temporarily stopping it with his heavy calibre bullet. But the enraged brute tossed its head up as though throwing off an irritation, then charged on. Although Clary's second shot from the side hit its neck, it was too high to kill the bull, but the buffalo went down in a cloud of red dust, letting out a loud bloodcurdling bellow as it hit the ground.

"Shoot again, Charlie!" shouted Clary, as he reloaded his big 450 Express rifle.

Charlie was quick with his final killing shot to the head, fired from just six yards away. But then he suddenly screamed, "There's another one!"

Out the corner of his eye, Clary caught a glimpse of another buffalo charging at them. It was very close, and slightly behind and to their left. Seeing the second buffalo bearing down on them, Charlie panicked and reloaded too quickly, jamming a round in the breech of his gun. He was also standing between Clary and the charging buffalo, so Clary could not take a clear shot.

At the last second, Charlie staggered to the right as Clary stepped left and fired two killing shots in quick succession, one bullet hitting the buffalo in the head and the other hitting it in the neck. The buffalo's head hit the ground first, and the black body summersaulted onto its back to land four yards away from Charlie, who was still trying to extract a bent cartridge from his gun.

"It will always be the unseen buffalo that kills you!" muttered Clary, as he walked up to admire the large horns of both dead animals and check that they were dead.

Charlie, still stunned from his near brush with death, said nothing. His hands were shaking so much that he couldn't work the bolt of his gun to extract the jammed cartridge.

Clary took Charlie's gun, extracted the bent shell, then led him by the arm and sat him under a tree, saying, "Wait here with the trackers, and I'll get the car".

While the gun bearers and trackers sat with Charlie, Clary walked the four miles alone to retrieve the car. His infallible guides on the way back to the buffaloes were the vultures already circling overhead the kill.

After taking a few posed pictures with the buffaloes, both animals were butchered and loaded into the car. Only the stomachs and dry blood were left for the waiting vultures.

With the car overloaded with more than a ton of fresh meat, they lurched back to camp. There, over stiff whiskies with ice for Clary and bourbon for Charlie, the client asked Clary for a cigarette, although Charlie did not smoke. The double buffalo charge had scared the daylights out of the man, and he was finally giving into his fear.

The whole sequence of events had been Clary's fault for not checking for the presence of another buffalo, or even several of the dangerous animals. It was a near fatal mistake that should not have occurred. It had all happened very quickly, and had called for a snap decision whether or not to shoot that first animal. Clary admitted that it was his mistake, but Charlie was still in a state of shock and did not react to the words. It was now Clary's duty as a professional hunter to help his client overcome his fear in order to avoid a nervous breakdown.

He managed it admirably with the help of copious amounts of bourbon and plenty of tales throughout the evening, comparing other men's foolhardy actions with Charlie's steady bravery. The therapy worked well, because in spite of a throbbing hangover, Charlie was ready and raring to go hunting the next morning.

Clary did not intend to stay at the Ruvu camp for the whole 30-day safari. He planned to check out his Losira and Kitwai Plains hunting grounds and move his camp there if he found sufficient water and abundant game.

A few days after the buffalo encounter, they left the Ruvu River at 4am with a fully provisioned Land Rover. Charlie was quite annoyed at having to get up at the ungodly hour of 3am to prepare to leave, but he was appeased by being served his favourite breakfast of a stack of pancakes with honey, followed by mugs of piping hot coffee.

It was ice cold driving in the open Land Rover, and everyone on board was glad to have a coffee and tea break to warm up as the sun rose over the land. The closer they got to the waterholes at Losira, the more they saw cattle tracks, and the less they saw game tracks. It was not a good sign, but in spite of their concern, they drove on.

When they finally reached the Losira waterholes and Clary saw them for the first time in about ten years, it was like being punched in the gut – only it hurt more. There were many herds of multi-coloured Maasai cattle being driven by a few tall, sweating men to the almost empty, muddy waterholes. Dust devils blew across the bare, overgrazed land, churning up grey dust and dry grass in long, twisting spirals. Destructive goats were nibbling at the last exposed grass roots, ensuring that grass would never grow here again. There were no water lilies, and no ducks or any other birds, except for a scavenging vulture pecking at the remains of a dead cow.

Clary walked over to the deep rocky waterhole, but then regretted doing so. The Maasai had built a heavy thorn stockade around it to stop wild animals from drinking there, because they were saving the muddy water for themselves and their livestock. A group of Maasai women, chatting to each other incessantly, were busy filling four-gallon tin cans with water, which they strapped onto grey lop-eared donkeys to carry back to their bomas.

The Kitwai Plains, Clary's former Utopia that had been shot to hell by the Kenyan hunter, was not far away. He was determined to see it once more, regardless of his gloomy suspicions about what state it would be in. He steered towards it, then realised that where there had been thick bush, there was now open bushland with one Maasai boma after another. Seeing the Kitwai Plains was like having two heavy punches to the gut, except it was even more painful. It was a barren dust bowl. A few forlorn Acacia trees and tufts of spinifex grass still dotted the plains, though no animals moved over them. Blowing dust blotted out the horizon and filled the air with a dry, choking grey powder. Clary had seen enough. It was time to leave and never come back.

On the solemn drive back to the Ruvu, Clary could not speak for a long time, not until they reached the denser bush that was avoided by Maasai cattle herders due to the presence of tsetse flies and where dangerous game could easily hide. Finally, they saw some game, and Clary's mood improved.

As the car rounded a bend, a herd of impala jumped over the road and disappeared into the bush. The last impala was a large male, well worth shooting. It was just visible through some light branches about 75 yards away.

"There he is, Charlie", whispered Clary. "He has a good head on him, and these bushes have only thin branches; your bullet will go through easily."

Charlie stepped out of the car and peered through the telescopic sights, aiming all around the bush as he looked for the impala.

"Shoot him. He's still standing there, but he won't be for long", Clary murmured again, slightly irritated.

"I can't see him. Where is he?" asked Charlie, annoyed at his inability to spot the animal.

"Right through there, you can just see his red chest and horns through the bush", said Clary, anxiously trying to point out the animal.

Charlie looked again through his scope, then, in a very frustrated loud voice, snapped, "I can't see the damn thing. Here, you shoot it."

Clary, just as annoyed as Charlie at his client's incompetence, grabbed the rifle, aimed quickly, and fired. They heard a loud "thump" from the bushes as the bullet hit something solid.

"There, I got it for you!" yelled Clary.

They walked through the bush to retrieve the dead impala, only to find instead a tall, red anthill sprouting a couple of dead branches, and a neat bullet hole just below the "horns". It was now Clary's turn to be embarrassed, and very embarrassed he was too, as they returned to the car.

Charlie broke the ice by saying, "At least it was a good anthill you shot! It's difficult to mount as a trophy, though. I think it's time we had a drink. Let's get back to camp."

By the time they reached camp, it was dark, with only a few kerosene lamps lighting the secluded campsite. Charlie urgently had to pee, so he jumped out of the car just as it came to a stop on the camp perimeter and ran a few yards into the three-foot-high long grass.

"Get outta here!"

Clary heard Charlie shout from somewhere out in the darkness. A minute later, Charlie walked into the mess area, grabbed a cold beer from the kerosene-run fridge, and sat on a camp chair next to Clary, telling him that he had chased away some animal lurking in the long grass.

"Hyenas", remarked Clary. "They are always hanging around camps trying to steal anything that smells edible. They once stole a bar of soap from in front of my tent. I found it in the morning with a big chunk bitten out, so I presume they don't like soap."

The next morning, it was already daylight when the hunters were ready to leave. As they drove out of camp, Clary saw some footprints in the sand, so they stopped to have a look. The footprints were lion spoor. He and Charlie followed the prints into the high grass to a spot where it was trampled down. A whole pride of lions had been prowling around camp the previous night, and Charlie had scared one off, as confirmed by the tracks of a running lion right next to a patch of Charlie's dried urine.

"The rest of the pride were probably hiding a few yards away", Clary mentioned casually to Charlie, who was beginning to look worried.

"Let's go hunt some kudu", declared Clary cheerfully, as they walked back to the car.

They drove to an area of open scrub thorn with only an occasional tall flat-topped Acacia tree for shade. They parked the hunting car under a tree and set out to search for their quarry.

Lesser kudu are such shy animals that they will flee at the slightest hint of danger. Their corkscrew horns and vertically striped, grey coat blends in so well with the surrounding dry bush that they become almost invisible to inexperienced hunters. Several times, Clary spotted these elusive animals browsing peacefully on thorn branch tips, but Charlie could not make them out. Even when peering through his high-powered telescopic sight, Charlie simply could not see them until they darted away.

At midday, the heat became so intense in the windless thickets that the hunters were forced to return to the car for a rest and to replenish the empty water bottles. The afternoon hunt proved to be just as frustrating as the morning hunt. Eventually, when it was getting late, the hunters and trackers headed back to the car.

However, just before they arrived, Clary saw some gerenuk – a dainty, thin, long-necked antelope. Gerenuk stand on their hind legs and brace their front feet high up onto trees so they can nibble the higher foliage that other browsers cannot reach.

"There is a very nice gerenuk. Take him", whispered Clary, as he pointed towards one standing on its hind legs not 60 yards away.

Charlie turned to him with a shocked look and said, "You want me to shoot one of those people?"

"They're not people; they only look like them when they are standing on their back legs", Clary replied with an amused smile.

Charlie looked back at the animal just as it got down on all four legs and strolled to another bush, where it again stood up on its hind legs to browse. Charlie quickly took the shot from 60 yards and brought down his trophy. All the meat from his gerenuk was consumed with great pleasure in camp, as it was tender and flavourful.

After spending two more frustrating days hunting the ghostly kudu, which always seemed to vanish into thin air, Clary opted to try another hunting method. If they could not hunt the elusive kudu by stalking them, they would let the animals come to the hunter instead. To this end, they found a long, open area in the bush with a lot of lesser kudu spoor, which indicated that the animals browsed here frequently.

Clary chose a place to hide under a low, bushy tree, from where they had a good view of both sides of the opening. They sat quietly in the dirt, waiting for the animals to show up. Pesky sweat bees and sand flies flew around their faces and into their eyes, noses, and mouths, making their wait uncomfortable at best. Swishing a hand over their faces to chase the bugs away brought only a few seconds of relief.

During one of these swishes, Clary saw a few kudu females browsing slowly amongst the trees at the far end of the open section. This time, Charlie could see them, too, but only when one started walking. They could not see any males in this herd, but more kudu were bound to appear soon. Sure enough, an old male with beautiful, wide, corkscrew horns, ambled into sight. It was almost 300 yards from them – still too far away to hit such a small target accurately from where the men sat.

Just as Clary was planning to stalk through one side of the thicket to get closer, another three young kudus walked out halfway along the opening. If they spooked these animals, then surely the big bull would run off, so there was no choice except to stay put. The kudu bull was moving in and out of the trees, browsing as he went, but he would soon move behind a long line of bushes and be out of sight. So as not to lose him, Clary decided to let Charlie take a long shot from where they sat, as it seemed like the only chance they had before the animal disappeared.

The tripod would not be steady enough for Charlie to take such a long-distance shot, so Clary took off his leather belt, strapped it around the trunk of the tree they were sitting under, then took Charlie's gun and twisted the barrel several turns through the belt, affixing it firmly to the tree trunk. Charlie could move the gun only a few inches up or down or left and right, yet that was all he needed in exchange for a steady rest.

He aimed for several long seconds before firing a perfect shoulder shot that dropped the animal where it stood. Lesser kudu meat is very flavourful, so they took the complete carcass back to camp. Over the next few days, the cook prepared a great variety of delicious meals using all parts of the kudu, and alternating it with the even tastier meat of the gerenuk.

One afternoon in camp, Clary was checking all of Charlie's trophies to make sure that they were properly salted or dry enough to pack away. Charlie was getting bored sitting in camp and wanted to go by himself with his shotgun to shoot some birds. Between the riverine forest where the camp was situated and the heavy thorn bush thickets, was an open grassy swath running parallel to the river. This little plain was about 200 yards wide and several miles long, and was filled with guinea fowl, spurfowl, bustards, francolin, and fat pigeons, who all liked to scratch in the grass for food.

Clary concluded that it was quite safe for Charlie to go alone in daylight along this grassy plain, so told him to stay in the open plain where he could walk east or west of camp for a few miles in either direction without getting lost. The staff saw Charlie walk out of camp and head west. About an hour later, they heard a few shots, and soon Charlie walked past the camp and continued on to the east, where he fired a few more shots.

A camp member who had been observing Charlie came to Clary and said he thought the client had gone mad, because he was shooting into the air at nothing. Puzzled, Clary walked with all his staff to the edge of camp and saw Charlie fire a shot into the air, then walk a hundred yards farther and fire into the air again. Charlie continued walking away from the camp until he was out of sight, then fired again. Fifteen minutes later, Charlie appeared once more, about half a mile away, firing into the air as before. He shot skyward once more before he came abreast of the camp, saw Clary and the curious camp staff watching him, and walked towards them with nary a single bird to show for all his shooting.

"I was lost. I couldn't find the camp anymore, so I was firing into the air hoping someone would come out after me", said Charlie sheepishly.

Indeed, the camp with its dark green tents was well hidden and difficult to see under the leafy canopy of trees, and it was no surprise to anyone that Charlie had lost sight of it.

Another episode in camp nearly ended in tragedy. They had been out hunting all day and returned to camp in the afternoon with nothing to show for their effort. After a nice, long, hot shower and some afternoon tea, Clary spotted a big baboon sitting guard at the very top of a Terminalia tree while his troop safely played and scratched around for food on the open grassland below.

A leopard's favourite prey are baboons. And since Charlie wanted a leopard, Clary decided this baboon would make perfect leopard bait. The distance from the camp to the tree was more than 300 yards, which was still in range for a 300 calibre telescoped rifle, so Clary asked Charlie if he thought he could hit that baboon from camp if he had a steady rest.

"I'll try", replied Charlie.

So the men set out a table with some folded blankets on top to use as a rest, and placed a chair behind it. Charlie now had a perfect, solid rest from which to shoot using a 300 Winchester rifle with a high-power telescopic sight. The shot rang out, and the baboon crashed to the ground, while the alarmed baboon troop screeched as they dashed for cover into the bush. The big male was collected and taken far away to be hung up as leopard bait.

Two afternoons later, Clary spotted another big baboon sitting in the same place as the first one. Charlie needed more leopard bait, because the first baboon had already been eaten by a big leopard. So, again they set up the table with some folded blankets. Charlie settled down to shoot with his trusty 300 and powerful scope.

He aimed carefully, then paused.

"Clary, that doesn't look like a baboon", said Charlie, somewhat confused as he looked through his scope.

Clary fetched his binoculars, came to the table, and looked at the baboon sitting in the Terminalia tree, 300 yards away.

"What the hell is that? It looks like a boy! It is a boy!" Clary gasped incredulously.

He sent a tracker to the tree to bring the boy back to camp. It was indeed the young boy who was hired to help clean the campsite. What was he doing up there? He had climbed up the tree to see where the baboons were hiding today because he wanted to earn Charlie's favour by showing him where they were. It was a close call, and a frightful reminder to be aware of the unexpected at any time.

Charlie also wanted to shoot an elephant. However, there was very little chance of finding a big tusker close to the Ruvu camp. Therefore, Clary opted to make a fly camp a whole day's drive away, deep into Maasailand.

They went in the go-anywhere Dodge truck, battering their way along game trails until they reached a small open plain where they found a few scraggly trees to site their camp. From here on, all the hunting had to be done on foot. The hunt was successful. Charlie shot a lone bull elephant with tusks weighing almost 100 pounds.

However, as they hunted, there was something that puzzled Clary about this open plain. On one side was a broad, low pile of stacked stones, about 20 feet square and a few feet high. It did not look like a natural landform, but rather looked man-made. Curiously, there were no stones in the area where the pile had been built. The only place from where the stones could have come was a small, low hill about a mile away. Clary and Charlie removed some of the stones, but underneath there was only bare earth.

When Maasai chiefs die, they are not left for hyenas to devour like common Maasai. Instead, they are buried under a pile of stones. However, there was no sign that any Maasai had been to this area, and in any event, the stone pile was much too big for a burial site. Since no other explanation was apparent, Clary put it down as the grave of a great Maasai chief.

Many years later, Clary found a more likely explanation for the stone pile. He was reading a book about the First World War in East Africa, and he came across a passage referring to a large pile of stones. The author described how the German commander, General von Lettow-Vorbeck, was being chased by British forces. In an attempt to cut him off at Tabora, a British platoon consisting of three officers commanding West African troops was ordered to march through the heart of Maasailand to try to reach Tabora before Lettow-Vorbeck got there. While the British expedition was somewhere in Maasailand, a dispatch rider was sent to stop the platoon from continuing the trek, because Lettow-Vorbeck had altered course and was heading away from Tabora. The platoon was ordered to stay put and await further orders. Idle soldiers are bad for morale, so the British officer ordered his men to look for stones nearby and carry them to the camp to build a wall. After a week of waiting and wall-building, another dispatch rider arrived with orders to abandon all nonessential material and march back to their base at Buiko, as quickly as possible.

According to dispatch papers, the nonessential items they carried were two completely disassembled motorcycles wrapped in oilcloth, as well as "officers' comforts", namely, whisky, brandy, and cigars, plus a few tinned luxury items. Before leaving their bivouac, the officers ordered their men to dig a big hole and bury all these items, then cover them with the stones they had gathered for the wall. The exact location was not marked on an ordinance map, only noted in dispatch papers as five days' march due west from their starting camp at Buiko.

Clary never had another opportunity to go back to that plain to look for the stone pile, but many years later, he was told that the area had been so overrun by Maasai cattle herders that it was no longer recognisable, and it was unlikely that he could find the exact place again.

This safari for the car dealer from Detroit was so successful and impressed him so much that he became an avid hunter, and would eventually return to Africa many, many times to hunt again.

As his safari ended, Charles promised that if he ever came back to Africa, he would bring Clary more gunpowder, except next time he would transport it safely in his gun case.

Chapter 58
Fight or Flight for Life

On another safari a few months later, Clary learned that elephants are tougher than he ever believed possible, when he and two of his clients were almost overwhelmed in heavy brush by one of the great animals.

Clary's two American clients, Hank and Vern, who were both in their late sixties, had been in the army as young men and still retained an air of toughness and fearlessness that had been drilled into them in the military.

This was to be their first of many future planned African safaris. They had come to hunt elephants with Clary, specifically due to his reputation for finding big tuskers for his clients.

The safari started in an area called Ndedo, to the west of Clary's usual Maasailand hunting grounds. Recent rains had caused the trees there to become very green, grow very dense, and very high. It was an ideal place for elephants, because in this lush environment they had a plentiful supply of fodder and were undisturbed, since few other animals, other than the occasional rhino or buffalo, ventured through the heavy bush. However, it was a nightmare to hunt in this dense bush.

Clary placed his well-equipped camp with his crew of 12 men a few hundred yards off a rarely used car track. They set up camp under a large stand of shady Commiphora trees, where there was a good supply of water from a spring that emerged from the base of a nearby hill.

On the first night, when everyone had gone to bed early after an exhausting day, a pride of lions came sniffing around the camp. Suddenly, the powerful, earth-shaking roar of a lion broke the silence of the night, too close to camp to be ignored. Expecting the lion to attack his camp, Clary grabbed his loaded 450 rifle from his bedside and a powerful flashlight, and dashed out of his tent. The roar had come from behind the staff sleeping tents, sending the occupants fleeing in panic from their beds.

Clary shouted to them, "Simama, simama" meaning "Stop, stop". Just as they were about to race to the other side of camp. Clary rushed up and shone his flashlight ahead of them. A bunch of shining yellow eyes reflected back at him, as the waiting lionesses waited hungrily for dinner to come running their way. The terrified men, who were mainly townspeople, gasped in horror at their near fatal mistake, then turned and ran towards the mess tent.

"AH! AH!" came a loud scream from the client's tent.

Clary swung about and saw a young camp helper ran out from beneath the tent, still screaming in panic as he rushed past Clary and dived headfirst into another tent. The situation was getting out of control as panicky men rushed in confusion all over the place. Someone was going to get hurt if this state of affairs continued.

So Clary strode towards the lion pride and fired two bullets into the earth at their feet. They howled and snarled with disapproval at this affront as they retreated into the night. Clary reloaded and fired one shot towards the old male who had bellowed so loudly and was the cause of this whole mess. Then, for good measure, he fired one more shot through the tree branches above the heads of the disappearing pride.

The crew heard a few more lion grunts, though thankfully they were quite far away, confirming that the pride had given up the attack – at least for tonight.

Hank and Vern emerged from their tent, laughing too jovially for such a serious event. Rather annoyed, Clary asked what the joke was, as this happened to be a serious matter.

When he could stop laughing, Vern said, "When the lion roared, we both woke up but were unsure of what to do, so we sat there listening to the commotion outside. Just then, something big crawled under our tent groundsheet. We thought it was one of the lions, so Hank grabbed his gun, and I grabbed a flashlight. Hank was about to shoot through the tent floor, but I stopped him and said, 'No, let me hit it with my shoe. That will be a much more interesting story.' So, I picked up my boot and hit the hump hard. When it screamed 'AH, AH', and ran out, I realised that it must have been one of the men hiding under there. Lucky that Hank didn't shoot."

To the amazement of the regrouping staff, all three men burst out laughing. When Clary told his men why he was laughing, they pointed to one very embarrassed young man who was rubbing his sore head and was not amused at almost being attacked by lions and then almost being shot, then being hit over his head. The camp personnel went back to their tents but lit two big fires on either side of the camp, which they kept burning brightly all night long just in case the lions came back.

A few days later, while they were out with the car hunting for kudu, they came across the very large spoor of a lone elephant that had passed that way only a few hours earlier. A track this size was worth following because it had been made by a very big elephant, and likely one that had big tusks. Clary considered it wise to take both trackers, as they knew this area fairly well and this hunt could take the whole day. It was quite safe to leave the hunting car unattended in this uninhabited area, but they took all the ammunition from the car just in case honey hunters came by. It meant that the trackers' haversacks would be a little heavier than usual.

The group of five set off, with Clary carrying his 450 Express rifle while Hank carried a new Winchester .375 magazine rifle, since he was to hunt the first elephant. Vern had to take a 300 Winchester, which was too small a calibre for hunting elephants, but Clary did not want it left in the car. Vern felt safer with a gun, as he did not want to go unarmed through the bush.

The two expert trackers, who had long ago forsaken their traditional loincloths for sturdy khaki jackets, trousers, and open sandals made of old car tyres, led the way. Each tracker carried a haversack with water bottles, biltong, and all the spare packets of ammunition.

Spooring the lone bull's deep imprints in the soft red soil was easy, but finding a way to manoeuvre between the spikey thorn bushes was hard work. Whereas the elephant had rambled straight through the thickets, the men had to find a passage around the dense bush. The green jungle was getting thicker, and it became increasingly difficult to find passage through it, although the spoor was still easy to see. Suddenly, the lead tracker held up his hand signalling, 'Stop'. Everyone froze, straining to hear any sound. The loud crack of a breaking branch signalled the presence of their quarry close by.

Clary took the lead, while a tracker followed him with his little cloth bag of ash, which he kept shaking to confirm the wind was still favourable for them. Hank, Vern, and the second tracker followed behind. From now on, there would be no more talking; all communication was only by hand signal as they slowly crept forward to get a glimpse of the animal's tusks.

About 50 paces from the elephant, Clary got down on his hands and knees to get a better look under the heavy bush at the animal. The elephant was eating and moving away a few steps at a time, while the hunters stayed crouching in the same place for at least ten minutes.

Very cautiously, Clary turned to Hank and whispered in his ear. "I could only see the feet under the bushes, but one time I got a quick glimpse of its tusks almost touching the ground. It is definitely a very big tusker, although I am not sure how big. We will take him."

Hank's eyes lit up as he turned to Vern and gave him a big grin. The hunting party could not get close in this heavy brush, so they kept a good distance away from the elephant until the bush thinned out a little and they could edge into shooting position. The wind was beginning to alter direction, which meant they had to shoot soon or risk losing the elephant if it scented them.

Hank's .375 rifle with solid bullets was heavy enough to kill any animal in Africa, except in this case the bullet would have to first penetrate 40 yards, or so, of brush before hitting the elephant's thick hide and entering a vital organ. If the bullet hit too many branches, it would slow down and not have enough power to kill the animal, perhaps only wound it. Clary's 450 bullets were heavier and had much more energy than a .375, though he would have the same penetration problem in this thick brush.

Clary whispered his concern to Hank about the .375's killing power. Hank understood the problem and was willing to take the risk of wounding the animal and accept the danger of following it afterwards, if he did not make a clean kill.

There was no opening in the thicket from which a clear shot could be made, so when the elephant entered a less dense patch of bush, Clary made the decision to shoot.

At about 40 yards away, Hank could make out the elephant's form through a tangle of Commiphora bushes, and aimed for the elephant's heart, then fired. Half a second later, Clary's 450 also boomed out. Trees crashed and dust blew all around them as the wounded elephant turned towards them instead of away. It screeched wildly as it swung left and right, trying to pinpoint the source of danger. It ran past them at no more than 15 yards, but due to the dust and the breaking trees, there was confusion amongst the hunters as to what it was doing and no one took another shot.

For over a minute, the hunters could hear the big elephant crashing through the dense thickets as it ran on and on, so they knew now that it was not fatally wounded. The men walked to where the elephant had been standing when they fired at it. Clary examined the bush and was dismayed to see that both his and Hank's bullets had hit some thick branches on their trajectory, so the shots had lost a lot of their power before hitting the elephant.

After a ten-minute break to sip water and calm their nerves, they began to follow the spoor. Dark red blood glistened brightly on green leaves, helping them track the injured animal. Broken branches oozed clear sap where they had been smashed by the fleeing creature. After a mile, the elephant had slowed to a fast walk, still dripping blood onto the bushes as it passed. A tracker remarked nervously that it was heading for a particularly dense patch of heavy green bush and tall trees.

Still following the spoor, the hunters stopped an hour later in a small clearing to rest and sip water. Suddenly they heard the whooshing sound of something big moving fast through the trees towards them. Before anyone could react, a high-pitched, blood-curdling screech split the air. The enraged elephant had got their wind and now bore down on them like a locomotive at full steam. A massive bush came crashing towards the men as the elephant hit it head-on, its enormous ivory tusks poking out the other side.

Without aiming, Clary fired his big gun into the advancing bush, temporarily stopping the charge. "Hank, shoot!" he shouted.

Hank fired at the huge grey body as it turned and ran past them, then saw a puff of dust fly up as his bullet hit the animal too far back to do much damage.

"Vern, you shoot, too", ordered Clary.

He knew that Vern's bullet could not penetrate the elephant's skull into the brain, but at this short range, a side shot would go deep enough to reach the animal's heart and lungs. Before he finished speaking, a huge grey mass appeared again above the surrounding thicket, fast coming their way.

All three rifle shots from the hunters sounded like one, hitting the elephant's forehead too high to be fatal but causing him to turn and run back. The three men stood, guns cocked and ready, straining to catch any noise that might indicate the whereabouts of their adversary.

After a minute, the three hunters and two trackers moved cautiously forward. They saw fresh blood on the branches, though it was too dark and there was too little of it to have come from a vital organ. They followed the big spoor again, stopping every five minutes to listen carefully for any sign of the animal's presence. When they passed under a tall tree, Clary asked a tracker to climb up as far as he could and scout out the bush to try to spot the elephant. The tracker had barely climbed halfway up when he started gesturing frantically that the elephant was charging again.

A long, loud, undulating squeal came from in front of them as the elephant surged towards the group. Long white tusks burst into view as thick bushes were swept aside by the oncoming rogue. Clary and Hank fired one after the other, turning the charging animal away, then Vern fired a broadside shot as the elephant crashed through the bush. The tracker, still watching from the tree, said softly that the animal had stopped about a hundred yards away and then a minute later, it fell over.

They were all deeply relieved, but Hank and Vern were visibly shaken, so Clary ordered a ten-minute rest before moving out to look at the dead elephant. But less than two minutes later, the tracker, who was still in his perch, cried out that the elephant was up and walking away slowly.

Perhaps the bullets from the two heavy guns had hit too high in the head and only given the animal a headache, thought Clary. Whatever the case, the elephant was not fatally injured, which meant they must continue to track him. Not wanting to be ambushed again, the hunters took extra precautions as they went, skirting the denser thickets for the less dense bush on the edges, then picking up the spoor again on the other side. They stopped to listen in complete silence every five minutes, and climbed every tall tree they passed to scout the bush ahead. Progress was agonisingly slow at this pace, but to keep everyone safe from another sudden attack, there was no alternative.

However, in spite of these precautions, they did not have to wait long before the next attack came. They all heard the behemoth coming, trumpeting with rage, as it crashed like a bulldozer through the dense bush from more than a hundred yards away.

"Get ready. Aim just above the tusk line and shoot when you see it", ordered Clary, as the three hunters stood in a line ready to face the onslaught.

Hank lost his nerve and fired too early into the shaking trees before the animal came into view. Vern, also very nervous, fired too. These shots simply turned the elephant away. There was dead silence as they strained their ringing ears, listening for any sounds from ahead.

"Do you think we've got it?" Vern's whispered words provoked an immediate attack, not from the front, where they were facing, but from behind, where they had just come from.

The bush was so dense here that the elephant would be on top of them before they could see it, so they fired a salvo into the swaying trees, again turning the maddened animal away. Seconds later, a tracker with excellent hearing pointed his finger straight ahead and said, "Ana kuja!" "He's coming!"

Another bloodcurdling scream from the elephant confirmed the tracker was right. Clary waited until the tree in front of him came down before firing two shots in quick succession. His double salvo merely turned the animal away. Once more, an anxious silence ensued as the jittery hunters listened through ringing eardrums for the next nerve-wracking assault. The place where they were making their stand was dangerous, because the thick bush obscured the charging elephant until it was almost on top of them.

Clary decided to risk a quick exit to find a more open area where they could see farther in all directions. They had not heard the elephant for many minutes, so he ordered everyone to silently run the 300 yards towards an area where the tracker had seen some tall trees and low bushes. They made it without a scare and stopped under a big old thorn Acacia where the bush was low and less dense, affording a good view for a few hundred yards all around.

Clary told Vern to climb up the old Acacia and keep a lookout for the elephant, while Hank sat below with his .375 Winchester at the ready. Clary and one tracker were going to another taller tree, 50 yards away from where they could see much farther into the distant patches of bush.

While sitting in the tree, Vern tore out a piece of paper from his pocket diary and wrote on it, "Say after me: Our Father, who is in heaven…", and dropped it down to Hank, who read it and started chuckling.

The tracker in his tree, scanned the whole area as far as he could see using Clary's powerful binoculars, but there was no elephant to be seen. It was already late afternoon, and they still had to walk many miles back to the car before it got dark.

Clary was contemplating giving up the chase for the elephant, as it was so late, and his clients were extremely nervous from the five charges they had withstood. When he came back to the tree where Hank and Vern were based, he found them laughing and without a trace of anxiety. Hank showed Clary the note that Vern had dropped to him and which explained their amusement. Both Hank and Vern insisted on continuing the hunt until they made their kill.

The problem with this thicket was that the green trees had soaked up plenty of water after the rains, swelling their branches with sap and making their interior fibres as strong as hemp rope. A bullet hitting even a small branch lost power because it had to displace the sap and cut through the tough fibres. By the time Hank's .375 bullet had passed through a few branches, its penetrating power had diminished to such an extent that it barely made it through the tough elephant hide, and certainly not to a vital organ. This thick green bush was giving the elephant a bulletproof vest.

Adding to the problem was the bush being so high that only the top of the elephant's head showed above it to shoot at. There is nothing in the top part of the head except spongy bone; the animal's brain is behind the eye. Despite this problem, they were determined to finish the job and not leave a wounded elephant to die in agony.

Hank and Vern were amazed that such a massive, heavy animal, weighing seven tons or more, could run so silently that it was barely audible as it ploughed through the brush. They expected to hear the loud crashing sounds of breaking trees and heavy pounding as colossal feet came charging towards them.

"No", said Clary, "elephants are like the fairies of the forest. They can move silently and swiftly if they want to, on their long legs and soft padded feet. I once watched a herd of 30 elephants pass me at 40 yards so quietly that they didn't even wake my resting client and the trackers next to me. They can also charge at an adversary with an ear-piercing scream that can curdle the thickest blood of any hunter, or attack as silently as a ghost."

The hunting party went back to where they had last seen the elephant and picked up its spoor, making wide semi-circles around the denser, taller bush, and picking up the spoor on the other side. They trudged on for an hour until they came to a large, dense patch of bush where they could not find any elephant tracks leading out. Their quarry was in there, and now they had to go in after it.

Carefully, they entered the thicket in single file and stayed close. They walked very delicately and slowly to avoid making any noise, stopping every minute to listen and check the wind, which was now calm and steady. Near the middle of the thicket, they came to a small grassy patch of ground surrounded by scrubby bushes. It was only 30 yards long by ten yards wide, but it meant that a charging elephant would be in full view for a second or two before it got to them.

One tracker, listening carefully, cocked his head to one side and pointed to the bushes on the left. Then the other tracker, listening too, pointed farther to the left. They both cocked their heads to one side and kept moving their pointing fingers leftwards as though following some invisible being. One tracker took out the little bag of ash, shook it, and watched the whitish dust drift slowly to the right. He gestured to Clary, indicating that the elephant was circling the bush trying to pick up their scent, and when it did, it would charge. He indicated with a puff of ash dust that the attack would come from their right.

When the charge came exactly as predicted, the hunters were lined up and ready to shoot. This time, the elephant came silently, with no screech of rage, just muffled pounding strides and ghostly whooshes as his great bulk parted the bush. He was charging with the intent to kill his pursuers.

The first salvo of heavy bullets fired at 35 yards stunned the animal, and it dropped to its knees behind some bushes. The downed elephant struggled and thrashed about, kicking its legs in the air, but then recovered enough to get up and stagger away. A few minutes later, it charged again, but this time the nerve-wracked hunters could not wait, and fired blindly into the quivering bush. Two more times, the great elephant charged the trapped and frightened hunters from different directions, and each time it was turned back by heavy bullets thumping harmlessly into its massive skull. When Clary reached into the haversack for more ammunition for his 450, he realised it was empty. He only had two rounds left in his gun.

"How much ammo have you got, Hank?" he asked.

Looking through his jacket pockets and the second haversack, Hank said, "Four bullets".

Vern had eight rounds of lightweight bullets, which were useless against a charging elephant. The hunters realised that their situation was now very, very serious. They all looked at Clary, expecting him to come up with a life-saving plan. He was thinking hard.

The elephant's last three attacks had come from their right, into the wind, so the next one was also bound to come from that direction, as the animal was hunting them by scent only. Clary quickly consulted his trackers about where the next assault was likely to come from, and which was the closest area of light bush to which they could run. They pointed in the direction they had come. Clary then told Hank and Vern that they would have to run for their lives to reach open bush to be safe. If the elephant charged them again, they were to follow the trackers and keep running until they reached open ground. Clary, with his two bullets, would stay behind and confront the attack alone, waiting until he could get a clear, close-up head shot before firing.

The only route out of the thicket was back the way they had come, along the elephant spoor. The two trackers would lead the way, followed by Vern and Hank. Clary would bring up the rear, from where an assault could be expected. They were to move quickly and as silently as possible, without stopping to listen for danger, only halting if a tracker held up his hand.

The solemn, silent, frightened group departed their bush prison at a fast walk as quietly as possible. Hearts thumped like bongo drums, blood pressure ran high, wide open eyes darted about seeking danger, ringing eardrums imagined they heard breaking branches on all sides.

They knew that somewhere close by or farther out, perhaps in front or behind them, to the left or to the right, was seven tons of enraged, wounded elephant in his natural element, hell-bent on revenge by death. Their death. They realised that they, the hunters, had now become the hunted, and they were running away like scolded dogs with their tails between their legs.

They stopped only once at Clary's command, when they heard the loud cracking of branches far behind them. The elephant had picked up their trail and was following them. Clary ordered a faster pace, for they now knew the whereabouts of their adversary. After an hour of fighting through heavy brush, they came upon a game trail that cut through the middle of a long, open stretch of low bushes and scattered thorn trees. However, the exhausted hunters could not maintain the fast pace set by the trackers, so they were forced to stop and catch their breath.

The clients' arms and faces were scratched and bleeding from racing through the thorns. Their faces were red and swollen from fatigue. Their eyes were wide open with fear, as they were still expecting another charge to come suddenly out of nowhere. Their cotton shirts and long trousers were ripped and cut to ribbons.

There was no time to attend to their injuries, because Clary did not want to make a last stand against the elephant if he could avoid it. He wanted to get everybody out of this dangerous situation and come back with more ammunition. He ordered them to move out at the double. They trotted along the game path which, thankfully, avoided the heavy thorn patches and eventually emerged at a waterhole. Daylight was fading fast, and the car was still far away, so there was no time to linger and rest. They knew that the elephant was still out there somewhere, still hunting them.

Clary ordered his two trackers to carry the clients' rifles, as he noticed that both Hank and Vern were completely done in by this time.

Clary took the lead, keeping a fast walking pace as the two bone weary clients struggled to keep up. The last mile to the car was in the pitch dark, but luckily, just as it got dark, they arrived at the track leading to the car, so the going was easier. The short drive back to camp was in complete silence, with everyone, including the tough trackers, too weary even to speak.

For the next two days, which were the last of the safari, they hunted plains game in open country. Neither Hank nor Vern had the courage to go back to the place where they had only just escaped with their lives. Clary understood their reluctance to face their fears again, so he did not push them to return. After the safari was over, he would go back on his own to hunt down their wounded elephant, because it was his duty to do so.

As scheduled, at the end of those two days, the safari was over, so Hank and Vern had to fly back home to the United States without their elephant.

As he said goodbye to them at the Tanga Aerodrome, Clary promised that he would go back to look for the animal. He reminded them that they had been charged 11 times and fired a total of 23 bullets at the elephant, most of them hitting the animal, so it must surely have died somewhere out there. The few times that the elephant tusks had been visible, Clary estimated their weight to be well over 100 pounds per side, so he really wanted to find the animal.

Five days after his clients left, Clary travelled back to Ndedo to pack up his camp and return to the battlefield, where he expected to find the big elephant lying dead. With his same two trackers, extra packs of ammunition, and a second heavy calibre rifle, he followed their faint footprints back to the thick bush where they had last encountered the elephant. They were very surprised to see that the elephant had followed their tracks almost until it reached the road where they had parked the car. This was one very angry, determined elephant to go to such lengths to hunt its tormentors.

There were no vultures circling anywhere over the land, no smell of a dead animal in the areas they passed through, nor any other indication that the wounded elephant had died in this part of the bushland. Clary went to the few Maasai bomas in the district and offered a big reward to anyone who found his dead elephant. He hoped that honey hunters, who still ranged throughout the district, would look for the elephant to claim the generous reward. However, his elephant was never found.

With 23 bullets in its body, it was unlikely to have survived for very long. The only conclusion was that the poor, disabled animal had gone far away into the thickest, densest part of his realm, and died. Its great body would be hidden from the prying eyes of scouting vultures by the thick, impenetrable Nyika bush for weeks while the hyenas devoured its rotting flesh by night, its massive ivory turning slowly to dust.

A year later, Clary received a letter from Vern, saying that Hank had been having severe nightmares for months after they had returned from the safari, and had eventually suffered a nervous breakdown. He spent a few weeks in hospital for treatment and recovered, but his thick head of brown hair had turned snow-white. His doctor said the breakdown and white hair was caused by his close encounter with a life-threatening situation, referring to the elephant hunt. They had cancelled their plans to return to Africa to hunt again.

The only trophy Hank has from that hunt is a framed piece of paper with the words "Say after me: Our Father, who is in heaven…"

Chapter 59
No Hollywood Fame, Then came the Rain

Clary's safari business was still struggling to show a profit, so when an opportunity came to participate in making a big Hollywood film with renowned stars John Wayne and Elsa Martinelli, he was elated. His reputation as a fearless hunter and savvy bushman had reached Hollywood, and now he was being asked for advice about making the film *Hatari*, which means "danger" in Swahili.

A location manager and an assistant director came to Tanganyika looking for filming locations, since they had been told that this country was more suitable for making such a film than the very popular neighbouring country of Kenya.

Clary took the two men to Mikumi, a verdant plain still teeming with wildlife that had recently been made a game-controlled area to strictly manage and minimise hunting activity there. The game and terrain they encountered in Mikumi were perfect for the film, which was about a wild animal trapping company that captured game and supplied them to zoos and circuses. At Mikumi, they found long, flat, open, grassy plains where game could easily be chased using an open top vehicle and captured by a daring man standing in the back with a neck noose. They saw undulating hills covered with picturesque vegetation and big, shady trees where lions rested during the day. Clary and the film team spent days going over the script so that the next day they could drive out and locate suitable sites for each scene.

After a week of scouting around Mikumi and finding good locations for every scene, the film team were so pleased that they decided that the film should definitely be made there.

However, there was just one hurdle to overcome before they could get a filming permit from the government. They would first need to get game department approval to chase and capture wildlife by car in this area.

Not expecting any problems in obtaining the required approval, Clary went alone to see the chief game warden in the capital, Dar es Salaam. He explained to him what they intended to do during filming, and how the Hollywood film would greatly benefit Tanganyika by putting it squarely on the tourist map as an exotic game-viewing destination. However, the game warden refused point-blank to give his approval for filming in Mikumi, saying that he intended to make it into a park in the near future. He was concerned that chasing game with a car would make the animals wary of cars for years to come, and tourists driving around would only see fleeing animals in the distance. He was adamant that there would be no filming in Mikumi under any circumstances.

On hearing the "no" verdict, both the location manager and the assistant director approached the chief game warden to persuade him that the free worldwide advertising from this film would offset any negative effects on the game. Being an old and stubborn British army officer, however, the game warden refused to be persuaded. Even the promise of a large donation to cover park operating expenses for several years fell on deaf ears.

The film directors eventually obtained permission for the film to be made at Momella near Arusha, in northern Tanganyika. They hired another hunter from Arusha to act as adviser, but had to rewrite the script to suit the Arusha conditions.

The film became a box office success.

Clary was disappointed by this loss of a golden opportunity to make money, but shrugged it off as bad luck and looked for something new.

A year later, he visited the small town of Bagamoyo, on the Tanganyika coastline. In its heyday, it had been a busy slave trading post and staging port for great expeditions into the African interior, but had since fallen onto hard times and much of the town was in ruins.

Just outside the town, Clary found a shoddily built, run-down beach hotel, and rented it. Its only attractions were its location on a low hill covered with tall waving palm trees, the magnificent views over the turquoise Indian Ocean, and the blinding white, fine sandy beach below. The previous hotel manager had failed to attract enough visitors to meet his expenses and make a profit, so after four years of losses he had given up.

However, Clary believed he could do better and make it profitable, although he had no experience of running a hotel, or running any business successfully for that matter. Nevertheless, he was determined to try. Unfortunately, he was soon to find out the hard way just why the previous owners had failed, and that it was through no fault of their own.

The weeks before Christmas and after New Year were the most lucrative for the hotel. It was the time when families from up-country came to spend some lazy days lying on the white sandy beaches, swimming in the warm Indian Ocean, drinking ice-cold Tusker beer, gorging themselves on freshly caught prawns, lobsters, and crabs, and being waited on hand and foot by the attentive staff.

In Clary's first year of operation and just before the first guests arrived for Christmas, unusually heavy rains came early, washing away all the small road bridges to the town. Little streams turned into raging torrents. Bagamoyo was cut off from the rest of the country for days, until temporary bridges were hastily constructed by the busy roads department. Luckily, Christmas celebrations at the hotel that year were saved by these temporary bridges. Then, just before the next rush of guests was due to arrive for the New Year festivities, the heavy rains came again, once more washing away all the bridges. However, this time they would not be replaced until the rainy season had ended at the end of May. Bagamoyo was cut off again.

All essential supplies for the town had to be sent in by dhow, a 12-hour, slow, uncomfortable boat ride from Dar es Salaam.

Clary almost went bankrupt in his first season but was saved by the few guests who did make it through for Christmas and New Year. During the rest of the year, a steady trickle of visitors from Dar es Salaam wanting a cheap beach holiday away from the big, impersonal, expensive town hotels, provided a small but steady cash flow. For the next three years, the rains spoiled every Christmas and New Year's holiday season, forcing Clary to admit defeat and give up. He abandoned the hotel and moved to the capital city of Dar es Salaam, 40 miles further south along the coast, to try to revive his beloved hunting safari business.

However, on the horizon loomed a massive black cloud that was sweeping across Africa and changing life for everyone, including the land, wildlife, and the forests.

Chapter 60
Change is in the Air

The British government and African politicians were discussing self-government and independence for its African colonies. Very few colonies were in a position to be properly governed by its indigenous staff, but the British government wanted to get out as quickly as possible, regardless of the consequences.

The British settlers and residents were advised to move out of Britain's African colonies if they felt insecure with an indigenous government. They could stay if they wished, but whatever they chose to do, they were told not to expect any help from the British government. Only British civil servants who had been sent out to Africa to work would be helped with their return to England. In other words, the British settlers who had struggled to make their little corner of Africa a thriving and prosperous place to live would now have no say in their future and no representation in a new government. They were being abandoned by their government who had urged them to make Africa their home in the first place.

For Clary, the choice was clear. He had been born in East Africa, grown up there and, except for four years of schooling in India, had never left the country, so he had no intention of leaving now. He was determined to stay in Africa, come what may.

Amongst the European population, the great uncertainty about their future in Tanganyika was on everyone's mind. Many of them sold everything they had at a great loss and moved on to another continent. Others were too poor or too old to start a new life in a foreign country, so their circumstances forced them to stay. A few took the "wait and see" approach; they sold most of their property, deposited their cash in overseas banks, were ready to move out quickly at the first hint of danger, yet stayed in the country to await developments.

All eyes were intensely focused on the first British West African colonies to gain independence, to see what happened there. The transition to an African government in the West went smoothly, and none of the expected rioting, looting, or acts of revenge took place. Life for the common people carried on as usual, and the British citizens, who were now foreigners in the new country, were welcome to stay and continue with their businesses. This was a huge relief for the 15,000 foreigners still living in East Africa, who now expected the independence of their country to go smoothly as well.

The next country to attain self-rule was the Belgian Congo in 1960. On the night independence was declared, a bloodbath of horrific proportions ensued that shook everyone to their core, whether they were black or white. The African population in the Congo had been treated very harshly by the Belgian colonialists, and the natives were not about to forget it. Ironically, the Belgian administrators in the Congo who were responsible for the cruel treatment of the African inhabitants, were the first to be repatriated before independence was granted. Those whites who remained were the missionaries, nurses, doctors, teachers, farmers, and businessmen who felt secure staying on, seeing as they had integrated well with the local people and had openly condemned the Belgian administrators for their inhuman treatment of Africans.

Starting on independence night in the Congo, large groups of vengeful Africans went on a killing, raping, and plundering rampage throughout the country, attacking any foreigner or African collaborator they found. They stopped fleeing vehicles on the roads out of the country, killing all the occupants, be they men, women, children, or babies. Even cats and dogs belonging to whites were slaughtered. The killers felt no remorse, no regret, no mercy, and no one was spared. The killing went on for weeks, even after a United Nations peacekeeping force arrived and tried to restore order.

Foreigners living in East Africa were in great turmoil, as they were next on the list of countries to be granted independence. If a killing orgy took place in the Congo, the same thing could happen to them, they reasoned. Uganda, another East African territory in line to gain independence, shared a long border with the Congo and had first-hand experience with traumatised fleeing European refugees into their country.

Any European in Tanganyika who had been unsure what to do now packed their belongings and fled the country, abandoning unsold property to the elements in their haste to flee.

One night Clary was sitting in a bar in Dar es Salaam having a farewell drink with some of his friends who were leaving. He told them that he was staying on, as he would rather die quickly at the hands of a panga-wielding thug than endure a slow, cold death in England. He added that the only thing he had in common with people in England was that they spoke the same language.

At midnight on the ninth of December, 1961, Tanganyika was the first of the three East African countries to be granted independence. No one was expecting any trouble from the peaceful African community. However, Clary felt uneasy because he still remembered the Mau attack on his family and their threat to one day rid the country of all Europeans. There were still some known Mau supporters in the country, and he feared they might go on a killing spree after midnight on Independence Day.

One day before Independence Day, Clary packed his Land Rover with camping equipment and enough food and spare petrol to last him a long time. Then he put all his guns and ammunition in the car – not to fight off hordes of attacking natives, but to supply himself with meat in the bush. His plan was that if any violence erupted that night, he would run to his old hunting grounds in Maasailand and hold out there until the troubles were over. If necessary, he could live off the land for years. He had no fear of reprisals from the Maasai, because they were an independent-minded people. They did not recognise the authority of the British government in Tanganyika, and they had no intention of recognising this new African government's authority either.

Clary waited at home all night listening to his old radio for news of unrest, but nothing unusual happened. The handover ceremony went peacefully. The only incidents that were reported on Independence Night were of some Africans storming into bars and posh restaurants that had previously been reserved for Europeans only, and ordering food and drinks. When the bill arrived, they realised that they could buy the same food and drinks in their own bars for half the price, and they stormed out again.

After independence, the hunting safari business in East Africa dropped to zero. Overseas clients were very wary of undertaking a safari in a newly independent African country, even if their favourite professional hunter assured them that it was safe to do so. Potential clients decided to wait a few years to see how the situation developed before committing themselves.

Clary had no income and no savings with which to tide him over until the safari business picked up again. Even the hardy overseas game viewing tourists whom he could take out on photo safaris were reluctant to risk visiting this new country. He was not only broke and very depressed, but was at a loss of what to do next.

Chapter 61
A Wet Safari and More Rain

Elephants, or better to say, ivory, had saved Clary from starving throughout his life, so they would now have to rescue him again. In the meantime, his eldest son, Michael, had returned from the United States after attending junior school there. Together, they would try to reopen the beach hotel in Bagamoyo and hunt elephants for ivory to help support the business. Although there were elephants within a short drive of Bagamoyo, they never grew big enough tusks to be worth shooting, so Clary and Michael always hunted elephants in Maasailand, where mighty tuskers still roamed.

After moving back to Bagamoyo and renovating the beach hotel to accommodate visitors, they desperately needed more money until the first guests arrived. A hunting trip for elephants was the only answer.

Clary, Michael, and two helpers packed the Land Rover station wagon with food and equipment and left Bagamoyo early one morning, bound for Maasai country. A few miles outside the town, it started to rain, and unbeknownst to the hunters, the rain would not stop for five days straight. They sped along in the downpour on a newly graded road that passed through good game country in lower Maasailand where they intended to hunt. They searched for a place along this road to pull off and make a camp, but both sides of the road were flooded with several inches of water. At one place that looked less wet than the surrounding countryside, they drove off the road to make a camp, and promptly got stuck in deep mud. The four-wheel drive mode on the Land Rover failed to extricate them from the muck. Eventually, they placed dead branches under the wheels for traction, and with all of them pushing the vehicle they managed to move the car a few yards forward bit by bit.

By evening, the car was still mired in red mud and was about 200 yards off the road. Wearily, they decided to make the best of it and set up camp then and there. They put up the tents in the mud and rain. The firewood they collected was soaked and would not light, so they ate cold tinned food for dinner.

The next morning, it was still drizzling and their tent was an inch deep in water, forcing Clary and Michael to stand on their beds to get dressed. The two African helpers slept quite well on their foam matrasses in the dry back of the empty Land Rover. Breakfast was cold tinned fruit. Hot tea was only a dream.

They tried to hunt in the bush around their camp, but the mud was deep and thick as glue, sticking so tenaciously onto their boots that walking was a struggle with each step. Their clothes were soaked through from the constant drizzle. Cardboard ammunition packs became waterlogged and burst open, spilling the cartridges into the bottom of the soaked haversacks.

They sloshed for miles through the thorny bush and sticky mud, hoping to find elephants or at least some fresh tracks to follow. When they finally found elephant tracks and began following them, the rain poured down so hard again that it washed away all traces of the spoor. Soaking wet, and dispirited at losing the tracks, they gave up and slogged and slipped and skidded back to camp through the endless mud. They tried hanging their clothes to dry inside their tent, but in the damp air, everything stayed wet. They doggedly continued hunting in these appalling conditions for five more days, hoping that the incessant rain would finally stop, and the red earth would dry out, but it was not to be. By the sixth day, everyone in camp was sneezing and coughing from colds and the flu.

Clary realized that it was hopeless to continue hunting, as everyone was ill, and he decided to give up and go home. They packed their tents and all the gear, even though everything was soaking wet, and stuffed it haphazardly into the car. When the drenched equipment was loaded up, they tried to drive back to the road, a mere 200 yards away, but the heavy vehicle had sunk too deep into the mud to move. Even brushwood packed in front of each wheel to improve traction, plus determined pushing by the men, failed to move the heavy Land Rover even a single inch. Trying to jack up a wheel to shove sticks right under only pushed the jack deep into the soft mud. Even a heavy log placed under the jack for support failed to raise the wheel out of the morass.

When it got too dark to see, they gave up trying to move the car and spent an uncomfortable night eating soggy biscuits, and dozing upright in the car plagued by hungry mosquitos. At first light the next morning, rheumy-eyed from fever and lack of sleep, they offloaded all the heavy, wet tents and equipment in the drizzling rain, dragged everything 200 yards through the mud, and piled it by the roadside. Now that the car was much lighter, they were able to dig a furrow for each tyre in the soft mud, fill it with sticks and brush, and drive 20 yards before it bogged down again.

By repeating this procedure nine more times, they managed to get the car onto the road by evening. The heavy rain had stopped, so at least they were able to load the wet equipment without getting soaked again. It was exhausting work for the four ailing men to manhandle the heavy, waterlogged equipment back into the car. By the time they finished loading the Land Rover and began the long drive home, night had fallen. The road was still wet and slippery, so they stayed in four-wheel drive and drove slowly until they reached a harder section of road. At the first village they came to in the dead of night, they hoped to buy something to eat, but all the huts were dark and shuttered.

It had not rained since that morning, so when they finally drove onto the main tarmac road, they were able to speed up and arrive back home in Bagamoyo to a beautiful cloudless morning. It had not rained there at all! Their tents and some wooden boxes were so wet and mildewed that they had to be thrown away. This safari had been one of the worst hunts Clary had ever experienced. Now they were even more broke than ever. Only a trickle of guests to the hotel throughout the year saved them from bankruptcy.

Two years later, his son Michael left again for the United States, where he would be sponsored to attend university and eventually make the United States his home. This left Clary on his own once more.

In 1963, Clary was hunting alone in Maasailand when the country experienced its heaviest rainfall in 50 years. Very heavy rain started in March and continued, on and off, until the end of May. Whole sections of main roads were washed away, making it impossible to travel between major towns. Mountainsides became so waterlogged that they simply slipped into the valley below, blocking the roads and rivers. Almost every small wooden bridge across every stream was swept away. Enterprising local natives set up a ferry service at the bridge locations, using their dugout canoes to ferry stranded passengers across the swollen streams, and charged them eye-watering fares. Stranded vehicles on the roads between the demolished bridges were pressed into carrying goods from one wash-out to the next, also for vastly inflated fees. Low-lying roads turned into fast-flowing rivers. Whole settlements in low-lying areas were swept away. Herds of cattle, sheep, and goats, unable to escape the rising waters, drowned in their enclosures.

Clary was able to drive around in the Maasailand because most of it consists of hard, stony ground that did not absorb much water. He had his four-wheel drive Land Rover to help him out of the muddy spots that he had to cross.

Along one flooded low road, far away from any river, he saw catfish swimming in the roadbed. He stopped and caught one, as he couldn't believe his eyes. One waterhole was so full that the water was flowing out of it instead of into it; he had never seen this before. He came to a long, open, grassy plain where he had previously hunted wildebeest and zebra. Now it was a lake filled with rainwater and teeming with birdlife.

A dry gully that he had driven through hundreds of times in the past was now a wide, flowing river that he could not cross. Far from the main river was a little stream that Clary used to step across without getting wet feet, but now it was a river 50 yards wide that was flowing backward up into the hills instead of down towards the main river.

Clary stayed in the bush for all of that rainy season, buying fresh vegetables from the local natives and shooting game for meat on his licence. When the rain finally stopped and the sun came out, the whole country burst into a bright green jungle, blooming with sprouting vegetation and roadside flowers. Rivers subsided, bridges were re-built. Dwellings were newly erected, roads were repaired, and the country got back to life as usual. Then Clary drove home to Bagamoyo.

Chapter 62
The End of Game in Maasailand

Around 1970, Clary made his last hunting trip by himself through the whole of Maasai steppe.

The area was overstocked with Maasai cattle, sheep, and goats. The vast open grass plains where he had hunted gazelles were now nothing but trampled dust bowls of overgrazed land. Herds of black and white cattle milled over the landscape as far as the eye could see. A lonely oryx drifted in and out of trees along the fringes, searching for some grass tufts to nibble on. Small groups of Grants gazelles browsed the last leaves off the thorn scrub that had been overlooked by voracious goats. Long-necked gerenuk and lesser kudu fared a bit better than many other gazelle, since they could still browse the branches that were out of reach of sheep and goats.

Old, dried rolls of elephant dung indicated that the great beasts had not been here for some time. Indeed, the droppings may have been from elephants who had just been passing through on their way to the river or heading back to seek thicker foliage. It seemed as though the prehistoric-looking rhinos had been driven out or become extinct, for Clary had had no sightings or signs of them for years. They had in fact been driven out of these plains and into the rugged, rocky, uninhabited foothills of the Usambara and Pare mountains, where few people ventured. Buffalo, which were once fairly common throughout the area, were direct competitors for grass with Maasai cattle, so they too had been driven out and now were rarely seen. Whereas before, large flocks of Guinea fowls were seen everywhere, now only a few scratched about under thorn trees, pecking at buried seeds and insects.

The biggest shock came as Clary was driving the last 50 miles north towards Arusha, when the bush suddenly ended. He slammed on the brakes so hard that his passenger hit his head on the windscreen. The bush and grass had been clear-cut right down to bare red earth. Old game trails were still visible on the naked ground, but shiny corrugated tin huts, congregated in small villages, reflected the sunlight over much of the barren landscape.

This sad land was fated to become bean farms. It would soon be tilled and planted to grow beans for export to Europe, where they would be turned into baked beans for world markets. The beans were meant to earn dollars for the country, not to feed its rapidly growing population.

Disgusted at the loss of his beloved game habitat, Clary continued on to Arusha, passing one newly cleared bean farm after another. There were plans to expand the bean growing area farther south if these first farms proved successful. In a developed world, wild animals and their land are given a protected place to live, but here they are pushed out to be the last in line for consideration, in spite of being one of its greatest assets. All too often, money comes first and foremost, and in Africa, money always comes above all else.

Clary hoped that a few places in the country remained where wild game still predominated. Those regions would likely be very dry with barren soil, unsuitable for growing any type of crop, and where tsetse flies were so prevalent that they discouraged livestock farming.

To find out if such places existed, Clary chartered a small, single-engine Cessna plane and a good pilot from Dar es Salaam, then spent three days flying low over the central part of the country, away from the towns and villages. To his great joy, he saw from the air that there were a few places that the Maasai and their massive cattle herds had not penetrated.

From the window of his low-flying Cessna, he could see waterholes exhibiting a mass of game footprints around them. Well-used game trails through the thickets confirmed that game was plentiful there. While flying over a remote location, Clary's keen eyes spotted a lone elephant covered in ochre red dust. He ordered the pilot to circle the animal once more to get a better look at its tusks. Clary was awestruck and his heart missed a few beats at the unbelievable size of this elephant's massive tusks. He estimated a weight of 200 pounds each side - an unheard of size. Just to be certain of his estimate, he asked the plane to circle once more, but even lower than before.

Detecting the roar of the plane's engine, the huge animal lifted its great head, thrusting its gigantic tusks skyward, then it ran for cover. Clary had seen all he needed to see. There was no mistake in his first estimate; it was a 200-pounder. Fortunately, the pilot was too busy concentrating on his flying to notice the elephant, so Clary could keep his find a secret. He vowed not to mention this elephant to anyone until he found a deserving client to hunt it.

Nevertheless, Clary never got the chance to go after the magnificent bull. Many years later, an off-duty African policeman shot this elephant far away from that spot yet well within the elephant's territorial range. The tusks weighed 190

pounds each, and are on display in the national museum in
Dar es Salaam.

Chapter 63
No More a Hunter

There still existed a lot of unexplored territory in western Tanganyika (now named Tanzania) which Clary wanted to survey by car, but due to the great distances he had to travel on poor roads, he opted for an aerial survey instead. He could not afford to pay the high charter fees again, so he invited two other acquaintances to come along to share the costs. Bouncing along in the low-level turbulence with the little Cessna was so tiring for the occupants that the pilot suggested they only fly in the early morning and late afternoon, when flying conditions were calmer. This option greatly reduced the passengers' queasiness from air sickness, and greatly increased their enthusiasm to continue their reconnaissance.

Areas of dense woodland hid all but the largest animals from aerial view, limiting the accuracy of their game count. Substantial stretches of open savannah and grassland showed evidence of use by large herds of game during the wet months, but a lack of surface water precluded its use during the dry season. One disturbing fact that Clary noticed over the region was the encroachment of new settlements into formerly uninhabited sectors, evidenced by palls of thick smoke from bush fires newly lit in an effort to quickly clear land for communal settlements.

These new villages were the result of a personal decision by the new president of Tanzania to make his country a socialist paradise. Sadly, this decision dragged the country down to one of the three poorest in Africa, and also proved to be the death knell for much of the wildlife in Tanzania, as vast tracts of bushland were cleared to make way for new settlements. Game near settlements became the main source of food as grand socialist schemes failed and did not provide the promised abundant food harvest for its inhabitants.

Having spent a lot of money to conduct the widespread aerial survey, Clary concluded that there were still a few regions where game was abundant enough for hunting safaris to be feasible. However, the whole venture proved to be in vain, because the government decided that independent hunters would not be permitted to operate in the country. Hunting safaris, which were slowly returning to East Africa, could only be undertaken by a newly formed government-run safari organisation. Clary was now out of the hunting business before he could begin again.

He tried to make a living by catching birds with fishing nets strung between trees in the forest next to his Ruvu river camp. He sold the birds he caught to a German businessman who exported exotic birds to Europe, though Clary failed to catch enough to make ends meet. Perhaps the real reason for his bird-catching experiment was so that he could live for a while longer in his beloved Maasailand amongst the wild animals, at least until he could think of his next move.

In between his bird-catching forays, he took ten days off and camped at Kijungu, hunting for the giant tusker that he had spotted from the air many months before. Since he could no longer hunt with his own clients, there was no point in keeping the great tusker for one of them. Although he saw a set of very large footprints that were definitely from the elephant he had spotted from the air, they were already months old, confirming that the elephant had been here but was no longer in the region.

Out of sheer financial desperation, he had to shoot an average-sized elephant just to get enough money to survive for a few more weeks. In the meantime, the price of an elephant licence had doubled, yet the price of ivory remained the same. So after selling the ivory, he ended up with less cash in his pocket than he had expected.

His bird-catching business was a total financial failure, forcing Clary to sell his Land Rover to survive. In the end, he had to take a low-paid job as an assistant manager at the newly established government hunting company called Tanzania Wildlife Safaris, or TWS.

He declined the position of professional hunter with the company, because Clary Palmer-Wilson, the great big game hunter, realised that he was getting older and slower. He could no longer walk through the sweltering dry heat for 20 to 30 miles a day, then get up early the next morning and do it again, as he had done in his earlier days. His eyesight was failing. He could no longer pick out a motionless grey kudu bull against a grey backdrop of dry trees at 300 yards and pierce its heart with a well-placed shot, as he had been able to in his youth. He needed glasses to read and needed another pair for long-distance vision, but was too embarrassed to wear them in front of strangers.

His asthma attacks were getting worse, and occurring more often. His reaction times in precarious situations were longer than the split seconds required of a good hunter. In addition, he fell asleep quite frequently when driving a long distance during the day, and managed to avoid an accident more by luck than driving skill. Therefore, he resigned himself to take the assistant manager's job and not the hunter's position.

Chapter 64
The Last Game Paradise in Africa

If miracles can still happen in Africa, then the following story has to be one of them.

There happened to be one great, unexplored, uninhabited, unknown game paradise in Tanzania. It was called the Selous game reserve, named after a South African hunter-explorer, adventurer, and World War One army scout who was killed by a sniper and buried in the reserve where he fell.

The Selous Game Reserve is a 19,000 square mile expanse of pristine bushland cut in half by the mighty Rufiji River and crisscrossed by numerous smaller rivers and streams. It contains eight large lakes and many more secluded bodies of water, which sustain herds of wildlife with fresh water the whole year round. It includes virgin forests that have never been harvested, and a petrified forest of 80 million-year-old trees hidden in an insignificant valley.

In this wild kingdom, protected by its isolation, lived some of the last great tuskers left in Africa. Other magnificent animals, left undisturbed for over a hundred years, had time to grow horns of record size. Most surprising of all was that this little piece of heaven existed only 80 miles from Dar es Salaam where Clary was living.

A newly appointed, middle-aged, English regional game warden was tasked with surveying this vast uncharted territory and coming up with a plan for its development into a revenue-producing unit. He first spent two-and-a-half years walking every inch of the reserve to make crude maps that indicated significant features, landscape types, and game numbers and conditions for them. His estimate of wildlife numbers later proved to be very accurate.

Fortunately for the Selous, the first idea, which was a government-suggested land resettlement scheme in the reserve for socialist communes, was declared untenable because of the poor soil and massive swarms of tsetse flies that occurred there.

The game warden's second idea for the area was to create a park for game-viewing tourists, but that proved unworkable due to the harsh terrain and difficulty of accessing most of the remote areas.

His third idea, which was implemented, was to turn the reserve into hunting blocks for the exclusive use of professionally guided safaris, in order to earn coveted foreign exchange for the newly formed government. With a very limited budget and a small workforce, the warden started to hack through the jungle, building simple roads into the easily accessible northern Selous before trying to expand southward into that inhospitable sector.

While managing the government hunting company, TWS, in Dar es Salaam, Clary had organised a few safaris for clients into the Selous. He heard stories from returning clients about the wealth of game they encountered in the new reserve, but he had never seen it for himself.

For three years, Clary managed the company's Dar es Salaam branch office, though he never stopped pestering the company directors to let him run his own safaris. Finally, they must have become tired of his pleading, so they relented and gave him a special permit to operate his own hunting safaris. Clary was elated and spent the next few days celebrating his victory with his acquaintances who he met in his usual hotels.

Clary resigned from TWS and formed his own hunting company in Dar es Salaam, but was not permitted to hunt in the Selous because it was reserved for TWS clients only.

Therefore, he had to be satisfied with taking out a few foreigners working in Dar es Salaam who were happy to shoot one or two animals on a week-long safari. At least it was a start for his new company. It took another eight months of harassing game department officials before he was permitted to take one of his short safaris into the northern Selous, and was given the closest block to Dar-es-Salaam to hunt, which he later discovered was Nirvana.

IMAGE 19: SELOUS AND LAKE SIWANDU. A PARADISE IN AFRICA.

The first time Clary drove his rattling old green Land Rover along one of the newly graded roads in the Selous reserve, his eyes widened in astonishment at the beauty of the land and the abundance of game. Herds of grazing impala eyed him curiously, as his noisy, green, stinky monster lurched by. They hardly stepped off the road, forcing him to drive slowly, bumping them a little on the rump to get them to move over. A herd of jet-black buffalo, perhaps a thousand strong, decided to cross the road in front of the car. They were in no hurry, so Clary had to switch off the engine and wait for 15 minutes in a cloud of fine dust until the last old stragglers wandered by.

Beautiful, ugly warthogs, with ivory tusks protruding from dark grey snouts, trotted along in lines of up to 20 animals in a group, their tails sticking straight up like radio antennas on a jeep. Zebras, with the blackest and whitest stripes he had ever seen, mingled freely with white chevroned wildebeest. Long-faced Lichtenstein's hartebeest, with their backward-pointing black horns, ran a few steps to acknowledge the disturbance by a car, snorted once, and then went back to eating grass.

Clary stopped on a yellow grassy plain just to drink in the beautiful landscape around him. Curious herds of wildebeest, zebras, and hartebeest came running up to see this new, strange, growling animal standing there. They snorted, grunted, threw their heads to one side in an open challenge, pawed at the loose earth with their long legs creating little dust clouds, and trotted around flicking their tails in anticipation of what this curious animal would do next. When this object of their curiosity did not move, they lost interest and galloped off at high speed, chasing each other in mock battles.

The tall giraffes looked down at the car with disdain from over the tree tops, unmoved and unimpressed by its passage. Clary saw, heard, and smelled elephant herds with their shrieking teenagers everywhere he went. Old elephant bulls, unable to stand the noisy herds, grazed contentedly in solitude on the abundant green vegetation all around them. Piles of bleached white bones, still containing ivory tusks, were spread out over the landscape, indicating that these elephants had lived their long lives here contentedly and had died a natural death, not a death caused by a poacher's poison arrow or hunter's bullet.

Each year while Clary had use of this block, between ten and 14 elephant tusks were picked up from naturally occurring deaths and handed over to the Selous Authority for a small reward. Richard, one of Clary's sons and also a professional hunter, kept a notebook in his top pocket to record the numbers of different animals seen each day. On the worst days, he noted only about 150 animals, and on any normal day, he counted 350 to 400. On the best days, he saw over 1500 animals, including two herds of buffalo, one of 300 animals and the other with about 800 individuals.

In this hunting block, there were five beautiful freshwater lakes, a big wide river, and many small streams. Each lake differed from the others in some unique way.

Lake Manze, full of fish and home to the odd crocodile and hippo, was a 300-yards long and 30-yards wide hidden gem in a forested low valley. Its water level rose and fell a few feet according to the seasonal rains.

The second lake, Mzizimia, was shallow and muddy, half water, half swamp. It was a birds' paradise, supporting every type of water bird that was found in this part of the country.

Whistling ducks, Egyptian geese, coots, and moorhens waded through pink and white water lilies, chasing green frogs, small fish, and swarms of insects for food. The early morning cacophony of waking birdlife was wild music to the ears of all who heard it. Succulent green water plants and fresh grass attracted elephants and buffaloes, who even spent the burning hot middays foraging in the cool water, occasionally covering their overheated bodies with a protective mud coating.

Lake Tagalala was mainly a very large swampy patch with deep muddy banks, covered in tall, razor-sharp swamp grass. This lake was home to mud-loving catfish, some of them the size of a boy. Snakes abounded here due to the abundance of frogs of all shapes and sizes. Mosquitoes by the trillion found ideal breeding conditions in the stagnant water. The females flew out each evening in huge, dark swarms to seek warm blood to drink to produce their eggs. At night, the blinking lights of fireflies flitting low over the swamp were more numerous and brighter than the stars above. Some brave crocodiles ignored the muddy conditions and lived in the deeper water, but they remained small because there were not enough fish for them to feed on. Any small land animal that ventured too close to this lake risked being sucked in and held captive in the lake's muddy prison, with no chance of parole.

The largest lake, Nzerakera, was almost two miles long and almost a mile wide. Along one side was a series of long, sandy beaches that sloped gently into the water, providing ideal sunning spots for the overcrowded crocodile population. On the opposite side was a muddy bank and deep muddy water, which easily concealed a crocodile as it waited for an unsuspecting animal to come down to drink. Fish were more abundant here, so Clary concluded that perhaps crocodiles just fancied game meat as a change from their fish diet.

Nzerakera was also the home of the hippos. There were dozens of pods of these fat creatures scattered throughout the lake, each keeping to their own territory. Their grunting could be heard throughout the day and in the early morning when they returned to the lake from their nightly feeding forays. It was quiet on the lake only during the night, when all the hippos waded out of the water and onto the wide, open grassland to eat. The hippos never made a sound when out on dry land.

Along the edges of this lake were thick, dense forests, providing perfect hiding places for elusive leopards and resting lions. Sausage trees, with their long, dangling seed pods, provided shade and food for elephants. Tamarind trees were never without a troop of monkeys gorging themselves on the sour fruit. Smaller ground animals came carefully to these trees to eat the leftover scraps of tamarind seedpods dropped by the monkeys, hoping too that the watchful monkeys above would warn them of any leopards close by.

Multi-stemmed doum palm trees flourished along the riverbanks and lakes. Well-worn trails led from one palm tree to the next, as animals, big and small, went looking for fallen nuts to eat. Great swathes of fan palms provided additional pleasant, shady hideaways for lions during the midday heat. A few massive baobab trees, hundreds of years old, made good landmarks, as they could be seen from miles away, towering over the lesser miombo bushland.

Siwandu, the fifth lake, was deep and still, 800 yards long and fed by an arm of the great Rufiji River. One side was dominated by a forest of tall Borassas palm trees, where baboons clambered up to harvest the edible red nuts while elephants scavenged below for fallen fruit. White-headed fish eagles used the upper branches as lookout perches from which to launch dive bomb attacks onto unsuspecting fish in the lake below. A wide sandy beach at one end was a favourite place for animals to come to drink, and a favourite waiting place for hungry lions to stalk thirsty prey. A small, five-acre island a few yards from the lake shore supported a small forest with a tree canopy so dense that no sunlight penetrated to the bare ground below. A constant breeze off the lake kept the area under the trees cool and salubrious throughout the seasons.

IMAGE 20: CAMP ON LAKE SIWANDU.

It was here that Clary chose to make his camp in his new Garden of Eden. He erected his six tents under the deep shade of the Moringa trees on the little offshore island.

In a hunter's view, living in a tent was the only way to appreciate the African jungle in all its visual and sensual glory. The thin canvas walls did not block out any sounds, allowing their occupants to hear even the faint footfalls of a passing leopard. The mighty roar of a lion caused the canvas sheets to vibrate and sent a chill down the spines of the sleeping guests inside. Little gauze covers over the tent windows let the myriad and mysterious smells of the jungle waft through unhindered and undiluted. A good tent in Africa kept mosquitoes, creepy-crawlies, and rain off those inside, but did not dilute the entry of sounds and smells.

Overhead in the trees, monkeys and a myriad of birds competed with each other for ripe red fruit and dark berries. A long, smooth, sandbank to the west of camp served as a convenient sunning spot for both the hippos and the crocs. There was abundant grassland around the lake shore, so the resident hippos were always well fed and content. Fish were so plentiful that none of the resident crocodiles ever starved or had to revert to catching game to survive.

Casting a fishing line in front of the camp, with a worm on the hook, caused the Tilapia fish to jump out of the water as they fought each other to get at the worm. A hook baited with fresh meat was irresistible to bottom-feeding catfish, who struck the bait within seconds after it was cast. A 20-foot long fishing net set in the lake for half an hour caught enough fat Tilapia fish to feed the camp for a week.

A client could spend the entire day sitting beside his waterfront tent, a cool drink in hand, watching the endless procession of game coming to drink on the wide, sandy shore of the opposite bank. With luck, he might witness a concealed lioness darting out of her hiding place to catch an unwary animal as it came to the water. She would then share her catch with the rest of her waiting pride.

A mile away from this campsite was a hard, flat expanse of open ground, suitable for hacking out a simple airstrip to serve the camp. There could never be a more perfect campsite in a more perfect location than there in the Selous Garden of Eden.

Clary had no intention of ever leaving this place and hoped to die here one day. With such an abundance of game and pleasant conditions, it would be easy for him to hunt here. Despite his old age and slow reaction time in dangerous situations, he believed that he was still an excellent hunter, so started hunting again with confidence. He never wanted to hunt anywhere in Tanzania again, so he settled in for the long run. He obtained from the Selous Authority a five-year concession (the maximum permitted) for the exclusive use of the block, with unlimited first priority extensions.

He intended to use this camp for hunting safaris and to conduct photo safaris when no hunters were booked. In order to keep the game from becoming shy, he enforced a one-mile no-shooting zone around camp, and refused to shoot at any animal from or within 200 yards of the hunting car. He could never understand how some professional hunters would let their clients shoot while sitting inside the car, which he believed was not hunting; it was just killing. These hunters would drive off the tracks and manoeuvre the car so close to an animal that their client did not have to step out of the car to shoot.

So as not to unduly harass the game, Clary insisted that there would be no hunting in his block for four months of the year, during the mating and calving times.

To the north of Lake Siwandu, was a two-mile stretch of land strewn with ghostlike black ebony trees. Some long dead tree trunks were thicker than a man's body and showed signs that they had withstood many bush fires over their lifetime, and were very likely to withstand many more. A few gnarled, old standing trees looked like dead wood, though they still sprouted green leaves and new shoots on a few branches. Young ebony saplings struggled to sprout through the dark soil next to their bigger cousins. Old stumps indicated that these trees had established a foothold here many hundreds, perhaps even thousands, of years ago. Scattered old, broken ebony branches littered the ground, where they could be collected and used for camp firewood by ignorant men who were unaware of its rarity.

In Clary's hunting block, the many open, grassy plains dotted with flat-topped Terminalia trees were an ideal habitat for all plains game. The trees provided shade all day, and the short grass enabled the animals to see a predator from afar. The many lakes and streams meant that water was plentiful and never far away from good grazing.

Just after the rainy season, this realm burst into bloom, turning Utopia into the Garden of Eden. The air was fresh, clean, and sweet. The sky turned a sparkling blue. Dust and smoke were washed out of the air by the rain, making distant objects visible with sharp clarity. Faraway hills seemed to draw closer. Even the light had a brighter, crisper clarity to it. Dormant flower buds sprang to life with a palette of colours that rivalled a rainbow. Dull brown little creepers covering the brown trees suddenly produced stunningly beautiful multi-coloured flowers that enveloped the entire host tree. Unassuming bushes brought forth such a mass of sweet-smelling flowers that no branch was left uncovered. Big old trees, not to be left out of the new life, endeavoured to smother themselves in stunning blossoms.

Every single flying nectar and pollen collecting insect was out in full force, buzzing like so many engines at full power, harvesting all that was on offer. Butterflies by the hundreds fluttered here and there, immersed in the joy of flight. Every ant, beetle, and other crawling insect climbed up every tree, every branch, every bush, and every plant to partake of this unlimited bounty. The whole area smelt like a giant perfume factory, producing odours of such intense fragrance that they put the most expensive French perfumes to shame. It was a sensual delight beyond words to simply walk around and treat your nose to such smells and your eyes to such visual delights.

Birds, too, took part in the bountiful offer of free food, flying or hopping around the trees. New fruits and berries springing out of old branches were plucked off in bunches by overfed birds and cast aside to become food for insects on the forest floor.

It was not only flora that renewed itself with new growth, but fauna, too. Young, agile, frolicking calves dashed about on their new spindly legs besides proud mothers, occasionally stopping for a suckle of milk. This was a time of plenty for all the wild animals, who could now afford to pick and choose as they nibbled only the most tender, juiciest parts of the new shoots. Brick red impala, with their young in tow, sauntered through the flowering shrubs as though taking a walk in the park. Zebras, with their rain washed black and white stripes, stood out starkly against the dark greens of the new grass.

On the south side of Lake Nzerakera was a flat, treeless grass plain that looked like a manicured golf course, only there were no golfers, just a 300 strong herd of shiny black buffalo who lounged around in the middle of the day, chewing their cud. Little snowy egrets perched on their backs or scampered around their feet, catching flying grasshoppers. A few waterbuck and some reedbuck trimmed the short grass between the dozing buffalo.

It was also a Nirvana for predators. The resident lions and leopards had ample cover in which to stalk and easily catch the innocent new-born animals who had no idea that such dangers existed. The young were such easy prey that some leopards had several uneaten carcasses hanging high up on tree limbs while they snoozed on a thick branch below their food stores. A group of lions with their cubs could devour a freshly caught baby wildebeest while the rest of the herd calmly browsed the short grass 100 yards away. Never far from the lions were the ever-present vultures, sitting on the tree tops with their heads hanging low, biding their time for their turn at the half-eaten carcass.

However, there was a downside in this Eden – as there always is – for the animals that lived there. All the new growth plants were soft and juicy, and were cropped by grazers and browsers alike. Among the new growth were some poisonous plants that were lethal to most animals. When young, these new shoots were odourless and tasteless, but they were just as lethal as the mature plant, and could cause a lingering, painful death if eaten. Young animals taking their first bites of vegetation sometimes ate the tender poisonous shoots, and would succumb to this terrible fate. So, the scavengers such as hyenas and jackals had their feast days on the dead and dying.

A month or so after the first pale green flush of growth, the landscape took on a dark green hue as the plants and trees matured, each at their own pace. A few months later came the dark green and dark gold time, when the leaves darkened and the green grass took on a dark golden colour, followed later by bright yellow gold hue. The green buffalo golf course became gold in colour. At the end of the dry season, the trees and bushes turned brown, and many lost their leaves. Only the forests and thickets along the water courses retained their greenery. During this dry time, the strong scents of wild sage, thyme, sweet basil, and many other aromatic herbs wafted through the air as they were crushed underfoot.

In this northern Selous Garden of Eden, there was no time of drought or of famine, or even a mere shortage of water and food for all its inhabitants. The biggest problem was the Tsetse flies that swarmed over all animals, people, and moving vehicles, easily biting through thick clothing with their long bloodsucking proboscis. It was the only inconvenience for people when walking or driving through this piece of heaven, but perhaps it was the reason that this area still existed and was not settled by humans with livestock.

Chapter 65
Years in Paradise

After Clary set up his camp, he tried to book some hunting safaris for himself. However, many overseas hunters were reluctant to come to Tanzania. The new government had decided that communism was the best way for the country to move forward, so capitalist hunters, the only ones able to afford the high hunting fees, stayed away.

Those overseas hunters who did dare come to Tanzania found the Selous to be one of the finest, most abundant game hunting areas they had ever seen, and they spread the word about their exceptional experience. They became Clary's best agents, recommending him to all their companions. Finally, more hunting safaris started to come his way. For the first time in his life, he had more safaris coming to him than he could handle. The Selous was a financial miracle for Clary.

When the first hunting client, Bob, arrived at Clary's private airstrip and drove the one mile in the open Land Rover towards camp, there was so much docile game to be seen on either side of the road that Bob asked if the hunting area was as good as this.

"This is the hunting area!" remarked Clary. "And you will be one of the first people to hunt this area in over 75 years!"

Then the client started to shake his head and chuckle in disbelief. By the time he got to camp, he was laughing uncontrollably.

"I just can't believe that this is a hunting area. I counted over a hundred animals and five species of game just on this short drive from the airstrip", he said.

"If you count those hippos over there and that crocodile, it makes seven species", answered Clary, as he pointed out the animals in the lake.

After Bob had settled into his luxury tent by the lake and taken in the breath-taking view from the camp, he was eager to start hunting. On the first afternoon hunt, they were driving through group after group of peacefully grazing impala just a few yards off the track when Bob asked how he was supposed to hunt them.

"I will drive right up to a big male, then you lean out the window with your gun and hit him hard over the head", said Clary, trying to conceal the smirk on his face.

"And if he's just out of range, should I jump out and strangle him?" joked Bob.

They parked the hunting car under some trees where the grass was short, and the Terminalia trees were widely spread out. They intended to walk from here for an hour in a wide semicircle, hunting less abundant and shy game as they went.

On the walk, Clary spotted a big bull eland browsing with his small group of females. The male had a good head and was worth shooting. But he was too far away to attempt a shot, so they had to get closer. Unfortunately, there were some impala, a small herd of zebra, and a few wildebeest close to the eland. They would raise the alarm as the hunters approached and scare off the eland, so Clary had to plan a stalk past these animals.

They stalked halfway round to the eland, when a group of waterbuck impeded their way. So, they had to re-route around the waterbuck. As they crept from cover to cover and edged closer to their quarry, they noticed a bunch of nosy giraffes eyeing them suspiciously, so they had to sit still for a while. When the giraffes finally got bored and moved on, the hunters continued stalking the eland.

However, the eland herd had moved farther on and were now next to a wildebeest herd. Clary would have to alter their plans again. The distance was still too far to chance a shot, so they decided to stay where they were and let the animals move apart before trying the next stalk. They sat behind some thick cover for 20 minutes before being discovered by a group of nosy impala, who raised the alarm, sending the eland running out of range to the open plain beyond.

"No eland today!" said Clary. "Let's go back to the car."

They went back to find the car surrounded by snorting wildebeest, upset by the intrusion of a strange metal thing into their midst. The curious animals stood 20 yards away as the hunters got into the car. As they drove away, the wildebeest ran after the car for a short distance, believing that they were chasing it away.

Clary realised that there was too much game around to hunt in the conventional way. He would have to change his hunting tactics. From then on, the hunters drove around looking for quarry that was either alone or with other game that was easily avoidable. If their quarry was in a difficult place to stalk, they would simply drive on to find another more convenient animal to hunt.

One time, they saw some kongoni very far away, right in the middle of a wide open plain. There was no cover within shooting range from which to stalk them, so hunting them in the conventional way would be a waste of time. Instead,

Clary noted the direction they were moving in, drove to a place far ahead of them, and stopped in their path. He sent the car away and hid in the trees and let the kongoni come to him. They waited for 40 minutes in the shade of a tree while the animals ambled into close shooting range, then Bob made a successful shot.

Another hunting technique that they often used was to drive to a convenient bush close to their quarry, stop the car for a few seconds to let the hunters out on the blind side, and then drive away. As the animal watched the car drive off, the hunter had time to aim carefully and shoot. Bob could have easily shot the 12 species of game on his licence within two days, but he drew out the hunt to last 14 days so that he could savour each day.

After Bob left, Clary had another client, Barney, who wanted to shoot a leopard as well as other animals. These big cats were plentiful in the forests that grew along the rivers and lakes, and could be heard coughing near the camp most nights. Clary put a leg of impala meat in a convenient tree on the edge of the forest for leopard bait, as it was the only sure way of getting a shot at one. Then, 20 yards away, he built a half-round hide of five-foot-high sticks and grass. He camouflaged the front of the hide with leafy branches, built a small peep hole from which to look out and shoot, and left the back open for easy access. They would hide in this blind and wait for the leopard to come for the bait. But first they needed to let the leopard find the bait and eat it in peace. They also wanted to let him satisfy his curious nature by leaving the hide empty. On the second night, they would hunt him.

When Clary and Barney inspected the bait in the morning, they saw that it had been completely eaten during the night, and the size of the paw prints indicated that it was a large male leopard. They put up another big piece of impala in the same tree. That afternoon at four o'clock, they drove to within a half mile of the bait, parked the car, and walked to the hide to wait in silence for the leopard to come for his dinner. However, the big cat did not come to the bait, so when it became too dark to shoot, they gave up for the night and returned to camp.

Next morning, they found the bait had again been eaten during the night, so they knew the leopard was still in the vicinity. That afternoon, they put up another piece of meat and went into the blind to await their leopard. An hour-and-a-half later, Clary heard some alarmed birds fly up from the forest behind the bait tree – a sure sign that the leopard was near. Expecting the leopard to jump up into the tree at any moment, Clary concentrated his full attention on the bait. He and Barney waited tensely but no leopard appeared.

After several tense minutes, a movement behind him caught Clary's eye. He turned his head very slowly and stared right into the face of their leopard, calmly sitting ten yards away, waiting patiently for the hunters to leave so he could get to his food. Clary froze for an instant, then turned ever so slowly, touched Barney on the shoulder and said in a very quiet, calm voice, "Your leopard is sitting right behind us. Take your gun and turn around very slowly, and be ready to shoot."

The twitchy client, thinking that Clary meant the cat was some distance behind them, turned around too quickly and suddenly was staring right into the big yellow eyes of the male leopard. Startled, the cat snarled viciously at being discovered.

The terrified client jumped up, grabbed his loaded gun, and aimed at where the cat had been. But the leopard was gone, and nothing but some flattened earth and a wisp of dust showed where it had been. For some reason, Barney was not so keen on shooting a leopard after that!

When he was in camp, Clary's only contact with the outside world was through a radiotelephone which had to be routed via a telephone operator to make a call. There were only two channels on which to call, and with hundreds of subscribers, it was difficult and time-consuming to get through to a telephone number in town.

During the rainy season, it could take eight hours to drive with the Land Rover from the Selous camp to Dar es Salaam, and vice versa, but it was only a 45-minute trip by small plane. Chartering a small Cessna from Dar es Salaam to his camp was not only expensive but also difficult, as it meant making an advance booking by radiotelephone, with the hope that the weather would be settled enough to fly on the chosen day.

A cheaper alternative for Clary was the Dar es Salaam Flying Club, where his son was a member. The club allowed Clary to hire a plane and pilot at a low rate, provided the flight was for his private use and not for his clients.

One day, Clary needed to attend to some urgent business in Dar es Salaam, so he hired the flying club's new four-seat high wing Cessna. The pilot who flew to the camp was a young, low time flying instructor, but he assured Clary that he knew the aircraft's performance well. In the aircraft, besides Clary and the pilot, were Donald, Clary's son from his first wife, and Donald's girlfriend, Margaret.

There had been heavy rain at the camp airstrip the day before, so on take-off the aircraft did not accelerate well due to the muddy ground. Halfway through the take-off run, the pilot still felt confident that he could make it despite the slowed performance, so he kept going along the runway. They never got airborne, and the aircraft smashed into the trees off the end at high speed. In the ensuing crash, the cabin wedged itself between the trees, and both wings snapped backwards, bursting the wing fuel tanks, and drenching the occupants in the back seats with 60 gallons of highly flammable aviation fuel. Luckily, there was no fire.

The aircraft only had two doors in the front. The one on Clary's side was blocked by trees, so he had to push the stunned pilot out the other door, and push a front seat forward so his son and girlfriend in the back seats could crawl out from under the broken wings. Donald and Margaret ran 30 yards away, but were unable to breathe properly because of the fumes rising from their soaked clothes, and they were shivering from the cold as the hot sun evaporated the fuel from their bodies. Clary then got out and joined the pilot, who had run away before anybody else was out. Luckily, they were not soaked in fuel. Only their shoes and socks were wet, because the cabin floor in the front had been several inches deep in fuel.

They heard a humming noise coming from the wrecked aircraft. The pilot refused to go back to the plane, stating that it could catch fire at any moment, as the ignition and electrical systems were still live. He urged them all to move farther away from the danger zone.

Although he knew very little about airplanes, Clary went back to the wreck, because his briefcase with all his documents was still in the luggage compartment, and if the plane caught fire he would lose them all. The pilot shouted to Clary from a safe distance to turn off the main switch, which was a red button on the left of the instrument panel, and turn the ignition key off and pull it out. The humming noise stopped.

Incredibly, nobody was hurt in the crash, since they had been wearing seat belts. Although the fuselage was a complete write-off, the engine and instruments of the aircraft were salvageable.

At the northern end of Clary's hunting block was a small permanent stream where hot springs spurted boiling water out of rocky crevices. The swimming pool-sized ponds in the stream let people choose any temperature of water between boiling and lukewarm to relax in. The pools were also used by other water-loving animals, such as buffalo and warthogs, who did not like human company. So visitors had to be on the constant lookout for the wildlife.

This stream eventually flowed into another watercourse fed by several other springs, assuring a permanent flow of water all year round. This little river, called the Beho-Beho River, was an elephant's heaven, for along its course grew thick forests of wild figs, brown tamarind, doum palms, sausage trees, Moringa, and many more trees that Clary did not recognise. The river eventually flowed into the swamps of Lake Mzizimia, itself an elephant's paradise.

Not far from this river, in a small sunlit clearing surrounded by tall doum palms, lay an insignificant broken concrete slab where the Selous's namesake was buried, at the spot where he had fallen to a sniper's bullet. His full name was Robert Courtney Selous.

One afternoon, when the sun was low on the horizon, Clary and a hunting client were cruising slowly in the hunting car across a wide-open grassy plain close to Selous' grave. Knee-high, bright golden grass waved gently to and fro in a soft breeze.

Clary stopped the car abruptly when he saw two majestic lions, tails swaying from side to side, come sauntering together through the waving grass. Their golden manes bobbed up and down in time with their footsteps. Their golden hides, touched by the low sun's rays, complimented and competed with the waving grass for beauty. It was one of the most beautiful, iconic African sights Clary had ever seen.

He and his client sat motionless in the open car for a long time, overwhelmed by the beauty of the scene. The two majesties paused for a cursory look at the hunters in their car, then continued their walk until they were swallowed up by the waving sea of grass. Although this was a hunting block and the client had a lion licence, there was never the slightest hint that he would contemplate shattering this tranquillity with a gunshot. Clary started the car and drove on in silence, as he and his client savoured the exquisite experience.

After this beautiful lion incident, Clary was reluctant to let any of his clients hunt in this sector of his hunting block. He felt its unique beauty needed to be protected from hunters, so he wrote a letter to the chief game warden and sent a copy to the Selous Authority, describing the beauty of this area and asking that it be declared a non-hunting area. The English game warden who had explored this sector on foot was the man in charge of the Selous Authority. He knew the charm of this place and accepted Clary's request to declare it exclusively a photographic safari area.

The big, shady trees of the Siwandu campsite had once been a favourite haunt for elephants. Since Clary had taken it over, the elephants had found other resting sites. One night, Clary heard an elephant walking past his tent but was too tired to get up to look at the animal. The next morning, when he stepped out of his tent, right in front of him was a fresh pile of elephant dung – a clear message from its maker saying, "I am back."

Sure enough, just behind the kitchen tent stood a bull elephant feeding tranquilly on some young saplings. It seemed as though it intended to stay by the camp, because when someone tried to chase it away, the elephant moved a little deeper into the bushes but remained nearby. This campsite was most probably his resting place in the past, so he was now reclaiming it.

Clary let it stay. When the animal got too close to the staff tents or kitchen area, someone would bang two cooking pots together to let it know it was too close. And it would wander away a short distance. Clary was enamoured by the bravery of this animal, residing in a hunter's camp, and named him "Roger the Lodger". In Clary's view, it became an unwritten agreement that Roger could saunter freely around the campsite at night, but during the day, he was to keep to his forested side of the island.

Elephants, however, are known to interpret agreements in their favour, so Roger believed that raiding the kitchen stores at night was included in his rights. One morning, the cook came to report the theft of all the potatoes and cabbages from the storage racks. Another time, all the fresh fruit had been stolen by the same culprit. After that, all fresh food was locked up in tin trunks out of Roger's reach, and the thefts stopped. Sometimes Roger would wander off to some place unknown, staying away for many weeks at a time, but he always came back to his island home. The agreement between Roger and the camp was honoured for all the years that Clary ran the camp.

A small plane circling the camp meant that something or someone needed to be picked up from the airstrip. Pilots were instructed to land, leave cargo under a tree, and then take off again. Camp staff would then walk to the strip and collect whatever had been dropped off. Whenever someone wanted to visit the camp, they had to call by radiotelephone before arriving, to be sure that someone was at the airstrip to pick them up.

One morning, while Clary was busy in camp and without any clients, a small plane circled overhead. He was not expecting anybody, but went to the airstrip anyway. The two passengers who disembarked were from the American Peace Corps, a non-governmental organisation helping with aid projects in Tanzania. They needed assistance, and Clary had been highly recommended to them as the only person who could help them solve the mystery of a young man missing somewhere in Maasailand. They related this eight-month-old story to Clary.

One Sunday afternoon, two young Peace Corps volunteers had gone hunting just a few miles away from the village in Maasailand, where they had been working on an aid project. One of them had shot and wounded an impala. The shooter told his companion to stay in the car, as the crippled impala could not be far away and he was going after it. About 20 minutes later, the waiting man heard a shot, which sounded a long way off. He waited in the car, thinking that his friend had finally killed the impala and would soon turn up. About one-and-a-half hours later, when the sun was going down, the hunter still had not returned.

Believing that his friend had lost his way, the waiting man took his shotgun and fired a signal shot into the air. There was no reply. Every 15 minutes until dark, he fired a shot into the air but never got an answer. Then he collected all the firewood he could find, lit a huge fire, left some food, water, and a blanket by the fire, and drove back to the village huts where he spent the night. Early the next morning, he went back to the bonfire to find nothing had been touched and no sign that his companion had been there. He then hurried back to the village, collected some helpers, and started a search for the missing man.

They found parts of an impala carcass that had been eaten by hyenas during the night, and presumed that this was the animal the hunter had shot. They searched the whole day, yet found no sign of the missing hunter or his gun. They eventually sought the help of over 100 tribesmen from the area, who searched for five days without finding even the slightest trace of the missing man. Neither did they see lion spoor or hear a lion, which they suspected could have killed the hunter.

The American Embassy eventually got involved in the search and offered a huge reward of 100 cows to anyone who could bring in any evidence of the missing man. The Maasai, who knew this land like the back of their hand, came by the hundreds to vie for the generous reward.

They searched for months and found nothing, absolutely nothing. The man had simply disappeared off the face of the earth. An international search was started, checking life insurance policies, bank accounts, girlfriends, his parents' and relatives' homes, but nothing showed up. He was listed as "missing" until proven otherwise.

It had now been eight months since the man disappeared. The Peace Corps men were hoping that Clary could come up with an idea about what could have happened to the lost man. He questioned them for hours about the disappearance and suggested possible scenarios, but they had investigated each and every one, and still come up with nothing. As they departed by plane back to Dar es Salaam, Clary promised that he would keep thinking about it and would contact them if he had any new ideas.

About three years after the Peace Corps meeting, Clary was talking to one of his American hunting clients who had been a Special Forces soldier in Vietnam. He talked about his jungle survival training in South America and his desert survival training in the United States. After listening to his client's description of survival training, Clary realised that he had a possible answer to the disappearance of the Peace Corps man. But first, he had to ask the United States Embassy an important question. Had the lost man ever been on a desert survival course?

A few weeks later, when Clary visited the Embassy, he was told yes, the man had done such a course just before he came to Africa. Clary was now sure of his theory and described the most likely scenario of what had taken place that fateful day three years before.

The hunter, having wounded the impala, followed the blood spoor for a long distance before seeing the animal again. He then fired at it, though did not kill it. This must have been the shot heard by the man in the car. The hunter either followed the impala for a while longer, or gave up and headed back to where his friend was waiting in the car. However, few amateur hunters know that injured game never run away in a straight line, but rather tend to circle back towards where they came from. Being unaware of this, the hunter very likely walked in the wrong direction, believing he was heading towards the car.

He was probably out of earshot when his companion fired the shotgun into the air. Realising that he was lost, and it was getting dark, he needed to find a safe place to spend the night. This is where the lost man's survival training kicked in. In this stretch of bush, there were only thorn trees, too small to climb to seek shelter for the night, so that was not an option. Then he sought shelter, as per his survival training, down a disused ant-bear hole, which are also sometimes used by hyenas and porcupines.

An ant-bear digs a hole at a shallow angle into the ground which is wide enough and long enough for a man to wriggle into. After making sure that there were no animals hiding inside, the missing man likely slid down into the hole, feet first, with his rifle pointing up. In here, he was protected from the cold night air and had a rifle to ward off any animals attacking from above. Little did he know that disused holes are favoured hiding places for one of Africa's deadliest snakes, the puff adder, whose bite can kill a grown man in minutes. As the hunter lay deep inside his refuge, warm and protected on all sides, a puff adder trying to get out of the hole to go night hunting may have bitten him with a full dose of poison.

The hunter was likely paralysed in seconds and died within minutes inside his hole, never to be found. None of the searchers had bothered to look into the hundreds of holes that were scattered about the area. The Embassy agreed with Clary that this was the most likely scenario, and said that some other game rangers had suggested the same theory. Years later, a young Maasai goat herder, grazing his animals close to the search area, handed in a piece of torn patterned cloth he had picked up that exactly matched the shirt that the hunter had been wearing when he disappeared. Nothing more of the man was ever found.

The abundance of game in the northern Selous was highlighted when a Romanian foreign minister was on an official visit to Tanzania. The minister was a keen hunter, and the Tanzanian government wanted to make a good impression by letting him shoot a few trophy animals.

Clary and his block were the best place to hunt from Dar es Salaam, so he was tasked with ensuring that the foreign minister had a good safari. Unfortunately, the minister only had one day free to hunt, and in fact, he only hunted for half a day because of delays in Dar es Salaam.

The Romanian minister, dressed in a dark suit and blue tie – together with his two tough-looking bodyguards, similarly dressed in dark clothes with blood red ties and wearing very dark sunglasses – arrived at Clary's airstrip at ten o'clock in the morning. An aide to the minister forgot to load his hunting rifle and ammunition on the plane, so he was obliged to make do with Clary's old but serviceable guns.

The minister had only hunted in Europe, where all game is shot from a tree hide, and he had never stalked game on foot, as was more common when hunting in Africa. Clary broke his own rules and permitted the minister to shoot from the car and inside the mile-wide no-shooting zone around the camp. On the short drive to camp, the minister was able to shoot one animal before reaching camp, and two more animals next to camp before lunchtime. He could have shot a larger variety of animal species, but a lot of time was employed in taking official pictures with each dead animal and various hangers-on who wanted their picture taken with the minister.

While the party was having lunch, Roger the Lodger came to feed on the lush vegetation around the camp. On seeing the elephant, one of the brave bodyguards pulled out his 9mm pistol and stood ready to defend his boss. Clary laughed at his well-meaning gesture and asked what he intended to do with his peashooter against an elephant. The guard looked at the towering hulk of Roger, then at his gun, laughed, and put it away.

Clary walked empty-handed towards Roger, said "Shoo", and walked back to his lunch as the elephant sauntered out of sight.

In the afternoon, the minister shot three other species of game within Clary's no-shooting zone, and then flew out with his entourage at 4pm. The Romanian minister commented that he saw over 500 hundred animals, and nine separate species, in his short stay. He could have shot many more, but in the end, he shot only six. He was very, very pleased with the results of his short hunting trip, and thanked Clary heartily.

However, it took Clary six months to get his safari costs refunded for this trip. The government was reluctant to pay him at all, saying that the hunt should have been free because it was an honour for Clary to hunt with the minister. Clary replied that if he could pay his licence fees and game fees with honour, he would agree with that statement.

There was so much game in Clary's two hunting blocks that he was able to conduct photographic safaris for clients when he had no hunting work. Due to his rule forbidding his clients to shoot from a vehicle or within 200 yards of one, the animals had lost their fear of cars, allowing him to drive his photographers right up to peacefully grazing herds of game.

At one time, he had two couples in camp who were sightseers from the United States. They were strong anti-hunting advocates and let him know in no uncertain terms their opinion of the industry, not only in Africa but in the whole world. Their only contact with wildlife back home had been visits to the local zoo, where the animals are well looked after and pampered, and trips to national parks to see wildlife in its natural state. This was their first trip to Africa, and they were thoroughly enjoying it. That is, until Clary told them that he was a professional hunter and had been for 50 years, and this was his hunting area.

The four Americans gaped at him in utter disbelief and then began a tirade of accusations of moral degeneration, malicious conduct, barbarous butchery, and many more such allegations that equated him with a blood-lusting killer. Clary kept his cool until the ranting and raving had subsided so that he could give his side of the discussion. Fortunately, his guests were intelligent enough to agree to listen to his side of the debate.

So, Clary started. "You city folk expect to have meat on your plate every day, but despise hunters for killing wild animals. Slaughterhouses kill thousands of animals each day, but as long as you don't see it being done, you don't mind. You too are hunters, only you find your meat already dead on the supermarket shelves. The fact that someone else killed those animals for you does not seem to worry you. You still hate hunters for what they do."

He continued, "A vegetarian is proud of himself because he does not eat meat, and he dislikes hunters more than anybody. Even so, he will insist on having leather shoes to buy, and leather belts, and leather handbags, and gloves. Does he think these products come from trees? Did he ever consider the thousands of insects, hundreds of birds, mammals, snakes, lizards, and other animals that were killed or poisoned to make way for food crops? With their habitat gone, these creatures will never come back. However, let a hunter kill one animal, and he will be hated for it, even if he leaves the habitat whole and intact, and another animal will be born to replace the lost one."

He paused while his guests pondered his words. Then he continued with the hunting side of the discussion.

"As for hunting safaris like I have been conducting all my life, think of it like this. A hunting safari is basically a luxury camping holiday in a few hundred square mile campsite. You have the whole place to yourself, with a staff of 12 to cater to all your wishes. You have the freedom to walk wherever you like with an armed and experienced guide to explore your domain. You can enjoy its unique solitude without man-made disturbances. You can breathe deeply in unpolluted air, scented only by the incomparable odours of nature. You can listen to the beautiful music of bird songs without interruption, or hear the patter of little feet on dry leaves as long-tailed lizards chase ants over the dry earth. You can drive through your private estate and take amazing pictures, or admire the unique natural beauty of its flora and fauna, uncompromised by man, and you can hunt the game if you wish."

He let his words sink in, then he went on with his description. "You must remember that humans, together with lions, leopards, hyenas, jackals, wolves, foxes, et cetera, have been hunters for, perhaps, millions of years, and we still are hunters At first, we hunted with sticks and stones, then developed bows and arrows and spears for killing our prey, since we lacked the teeth, claws, and speed of our competitors. We used our intelligence to increase our skills and become better hunters, as we were part of the food chain with other carnivores.

"It is only since the invention of the gun that man has gained an advantage over other hunters. Some men have misused the gun to enrich themselves at the expense of certain animals, such as elephants, but I condemn those people as money mongers. The animals that we hunt here are in their element; it is their home. Their eyesight, hearing, sense of smell, and running speed are far better than any human can manage. They have the advantage. We only have a gun and superior intelligence to hunt with; though, with some men, I am not sure about the intelligence part", joked Clary, trying to lighten the mood.

He continued, "Driving about to shoot animals from the car does not require skill; it is not hunting, it is just shooting. I only use my car to get to an area to hunt, not to shoot. No real hunter will ever kill for pleasure. The pleasure in hunting is the excitement and thrill of the chase, not the killing. It begins with walking silently through the bush in search of a potential prey. Sometimes you find your quarry, sometimes not. When an animal is spotted, the real excitement begins. You plan a stalk, taking into account the available foliage for cover and the prevailing wind, so as to get close enough to judge if the animal is old enough and big enough to shoot. Nine out of ten times, the stalk ends in failure, as your quarry sees, smells, or hears you before you get close enough, or it turns out to be too young or small-horned to shoot. If the animal is just right, you still have to edge close enough, without being detected, to make a clean shot without hitting a branch or other object in the way."

He went on, "Killing the animal with a perfect shot through the heart is the culmination of a successful hunt, but it is not the end of the story. There will be pictures taken to mark the occasion for posterity, and the dead animal will be taken back to camp, where all the meat will be eaten. The skull and skin will be carefully removed, salted, and dried, then shipped to a taxidermist to be mounted in a natural pose. The client will hang this trophy on his wall as a souvenir of

Africa, and the experience will never be forgotten. Any time the client looks at this trophy or his pictures, the memory of his safari, and in particular this hunt, will come flooding back to him in all its details, including the excitement he felt and the sights, sounds, and smells he experienced."

He paused again briefly, then went on, "In this hunting block, there are an estimated 8000 animals, 75 of which will be shot by hunting clients each year. However, that amount is minute in comparison to the off-take by the other carnivores and the death rate from natural causes, which is in the thousands. Poaching is kept under control by the zealous game scouts, so it has little impact on the game. Due to 'selective shooting', game numbers in my blocks are increasing each year." There was another brief pause.

"And the most important element about hunting is the fact that in this new Africa, wild animals have to pay a price to survive. If they didn't contribute money to the system, they would have no value and there would be no reason to protect them from slaughter. The few game-viewing tourists who come here contribute a pittance to the upkeep of this area, while a single hunting safari brings in many thousands of desperately needed dollars. That is the reality of the situation." So ended Clary's elucidation of hunting.

The only illegal hunting Clary did during his six-year stewardship of his hunting blocks in the Selous was to permit clients to shoot two large, very old male greater kudus, which were a protected species here. He allowed it because they were past breeding age, yet each still controlled a small group of females who produced no offspring. There were only three other kudu bulls and about nine females in this block, which was far too few to allow them to be legally hunted. However, after the two old males were removed from their herds, the remaining bulls joined the female groups, producing 16 offspring that year.

Three years later, he counted 27 kudus in the block, which was sufficient to assure a continued increase of animals in the following years.

Chapter 66
Hunting to Save the Game

Before Clary was granted hunting rights in his blocks in the Selous, a rough game census was conducted to determine how many of each species were in the area so that a shooting quota could be established. The quota was purposely set very low so that the impact of hunting on the wildlife could be observed without risking any overhunting. When the game population was not unduly affected, the shooting quota was increased slightly. Each year, Clary conducted eight to ten short safaris of ten days or less, in his two blocks, which had little negative impact on the game numbers. And only two or three safaris of three weeks duration in other blocks. In fact, the amount of game actually increased quite significantly.

After Clary had hunted his northern blocks for five years, a zoologist named Rogers took another game census and came to the conclusion that, in spite of all the hunting, the game numbers had ballooned significantly for almost all species. In camp one evening, Rogers explained to Clary why the numbers were up and not down. In the first game count he made, there were an estimated 3000 impala, and now there were over 5000 impala. Large impala herds consisting of up to 50 females were dominated by the strongest males who, during the breeding season, spent all their time fighting off rivals instead of mating. By shooting the old alpha male with his impressive trophy horns, which Clary's clients preferred, the young males had more opportunity to attract their own smaller herds and mate with all the females in them. As a result, all 50 females had young that year. The same circumstances applied to wildebeest, kongoni, waterbuck, and eland, all of which had increased in numbers due to Clary's selective shooting.

Buffalo numbers had stayed the same, although the herds looked healthier now. The reason for this was probably because only the lone bulls who had left the herds and were past breeding age were hunted. The big herds with breeding bulls had not been hunted.

Elephants had increased slightly due to the presence of hunters in the area and game scouts who constantly patrolled the blocks to keep the poachers away.

Another factor that influenced game numbers was the fact that shooting one leopard saved 52 mostly young animals from being caught and eaten by the big cat each year. That figure was based on one kill per week, since leopards must eat at least once a week to survive.

Chapter 67
The Last Safari and the End of Paradise

Clary was so pleased with the abundance of game in his northern Selous hunting blocks that for the first three years he had no interest in hunting anywhere else in Tanzania, not even the areas south of the Rufiji River where large elephants still roamed. But after three years of hunting exclusively in his northern blocks, Clary wanted to see the southern areas, whose reputation as a last stand for big elephants intrigued him.

The best and most sought-after elephant hunting blocks in the southern Selous had been awarded to a newly established French company, whose owner was a representative of the French government's foreign aid panel. He saw to it that hundreds of millions of dollars in French aid money flowed into the Tanzanian government's coffers, with no questions asked regarding where it went. This company's exclusive French clientele shot over 20 elephants with tusks weighing over 100 pounds each in these particular blocks. They also shot many more magnificent elephants with tusks that were just under that weight.

Clary had a special client from California who had made several successful safaris with him, and whose last wish before he hung up his guns forever was to hunt a big elephant. It took Clary two years of pleading and begging, as well as a large monetary donation from his rich client, for the Selous Authority to grant him a hunting block where there was a reasonable chance of finding a big tusker. The block he desired most for his special client had, five years previously, yielded an enormous 160-pounder elephant, the largest ever shot in the Selous. To his relief, Clary was eventually granted a one month permit to hunt in the assigned block.

Clary set up a comfortable camp in the middle of this block, and they hunted for only ten days before they located and shot a magnificent 120-pounder elephant. The client had fulfilled his dream and now could retire his guns.

Clary did not know at the time that this was his last elephant hunt, and in fact, it was his last safari, too.

Hunting was about to end.

Fire and human greed are two of the most destructive elements on earth, and the beautiful Selous would become a victim of both.

Much to Clary's irritation, the game rangers in the reserve started setting fire to the dry grassland just before the start of each rainy season. They intended to make room for new grass to shoot up with the first rain showers, which they knew would attract the game.

Yet in the years before the fires came, old dead grass, bushes, and fallen trees, rotted away on the ground to become ant fodder or humus for new plants to grow. The Selous had never experienced bushfires because there were no people living here to light them, and almost all fires in East Africa are man-made. Very few fires are started by lightning.

These newly set fires burned the old thick layers of dry grass so fast that antelope caught out in the fields had a hard time outrunning the flames. For the insects, there was no escape; they died in the millions. Only burrowing lizards, rodents, and beetles sometimes survived these blazes in their underground burrows. The infernos burned so rapidly that they only singed the bark and lower leaves of green trees, leaving taller trees unscathed.

In some of the southern Selous blocks, the grass was burned off by the first hunting parties to arrive after the rainy season. These fires were set to burn away the high grass so that the game could be seen and hunted easily. The burning was done every year and was encouraged by the Selous Authority as a way to increase the amount of game seen, and thereby increase the hunters' kill quota.

To increase the revenues for the Selous, the quota for all species was raised, and the number of animals killed increased, too. However, this increase in kills started to reverse a few years later as game numbers declined, not from over-hunting but loss of vegetation for food.

Due to the many fires, Clary noticed the decline of game and bird life in his little corner of the Selous and was determined to do something about it. He tried to stop the local game rangers from subjecting his northern area to the ravages of fire, but to no avail. He noticed during the subsequent years of hunting that there were fewer tsetse flies following his car, and fewer insects flying around the lamps at night in camp. The delightful bird chatter in the early mornings was less than in previous years. A walk through the short scrub bushland while hunting no longer included the pleasant aroma of wild herbs. Instead, there was only grey, choking, fine dust. Slow growing, delicate herbs had all been burned to ashes and scattered by the wind. Their hard-won space was taken over by quick growing spiny grass.

Where layers of old grass had dampened a hunter's footfalls, now bare, hard, dry earth reverberated to his noisy steps. The seeds of mighty trees that had in former years been scattered onto decomposing fallen leaves to bring forth new life, now fell on bare ground, where they were swept away by gusts of hot wind and piled into dry heaps where they withered and died. Dry season dust devils, which once carried small seeds, spores, and pollen in twisting wind spirals to deposit in distant fertile ground, were now whirling black dust devils depositing charcoal ashes onto barren land. Big, fat, well-nourished game and their healthy offspring that roamed contentedly a few years ago now looked thin and hungry at the end of the dry season, viciously fighting each other for the few patches of meagre grazing. Undernourished yearlings either lay down and died or, being unable to run far, become easy prey for big cats.

The Selous game reserve, a unique ecological unit, was a marvellous work of nature that had been left untouched by humans for 100 years. It was now starting to fall apart in just five short years as a result of human ignorance. Before man arrived, fire was an unknown phenomenon in the Selous, so it never needed to be accounted for in nature's calculations.

A paradise like the Selous only existed because of a delicate balance between give and take. Any excess taken on one side had to be compensated for by giving more on the other side. An excess of hunting should have been compensated for by a longer closed season. Fires could have been set in selected sectors then left unburnt for several years. The ecological balance was not being respected so the mighty Selous reserve was in decline.

With intelligent management, the decline could have been reversed. However, a new delegation tasked with its care were totally inexperienced in wildlife management and only saw the monetary potential in the future of this unique area. The new managers doubled the licence fees, doubled the game quotas for each block, and doubled the number of hunting blocks by making two blocks out of one old block. Then every few years, they increased the fees and increased the game quotas, even if they were told that the block could no longer sustain the off-take. When revenues from hunting diminished, they simply increased the block numbers by making each one smaller and adding extra charges for hunters. The game in the Selous was declining rapidly, and nobody in authority cared. They only had money on their minds.

Clary spent many sleepless nights alone in camp, deep in meditation as he contemplated not only his own future and that of the beautiful Siwandu camp, but also the future of wildlife in this new, ever-changing country. News from all quarters described policies that were detrimental to the preservation of wildlife and its habitat. The good old days of abundant wildlife and hunting were gone forever and would never return. Despite the gloomy outlook, Clary thought perhaps the present status quo could be preserved. With the help of his rich and influential American clients, Clary was determined to do something about it.

But it was too late.

In June of 1973, in one of his weekly pep talks to the nation, the vice president announced the banning of game hunting in the country. It was the middle of the hunting season. No warning was given. No one was expecting it, and no grace period to finish a hunt was given. Hunting had to stop immediately.

After existing for 60 years, the professional hunting industry in the country, and everyone involved in it, came to an abrupt end that day. Turmoil and uncertainty reigned over the hunting community. The game department in charge of wildlife matters had not been informed and had no idea of what to do, only suggesting that all hunters wait and see while they sought clarity from the vice president's office about the ban. After all, hunting was Tanzania's third largest source of desperately needed foreign currency.

Sadly, it was a countrywide, permanent hunting ban. There were no exceptions. Hunting was now closed. Tanzania did not want the money generated by hunting. The vice president said that all wild game was considered a natural resource to be exploited as needed only by the local population. The Swahili word for wild game is "nyama wa porini", which translates to "bush meat", meaning that to the local people it was just food for the taking. The slaughter could begin. The end of the game had started.

The courageous game department rangers tried their best to keep poachers out of game reserves, and managed to partially protect the most vulnerable areas from the ravaging hordes. It was rumoured that large numbers of elephants were killed to help pay for a new Chinese-built railway line in the country. In one northwest region, substantial amounts of wildlife were slaughtered to feed starving villages in a failed communist collective agricultural project. Most outlying army camps were ordered to substitute wild game in place of their meagre beef rations to feed their troops.

Tanzania had only been independent for 11 years and was struggling to survive economically. In order to help the country, foreign aid came pouring in from Western countries trying to stem the influence of Eastern communist countries. Conversely, the Eastern European countries came with their aid schemes, hoping to get a foot in the door. The government of Tanzania learned that by playing off the West against the East, they could increase their foreign aid income from the West tremendously and still accept aid from the East. The whole country was awash in aid money. Therefore, there was no need to preserve wild game and its habitat, and certainly no need to allow foreigners to run around the country shooting animals with guns, just to earn a few more dollars.

Chapter 68
A Hunter Gone

Clary's world shattered around him on hearing this edict. He was 66, too old to learn a new profession and too old to move to another country to start hunting safaris again. He had been a hunter in Tanzania for 52 of his years, and was at a total loss as to what to do next. The final decision about what to do was forced upon him.

He was denied a permit to use his Selous camp for photographic safaris, and was ordered to remove it permanently. His permit to remain in Tanzania was suspended, in spite of his having lived there permanently all his life. His small farm in the Usambara Mountains was nationalised without any compensation, and finally, his house in Dar es Salaam, which he had just bought and where he was living, was taken from him in the name of socialism. He was literally being thrown out of his homeland.

The end had come for Clary Palmer-Wilson.

Clary's son Donald was given the task of removing the Selous camp, selling off all the safari equipment, and disposing of the fourteen hunting rifles and a few thousand rounds of ammunition stored in the armoury. Donald was denied an export permit for the rifles and ammunition that he was hoping to sell in neighbouring Kenya, where hunting was still permitted. He was ordered to give his guns and ammunition to the local people, because all the game belonged to them now. However, he did not give away any guns; instead, he secretly took all 14 of them in a canoe to a very deep part of a muddy lake in the Selous and threw them overboard. The thousands of rounds of ammunition he buried deep in a sandy hole, where dampness and corrosion would quickly render them useless and harmless. The safari equipment, unusable for anybody now, was auctioned off for no more than a bag of peanuts.

At the invitation of an old hunting client, Clary agreed to come to the United States, believing it to be a temporary move. He expected that one day the Tanzania government would realise that communism was a failure and life would revert to normal in the country. Then he could return to his beloved homeland in East Africa, to live out his last years and perhaps even hunt once more.

Clary flew from Dar er salaam to Nairobi and spent his last night in Africa with an acquaintance in the town of his birth. The next evening, as he reluctantly boarded his flight to exile, he turned to his host and said, "I never believed that this day would come, even though I said always expect the unexpected." He turned his head away to hide his welling tears and walked onto the plane.

As the four-engined Boeing jet took off from Nairobi's runway 09 and thrust its way up at full power into the starry night, Clary, sitting by a right-hand side window seat, looked out and saw the unmistakeable silhouette of Kilimanjaro, its white snowcap glistening in the bright sky. At that moment he longed to be on the ground in his beloved country again, come what may, yet it was to be his last view of Africa. His genuine tears of very deep sorrow rolled down his cheeks in rivers and onto his light green shirt. As the plane continued turning north, he lost sight of the mountain and the tears continued to flow.

After arriving in the United States, he bought a little wooden shack, which was all he could afford, in a small town in Oregon, where he lived alone for 18 years, like a withered old tree unable to put down roots. During his first ten years in Oregon, Clary hoped to return to Africa once more, yet the news he received from his beloved country was so disheartening that eventually he made up his mind never to return.

He lived the last six months of his life on a ranch in Utah owned by his oldest son. He passed away peacefully one morning. His ashes were scattered in a national park close to where he spent his last months.

There is an old African saying that goes, "Old hunters never die; they just stop telling stories when no one listens."

After Clary died, a letter was found amongst his belongings that he had written to a friend in Africa but never posted.

In February 1990,

Dear (friend),

I have lived in old Africa at its finest, when game roamed unhindered over the whole country. I have walked for weeks through uncharted, unspoiled territory without meeting another human being. Where untamed rivers flowed freely before man's interference with them, they harboured hippos, crocodiles, and fish in over-abundance.

I have tramped through virgin forests whose giant trees had never been harvested and grew so dense that I needed a flashlight to light the way.

I have passed through villages big and small and been welcomed by the proud Africans into every one, and was treated as a guest.

I have sat on a hill for hours and watched hundreds of elephants, those gentle giants of Africa, walk slowly past me following the rainfall. I have seen herds of buffalo so large that they covered a hillside in a black moving mass. I have visited the steppes so overrun with such a variety of wild game that it would take a month to count them all.

I have learned the laws and ways of the bush all by myself, not from reading any books or taking courses. Hunting was a natural way of life for me. I just needed to let my inborn instinct run free.

I have witnessed the beginning of the end of the game, and I don't want to see the end.

I don't want to see the last elephants slaughtered for their tusks.

I don't want to see the last forests cut down for timber.

I don't want to see the last bush cleared for farms.

I don't want to witness the slaughter of the last wild animals for meat. I don't want to know when the last great plains are grazed down by cattle to dust bowls.

But let me tell you, I know that when the last African hunter is banished from his jungle, then the last of the wild game will not be far behind him, and the mighty roar of the last wild lion will be silenced forever.

The memories I have of Africa are still strong and vivid in my mind.

I had a wonderful life, filled with more adventure than most men could have in ten lifetimes.

I have never regretted choosing this way of life and never regretted any decision I made.

My real home was where my heart longed to be, and that was anywhere in the bush in a tent under a thorn tree. That was where I was happiest.

The only regret I have is that I won't be able to die under that thorn tree in Africa.

I predict that in 30 to 40 years' time, there will be no more wild and free game in East Africa, just a few representative species trapped in little parks for tourists to admire.

I am one of the last of the old hunters of Africa, and I am proud of it.

I am proud to have helped preserve the wildlife of this country for future generations.

I will never return to Africa. I will die here, with my memories of a bygone era vividly intact.

Sincerely,

Clary Palmer-Wilson

Clary was wrong about the game being gone in 30 years. There is still ten per cent of it left.

THE END

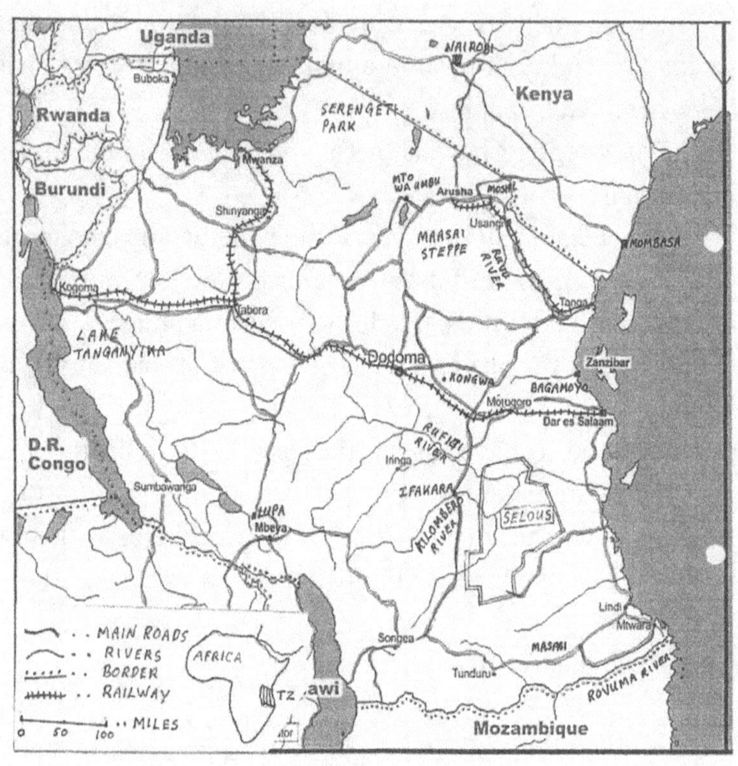

IMAGE 21: MAP DATA:D-MAPS.COM. AFRICA, TANZANIA.

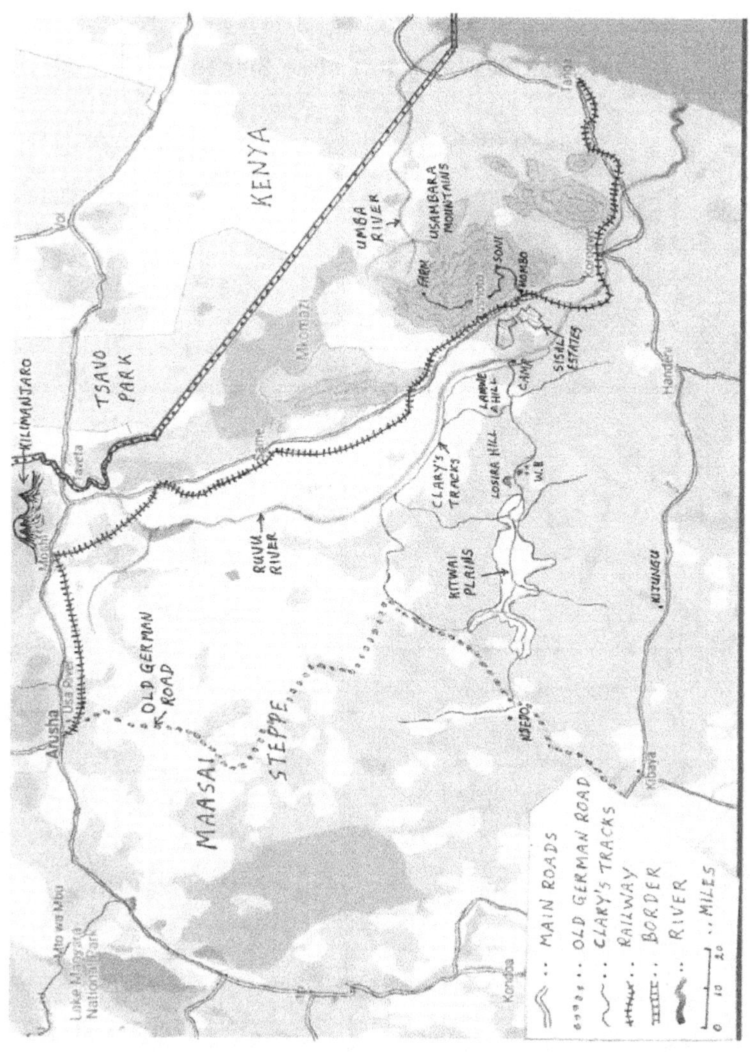

IMAGE 22: MAP SHOWING CLARYS TRACKS THROUGH MAASAILAND.

www.ingramcontent.com/pod-product-compliance
Lightning Source LLC
LaVergne TN
LVHW051218200726
843510LV00011B/1415